THE COMPLETE BOOK OF
# COOKIES

# THE COMPLETE BOOK OF
# COOKIES

Over 425 quick and easy recipes, plus expert tips

on mixing, baking and storing

EDITED BY
Deborah Gray

CONTRIBUTING AUTHORS:
Catherine Atkinson; Kathryn Hawkins; Dawn Stock; Janet Mannings; Katy Holder;
Fiona Hunter; Emma Patmore; Alison Austin

APPLE

A QUINTET BOOK

Published by Apple Press

ISBN 1 84092 400 4

This book was designed and produced by
Quintet Publishing Limited
6 Blundell Street
London N7 9BH

Art Director: Paula Marchant
Designers: Siân Keogh and
Sandra Marques at Axis Design
Managing Editor: Diana Steedman
Senior Project Editor: Toria Leitch
Editor: Jane Donovan
Photographer: Ferguson Hill
Food Stylist: Labeena Ishaque

Creative Director: Richard Dewing
Publisher: Oliver Salzmann

Material in this book also previously appeared in
Breakfast Bakes; The Complete Biscuit and Cookie
Book; New Jewish Cooking, Elizabeth Wolf Cohen; The
Complete Book of Gingerbread, Valerie Barrett; High
Fibre Cooking, Rosemary Moon; Kids' Kitchen Sugar
and Spice, Nicola Fowler

Typeset in Great Britain by
Central Southern Typesetters, Eastbourne
Manufacturered in Hong Kong
Printed in China

# Contents

# Introduction

Seeping out from the corners of every shopping centre, every pavement café and every bakery comes wafting the irresistible scent of baking butter, sugar, chocolate and vanilla. Cookies, ever-popular in America, can now be found everywhere. With the purchase of this book, the aromas from your kitchen can pervade your neighbourhood. The fruits of your labours can fill jars on the worktop, be displayed at bring-and-buy sales, be donated to parties, wing their way to distant relatives in the post, all to the delight of cookie fiends everywhere. For who can resist a cookie? Cookies seem to appeal to the child in us. They appear sweeter and more intensely flavoured than most cakes, they are crunchy and soft, nutty and chocolatey, and are easy to handle – the perfect comfort food.

Take comfort in the knowledge that this book is the only cookie book that you will ever need to own. It contains a unique collection of favourites from all over the world. The word "cookie" comes from the Dutch "koekje" meaning little cake, and this book includes recipes from Holland as well as France, Italy, Scandinavia, Eastern Europe and Australia. Every culture, it seems, has its cookies characterized by the availability of local ingredients and the temperament of its inhabitants. So rustic oaty cookies come from northern Europe, almond-studded biscotti from Italy, spicy Lebkuchen from Eastern Europe and delicate madeleines from the elegance of Marcel Proust's Paris. Then, of course, there are the American cookies themselves. Many of these are jumbo cookies stuffed with goodies or smaller, simpler cookies baked straight from the refrigerator. Here you will find recipes for family favourites and elegant classics alongside new ideas for the new millennium.

A comprehensive introduction provides all the background information in the art of cookie baking to turn you into a master of the art. Take time out to read this section before you begin, then return to your kitchen and enjoy yourself. If you have kids at hand rope them in too, they will enjoy the process of baking cookies and it's a good way to have fun with them on wet afternoons. Get them involved in the decorating, especially at holiday times, and your cookies will take on a certain home-made charm. No kids? Then why not bake with a friend? That way you'll have twice the choice without extra effort and have lots of laughs in the process. After all, you can be really serious about cookies, but who can deny that part of their charm lies in their frivolity.

The only problem with this book is the amazing choice it offers, and the wonderful photographs make all the cookies look so tempting. Maybe go for the Toll House Cookie, or the original recipe for the ever-popular Chocolate Chip Cookie or perhaps the White Chocolate and Apricot – eat one with a glass of cold milk to make the perfect snack while browsing through the other recipes to select your next cookie.

Be assured that whichever recipe you choose, the instructions are clearly written and easy to follow and the ingredients are listed in order of use. With this fabulous cookbook to guide you, you can't go wrong.

## THE INS AND OUTS OF COOKIE MASTERY

By simply following the recipe instructions on the following pages you will be able to bake a huge variety of sensational cookies, but it does help to know a little about the equipment and techniques you will be using. You might want your cookies just that little bit larger, chewier or crisper than the recipe suggests and by understanding the principles of cookie production you will be able to fine tune your baking to suit your taste.

## TOOLS OF THE TRADE

These are listed roughly in the order of use.

● Scales, a set of measuring spoons, and a measuring jug are all essential. Cooking is chemistry, and in order to get the optimum results careful attention should be paid to measuring the ingredients accurately. With spoon measurements, you should level the ingredient with the straight edge of a knife.

● A set of mixing bowls, preferably microwave-safe for melting butter and chocolate in the microwave as well as on top of a double boiler.

● A food mixer and/or food processor. A food mixer is great for combining butter and sugar and beating in eggs. It is still best to fold in dry ingredients by hand as it is easy to over-mix in a machine and risk making the dough tough. A food processor will blend the butter and sugar easily but will not produce quite as light, fluffy a mixture as a food mixer. However, it is probably preferable to doing it by hand with a wooden spoon, which can be quite hard on the arms. The food processor is brilliant for chopping and grinding nuts, chopping fruit and for making shortbread and pastry dough.

● A sifter or sieve.

● A wire whisk, or two – one large and one small.

● A grater for grating the rind from citrus fruits and for grating fresh ginger and nutmeg.

● Spoons. A wooden one, plus several teaspoons and tablespoons for mixing and measuring.

● Knives. A sharp pointed knife and a straight knife for levelling are both useful.

a large baking sheet they tend to burn. To avoid this use a small baking sheet or try turning a 20 x 20-cm/8 x 8-in baking tin over and baking on the back. Avoid using tins with edges such as Swiss roll pans, since they prevent good air circulation around the cookies as they bake.

For baking bar cookies a non-stick 32.5 x 23-cm/ 13 x 9-in and 20 x 20-cm/8 x 8-in tins are required. Some recipes also call for a Swiss roll tin. If you have to use an ovenproof glass baking dish for bar cookies, then be aware that glass retains more heat while cooking than metal. Avoid overcooking and scorched edges by reducing the oven temperature very slightly.

● A metal spatula for removing cookies from the baking sheet. Use thin, heatproof plastic if your non-stick surface will be damaged by metal.

● A timer.

● At least two wire cooling racks.

● A pastry brush.

● Two or three baking sheets. There are a lot out there to choose from. Heavy-gauge aluminium sheets are excellent as they conduct heat evenly and swiftly. Non-stick sheets are good too, but avoid those that are very dark in colour as they absorb too much heat which means that cookies may burn more easily. If yours are dark, compensate by cooking your cookies on a sheet of foil. Insulated baking sheets are not as good as they are cracked up to be – they consist of two layers of aluminium separated by a locked-in air space. Crisp cookies do not crisp well on them, and soft cookies spread out too much on them. If you are using insulated sheets, allow a minute or two extra cooking time and mound cookies generously before cooking.

To maintain optimal air circulation in the oven, baking sheets should be ten centimetres/four inches shorter and narrower than the oven. Heat circulation being what it is, if there are too few cookies placed on

## COOKIE TYPES

The ingredients for most cookies are pretty much the same – sugar, butter and a little egg, bound with flour and flavoured with vanilla, spices, chocolate, fruit or nuts. However, the proportions and treatment of these basic ingredients differ, resulting in a range of cookies with various textures and flavours.

### Drop Cookies

These are probably the simplest and most versatile type of cookie. They are called drop cookies as the dough is soft enough to drop off the spoon and onto the baking sheet. Use the size of spoon recommended in the recipe and encourage the mixture to drop off the spoon by pushing with a second teaspoon. The basic batter usually consists of butter (or margarine or white vegetable fat) and sugar beaten together until light and fluffy. Eggs are then beaten in, followed by flour com-

bined with leavening ingredients and flavourings, either subtle or robust. In addition, textual ingredients are added, the most common of these being oats, coconut, nuts or chocolate chips.

Space the cookies according to the instructions which will take account of the cooking spread, and bake in a moderate oven. For soft or cakey cookies the mixture should be left well mounded on the cookie sheet. For a cookie with a deliciously soft, chewy centre and a crisp edge, remove the cookies from the oven as soon as the edges turn golden and while the middles are still soft and paler in colour. The more even the colour and the firmer the cookie to touch, the crisper the cookies will be. If you want to make crisper cookies, spread the mixture out a little using the back of the spoon before baking. Some very crisp drop cookies such as Florentines require that the butter and sugar are first melted together to begin the caramelization prior to baking, others replace some or all of the sugar with syrup. Such cookies generally contain very little flour which helps them to spread out on the baking sheet. Make sure you space these cookies far apart on the baking sheet.

### Refrigerator Cookies

The advantage of refrigerator cookies is that the ingredients used to make up the dough can be made in advance and kept in the refrigerator for up to two weeks before being cooked. This encourages cooking on demand so that wonderful fresh cookies can be cooked as and when required without the need to prepare fresh dough each time you want to bake a batch. These are the perfect cookies for those who only have time to prepare food and bake at the weekend, or for anyone who doesn't have the self control necessary to leave half a batch of cookies in the storage tins!

The dough for refrigerator cookies is quite stiff, so it is easiest prepared in the food mixer or food processor. The dough is then moulded into a log or into a thin, oblong brick and wrapped in clingfilm. Due to its high fat content, the dough must then be chilled for at least 3 hours to firm up so that the cookies hold their shape and become crisp when cooked. Slice the cookies according to the instructions given in the recipe using a thin, sharp blade. Space 2.5 cm/1 in or so apart on the baking sheet in a moderate oven. If you decide to increase the thickness of the cookies, decrease the temperature of the oven slightly to ensure that the cookies are crisp throughout. The best way to check that these cookies are ready is to sacrifice one and break it in half. Check to see that there is no dark, doughy strip in the centre of the cookie and that the texture is even throughout.

## Rolled Cookies

Rolled cookies are the delight of Christmas cooks. These tempting cookies can be rolled out and cut into shapes using cookie cutters, or simply cut into discs using the top of a drinking glass. Rolled cookie dough is similar to that made for refrigerator cookies and often requires refrigerating before rolling and pressing. After chilling, roll the dough on a lightly floured board to a thickness of 3 to 5 mm/⅛ to ¼ in. Some cooks prefer to roll the dough between two sheets of thicker quality clingfilm so that the dough can be returned to the refrigerator before cutting. Dip the cookie cutter into flour before pressing through the dough, then press down firmly to ensure that the dough is cut right through. Gently pull away any scraps, which can be combined and re-rolled. These cookies are cooked in a moderate to moderately hot oven until very slightly golden around the edges and firm to the touch. They tend to be very fragile and need to be removed from the baking sheets after they have cooled for one or two minutes. Use a thin metal spatula or fish slice to transfer the hot cookies to cooling racks. Rolled cookies freeze well for up to 1 month so they can be made before Christmas and decorated when required.

## Pressed Cookies

A plate of delicate pressed cookies always looks fancy but they are simple to make using a commercial cookie press. They are the perfect cookie for those who would love to make festive cookies, but lack the skill or time to do the fancy decorations.

The dough for pressed cookies needs to be soft enough to be squeezed through a cookie press but firm enough to hold its shape. Extra care must be taken to ensure that the butter and sugar are beaten until really light and fluffy and the flour should be gently folded in

producing a denser and moister bar. For this reason the bars with a crumb or shortbread base often require that the oven temperature be reduced after an initial part-cooking of the base. Always cook bar cookies in the tin size recommended. Using a smaller tin will produce thicker cookies which will need a longer cooking time and would alter the proportions of crust to cake.

As a general rule these cookies are ready when a cocktail stick inserted into the centre of the tin comes out clean. However, some bar cookies, such as brownies, are best slightly softer and fudgier than most others. Remove from the oven as soon as the centre is set and the brownies are just beginning to pull away from the edges of the tin. Most soft, chewy brownies can be cut with a sharp, serrated knife when cooled. Crisp bar cookies, however, must be cut after five to ten minutes before they become firm and difficult to cut without breaking up. Do not cut bar cookies too big. Eight-centimetre/three-inch squares are ample, after all they are supposed to be cookies. Generally bar cookies keep well if left in the baking tin covered with an airtight lid or a piece of foil.

by hand. If the mixture is too stiff to press, then add a few drops of milk; if it is too soft, then place in the refrigerator until firm enough to hold its shape. For spritz-type cookies, the dough is generally pressed out onto ungreased, cold baking sheets and dredged with coloured sugar or decorated with nuts prior to cooking. To prevent the cookies from spreading and loosing their shape, the baking sheets are placed in the refrigerator to allow the cookies to firm up before baking in a moderate oven. Remove from the oven and transfer to the cooling racks as for rolled cookies.

## Bar Cookies

These cookies fall halfway between a cake and a cookie. They can be thick and chewy, thin and crispy, or light and cakey. Some combine two textures having a crispy outer shell (usually shortbread or crumb based) and a rich, soft centre. Most of these cookies are baked in a moderate to moderately low oven; the cooler oven slows the process of aeration called for in lighter cakes

## To Market

It goes without saying that good-quality ingredients make the best cookies but most of the ingredients required for the cookies in this book can be bought in the average grocery and are not expensive. The most important thing is to make sure that the ingredients are fresh – nuts left over from last Christmas and rock-hard apricots should be replaced, as should spices kept in a warm kitchen in full sunlight.

## Flour

Most recipes call for plain flour which you can buy bleached and unbleached (the latter is probably preferable;) sifted or unsifted. It is just as well to sift even pre-sifted flour as it tends to settle when left standing on the shelf for any length of time. Always sift flour when told to do so by the recipe. Note that even the same brand of flour can vary from season to season, so the amount of liquid used in some recipes to bind the ingredients can alter slightly. Do not use self-raising flour unless it is specifically mentioned in the recipe, as this already contains leavening agents and could create dramatic eruptions in the oven if used in conjunction with other leavening agents. Substitute 120 g/4 oz of plain flour plus 1½ tablespoons baking powder and a pinch of salt for 120 g/4 oz self-raising flour.

## Butter

This one is a soul-searcher. Butter has an incomparable flavour in baked goods but we all know that butter is high in saturated fat and cholesterol, both of which should be avoided. The problem is that the only substitute is regular, non-diet margarine and this is not much healthier. The process which turns liquid polyunsaturated oils into the solid fats found in margarine causes the fats to saturate, making them no better than those found naturally in butter. The softer margarines and spreads are healthier but have a greatly increased liquid content than should be used in baking. In some recipes with plenty of other flavours, hard margarine may be substituted for butter although the resulting cookie will be a little softer due to the higher water content of even hard margarine. However, where the butter is absolutely essential for a recipe, such as in shortbread, there is really no substitute. Maybe the solution is to make smaller buttery cookies and eat fewer of them.

Unsalted butter is best for baking as it allows the cook to fine tune the salt content of the cookies themselves. Always use unsalted butter when recommended in the recipe. If you only have salted butter to hand, then cut the amount of salt in the recipe by at least half. Salt was originally added to butter as a preservative, so surplus unsalted butter is best kept in the freezer in order to retain its freshness. Use butter at room temperature when making cookies that need initial beating of butter and sugar, particulary if you are beating by hand as this will cut out some of the hard work. If you need to do this quickly, place the butter on a dish and put it in the microwave on Medium and heat for 10 to 15 seconds (the exact timings vary with machines.) In other recipes where the butter is cut into the flour, very cold butter is essential as the small particles of butter in the mixture melt

while cooking creating tiny air pockets resulting in the characteristic light, crunchy texture.

A few recipes call for lard, which comes from pork, or for white vegetable fat, both of which create short, flaky pastries and cookies. Use as directed on the packet. If you wish to substitute white vegetable fat for butter, then reduce the amount used by 20%.

## Sugar

Sugars add flavour and texture as well as sweetness to the cookies. Use the type of sugar indicated in the recipe. Brown sugar is white sugar with syrup added to it, molasses in the case of brown sugar and generally a lighter syrup in conjunction with a little molasses in light brown sugar. Consequently, brown sugar tends to make moister cookies than white sugar. The darker the sugar the moister and more intense the flavour. Store brown sugar in airtight containers to prevent it drying out. To soften brown sugar that has gone hard, put the sugar with a slice of apple in a plastic container for a few days; alternatively, heat gently in the microwave, checking frequently until softened but not melted.

Many recipes call for granulated sugar or for the finer caster sugar. The sugar crystals in caster sugar are very small and will melt quicker than those in granulated sugar, so do not substitute.

Vanilla sugar may be asked for especially as a decoration. To make vanilla sugar simply place a vanilla pod or two in a sealed container and add about 350 g/12 oz sugar. Leave for a week to allow the flavour to infuse; add additional sugar as required and replace the vanilla pods about once every six months.

## Eggs

The eggs used in this book are large unless otherwise specified. It is important to use the correct size of egg or the mixture will be too dry or too wet. Eggs are easier to separate when they are cold but are best used in baking when at room temperature. Very cold eggs tend to curdle the mixture. If you forget to bring eggs up to room temperature, place in a bowl of warm water for a few minutes. Egg whites should always be used at room temperature to ensure that they whisk to their maximum volume. Always whisk egg whites in a clean bowl that is completely dry and free of grease. If there is even a speck of egg yolk remaining with the white it will not whisk satisfactorily. Start again with a new egg.

## Chocolate

The brand of chocolate you select is a matter of taste (and budget); some swear by readily available brands, others purchase special chocolate by mail order. What is not interchangeable is the type of chocolate you choose. If the recipe calls for plain chocolate that is what you should use. Be particularly careful when buying white chocolate chips that you are indeed buying chocolate and not vanilla-flavoured chips. Different chocolates contain different quantities of cocoa butter and sugar so altering the chocolate alters the chemistry of the cookie. Always melt chocolate very

slowly over a double boiler or on a Medium heat in the microwave (initially for 1 minute then in 20-second bursts); either way, remove the chocolate from the heat when it is about half melted and stir well until the remainder dissolves.

Cocoa powder must be the pure thing, not cocoa or chocolate drink mixes. Dutch cocoa is probably the best type to use as it has been processed with a small amount of alkali making it less bitter to taste and darker than its untreated counterpart.

## Nuts

It is important that nuts be as fresh as possible since they do go rancid over time. Buy whole nuts which keep their flavour longer, and chop in the food proces-

sor or by hand as required. Store in airtight containers, in the refrigerator if you have space. If nuts soften, place in a 300°F/150°C/Gas mark 2 oven for a few minutes to re-crisp. Some recipes call for nuts to be toasted to give a richer flavour. This is best done in an ungreased frying pan on the stovetop where they can be stirred and watched continuously. Otherwise, place on a baking sheet in a 350°F/175°C/Gas mark 4 oven and cook for about 15 minutes, stirring occasionally and watching carefully, especially towards the end of cooking as nuts burn quickly and seemingly without warning. Coconut and oats can be treated in the same way.

## Dried Fruit

As with nuts, the fresher the better. As a preference, buy dried fruit loose from a reputable health shop with a good selection and a regular turnover, as this is likely to be fresher than the packaged fruit (and nuts) (this is also true for nuts and special grains as well.) You are also much more likely to find fruits that have not been treated with sulphur in the health shop. Try to avoid fruit drying out by storing it in the appropriate containers and always sealing the packet when you put it away. To re-hydrate fruit, seep hot water on to it for 10 to 15 minutes.

## Crystallized Fruit

This is best bought in specialist shops, so you can be sure of buying good-quality, fresh ingredients.

## Oats and Muesli

Do not confuse quick oats with rolled oats. Quick oats are rolled oats chopped finer and they absorb more liquid during cooking. Use the type specified in the recipe. Usually the recipes call for plain muesli without fruit unless otherwise stated.

## Flavourings

Spices loose the intensity of their flavour quite quickly so need replacing frequently. To prolong their life keep in a cool, dark place and certainly out of direct sunlight. Use pure vanilla essence not artificial flavouring as this does not come close to the real thing. Similarly, freshly squeezed lemon and orange juice and freshly grated rind are an absolute must. Bottled juice is a poor flavour substitute.

## PREPARING YOUR TIN

There are several schools of thought with regard to tin preparation. Some prefer to very lightly brush their baking sheets with a little oil using a pastry brush or mister spray, and find that sufficient to stop their cookies from sticking. Others grease with white vegetable fat using kitchen paper. However, avoid butter as it burns at a relatively low temperature and salted butter tends to make cookies stick to the sheet. Or you can line the sheets with foil, which needs oiling, or with non-stick baking parchment paper which does not. Using liners allows you to prepare all the cookies at once then simply slide onto the baking sheets as soon as they become available. Never slide a sheet of prepared cookies onto a warm baking sheet. The sheet must be absolutely cold before it is reused or the fat in the cookies will melt and the cookies spread before they reach the hot air of the oven.

## INTO THE OVEN

Cookies must be put into a pre-heated oven. Most ovens take 10 minutes to heat up to temperature so switch your oven on when you begin preparation. Every oven is different, so the times given in this book may be a little different from those in your oven. Trust your eyes and your commonsense. If you persistently find the timings at variance, test the temperature of your oven using a cooking thermometer then calibrate with the thermostat reading; alternatively call for an engineer to check your oven. For optimum heat circulation, cook one cookie sheet at a time in the centre of the oven. If you cook two sheets simultaneously, then reverse the sheets halfway through the cooking time, working quickly to prevent the oven temperature falling too dramatically. When cooking two sheets at once, the cookies will need a little extra cooking time.

For evenly cooked cookies, space as directed in the recipe for consistent air circulation.

| INGREDIENT | ALTITUDE | | |
|---|---|---|---|
| | 3,000ft | 5,000ft | 7,000ft |
| Reduce baking powder<br>For each teaspoon reduce by | ⅛ teaspoon | ⅛ to ¼ teaspoon | ¼ teaspoon |
| Reduce sugar<br>For each 125 g/4 oz reduce by | 0–1 tablespoon | 0 to 2 tablespoons | 1 to 4 tablespoons |
| Increase liquid<br>For each cup 225 ml/8 fl oz | 1 to 2 tablespoons | 2 to 4 tablespoons | 3 to 4 tablespoons |
| Increase temperature by | 0–10°F/0–5°C/Gas ½ | 10–25°F/5–15°C/Gas 1 | 25–35°F/15–20°C/Gas 1½ |

## ARE THEY READY YET?

Check the cookies a couple of minutes before the suggested cooking time is up to make sure that the cookies are not already cooked. Observe the colour and touch the cookies gently to see if they spring back or feel soggy. Different types of cookies have different tell-tale signs that indicate they are ready and these will be given in the recipe. Also, follow the cooling instructions closely as some need to stay on the baking sheet to continue cooking for a few minutes while others need to get onto a wire rack fairly quickly to prevent sticking. Cut bar cookies according to the directions using a serrated knife and a gentle sawing motion. This method is less likely to rip the dough than cutting directly through the cake with a sharp knife.

## HIGH-ALTITUDE COOKING

Many sea-level cookie recipes work well without adjustments. However, above 9,800 metres/3,000 feet the atmospheric becomes pressure lower, liquid boils quicker and evaporation is therefore greater, which concentrates the flavour more, particularly sugars; in practical terms this means that chocolate chip and other drop cookies are slightly flatter and sweeter than at sea level. To compensate, adjust the recipes if necessary using the chart above as a guide. Reducing the quantity of fat and/or increasing the quantity of flour may help too. For soured cream-based doughs do not reduce the leavening beyond ½ teaspoon per 125 ml/4 fl oz soured cream. Avoid using self-raising flour as this already contains leavening agents (120 g /4 oz of self raising flour contains 1½ table-spoons of baking powder and a pinch of salt). Getting the recipe just right may require some element of trial and error – begin with small incremental changes until the cookies are baked to perfection.

## KEEPING COOKIES FRESH

With a few exceptions, cookies are best eaten on the day that they are cooked.

# WHAT WENT WRONG

**The following are the most common causes for disappointment.**

| PROBLEM | REASON | REMEDY |
|---|---|---|
| Cookies stick to baking sheet<br>Cookies too cool | Baking sheet not greased or unevenly greased<br>Greasing with salted butter | Cookies should be removed from baking sheet 1 to 2 minutes after cooking. Return to the oven for a couple of minutes and remove from sheet immediately. Follow instructions below for over-greased sheets. Salted butter can make cookies stick to baking sheets. |
| Cookies break or crumble when removed from baking sheet | Delicate butter-rich cookies can be very fragile | Leave on baking sheet for 2 minutes before removing to cooling rack. Lift carefully with thin metal spatula. |
| Cookies too Dry<br>Cookies are Over-baked | Oven too hot | Check oven thermostat. Check cookies a few minutes before suggested cooking time is up. Trust your judgement when testing. Place half an apple in the storage tin with the cookies to moisten. |
| Cookies too moist | Cookies are underdone | Check oven thermostat. Do not remove from oven unless the cookies test ready even if the cooking time is up. Return to the oven for a few minutes. |

| PROBLEM | REASON | REMEDY |
| --- | --- | --- |
| **Dough too soft** <br> **Won't roll or hold its shape** <br> **Dough too wet** <br> **Dough too warm** | Maybe too much liquid or fat or insufficient flour | Measure the ingredients carefully. Add extra flour. Place in the refrigerator for 30 minutes. |
| **Dough won't hold together and is crumbly** <br> **Dough too dry** | Too much flour, or insufficient fat or liquid | Check that the correct size of eggs has been used. Measure ingredients carefully. Add a little soft butter or a little milk. |
| **Cookies spread across baking sheet and touch each other** | Cookies placed too close together <br> Baking sheet over-greased <br> Cookies placed on warm baking sheet | Follow recipe instructions for spacing. Use a pastry brush dipped in vegetable oil and wipe the sheet thinly and evenly with oil. Allow baking sheets to cool between batches. |
| **Cookies are not evenly cooked** | Cookies of uneven sizes on one sheet <br> Oven cooks unevenly | Always cook cookies of a similar size on one sheet. Turn cookie sheets round during cooking and reverse sheets if cooking two at a time. |
| **Cookies burnt on bottom but not top** | Poor baking sheets <br> Over-greasing <br> Greasing with butter <br> Cooking too low in oven | Avoid very thin or very dark baking sheets or line such sheets with foil. This causes cookies to spread too much. Butter burns at a lower temperature – use oil or white vegetable fat. Cookies are best cooked on the middle shelf. If cooking two sheets, reverse half way through cooking time. |

Cookie dough, for all but cakey cookies that contain leavening ingredients (baking powder, bicarbonate of soda, self-raising flour or cream of tartar,) will keep in the refrigerator at least overnight, some types for as much as two or three days.

Cool cookies completely before wrapping and storing to prevent them from going soft.

Dough can be safely frozen for up to four months. The flavours do become less intense after the first month after which the dough may also pick up that characteristic freezer taste. Be sure to wrap the dough well, then place in an airtight plastic container. When freezing iced cookies, place a sheet of greaseproof paper between the layers.

Store cookies in airtight containers to prevent soft cookies becoming hard and crisp cookies becoming soft. If possible store in the refrigerator to retain the freshly baked flavour. For crisp cookies do not shut the container completely – a slight air flow helps them stay crisp in all but the most humid climates. For this reason, crisp cookies are the best type to keep in ceramic containers. A little crumpled, clean tissue paper placed at the bottom of the jar to absorb moisture also helps keep them crisp. If you must keep soft cookies in jars, place them first in self-sealing plastic bags. Never mix crisp and soft cookies when storing.

To re-crisp cookies, place in a 300°F/150°C/ Gas mark 2 oven for a few minutes, remove and cool. To revitalize soft cookies that have hardened, place a piece of apple or a slice of bread in the container. Replace every day or two. This trick can be used to prolong storage, particularly in very dry climates.

Cookies keep best in the refrigerator in plastic containers. Defrost cookies in their wrappings for between 15 to 30 minutes. To accelerate the defrosting process, defrost in the microwave on Medium for about 40 to 60 seconds.

## DECORATIONS GALORE

This is the point where the great cookie cook and the artist shoot off in different directions. For some, decoration means a dollop of icing or a sprinkling of sugar; others take pride in their decorating skills and pipe fancy lines and designs of great beauty.

## A BASIC DECORATOR'S ICING

225 g/8 oz icing sugar

½ tsp vanilla essence

2 Tbsp milk

Beat together the ingredients until of spreading consistency and colour.

This quantity is sufficient to decorate 3 to 5 dozen cookies. Thin this mixture down a little and it becomes a useful cookie paint.

Another option is to use an egg wash. Mix together 1 egg yolk and ½ tsp water. Divide the resulting mixture if desired and tint with food colouring. This mixture can then be painted onto cookies prior to cooking. For a blue tint use egg white in place of yolk. Tinted evaporated milk can also be used as a subtle glaze in place of egg wash.

The recipes in this book give you the information needed to decorate the cookies, but when out shopping look for unusual decorations, such as coloured sugars, sprinkles, shaped chocolate pieces and crystallized flowers that might come in handy. Small seasonal templates can be used as a stencil and dusted with icing sugar coloured with decorator's colouring dust for effective, simple decorations.

## COOKIES BY POST

Cookies make the perfect gift, whatever the occasion. Wrapped in gift boxes or bags, or in seasonal storage tins they are always greeted with delight. For cookies by post, line a sturdy box or tin with foil or cellophane and place some crumpled tissue paper or cellophane on the base. Select cookies that will withstand the journey such as drop or bar cookies, or those containing fruit. Thin, delicate crisp cookies decorated with the finest piping make the worse travellers – if you must send these, place a few cookies on a piece of card, then wrap securely with clingfilm. Place plenty of crumpled tissue in between the cardboard layers in the box and around the edges. Pack other more robust cookies in layers separating each with a layer of paper or cellophane. Then pack crumpled paper in the top of the box and in any gaps around the edges. Place the box in a plastic bag and seal well (in case the package encounters inclement weather) then pack in a larger, sturdy box surrounded by a layer of packaging foam pieces or crumpled paper. Make sure that the box of cookies does not move around at all. Send for next-day delivery if possible, although most cookies can cope with a few days in the post.

# All-day Cookies

Who says you can't eat cookies at any time of the day? In this chapter there are cookies for breakfast, brunch, morning coffee, lunch boxes, afternoon tea, after dinner, and night-time nibbles. Many of the cookies are quick to make, so there is no excuse – get baking and enjoy them fresh from the oven.

## Breakfast

*Try not to miss this most important meal of the day and there is no excuse now with this selection of tempting, nutritious cookies.*

## Brunch

*Substantial cookies for a late brunch at weekends.*

## Morning Coffee

*Delight your friends with the smell of freshly baked cookies when they come for coffee. These cookies make a perfect snack.*

# Lunch Box

The cookies in this section are hearty enough for brunches or lunches, or whenever you need an energy-giving snack. They are portable too and ideal for when you have a busy schedule but still need a quick bite to eat.

# Afternoon Tea

The cookies featured in this part of the book are generally smaller and more delicate than the cookies for brunch or lunch. These cookies have also been chosen as their flavours complement the different tasting teas such as Earl Grey.

# After-dinner Delicacies

These cookies are small, delicate, and bite sized; ideal to serve up after a meal of several courses with coffee when entertaining. They may be small, but they are very tempting so make a good selection for your guests to choose from.

# Night-time Nibbles

# Muesli Bars

*Preparation time: 15 minutes ● Cooking time: 25 minutes ● Makes: 12 bars*

**Ideal for those who need to eat breakfast on the move, grab a bar and a piece of fruit and this will set you up for the day.**

### INGREDIENTS

*125 ml/4 fl oz clear/runny honey*

*120 g/4 oz margarine*

*50 g/2 oz dark brown sugar*

*50 g/2 oz light brown sugar*

*225 g/8 oz rolled oats*

*3 Tbsp flaked almonds*

*3 Tbsp chopped walnuts*

*40 g/1½ oz raisins*

*40 g/1½ oz chopped dried dates*

*40 g/1½ oz chopped dried apricots*

Pre-heat oven to 350°F/175°C/Gas mark 4. Grease a shallow 28 x 18-cm/11 x 7-in baking tin or line with a sheet of non-stick baking parchment.

● Gently melt the honey, margarine and sugars in a saucepan until well combined, taking care not to boil the mixture. Stir in the oats, nuts and dried fruits, mixing well.

● Press the mixture into the baking tin and bake in the centre of the oven for about 25 minutes, until golden. Leave to cool in the tin for 5 minutes. Cut into bars.

● Leave to cool completely before removing muesli bars from the tin. Store in an airtight container.

# Maple Syrup Cookies

*Preparation time: 15 minutes ● Cooking time: 12 to 15 minutes ● Makes: About 12 to 14*

**These simple cookies are delicately flavoured with maple syrup.**

### INGREDIENTS

*120 g/4 oz lightly salted butter*

*120 g/4 oz light brown sugar*

*1 egg, beaten*

*175 g/6 oz plain flour*

*2 Tbsp maple syrup*

Pre-heat oven to 350°F/175°C/Gas mark 4. Grease two large baking sheets or line with non-stick baking parchment.

● Beat the butter and sugar together in a mixing bowl. Beat in the egg, then add the flour and maple syrup.

● Place 12 to 14 equal-sized spoonfuls of the mixture onto the baking sheets, allowing 8 cm/3 in for spreading. Flatten the mounds of mixture a little with the back of the spoon. Bake in the oven for about 12 to 15 minutes, until pale golden. Remove from the oven and allow to cool for one minute to allow the cookies to firm, before removing with a thin metal spatula to a wire rack to cool completely. Store in an airtight container.

# Banana Cookies

*Preparation time: 15 minutes* ●
*Cooking time: 10 to 12 minutes* ● *Makes: 12*

**Great served with a quickly whizzed smoothie or shake.**

### INGREDIENTS

| |
|---|
| *120 g/4 oz lightly salted butter* |
| *120 g/4 oz light brown sugar* |
| *1 egg, beaten* |
| *175 g/6 oz plain flour* |
| *150 g/5 oz dried banana chips, chopped* |

Pre-heat oven to 350°F/175°C/Gas mark 4. Grease two large baking sheets or line with non-stick baking parchment.

● Beat the butter and sugar together in a mixing bowl until pale and fluffy. Beat in the egg and flour. Stir in three-quarters of the chopped banana chips and place twelve equal-sized spoonfuls of the mixture onto the baking sheets, allowing 8 cm/3 in for spreading. Flatten the mounds of cookie mixture a little using the back of the spoon.

● Sprinkle the remaining banana chips equally over the twelve cookies and press in very lightly. Bake for about 10 to 12 minutes, until pale golden. Remove from the oven and allow to cool for one minute to allow the cookies to firm, before removing with a thin metal spatula to a wire rack to cool completely. Store in an airtight container.

# Pine Nut Oaties

*Preparation time: 10 minutes* ●
*Cooking time :10 to 12 minutes* ● *Makes: 12*

**A high fibre start to the day.**

### INGREDIENTS

| |
|---|
| *5 Tbsp dark brown sugar* |
| *200 g/7 oz rolled oats* |
| *40 g/1 oz oatmeal* |
| *200 g/7 oz pine kernels* |
| *125 ml/4 fl oz peanut oil* |
| *1 egg, beaten* |

Pre-heat oven to 375°F/190°C/Gas mark 5. Grease two large baking sheets or line with non-stick baking parchment.

● Place the sugar, oats, oatmeal and pine kernels in a mixing bowl and mix together. Add the peanut oil and egg and mix all the ingredients together thoroughly to form a crumble mixture.

● Place small tablespoonfuls of the mixture 10 cm/4 in apart on the baking sheets and flatten with a fork to make 8 cm/3 in circles. If necessary, bring the crumble mixture together and place any loose pine kernels back on top of the cookies. Bake in the oven for 10 to 12 minutes or until golden-brown. Leave for 1 minute to firm before removing with a thin metal spatula to cool on a wire rack. Store in an airtight container.

# Apricot Slices

*Preparation time: 45 minutes • Cooking time: 25 to 30 minutes • Makes: About 12*

**The fresh tang of apricots combined with the comforting oats makes this a great breakfast cookie.**

### INGREDIENTS

*40 g/1½ oz dried apricots*

*2 Tbsp granulated sugar*

*150 ml/5 fl oz unsweetened clear apple juice*

*120 g/4 oz plain flour*

*1 tsp bicarbonate of soda*

*200 g/7 oz rolled oats*

*50 g/2 oz light brown sugar*

*120 g/4 oz lightly salted butter*

Pre-heat oven to 375°F/190°C/Gas mark 5. Grease a shallow 28 x 18-cm/11 x 7-in baking tin or line with non-stick baking parchment.

● Chop the apricots into quarters and place in a saucepan with the granulated sugar and apple juice.

Bring to the boil, cover and simmer for 15 minutes or until the apricots have softened and absorbed nearly all of the apple juice. Leave to cool completely, then place in a blender and process until smooth.

● Mix together the flour, bicarbonate of soda, oats and brown sugar in a mixing bowl. Blend in the butter using fingertips, until the mixture resembles breadcrumbs.

● Press half of the crumbly oat mixture over the base of the baking tin. Spread the apricot purée evenly over the oat mixture, using a thin metal spatula wetted with a little cold water to help ease of spreading. Cover with the remaining oat mixture, pressing the mixture down lightly. Bake in the oven for 25 to 30 minutes, until pale golden. Leave to cool in the tin before cutting into 12 equal-sized bars. Store in an airtight container.

# Pumpkin Seed and Bran Cookies

*Preparation time: 10 minutes* ● *Cooking time: 10 to 12 minutes* ● *Makes: 12*

**Packed with goodness, try these deliciously crunchy cookies any time of day.**

## INGREDIENTS

| |
|---|
| *120 g/4 oz lightly salted butter* |
| *120 g/4 oz light brown sugar* |
| *120 g/4 oz dark brown sugar* |
| *1 egg, beaten* |
| *150 g/5 oz plain flour* |
| *75 g/3 oz bran* |
| *40 g/1½ oz pumpkin seeds* |

Pre-heat oven to 350°F/175°C/Gas mark 4. Grease two large baking sheets or line with non-stick baking parchment.

● Beat the butter and sugars together in a mixing bowl until the mixture turns pale and fluffy. Beat in the egg, flour and bran. Stir in three-quarters of the pumpkin seeds.

● Place 12 equal-sized spoonfuls of the mixture onto the baking sheets, allowing 8 cm/3 in for spreading. Flatten the mounds a little with the back of the spoon and sprinkle the remaining pumpkin seeds evenly over the cookies. Bake for about 10 to 12 minutes, until golden and just firm. Remove from the oven and allow to cool for one minute, then remove with a thin metal spatula to a wire rack to cool completely. Store in an airtight container.

# Lime Cookies

*Preparation time: 15 minutes* ● *Cooking time: 12 to 14 minutes* ● *Makes: 12*

**Lime adds a tang to wake up your tastebuds.**

### INGREDIENTS

*120 g/4 oz lightly salted butter*

*120 g/4 oz granulated sugar*

*1 egg, beaten*

*175 g/6 oz plain flour*

*Finely grated rind of 1 lime*

*2 Tbsp fresh lime juice*

### FILLING

*75 g/3 oz unsalted butter, softened*

*175 g/6 oz icing sugar, sifted*

*1 Tbsp grated rind of 1 lime*

*2 tsp fresh lime juice*

Pre-heat oven to 350°F/175°C/Gas mark 4. Grease two large baking sheets or line with non-stick baking parchment.

● Beat the butter and sugar together in a mixing bowl until pale and fluffy. Beat in the egg, flour, lime rind and lime juice.

● Place 12 equal-sized spoonfuls of the mixture onto the baking sheets, allowing 8 cm/3 in all round for spreading. Flatten the mounds of mixture a little using the back of the spoon. Bake the cookies in the oven for about 12 to 14 minutes, until pale golden. Remove from the oven and allow to cool for one minute to allow the cookies to firm, before removing with a thin metal spatula to a wire rack to cool completely.

● To make the filling, in a small bowl beat together the butter and icing sugar until soft and stir in the lime rind and juice for a soft icing. Sandwich the cookies together with the filling.

● Store in an airtight container.

# Honey and Oat Cookies

*Preparation time: 15 minutes • Cooking time: 10 to 12 minutes • Makes: 14*

**Sweet and delicious honey and oats make these a good breakfast choice.**

### INGREDIENTS

*120 g/4 oz lightly salted butter*

*120 g/4 oz light brown sugar*

*2 Tbsp clear/runny honey*

*1 egg yolk*

*175 g/6 oz self-raising flour*

*Pinch mixed spice*

*75 g/3 oz rolled oats*

Pre-heat the oven to 350°F/175°C/Gas mark 4. Meanwhile, grease two large baking sheets.

● Beat together the butter and sugar in a mixing bowl until pale and fluffy. Beat in the honey and egg yolk, then stir in the flour, mixed spice and oats until well combined.

● Divide the mixture into 14 equal-sized pieces and roll into balls using your fingertips. Place the cookies onto the baking sheets 8 cm/3 in apart, to allow for spreading. Bake for 10 to 12 minutes until golden and just firm. Leave to cool for one minute to allow the cookies to firm, before removing them with a thin metal spatula to a wire rack to cool. Store in an airtight container.

# Sesame Seed Sensations

*Preparation time: 10 minutes ● Cooking time: 12 to 15 minutes ● Makes: About 12*

**Sesame seeds have a strong flavour which bursts through the oat base in this cookie.**

### INGREDIENTS

| |
|---|
| *5 Tbsp light brown sugar* |
| *200 g/7 oz rolled oats* |
| *40 g/1½ oz oatmeal* |
| *40 g/1½ oz sesame seeds* |
| *125 ml/4 fl oz peanut oil* |
| *1 egg, beaten* |

Pre-heat oven to 375°F/190°C/Gas mark 5. Grease two large baking sheets or line with non-stick baking parchment.

● Place the sugar, oats, oatmeal and sesame seeds in a mixing bowl and mix. Add the peanut oil and beaten egg and mix all the ingredients thoroughly to form a crumble mixture.

● Place small tablespoons of the mixture 8 to 10 cm/ 3 to 4 in apart on greased baking sheets and flatten with a fork to make 8-cm/3-in circles. Bake in the oven for 12 to 15 minutes or until golden-brown. Leave on the baking sheets for 1 minute to firm before carefully removing with a thin metal spatula to cool the cookies on a wire rack. Store in an airtight container.

# Orange Shortbread

*Preparation time: 10 minutes ● Cooking time:*
*1 hour ● Makes: About 16*

**Home-made shortbread is crisp and light and this
version is delicately flavoured with orange rind.**

### INGREDIENTS

*120 g/4 oz lightly salted butter*

*120 g/4 oz plain flour*

*50 g/2 oz icing sugar*

*50 g/2 oz cornflour*

*Grated rind of 1 orange*

Preheat oven to 325°F/160°C/Gas mark 3. Grease a
shallow baking tin measuring 18 x 18-cm/7 x 7-in
or line with non-stick baking parchment.

● With fingertips gently work the butter, flour, icing
sugar, cornflour and orange rind together in a mixing
bowl. Bring the mixture together to make a soft dough.

● Press the mixture evenly into the pan and smooth the
surface. Lightly prick the surface evenly all over with a
fork. Bake for 40 minutes then reduce the temperature
to 275°F/140°C/Gas mark 1 and bake for a further
15 to 20 minutes, or until lightly browned. Leave to cool
completely in the tin and cut into 16 equal-sized bars
with a sharp knife. These cookies are best eaten on the
day they are made.

# Currant and Almond Cookies

*Preparation time: 15 minutes + chilling ●*
*Cooking time: 8 to 10 minutes ● Makes: 16*

**The combination of currents and nuts in these cookies
makes them both crunchy and chewy – delicious.**

### INGREDIENTS

*225 g/8 oz lightly salted butter*

*120 g/4 oz light brown sugar*

*175 g/6 oz self-raising flour*

*50 g/2 oz flaked almonds*

*75 g/3 oz currants*

Preheat oven to 400°F/200°C/Gas mark 6. Grease
two large baking sheets with non-stick baking
parchment.

● Beat together the butter and sugar in a mixing bowl
until pale and fluffy. Beat in the flour and almonds then
stir in the currants. If the dough is too soft to handle,
cover and chill in the refrigerator for 30 minutes.

● Form the cookie dough into a roll about 5 cm/2½ in
in diameter. Cut into 1-cm/½-in slices and place well
apart on the baking sheets to allow for spreading.

● Bake the cookies in batches in the oven for 8 to 10
minutes, until light brown. Leave to cool for five minutes
on the sheets before removing with a thin metal spatula
to a wire rack to cool completely.

# Cornflake and Sultana Cookies

*Preparation time: 25 minutes ● Cooking time: 10 to 15 minutes ● Makes: 18*

**Soft chewy cookies that are very easy to make.**

## INGREDIENTS

120 g/4 oz soft margarine

120 g/4 oz light brown sugar

1 egg, beaten

150 g/5 oz self-raising flour

60 g/1½ oz cornflakes

75 g/3 oz sultanas

Preheat oven to 350°F/185°C/Gas mark 4. Grease several baking sheets or line with non-stick baking parchment.

● Beat together the margarine and sugar in a mixing bowl until pale and fluffy. Beat in the egg. Stir in the flour with the cornflakes and golden raisins and mix everything together until well combined.

● Place mounds of the mixture onto the baking sheets, leaving big spaces in between to allow for spreading.

● Bake the cookies in the oven for 12 to 15 minutes, until golden brown. Lift onto wire racks to cool completely. Store in an airtight container.

# Double Banana Cookies

*Preparation time: 25 minutes ● Cooking time: 12 to 15 minutes ● Makes: 16*

**These wholesome cookies contain oats, banana chips and fresh chunks of banana.**

## INGREDIENTS

120 g/4 oz soft margarine

120 g/4 oz light brown sugar

1 egg, beaten

175 g/6 oz self-raising flour

25 g/1 oz porridge oats

25 g/1 oz chopped candied pineapple

25 g/1 oz crumbled banana chips

1 banana, chopped

Preheat oven to 350°F/175°C/Gas mark 4. Grease several baking sheets or line with non-stick baking parchment.

● In a mixing bowl beat together the margarine and sugar until pale and fluffy. Beat in the egg. Stir in the flour with the oats, candied pineapple, banana chips and fresh banana and mix everything together until well combined.

● Place mounds of the mixture onto the baking sheets, leaving big spaces in between to allow for spreading.

● Bake the cookies in the oven for 12 to 15 minutes, until golden brown. Lift onto wire racks to cool completely. Store in an airtight container.

# Cream Cheese Puff Swirls

*paration time: 10 minutes* ● *Cooking time: 12 to15 minutes* ● *Makes: About 18*

**These cookies are so simple to make and look exquisite.**

### INGREDIENTS

*225 g/8 oz ready-rolled puff pastry, thawed, if frozen*

*120 g/4 oz chopped dried apricots*

*120 g/4 oz cream cheese*

Pre-heat oven to 425°F/220°C/Gas mark 7. Grease two large baking sheets or line with non-stick baking parchment.

● Place the puff pastry on a lightly floured surface and roll to make a rectangle measuring 28 x 23 cm/11 x 9 in.

● In a bowl mix the apricots and cream cheese together thoroughly. Spread the mixture evenly all over the surface of the pastry. Holding one of the short sides, roll the pastry up to make a roll. Cut across the pastry roll with a sharp knife to make 2.5-cm/1-in thick slices.

● Place the pastry swirls onto the prepared baking sheets allowing 2.5 cm/1 in in between them for spreading. Bake for 12 to 15 minutes, or until the pastry is golden-brown and crisp. Best if eaten warm when freshly made, but can be cooled and kept in the refrigerator for 24 hours.

# Nut Chewies

*Preparation time: 25 minutes + cooling ● Cooking time: 12 to 15 minutes ● Makes: About 36*

**This cookie is almost all nuts and fruit. They are soft and chewy and don't last long – especially at a picnic.**

## INGREDIENTS

| |
|---|
| *120 g/4 oz unblanched whole almonds* |
| *50 g/2 oz pecan or walnut halves* |
| *50 g/2 oz blanched hazelnuts* |
| *120 g/4 oz plain flour* |
| *1 tsp bicarbonate of soda* |
| *¼ tsp salt* |
| *120 g/4 oz unsalted butter* |
| *120 g/4 oz granulated sugar* |
| *3 Tbsp dark brown sugar* |
| *1 egg* |
| *1 tsp vanilla essence* |
| *75 g/3 oz raisins* |
| *75 g/3 oz sultanas* |

Preheat oven to 375°F/190°C/Gas mark 5. Place nuts on a large baking sheet and toast until golden and fragrant, 5 to 7 minutes, stirring occasionally. Pour onto a plate and cool completely, then roughly chop. Grease two large baking sheets or line with non-stick baking parchment.

● Into a small bowl, sift together the flour, bicarbonate of soda and salt. In a large bowl, beat the butter until soft, beat in the sugar until the mixture becomes light and fluffy. Beat in the egg and vanilla until combined. Stir in the flour mixture followed by the raisins, sultanas and nuts until evenly distributed.

● Drop heaped tablespoons of the mixture, at least 5 cm/2 in apart onto baking sheets. Bake in the oven until set and golden, 12 to 15 minutes, rotating the baking sheets during cooking. Cool the cookies slightly, then transfer to wire racks to cool completely. Store in an airtight container.

# Maple Syrup Tartlets

*Preparation time: 30 minutes + chilling ● Cooking time: 15 to 20 minutes ● Makes: About 17*

**These little tartlets are delicious served warm with more maple syrup poured over the top.**

INGREDIENTS

FOR THE PASTRY BASE

*120 g/4 oz margarine*

*1 Tbsp milk*

*175 g/6 oz plain flour*

FILLING

*150 ml/5 fl oz maple syrup*

TOPPING

*50 g/2 oz margarine*

*50 g/2 oz light brown sugar*

*6 Tbsp self-raising flour*

*½ tsp baking powder*

*¼ tsp vanilla essence*

*1 egg, beaten*

*1 Tbsp milk*

Pre-heat oven to 375°F/190°C/Gas mark 5. Grease two shallow bun tins or eight 9-cm/3½-in individual tartlet tins.

● To make the pastry base, place the margarine, milk and flour together in a bowl and mix together to make a dough. If the pastry is too soft to handle, cover and refrigerate for at least 30 minutes to become firm.

● On a lightly floured surface, roll out the pastry thinly and cut into 8-cm/3-in circles using a fluted pastry cutter. Re-roll and cut the pastry to make as many pastry circles as possible. Line the tartlet tins with the pastry circles. Place one teaspoonful of maple syrup in each small pastry shell.

● To make the topping, beat together the margarine and sugar until pale and fluffy. Add the flour, baking powder, vanilla essence, egg and milk, mix thoroughly. Divide the mixture evenly over the maple syrup-covered tartlet bases. Bake in the oven for 15 to 20 minutes, until golden. Eat warm, served with more maple syrup or cool and store in an airtight container.

# Spiced Orange Cookies

*Preparation time: 40 minutes* ● *Cooking time: 25 minutes* ● *Makes: About 96*

**A very tangy cookie that never loses its appeal. These are great for brunch or for social parties at school, church or tennis club, for example.**

## INGREDIENTS

| | |
|---|---|
| *350 g/12 oz plain flour* | *Grated rind of 1 orange* |
| *½ tsp mixed spice* | *50 ml/2 fl oz freshly squeezed orange juice* |
| *¼ tsp salt* | *½ tsp almond essence* |
| *350 g/12 oz unsalted butter* | *4 Tbsp orange marmalade* |
| *200 g/7 oz caster sugar* | *Flaked almonds, to decorate* |

Pre-heat oven to 375°F/190°C/Gas mark 5. In a medium bowl, sift together flour, spice and salt. In a large bowl beat butter until creamy. Add the sugar and continue beating until light and fluffy. Beat in egg, orange rind and orange juice until well blended. Stir in flour until well combined.

● Divide the dough into quarters. Working with one-quarter at a time, fill a cookie press fitted with a ribbon or bar plate. Press 30-cm/12-in strips overlapping lengthwise, onto one side of an ungreased baking sheet, making a base about 8 cm/3 in wide. Pat down strips to flatten. Refill the press with dough, if necessary, and press a border along each side of strips, leaving a shallow trough in the centre. Press out a little dough

and use to make 2 ends (this will prevent the marmalade from oozing out onto the baking sheet.)

● Bake strips for 15 minutes. Remove baking sheets from oven, and using the back of a spoon, press down a centre trench in each strip. Fill with marmalade to just below the edges.

● Return the baking sheet to the oven and bake until the edges are golden and the marmalade bubbling, 10 to 12 minutes. Remove baking sheets to wire rack and cool until set, about 3 minutes. Using another baking sheet or long metal spatula, slide each long strip onto a wire rack to cool for about 5 minutes. Slip each strip onto a work surface and while still warm, trim the edges and cut into 2.5-cm/1-in cookies.

# Jam Thumbprints

*Preparation time: 20 minutes + chilling* ● *Cooking time: 15 to 17 minutes* ● *Makes: 14*

**A cookie classic. Using a selection of jams or preserves makes a plate of these look really pretty.**

### INGREDIENTS

*150 g/5 oz lightly salted butter*

*5 Tbsp light brown sugar*

*1 egg yolk*

*225 g/8 oz plain flour*

*14 tsp seedless fruit jam*

Grease two large baking sheets or line with non-stick baking parchment.

● Beat together the butter and sugar until light and fluffy. Beat in the egg yolk and stir in the flour. Cover and refrigerate for about an hour, or until firm enough to handle. Pre-heat oven to 350°F/175°C/Gas mark 4, then divide the mixture into 14 equal-sized pieces and roll into balls using your hands. Place at least 2.5 cm/ 1 in apart on the baking sheets. Press your thumb into the centre of each cookie ball to make a hollow indentation.

● Bake in the oven for about 10 to 12 minutes until pale brown and just firm. If the centres of the cookies have risen slightly, gently pat back down with the back of a teaspoon. Fill each hollow with a teaspoon of jam or preserves and bake for a further 5 minutes. Remove the cookies to a wire rack to cool using a thin metal spatula. Store in an airtight container.

# Crunchy Cheese Bites

*Preparation time: 10 minutes* ● *Cooking time: 20 minutes* ● *Makes: 10*

**A great favourite with children and adults alike.**

### INGREDIENTS

*50 g/2 oz margarine*

*50 g/2 oz plain flour*

*½ tsp paprika*

*120 g/4 oz freshly grated Parmesan cheese*

*75 g/3 oz Rice Crispies*

*1 egg, beaten*

Pre-heat oven to 350°F/175°C/Gas mark 4. Grease a large baking sheet or line with non-stick baking parchment.

● Beat together the margarine, flour, paprika and Parmesan to make a crumbly mixture.

● Stir in the cereal and egg, until combined, taking care not to crush the cereal. Shape into 10 equal-sized balls and place on the baking sheet. Bake for 20 minutes, until lightly browned. Eat warm, or cool on a wire rack. These are best eaten on the day they are made.

# Ginger Bites

*Preparation time: 10 minutes* ● *Cooking time: 15 minutes* ● *Makes: About 12*

**Ginger cookies go well with cappuccino.**

### INGREDIENTS

| |
| --- |
| *4 Tbsp light brown sugar* |
| *50 g/2 oz lightly salted butter* |
| *2½ Tbsp treacle* |
| *175 g/6 oz self-raising flour* |
| *1 tsp ground ginger* |
| *½ tsp baking powder* |

Pre-heat oven to 350°F/175°C/Gas mark 4. Grease two large baking sheets or line with non-stick baking parchment.

● Beat together the sugar, butter and treacle until it becomes lighter in colour and fluffy. Mix in the flour, ginger and baking powder until well combined. Roll the mixture into walnut-sized balls using your hands and place 5 to 8 cm/2 to 3 in apart on the baking sheets to allow for spreading. Flatten the cookies slightly using your fingers or the back of a fork. Bake in the oven for about 15 minutes, until flattened and slightly firm to the touch. Leave to cool on the baking sheets then remove and store in an airtight container.

# Popcorn Cheese Balls

*Preparation time: 10 minutes ● Cooking time: 20 minutes ● Makes: 8*

**The popcorn adds an airy crunch to these cookies.**

### INGREDIENTS

| |
|---|
| 50 g/2 oz margarine |
| 6 Tbsp plain flour |
| 50 g/2 oz grated Cheddar cheese |
| 25 g/4 oz grated Parmesan cheese |
| 2 eggs, beaten |
| 175 g/6 oz ready-made plain or salted popcorn |

Pre-heat oven to 350°F/175°C/Gas mark 4. Grease a large baking sheet or line with non-stick baking parchment.

● Beat together the margarine, flour and cheeses in a large mixing bowl to make a crumbly mixture. Stir in the egg. Add the popcorn and mix thoroughly, so that the cheese mixture coats the popcorn. The mixture will combine sufficiently so that it will form balls.

● Make 8 equal-sized ball-shaped cookies with the mixture and place on the baking sheet. Bake for about 20 minutes, until lightly browned. Serve immediately, while warm.

# Butter, Currant & Coconut Cookies

*Preparation time: 15 minutes + chilling ● Cooking time: 8 to 10 minutes ● Makes: 16*

**These cookies are crisp on the day they are made, but if stored in an airtight container they soften and become quite chewy – both are delicious.**

### INGREDIENTS

| |
|---|
| 225 g/8 oz lightly salted butter |
| 175 g/6 oz light brown sugar |
| 175 g/6 oz self-raising flour |
| 75 g/3 oz sweetened flaked coconut |
| 125 g/4 oz currants |

Pre-heat oven to 400°F/200°C/Gas mark 6. Grease two large baking sheets or line with non-stick baking parchment.

● Beat together the butter and sugar in a mixing bowl until pale and fluffy. Beat in the flour and coconut. Stir in the currants. If the dough is too soft to handle, cover and chill in the refrigerator for about 1 hour to firm.

● Form the cookie dough into a roll about 6 cm/2½ in in diameter. Cut into 1-cm/½-in slices and place well apart to allow for spreading as the cookies double in size. Reshape into neat rounds, if necessary.

● Bake the cookies in batches in the oven for about 8 to 10 minutes, until light brown. Allow to cool for 5 minutes to firm on the baking sheet, before removing with a thin metal spatula to a wire rack to cool.

# Pear Cookies

*Preparation time: 15 minutes ● Cooking time: 12 to 14 minutes ● Makes: About 12 to 14*

**You will want to add dried pears to many more recipes after enjoying these cookies. Other dried fruit such as apricots, can also be substituted.**

## INGREDIENTS

*120 g/4 oz lightly salted butter*

*120 g/4 oz light brown sugar*

*1 egg, beaten*

*175 g/6 oz plain flour*

*150 g/5 oz chopped ready-to-eat dried pears*

Pre-heat oven to 350°F/175°C/Gas mark 4. Grease two large baking sheets or line with non-stick baking parchment.

● Beat the butter and sugar together in a mixing bowl until pale and fluffy. Beat in the egg and flour. Stir in the chopped pears.

● Place 12 to 14 equal-sized spoonfuls of the cookie mixture onto the baking sheets, allowing 5 to 8 cm/2 to 3 in for spreading. Flatten the mounds of mixture a little using the back of the spoon. Bake the cookies in the oven for about 12 to 14 minutes, until pale golden. Remove from the oven and leave to firm on the baking sheets for one minute, before removing with a thin metal spatula to a wire rack to cool completely. Store in an airtight container.

*Chocolate Swirls*

# Chocolate Swirls

*Preparation time: 5 minutes ● Cooking time: 10 to 12 minutes ● Makes: About 18 to 20*

**Using ready made puff pastry makes these cookies very quick and easy to make.**

## INGREDIENTS

*225 g/8 oz ready-made rolled puff pastry, thawed if frozen*

*3–4 Tbsp chocolate spread*

Pre-heat oven to 425°F/220°C/Gas mark 7. Grease two large baking sheets or line with non-stick baking parchment.

● Place the puff pastry on a lightly floured surface and if necessary roll to make a rectangle measuring 28 x 23 cm/11 x 9 in. Spread the chocolate spread evenly all over the surface of the pastry. Holding one of the short sides, roll the pastry up to make a long roll. Cut across the pastry roll with a sharp knife to make 5-mm/¼-in thick slices.

● Transfer the pastry swirls onto the baking sheets allowing a little space for spreading. If necessary, reshape into neat circles and pat down slightly. Bake for 8 minutes in the centre of the oven until golden-brown, then carefully turn the pastries over and bake for a further 2 to 4 minutes until golden. Using a thin metal spatula, remove the chocolate swirls to a wire rack to cool completely.

# Cheese and Peanut Shortbread Bars

*Preparation time: 15 minutes • Cooking time: 50 minutes • Makes: 10 bars*

**These filling bars are tasty served with more sliced cheese or spread with peanut butter.**

### INGREDIENTS

*225 g/8 oz lightly salted butter*

*225 g/8 oz plain flour*

*120 g/4 oz grated mature Cheddar cheese*

*50 g/2 oz freshly grated Parmesan cheese*

*225 g/8 oz salted peanuts, toasted*

Pre-heat oven to 350°F/175°C/Gas mark 4. Grease a shallow 28 x 18-cm/11 x 7-in baking tin.

● Beat together the butter and flour in a mixing bowl until well combined. Add the cheeses and three-quarters of the peanuts and using your hand, lightly bring the mixture together to form a soft dough.

● Press the mixture into the prepared tin with a lightly floured hand and smooth the surface. Evenly sprinkle over the remaining peanuts and lightly press into the top of the shortbread mixture. Bake for about 50 minutes, until a pale, golden-brown and firm to touch.

● Leave to cool completely in the tin before cutting into 10 even-sized bars. Store in an airtight container. Best eaten on the day made but can be kept in the refrigerator for 2 to 3 days.

# Ginger and Coffee Creams

*Preparation time: 30 minutes ● Cooking time: 15 to 20 minutes ● Makes: About 25*

**Crisp ginger nut cookies sandwiched together with a coffee cream; perfect with a large mug of steaming coffee.**

## INGREDIENTS

*175 g/6 oz plain flour*

*2 tsp baking powder*

*1 tsp bicarbonate of soda*

*2 tsp ground ginger*

*1 tsp mixed spice*

*1 Tbsp caster sugar*

*120 g/4 oz lightly salted butter or margarine*

*125 ml/4 fl oz golden syrup*

### ICING

*120 g/4 oz unsalted butter, softened*

*3 Tbsp caster sugar*

*1 tsp coffee essence*

*7 Tbsp icing sugar*

Pre-heat oven to 375°F/190°C/Gas mark 5. Grease or line two baking sheets with non-stick baking parchment.

● Sift together the flour, baking powder, bicarbonate of soda, ginger and mixed spice. Stir in the sugar and make a well in the centre. Melt the butter, then stir in the golden syrup and pour the mixture into the well. Mix to a soft but not sticky dough.

● Take half teaspoons of the mixture and roll into balls. Place on the baking sheets leaving space between the cookies as they will spread while cooking. Flatten them slightly. Bake for 15 to 20 minutes until set. Leave to cool for a few minutes, then transfer onto wire racks to cool completely.

● To prepare the icing, beat the butter and caster sugar together with the coffee essence until well blended. Gradually beat in the icing sugar and mix to a stiff paste. Sandwich the cookies together with the icing. Best eaten on the day they are filled, but may be stored in an airtight container for 2 to 3 days although the filling will make the cookies soften.

# Apricot and Cheese Cookies

*Preparation time: 15 minutes ● Cooking time: 15 to 18 minutes ● Makes: About 14*

**Tangy sweet apricots complement these cheese cookies.**

### INGREDIENTS

*150 g/5 oz no-soak, dried apricots, finely chopped*

*75 g/3 oz lightly salted butter*

*225 g/8 oz plain flour*

*6 Tbsp grated Cheddar cheese*

*1 egg, beaten*

*3–4 Tbsp milk*

Pre-heat oven to 375°F/190°C/Gas mark 5. Grease two large baking sheets or line with non-stick baking parchment.

● Cut the dried apricots into small pieces. In a mixing bowl, blend the butter into the flour to resemble breadcrumbs. Stir in two-thirds of the grated cheese, three-quarters of the chopped dried apricots and the egg. Add enough milk to form a dough.

● On a lightly floured surface, roll the cookie dough out to 5 mm/¼ in thick and cut the dough into 5 x 8-cm/2 x 3-in rectangular cookies. Re-roll and repeat. Place the cookies on the baking sheets, brush with any remaining milk and sprinkle over the reserved grated cheese and apricots. Bake for about 15 to 18 minutes, until golden-brown. Remove from the baking sheet with a thin metal spatula and cool on a wire rack. Store in an airtight container in the refrigerator for up to 2 days.

# Apple and Cinnamon Cookies

*Preparation time: 15 minutes + chilling ● Cooking time: 25 minutes ● Makes: 12*

**These cookies are best eaten the same day, but can be stored in an airtight container for 2 days.**

### INGREDIENTS

*225 g/8 oz lightly salted butter*

*120 g/4 oz icing sugar*

*4 drops vanilla essence*

*1 tsp ground cinnamon*

*225 g/8 oz plain flour*

*150 g/5 oz cornflour*

*3 Tbsp apple sauce*

*1 eating apple, peeled, cored and diced*

Pre-heat oven to 350°F/175°C/Gas mark 4. Grease two large baking sheets or line with non-stick baking parchment.

● Beat the butter, icing sugar, vanilla essence and cinnamon until well combined. Stir in the flour, cornflour, apple sauce and diced apple until it forms a well mixed but crumbly dough. If the mixture is soft and sticky, refrigerate for at least 30 minutes to firm.

● Divide the mixture into 12 equal-sized pieces and using your hands shape into balls. Place the cookie balls onto the baking sheets, 8 cm/3 in apart and flatten slightly with a fork. Bake in the oven for about 25 minutes, until golden. Leave to cool on the baking sheet for 5 minutes to firm before removing with a thin metal spatula to a wire rack to cool completely.

# Chocolate and Cream Cheese Marble Fudge Bars

*Preparation time: 20 minutes* ● *Cooking time: 40 to 45 minutes* ● *Makes: 12*

**These are very rich and sticky fudge bars which can be wrapped in greaseproof paper and make wonderful lunch box fillers.**

### INGREDIENTS

### FOR THE CHOCOLATE BASE

*175 g/6 oz lightly salted butter*

*75 g/3 oz plain chocolate*

*175 g/6 oz light brown sugar*

*175 g/6 oz dark brown sugar*

*2 eggs, beaten*

*120 g/4 oz plain flour*

*6 drops vanilla essence*

### TOPPING

*175 g/6 oz cream cheese*

*75 g/3 oz light brown sugar*

*1 egg, beaten*

*4 drops vanilla essence*

Pre-heat oven to 350°F/175°C/Gas mark 4. Grease a shallow 18 x 28-cm/7 x 11-in baking tin, line with non-stick baking parchment and then grease again.

● To make the chocolate base, melt the butter and chocolate in a small saucepan over a gentle heat, taking care not to boil the mixture.

● In a mixing bowl, whisk together the light and dark brown sugars with the eggs until well combined, then whisk in the melted butter and chocolate mixture. Stir in the flour and vanilla essence. Pour the mixture into the prepared tin.

● Make the topping. Beat together the cream cheese, sugar, egg and vanilla essence until the mixture thickens to a spooning consistency. Randomly place spoonfuls of the mixture over the chocolate mixture in the baking tin and, using the tip of a sharp knife, make swirling patterns drawing the knife through the two mixtures to combine lightly. Bake in the oven for about 40 to 45 minutes, or until the mixture is firm to touch and the tip of a sharp knife comes out clean when inserted into the centre of the cookie mixture. Cool in the tin and cut into 12 equal-sized bars. Store in an airtight container in the refrigerator for up to 2 days.

# Spiced Molasses Drops

*Preparation time: 15 minutes ● Cooking time: 14 to 20 minutes ● Makes: About 40*

**These cookies are bite-size, and packed with a rich spicy flavour**

### INGREDIENTS

120 g/4 oz plain flour

1 tsp ground cinnamon

¹/₂ tsp ground ginger

¹/₂ tsp ground nutmeg

¹/₄ tsp ground cloves

¹/₂ tsp bicarbonate of soda

¹/₂ tsp salt

50 g/2 oz butter or margarine, softened

120 g/4 oz shortening

4 Tbsp molasses

120 g/4 oz dark brown sugar

1 egg

### GLAZE

175 g/6 oz icing sugar

3 tsp water

¹/₂ tsp vanilla essence

Preheat oven to 375°F/190°C/Gas mark 5. Grease two large baking sheets or line with non-stick baking parchment.

● In a medium bowl, sift together flour, cinnamon, ginger, nutmeg, cloves, bicarbonate of soda and salt. In a large bowl beat the butter or margarine, shortening, molasses, brown sugar and egg until well blended. Stir in flour-spice mixture until combined.

● Drop teaspoons of mixture 2.5 cm/1 in apart onto 2 large ungreased baking sheets. Bake until crisp and golden, 7 to 10 minutes. Cool slightly on wire racks, then remove cookies onto wire racks to cool completely. Repeat with remaining mixture.

● For the glaze, mix the icing sugar, water and vanilla until smooth. Arrange cookies on a rack over a baking sheet (to catch drips) and drizzle with glaze. Allow glaze to dry completely. Store in an airtight container.

# Milk Cookies

*Preparation time: 15 minutes* ●
*Cooking time: 15 to 20 minutes* ● *Makes: About 14*

**Serve milk cookies spread with savoury toppings such as cream cheeses and pâtés.**

### INGREDIENTS

| |
|---|
| *25 g/1 oz margarine* |
| *150 ml/5 fl oz milk* |
| *225 g/8 oz flour* |
| *1 tsp baking powder* |
| *Pinch of salt* |

Preheat oven to 350°F/175°C/Gas mark 4. Grease two large baking sheets or line with non-stick baking parchment.

● Place the margarine and milk in a small saucepan and heat gently to melt the margarine, taking care not to boil the milk. Leave to become tepid. Place the flour, baking powder and salt in a mixing bowl and add sufficient of the cooled milk and melted margarine mixture to form a dough. Knead the mixture until smooth.

● On a lightly floured surface, roll out the dough to 2-mm/⅛-in thick. Using a plain 8-cm/3-in round cutter, cut out the cookies and place on the baking sheet. Re-roll and cut out the dough to make as many cookies as possible.

● Lightly prick the surface of each cookie with the prongs of a fork several times. Bake in the oven for 15 to 20 minutes, until lightly golden all over. Remove the cookies with a thin metal spatula to a wire rack to cool completely. Store in an airtight container.

# Peanut and Lemon Crunch Bars

*Preparation time: 10 minutes + chilling*
● *Makes: About 6 bars*

**Peanut butter is a certain favourite and makes these cookies a nutritious treat.**

### INGREDIENTS

| |
|---|
| *50 g/2 oz lightly salted butter* |
| *50 g/2 oz light brown sugar* |
| *3 Tbsp honey* |
| *3 Tbsp crunchy peanut butter* |
| *Grated rind of 1 lemon* |
| *50 g/2 oz crisp rice breakfast cereal* |
| *50 g/2 oz cornflake breakfast cereal* |

Grease a 20-cm/8-in square, shallow baking tin or line with non-stick baking parchment.

● Place the butter, sugar, honey and peanut butter into a large saucepan and heat gently to melt the butter and dissolve the sugar. Do not boil the mixture. When the ingredients are melted and well combined, remove from the heat.

● Stir the lemon rind, crisp rice and cornflake breakfast cereals into the melted mixture carefully so as not to crush the cereals. Mix well. Spoon the mixture into the pan and level the surface. Leave to set for at least 30 minutes in a cool place, then cut into 6 equal-sized bars. Store in an airtight container.

# Cranberry Crunchies

*Preparation time: 15 minutes • Cooking time: 10 to 12 minutes • Makes: 14*

**Dried cranberries are full of flavour and would go well with a cup of lemon herb tea.**

## INGREDIENTS

*120 g/4 oz lightly salted butter*

*120 g/4 oz light brown sugar*

*2 Tbsp honey*

*1 egg yolk*

*175 g/6 oz self-raising flour*

*50 g/2 oz rolled oats*

*75 g/3 oz dried cranberries*

Pre-heat oven to 350°F/175°C/Gas mark 4. Grease two large baking sheets or line with non-stick baking parchment.

● Beat together the butter and sugar in a mixing bowl until pale and fluffy. Beat in the honey, egg yolk, flour and oats until well combined. Stir in the cranberries.

● Divide the mixture into 14 equal-sized pieces and roll into balls using the fingertips. Place the cookies 5 to 8 cm/2 to 3 in apart to allow for spreading onto the prepared baking sheets. Bake in the oven for about 10 to 12 minutes until golden and just firm. Leave to cool for one minute to allow the cookies to firm, before removing them with a thin metal spatula to a wire rack to cool. Store in an airtight container.

# Maple Walnut Drops

*Preparation time: 30 minutes + chilling* ● *Cooking time: 13 to 15 minutes* ● *Makes: About 48*

**These cookies are bursting with flavour and make a great cookie to come back to after an afternoon out.**

### INGREDIENTS

| |
|---|
| *120 g/4 oz raisins* |
| *300 g/10 oz plain flour* |
| *1 tsp salt* |
| *½ tsp baking powder* |
| *¼ tsp bicarbonate of soda* |
| *1 tsp ground cinnamon* |
| *½ tsp ground nutmeg* |
| *175 g/6 oz unsalted butter* |
| *120 g/4 oz dark brown sugar* |
| *2 eggs* |
| *½ Tbsp maple syrup* |
| *5 Tbsp cold, strong black coffee* |
| *150 g/5 oz coarsely chopped walnuts* |

In a small bowl, cover the raisins with hot water, stand for 15 minutes to plump. Drain the raisins and pat dry; set aside. Into a medium bowl sift together the flour, salt, baking powder, bicarbonate of soda, cinnamon and nutmeg.

● In a large bowl, beat the butter until soft, then beat in the sugar until light and fluffy. Beat in the eggs one at a time, beating well after each addition, then beat in the maple syrup.

● In three batches add the flour mixture and the black coffee ending with the flour. If the mixture seems to stiff, add a little extra coffee or water, but the mixture should be thick enough to drop. Stir in the walnuts and raisins and refrigerate until chilled, at least 30 minutes.

● Pre-heat oven to 350°F/175°C/Gas mark 4. Grease or line two baking sheets with non-stick baking parchment.

● Drop dough by heaped teaspoon on the baking sheets 5 cm/2 in apart (keeping the remaining dough refrigerated). Bake until golden and firm to the touch, 13 to 15 minutes. Rotate baking sheets halfway through cooking. Remove the baking sheets to wire racks to allow to cool slightly, then, using a metal spatula, remove the cookies onto wire racks to cool completely. Store in an airtight container.

# Blueberry Streusel Bakes

*Preparation time: 20 minutes* ● *Cooking time: 55 to 60 minutes* ● *Makes: 12 bars*

**This recipe uses blueberry jam, but plum, apricot, or even pineapple jam would be equally delicious.**

### INGREDIENTS

### BASE

*120 g/4 oz lightly salted butter*

*120 g/4 oz light brown sugar*

*120 g/4 oz plain flour*

### FILLING

*7 Tbsp blueberry jam*

### TOPPING

*150 g/5 oz plain flour*

*½ tsp baking powder*

*5 Tbsp light brown sugar*

*120 g/4 oz lightly salted butter*

*40 g/1½ oz chopped almonds*

*Grated rind of 1 lemon*

Pre-heat oven to 350°F/175°C/Gas mark 4. Grease an 18 x 28-cm/7 x 11-in baking tin.

● To make the base, beat together the butter and sugar in a mixing bowl until pale and fluffy. Stir in the flour to form a soft dough. Press the mixture down evenly over the base of the baking tin using the back of a spoon or lightly floured hand. Lightly prick the dough with a fork several times. Bake the dough in the oven for 15 minutes, until just firm. Remove from the oven and spread the blueberry jam over the dough base.

● To make the topping, place the flour, baking powder and sugar in a mixing bowl and blend in the butter, until the mixture resembles even-sized crumbs. Stir in the almonds and grated lemon rind. Sprinkle the topping over the jam. Bake in the oven for about 40 to 45 minutes until golden. Cool before cutting into bars. Store in an airtight container.

# Coconut Cookies

*Preparation time: 15 minutes ● Cooking time:*
*10 to 12 minutes ● Makes: About 24*

**An old-fashioned tea-time favourite.**

### INGREDIENTS

120 g/4 oz light brown sugar

225 g/8 oz lightly salted butter

350 g/12 oz plain flour

50 g/2 oz sweetened flaked coconut

Pre-heat oven to 375°F/190°C/Gas mark 5. Grease two large baking sheets or line with non-stick baking parchment.

● Place the sugar, butter and flour in a mixing bowl and with fingertips, blend the mixture together until it resembles breadcrumbs. Add the coconut and work the mixture together to form a dough. Do not be tempted to add any liquid as the crumb mixture, once kneaded, will come together to make a smooth dough.

● On a lightly floured surface, halve the mixture and make two long rolls about 3 to 4 cm/1¾ to 1⅓ in in diameter. Cut into 1-cm/½-in slices. Place the cookies on the baking sheets, 2.5 cm/1 in apart to allow for spreading during baking. Bake in the oven for 10 to 12 minutes, until a pale light brown. Allow to cool for 1 minute before removing to a wire rack to cool completely. Store in an airtight container.

# Cinnamon Palmiers

*Preparation time: 10 minutes ● Cooking time:*
*10 to 12 minutes ● Makes: 18 to 20*

**A variation on the French classic.**

### INGREDIENTS

225 g/8 oz ready-rolled puff pastry, thawed, if frozen

3 Tbsp dark brown sugar

1 tsp ground cinnamon

Pre-heat oven to 425°F/220°C/Gas mark 7. Grease two large baking sheets or line with non-stick baking parchment.

● Place the pastry on a lightly floured surface and if necessary roll out to a 28 x 23-cm/11 x 9-in rectangle.

● In a small bowl mix together the sugar and cinnamon. Sprinkle two-thirds of the cinnamon mixture evenly over the surface of the pastry. Fold each of the shortest pastry sides into the centre, press down and sprinkle over the remaining cinnamon mixture. Fold each pastry side in half again so they meet in the centre. Brush the pastry with cold water and fold over to make a long roll. Cut across the roll to make 5-mm/¼-in slices and place on the baking sheets 2.5 cm/1 in apart to allow for spreading.

● Bake in the oven for 8 minutes until golden, then carefully using a thin metal spatula, turn the palmiers over and cook for a further 3 to 5 minutes to brown and crisp the other side. Remove from the baking sheet with a thin metal spatula and cool on a wire rack. Best eaten when made, but can be kept in an airtight container for a few days, although they will lose their crispness.

# Mini Florentines

*Preparation time: 25 minutes* ● *Cooking time: 10 minutes* ● *Makes: About 16*

**Don't reserve these fantastic cookies for the festive season.**

## INGREDIENTS

| |
|---|
| *50 g/2 oz lightly salted butter* |
| *2 Tbsp light brown sugar* |
| *2 tsp treacle* |
| *50 g/2 oz finely chopped glacé cherries* |
| *2 Tbsp finely chopped walnuts* |
| *2 Tbsp raisins* |
| *2 Tbsp candied citrus peel* |
| *25 g/1 oz plain flour* |
| *2 oz plain chocolate* |

Pre-heat oven to 325°F/160°C/Gas mark 3. Grease and line a large baking sheet with non-stick baking parchment. In a small saucepan, melt the butter, sugar and treacle over a low heat, taking care not to boil the mixture. When the ingredients are melted and well combined, stir in the cherries, walnuts, raisins, candied mixed peel and flour. Mix thoroughly.

● Place small heaped teaspoonfuls of the mixture onto the baking sheet at least 2.5 cm/1 in apart to allow for spreading. Bake in the oven for about 10 minutes, until the mixture has spread slightly and is bubbling. Remove the cookies from the oven and allow to cool slightly to firm, before lifting off with a thin metal spatula and placing on a wire rack to cool completely.

● Break the chocolate into small pieces and place in a small bowl over a pan of hot water. Melt the chocolate very slowly, taking care not to boil or get water in the chocolate. When the chocolate has melted, stir and remove from the heat. Using a pastry brush, cover the base of each Florentine with a little of the melted chocolate and leave chocolate side up on the wire rack until set. If desired, when the chocolate is very nearly set, make a wavy line pattern with the back of a fork on each chocolate Florentine. When the chocolate has set, store the Florentines in an airtight container.

# No-bake Chocolate Delights

*Preparation time: 15 minutes + setting* ● *Makes: About 18 to 20*

**A cross between a cookie and a truffle – and so easy to make.**

## INGREDIENTS

*150 g/5 oz sponge cake crumbs*

*75 g/3 oz glacé cherries, quartered*

*50 g/2 oz raisins*

*50 g/2 oz plain chocolate*

*50 g/2 oz lightly salted butter*

*2 Tbsp milk*

Place the cake crumbs, quartered glacé cherries and raisins into a mixing bowl. Break the chocolate into small pieces and place in a small heatproof bowl with the butter and milk over a saucepan of hot, but not boiling, water. Carefully melt all of the ingredients and stir into the sponge and fruit mixture. Mix together thoroughly to combine all of the ingredients and then leave to cool for a short while until the mixture is cool enough to handle.

● Using a teaspoon, place heaped spoonfuls of mixture on greaseproof paper in a single layer on a baking sheet. Chill the chocolate cookies in the refrigerator for at least 1 hour, to firm. Remove from the greaseproof paper and store in an airtight container.

# Minute Meringues

*Preparation time: 10 minutes* ● *Cooking time: 45 minutes* ● *Makes: 26*

**Tiny bubbles of airy sugar – irresistible!**

### INGREDIENTS

*1 egg white*

*50 g/2 oz light brown sugar*

*1 tsp cornflour*

Pre-heat oven to 275°F/140°C/Gas mark 1. Line two baking sheets with edible rice paper or non-stick baking parchment.

● Place the egg white in a grease-free mixing bowl and whisk until soft peaks form. Whisk in half of the sugar and all of the cornflour, until well combined. Add the remaining sugar and whisk until shiny and fairly stiff.

● Spoon the meringue mixture carefully into a piping bag fitted with a small star nozzle and then pipe small wavy lines about 5 cm/2 in long and small rosettes directly onto the lined baking sheets, leaving 2.5 cm/1 in between them to allow for a little spreading during the cooking process. Bake in the oven for about 45 minutes, until pale brown and crisp. Remove from the oven and cool completely, before removing from the baking parchment. If using rice paper, remove as much as possible, but any left on the base of the meringues is edible. Store in an airtight container.

# Maple Pecan Wafers

*Preparation time: 25 minutes* ● *Cooking time: 48 minutes* ● *Makes: About 24*

**These elegant wafers are ideal served with ice cream. Be sure to use real maple syrup, not the artificial flavouring – it makes a big difference.**

### INGREDIENTS

*175 g/6 oz pecan halves*

*50 g/2 oz unsalted butter*

*225 g/8 oz dark brown sugar*

*75 g/3 oz plain flour*

*1 tsp maple syrup*

*¼ tsp salt*

*1 egg, lightly beaten*

Pre-heat oven to 375°F/190°C/Gas mark 5. Line a large baking sheet with foil. Set aside 24 perfect pecan halves, then chop the remaining nuts.

● In a medium saucepan over a low heat, melt the butter. Remove from the heat and stir in the sugar, flour, maple syrup, salt and egg until well blended. Drop tablespoonfuls, at least 8 cm/3 in apart on the baking sheet, place a reserved pecan halve into the centre of each.

● Bake the wafers for 12 minutes, remove the baking sheet to a wire rack to cool slightly, then transfer the cookies onto a wire rack to cool completely. Cook the baking sheet and re-line, then repeat with another batch of cookies. When the wafers are cool, peel off foil and store in an airtight container with greaseproof paper between the layers.

# Cardamom Cookies

*Preparation time: 10 minutes ● Cooking time: 15 minutes ● Makes: 14*

**Fresh cardamom seeds have a distinctive but subtle flavour characteristic of the Eastern Mediterranean.**

### INGREDIENTS

*120 g/4 oz lightly salted butter*

*50 g/2 oz icing sugar*

*125 g/4 oz plain flour*

*3 drops almond essence*

*6 cardamom pods, split and seeds lightly crushed*

*25 g/1 oz chopped walnuts*

Pre-heat oven to 350°F/175°C/Gas mark 4. Grease two large baking sheets or line with non-stick baking parchment.

● Place the butter, icing sugar and flour in a large mixing bowl and beat together thoroughly. Stir in the almond essence, crushed cardamom seeds and chopped walnuts until well combined and the dough has a firm texture.

● Using your hands, shape the dough into 14 equal-sized balls and place 5 cm/2 in apart on the baking sheets. Bake in the oven for about 15 minutes, or until lightly browned. Remove with a thin metal spatula to a wire rack to cool completely. Store in an airtight container.

# Chocolate Prezels

*Preparation time: 40 minutes + chilling* ●
*Cooking time: 10 to 15 minutes* ● *Makes: 30*

**These delicious prezels are surprisingly easy to form.**

### INGREDIENTS

*175 g/6 oz plain flour*

*¼ tsp salt*

*3 Tbsp unsweetened cocoa powder*

*120 g/4 oz unsalted butter*

*125 g/4 oz caster sugar*

*1 egg, beaten*

*1 tsp vanilla essence*

### GLAZE

*1 egg white, lightly beaten*

*Sugar crystals, for sprinkling*

Sift together the flour, salt, and cocoa powder. In a separate bowl, beat the butter until creamy, add the sugar and beat until light and fluffy. Beat in the egg and vanilla essence until blended. Gradually add the flour mixture until combined. Turn onto a piece of clingfilm and seal. Refrigerate until firm.

● Pre-heat oven to 375°F/190°C/Gas mark 5. Grease two baking sheets or line with non-stick baking parchment.

● With lightly floured hands, roll dough into about 30 4-cm/1½-in balls. Roll into a "rope" about 23 cm/9 in long. Bring each end of the "rope" together to meet in the centre. Twist the ends together, and press to the middle of the "rope" to form the prezel shape. Transfer to the baking sheets.

● Brush each prezel with egg white to glaze, then sprinkle with sugar crystals. Bake until firm, 10 to 12 minutes. Cool and tranfer to wire racks to cool completely. Store in an airtight container.

# Nut Rocks

*Preparation time: 20 minutes + chilling* ●
*Cooking time: 15 minutes* ● *Makes: 12*

**Crunchy cookies with a hint of oranges and almonds.**

### INGREDIENTS

*120 g/4 oz lightly salted butter*

*50 g/2 oz light brown sugar*

*Grated rind of 1 orange*

*1 egg, separated*

*120 g/4 oz plain flour*

*50 g/2 oz ground almonds*

Beat the butter and sugar together in a mixing bowl until pale and fluffy. Beat in the orange rind, egg yolk, and flour. Refrigerate for at least 30 minutes.

● Pre-heat oven to 350°F/175°C/Gas mark 4. Grease two large baking sheets or line with non-stick baking parchment. Using your hands, divide the cookie dough into 12 equal-sized balls and roll each in the lightly beaten egg white then in the ground almonds to coat evenly. Place the almond-covered balls on the baking sheets at least 2.5 cm/1 in apart. Bake for about 15 minutes, until just firm and light brown. Remove the cookies immediately from the baking sheet with a thin metal spatula, to prevent them from sticking, and cool on a wire rack. Store in an airtight container.

# Tropical Fruit Cookies

*Preparation time: 15 minutes* • *Cooking time: 12 to 15 minutes* • *Makes: 12*

**Almost every fruit under the sun is now available dried – try a new flavour or use your favourites, the choice is yours.**

### INGREDIENTS

*120 g/4 oz lightly salted butter*

*120 g/4 oz granulated sugar*

*1 egg, beaten*

*75 g/3 oz plain flour*

*75 g/3 oz chopped ready-to-eat dried exotic fruit (papaya, mango, pineapple or melon)*

Pre-heat oven to 350°F/175°C/Gas mark 4. Grease two large baking sheets or line with non-stick baking parchment.

● Beat the butter and sugar together in a mixing bowl until pale and fluffy. Beat in the egg and flour. Stir in the chopped exotic fruit mix.

● Place 12 equal-sized spoonfuls of the mixture onto the baking sheets, allowing 5 to 8 cm/2 to 3 in in between them for spreading. Flatten the mounds of mixture a little with the back of the spoon. Bake in the oven for about 12 to 15 minutes, until pale golden. Remove from the oven and leave to firm for one minute. Transfer to a wire rack and cool completely. Store the cookies in an airtight container.

# Honey and Date Comforts

*Preparation time: 10 minutes* ● *Cooking time: 12 to 15 minutes* ● *Makes: About 12 to 14*

**Comfort food at bedtime.**

### INGREDIENTS

*125 g/4 oz lightly salted butter*

*250 g/8 oz light brown sugar*

*1 egg, beaten*

*175 g/6 oz plain flour*

*2 Tbsp honey*

*75 g/3 oz chopped dried dates*

Pre-heat oven to 350°F/175°C/Gas mark 4. Grease two large baking sheets or line with non-stick baking parchment.

● Beat the butter and sugar together in a mixing bowl until pale and fluffy. Beat in the egg, flour and honey. Stir in the chopped dates.

● Place 12 to 14 equal-sized spoonfuls of the mixture onto the baking sheets, allowing 5 to 8 cm/2 to 3 in in between for spreading. Flatten the mounds of mixture a little with the back of the spoon. Bake in the oven for about 12 to 15 minutes, until pale golden. Remove from the oven and leave to firm for one minute on the baking sheets before removing with a spatula to a wire rack to cool completely. Store in an airtight container.

# Around the World

The cookie is not a new phenomenon and most countries have little treasures that are loved by their people. Looking at the following selection, it is clear to see national influences such as almonds from Italy, spices from the Middle East, thick cream from Britain, and pecans and maple syrup from North America. There are stunning similarities too, in the use of butter, sugar, and spices which are used universally to create a treat that's always a pleasure to eat.

These cookies make excellent desserts. Espresso Biscotti would make a delightful finale to an Italian meal, serve the Spanish Churros after paella, and the Coconut Fortune Cookies after a stir-fry.

## North America

*The American nation has taken the idea of the cookie and run with it. Cookies are everywhere, and they are bigger, more action-packed and more adventurous than their traditional ancestors.*

## Britain

*Known as biscuits rather than cookies in Britain, these are usually served with morning coffee or afternoon tea.*

# Western Europe

*Steeped in history and culture, Western Europe has a long culinary tradition as clearly exemplified in its magnificent cookies as in any of its fancy sauces.*

# Further Afield

*Eastern Europe, Scandinavia, Australia, New Zealand, India and China all have their own traditional cookie recipes. Typical ingredients include nuts, sour cream, fresh fruit juice and all kinds of spices.*

# Pennsylvanian Shoofly Slices

*Preparation time: 40 minutes* ● *Cooking time: 35 minutes* ● *Makes: 14 slices*

**This cookie owes its origin to the shoofly pies popular in America's Southern States.**

### INGREDIENTS

175 g/6 oz plain flour

pinch of salt

2 Tbsp icing sugar

120 g/4 oz lightly salted butter

### FILLING

3 Tbsp golden syrup

3 Tbsp treacle

150 ml/5 fl oz boiling water

1 tsp bicarbonate of soda

275 g/10 oz plain flour

1 tsp ground ginger

1 tsp ground cinnamon

120 g/4 oz lightly salted butter

175 g/6 oz light brown sugar

Pre-heat oven to 350°F/175°C/Gas mark 4. Lightly grease a 28 x 18-cm/11 x 7-in tin. Sift the flour, salt and icing sugar into a mixing bowl. Blend in the butter until the mixture resembles fine breadcrumbs. Add enough cold water to make a firm dough. Roll out on a lightly floured surface and use to line the base and sides of the tin. Chill the dough in the refrigerator while making the filling.

● Put the golden syrup and treacle in a heatproof jug and pour over the boiling water. Stir until well-mixed, then add the bicarbonate of soda and mix again. Leave to stand for 5 minutes.

● Sift the flour, ginger and cinnamon into a bowl. Blend in the butter until the mixture resembles breadcrumbs. Stir in the light brown sugar. Spoon half the crumb mixture evenly over the base of the tin. Slowly pour over the syrup and treacle mixture, then spoon over the remaining crumb mixture.

● Bake immediately for 35 minutes, or until lightly set. The mixture will rise a little as it cooks, but will sink again as it cools. Leave to cool in the tin. Divide the baked mixture into 14 slices.

# New Orleans Oat Cookies

*Preparation time: 20 minutes ● Cooking time: 10 minutes ● Makes: 20*

**The food of New Orleans has been influenced by African, Spanish and French cuisines as seen in these delicious cookies.**

## INGREDIENTS

*120 g/4 oz lightly salted butter*

*120 g/4 oz light brown sugar*

*1 egg, beaten*

*175 g/6 oz self-raising flour*

*5 Tbsp fine oatmeal*

*175 g/6 oz rolled oats*

*3 Tbsp pumpkin seeds*

*Pumpkin seeds, to decorate*

Pre-heat oven to 375°F190°C/Gas mark 5. Lightly grease two baking sheets.

● Beat the butter and sugar until light and fluffy. Add the beaten egg, a little at a time, beating between each addition. Sift the flour over the butter mixture and work into the butter mixture with the oatmeal, oats and pumpkin seeds.

● Roll out on a lightly floured surface to about 5 mm/¼ in thick. Stamp out rounds with a 6-cm/2½-in plain cutter. Place on the baking sheets, spacing slightly apart. Press a few pumpkin seeds on the top of each to decorate. Bake for 10 minutes, until golden brown. Leave on the baking sheets for 5 minutes, then remove and cool on a wire rack. Store in an airtight container.

# Peanut Butter and Jelly Cookies

*Preparation time: 25 minutes + chilling* ● *Cooking time: 15 minutes* ● *Makes: 24*

**The classic American combination of peanut butter and jelly (jam) not only appears as a sandwich filling, but in these giant crunchy cookies as well.**

## INGREDIENTS

*75 g/3 oz unsalted peanuts*

*120 g/4 oz unsalted butter*

*120 g/4 oz caster sugar*

*5 Tbsp light brown sugar*

*1 Tbsp seedless raspberry jam*

*120 g/4 oz  smooth or crunchy peanut butter*

*1 tsp vanilla essence*

*1 egg, beaten*

*175 g/6 oz plain flour*

*2 tsp baking powder*

Pre-heat oven to 350°F/175°C/Gas mark 4. Lightly grease 2 baking sheets or line with non-stick baking parchment. Spread the peanuts on a baking sheet and roast in the oven for 5 minutes, until beginning to turn brown. Allow to cool, then roughly chop.

● Beat the butter and sugars until light and fluffy. Add the jam, peanut butter and vanilla essence, then beat until thoroughly mixed. Gradually add the egg, a little at a time, beating well after each addition. Sift the flour and baking powder into the bowl. Stir into the mixture with the chopped nuts to make a soft dough. Wrap the dough in clingfilm and chill in the refrigerator for 1 hour.

● Divide the dough into 24 pieces. Roll each piece into a ball the size of a walnut. Put the cookies onto the prepared baking sheets, spacing them well apart. Flatten slightly with a fork. Bake for 15 minutes or until golden brown. Leave on the baking sheets for 3 to 4 minutes, then remove with a thin metal spatula and cool on a wire rack.

## VARIATION

### Hazelnut Cookies

● Add 120 g/4 oz hazelnut butter and 75 g/3 oz chopped roasted hazelnuts instead of the peanut butter and unsalted peanuts.

# Rocky Road

*Preparation time: 25 minutes* ● *Cooking time: 10 minutes* ● *Makes: 18*

**Both children and adults love this sumptuously wicked treat.**

## INGREDIENTS

| | |
|---|---|
| 75 g/3 oz plain flour | |
| 2 Tbsp unsweetened cocoa powder | |
| 25 g/1 oz icing sugar | |
| 50 g/2 oz lightly salted butter | |
| 1 egg yolk | |
| 1 Tbsp milk | |

### TOPPING

| |
|---|
| 400 g/14 oz plain chocolate |
| 120 g/4 oz unsalted butter |
| 25 g/1 oz glacé cherries |
| 50 g/2 oz mini marshmallows |
| 5 Tbsp unsalted peanuts |

Pre-heat oven to 350°F/175°C/Gas mark 4. Grease and line the base of an 18 x 28-cm/7 x 11-in tin with non-stick baking parchment.

● Sift the flour, cocoa powder and icing sugar into a bowl. Cut the butter into small pieces and blend in until the mixture resembles breadcrumbs. Add the egg yolk and milk to the dry ingredients and mix to a firm dough. Knead on a lightly floured surface until smooth, then press into the base of the tin. Prick all over with a fork, then bake for 10 minutes. Leave to cool while making the topping.

● Break the chocolate into pieces and put in a bowl with the butter over a saucepan of near-boiling water. Heat gently until melted, stirring occasionally. Remove from the heat and allow to cool for 3 minutes. While the chocolate is melting, snip the cherries into quarters with oiled scissors. Stir into the chocolate with the mini marshmallows and peanuts.

● Quickly pour the topping over the base, gently shaking the tin to spread the mixture. Leave to set at room temperature. Cut into small squares and store in the refrigerator until ready to serve.

# Raisin Rockies

*Preparation time: 20 minutes ● Cooking time: 15 minutes ● Makes: 16*

**The raisins in these tasty cookies are soaked in orange juice to make them plump and juicy.**

## INGREDIENTS

*50 g/2 oz raisins*

*2 Tbsp orange juice*

*120 g/4 oz lightly salted butter*

*50 g/2 oz caster sugar*

*50 g/2 oz light brown sugar*

*Grated rind of ½ orange*

*1 egg, beaten*

*175 g/6 oz plain flour*

*½ tsp bicarbonate of soda*

Put the raisins in a small bowl. Sprinkle over the orange juice, stir, cover with clingfilm and leave to soak for at least 2 hours, or overnight in the refrigerator.

● Pre-heat oven to 350°F/175°C/Gas mark 4. Lightly grease two baking sheets. Beat the butter, sugars and orange rind together until light and fluffy. Gradually add the egg, beating well between each addition. Sift the flour and bicarbonate together and work into the butter mixture with the soaked raisins to make a soft, dropping mixture.

● Drop heaped teaspoonfuls onto the prepared baking sheets, spacing well apart. Bake for 15 minutes until lightly browned. Leave on the baking sheets for 5 minutes, then remove and cool on a wire rack. Store in an airtight container.

## VARIATION

**Apricot and Almond Rockies**

● Substitute 50 g/2 oz chopped dried apricots for the raisins and mix in 25 g/1 oz chopped blanched almonds.

# Refrigerator Cookies

*Preparation time: 20 minutes* ● *Cooking time: 10 to 12 minutes* ● *Makes: 40*

**This cookie dough will keep for up to a week in the refrigerator.
It freezes well too so you can make it ahead and bake as necessary.**

## INGREDIENTS

| |
|---|
| *225 g/8 oz plain flour* |
| *1 tsp baking powder* |
| *120 g/4 oz lightly salted butter* |
| *50 g/2 oz caster sugar* |
| *1 egg* |
| *½ tsp vanilla essence* |

Sift the flour and baking powder into a mixing bowl. Cut the butter into small pieces and blend in until the mixture resembles breadcrumbs. Stir in the sugar. Beat the egg with the vanilla essence, add to the dry ingredients and mix to a firm dough. Shape into a roll about 5 cm/2 in in diameter and wrap in clingfilm or foil. Chill in the refrigerator for at least 2 hours, or until needed.

● When ready to bake the cookies, pre-heat oven to 375°F/190°C/Gas mark 5. Lightly grease three baking sheets or line with non-stick baking parchment.

● Unwrap the dough and cut into 5-mm/¼-in slices. Arrange on the baking sheets, spacing slightly apart. Bake for 10 to 12 minutes or until golden-brown. Leave on the baking sheets for 5 minutes, then transfer to a wire rack to cool.

## VARIATIONS

### Fruit and Nut

● Stir 50 g/2 oz chopped raisins and 50 g/2 oz chopped walnuts into the dry ingredients. Replace the vanilla essence with almond essence.

### Cherry and Almond

● Stir 25 g/1 oz chopped glacé cherries and 50 g/2 oz chopped blanched almonds into the dry ingredients. Replace the vanilla essence with almond essence.

### Double Chocolate Chip

● Replace 50 g/2 oz flour with 50 g/2 oz unsweetened cocoa powder and stir 50 g/2 oz plain or white chocolate chips into the dry ingredients.

# Pecan Tassies

*Preparation time: 30 minutes* ● *Cooking time: 20 minutes* ● *Makes: 24*

**These American tassies from the Southern Pecan-growing regions taste as delicious as they sound. Considered a "cookie" it is really a mini tartlet. Tender cream cheese pastry filled with a caramelized pecan centre.**

## INGREDIENTS

### CREAM CHEESE PASTRY

| |
|---|
| 120 g/4 oz plain flour |
| 1 Tbsp sugar |
| ¼ tsp salt |
| ¼ tsp ground nutmeg |
| 120 g/4 oz unsalted butter, softened |
| 50 g/2 oz full-fat soft cheese, softened |

### PECAN FILLING

| |
|---|
| 1 egg |
| 5 Tbsp dark brown sugar |
| 1 tsp vanilla essence |
| 25 g/1 oz unsalted butter, melted |
| 50 g/2 oz chopped toasted pecan nuts |
| 24 pecan halves, for decoration |

First, lightly and evenly butter two 12-bun or one 24-bun bun tins.

● Into a medium bowl, sift the flour, add the sugar, salt and nutmeg. Add the butter and cream cheese and, using your fingertips or a food processor, blend together until a soft dough forms. Cover the bowl and refrigerate until just firm enough to roll out, about 10 minutes.

● On a lightly floured surface, roll the pastry to 8 mm/ ⅓ in thick. Using a 6-cm/2½-in cutter cut out 24 circles. Carefully line the bun tins with the pastry circles, gently pressing pastry onto the bottom and sides. Refrigerate for 20 to 30 minutes. (If using a12-bun tin, refrigerate remaining dough and cut out once the first batch is cooked.)

● In a medium bowl, beat the eggs until foamy. Gradually beat in the brown sugar, vanilla essence, and melted butter. Sprinkle an equal amount of chopped pecans into each cup. Carefully distribute the filling in the bun tin, and top with a pecan half.

● Bake the tassies until the tops are puffed and the filling set with golden pastry edges, about 20 minutes. Remove to a wire rack to cool, 20 to 30 minutes. Using the top of a sharp knife, gently loosen the edge of the pastry from each bun tin and unmould each tassie. Either serve warm or cool completely, then store in an airtight container.

### TIP

Filling can be made with toasted chopped walnuts, hazelnuts, macadamias or even pine nuts, but pecan nuts are traditional.

# Grantham Gingerbread

*Preparation time: 15 minutes ● Cooking time: 35 minutes ● Makes: 25*

**These crisp pale spiced cookies are also known as White Buttons in the Norfolk fenlands
where they are rolled in sugar after cooking.**

### INGREDIENTS

*120 g/4 oz lightly salted butter*

*400 g/14 oz caster sugar*

*1 egg, beaten*

*250 g/9 oz self-raising flour*

*1 tsp ground ginger*

*¼ tsp ground cinnamon*

Pre-heat oven to 300°F/150°C/Gas mark 2. Lightly grease two baking sheets or line with non-stick baking parchment.

● Beat the butter and sugar together until pale and fluffy. Gradually add the egg, beating well after each addition. Sift the flour and spices into the mixture and work in to make a firm dough.

● Roll into small walnut-sized balls and place on the prepared baking sheets, spacing slightly apart. Bake for 35 minutes, or until well-risen, crisp and golden. Leave on the baking sheets for 2 to 3 minutes, then remove and cool on a wire rack.

### VARIATION

● For spicier cookies, sprinkle with 2 tablespoons caster sugar and ¼ teaspoon of ground ginger and cinnamon.

# Wholemeal Digestives

*Preparation time: 20 minutes* ● *Cooking time: 20 minutes* ● *Makes: 20*

**These are sometimes spread with butter and served with cheese.**
**The amount of sugar may be varied, depending how sweet you like them.**

## INGREDIENTS

*225 g/8 oz plain wholemeal flour*

*50 g/2 oz fine oatmeal*

*½ tsp salt*

*50 g/2 oz lightly salted butter*

*50 g/2 oz white vegetable fat*

*4 Tbsp soft light brown sugar*

*½ beaten egg*

*2 Tbsp milk*

*2 Tbsp fine oatmeal, for sprinkling*

Pre-heat oven to 350°F/175°C/Gas mark 4. Lightly grease two baking sheets or line the base with sheets of non-stick baking parchment.

● Put the flour, oatmeal and salt in a bowl and stir together. Blend in the butter and white vegetable fat until the mixture resembles fine breadcrumbs. Stir in the sugar. Add the beaten egg and mix to a firm dough. Lightly knead for a few seconds until smooth.

● Roll out the dough on a floured surface to a thickness of 3 mm/⅛ in. Cut into rounds using a 6-cm/2½-in plain cutter and lift onto the prepared baking sheets.

● Brush the rounds very lightly with milk and sprinkle with the oatmeal. Prick all over with a fork and bake for 20 minutes, until slightly darkened. Leave on the baking sheets for 2 minutes, then remove and cool on a wire rack.

# Scottish Shortbread

*Preparation time: 15 minutes+ chilling time* ●
*Cooking time: 30 to 40 minutes* ●
*Makes: One 18-cm/7-in shortbread round*

**Generations of Scots have baked this simple delicious recipe. As with all "traditional" recipes there are many variations, but it is always made with butter.**

### INGREDIENTS

| |
|---|
| *120 g/4 oz lightly salted butter* |
| *2 Tbsp caster sugar* |
| *150 g/5 oz plain flour* |
| *3 Tbsp semolina or ground rice* |
| *1 Tbsp caster sugar, for dusting* |

Lightly grease a baking sheet or line with non-stick baking parchment.

● Put the butter in a mixing bowl and beat until soft and creamy. Stir in the sugar. Sift in the flour and mix in with the semolina or ground rice. Lightly knead on a floured surface for a few seconds until smooth.

● Roll out the dough to a 15-cm/6-in circle, then press into an 18-cm/7-in shortbread mould. Unmould onto the prepared baking sheet. If you haven't got a shortbread mould, press the mixture into an 18-cm/7-in loose-bottomed pie tin. Prick all over and mark into 8 wedges. Chill in the refrigerator for 1 hour.

● Pre-heat oven to 325°F/160°C/Gas mark 3.

● Bake for 35 to 40 minutes, or until pale golden-brown. Remove from the oven and dust with caster sugar. Leave on the baking sheet or remove from the tin, leaving the shortbread on the base for 15 minutes, then cool on a wire rack. Store in an airtight container.

# Cornish Fairings

*Preparation time: 15 minutes* ●
*Cooking time: 12 to 15 minutes* ● *Makes: 16*

**Cornish Fairings were sold in the market town of Launceston at the annual fair where maids were hired.**

### INGREDIENTS

| |
|---|
| *175 g/6 oz self-raising flour* |
| *1½ tsp ground ginger* |
| *Pinch of freshly grated nutmeg* |
| *75 g/3 oz lightly salted butter* |
| *5 Tbsp light brown sugar* |
| *3 Tbsp golden syrup* |
| *3 Tbsp treacle* |
| *1½ tsp bicarbonate of soda* |

Pre-heat oven to 350°F/175°C/Gas mark 4. Lightly grease two baking sheets or line with non-stick baking parchment.

● Sift the flour, ginger and nutmeg into a large mixing bowl. Blend in the butter until the mixture resembles find breadcrumbs. Stir in the sugar.

● Gently warm the golden syrup and treacle in a small pan. Stir in the bicarbonate, then immediately add to the dry and mix together to a soft dough.

● Roll the dough into walnut-sized balls and place on the prepared baking sheets. Flatten with a thin metal spatula to about 1 cm/½ in thick. Bake for 12 to 15 minutes until slightly darkened and cracked in appearance. Leave on the baking sheets for 10 minutes, or until firm, then cool on wire racks.

# Amaretti

*Preparation time: 15 minutes* ●
*Cooking time: 12 minutes* ● *Makes: 30*

**Wrap these almond cookies in pairs with pretty pastel tissue paper for an authentic Italian presentation.**

### INGREDIENTS

*1 egg white*

*2 tsp amaretto liqueur*

*¼ tsp almond essence*

*175 g/6 oz ground almonds*

*120 g/4 oz icing sugar*

*2 Tbsp icing sugar, for dusting*

Pre-heat oven to 350°F/175°C/Gas mark 4. Line two baking sheets with non-stick baking parchment.
● Lightly whisk the egg white with a fork until slightly frothy. Add the amaretto liqueur and almond essence and whisk again.
● Put the ground almonds in a bowl and sift in the icing sugar. Make a well in the centre, add the egg white mixture and stir to a stiff dough. Divide the dough into 30 pieces, then roll each into a ball. Place on the prepared baking sheets, spacing slightly apart.
● Bake for 12 minutes, or until the cookies are golden-brown. Dust with icing sugar. Leave on the baking sheets for 2 minutes, then transfer to a wire rack to cool. When completely cold wrap in pairs in coloured tissue paper.

### TIP

Amaretto is a sweet almond liqueur. An orange or coffee liqueur may be used instead.

# Fior di Mandorle

*Preparation time: 20 minutes + chilling* ●
*Cooking time: 15 minutes* ● *Makes: 20*

**These sweet almond cookies, flavoured with cinnamon, are Arabic in origin, but are made throughout Sicily.**

### INGREDIENTS

*150 g/5 oz lightly salted butter, softened*

*120 g/4 oz caster sugar*

*1 Tbsp honey*

*120 g/4 oz plain flour*

*½ tsp ground cinnamon*

*¾ cup ground almonds*

*Caster sugar and cinnamon, for dusting*

Pre-heat oven to 350°F/175°C/Gas mark 4. Lightly grease two baking sheets or line with non-stick baking parchment.
● Beat the butter, sugar and honey together until light and fluffy. Sift the flour and cinnamon into the bowl and work into the butter mixture with the ground almonds. Lightly knead on a floured surface until smooth. Wrap in clingfilm and chill in the refrigerator for 30 minutes.
● Roll out the dough on a floured surface to a thickness of 5 mm/¼ in and cut into 8-cm/3-in squares. Carefully transfer to the prepared baking sheets, spacing slightly apart. Chill for a further 30 minutes.
● Bake for 15 minutes, or until light golden-brown. As soon as the cookies come out of the oven, dust with a little caster sugar and ground cinnamon. Leave on the baking sheets for 5 minutes, then remove with a thin metal spatula and cool on a wire rack. Store in an airtight container.

# Espresso Biscotti

*Preparation time: 20 minutes* ● *Cooking time: 30 minutes* ● *Makes: 00*

**They're wonderful served with steaming black coffee or cappuccino, although traditionally they are dipped into chilled sweet wine.**

## INGREDIENTS

*75 g/3 oz unblanched almonds*

*250 g/9 oz plain flour*

*1½ tsp baking powder*

*Pinch of salt*

*75 g/3 oz unsalted butter*

*120 g/4 oz caster sugar*

*2 eggs, beaten*

*2 Tbsp strong espresso coffee, cooled*

Pre-heat oven to 350°F/175°C/Gas mark 4. Grease a baking sheet or line with non-stick baking parchment.

● Place the almonds on a baking sheet and toast in the oven for 5 minutes. Allow to cool, then grind in a nut grinder or food processor until fine.

● Sift the flour, baking powder and salt into a mixing bowl. Cut the butter into small pieces and blend into the flour until the mixture resembles breadcrumbs. Stir in the sugar and ground almonds. Make a well in the centre. Mix the egg and coffee together and add to the dry ingredients. Mix to a firm dough.

● Lightly knead on a floured surface for a few seconds until smooth, then shape into 2 rolls about 6 cm/2½ in in diameter. Transfer to the prepared baking sheet and bake for 20 minutes until lightly browned. Leave to cool for 5 minutes, then cut with a serrated knife into 5-mm/½-in slices. Arrange on the baking sheet, cut-side down and bake for a further 10 minutes, until golden brown and dry to the touch. Store the biscotti in an airtight container for at least 24 hours before serving.

# Panforte di Siena

*Preparation time: 35 minutes ● Cooking time: 40 minutes ● Makes: 12 slices*

**A speciality of Siena in Italy, thin slices of this rich fruit and nut cookie are traditionally served at Christmas.**

### INGREDIENTS

| |
|---|
| 50 g/2 oz candied citrus peel |
| 50 g/2 oz crystallized pineapple |
| 25 g/1 oz glacé cherries |
| 50 g/2 oz papaya or mango |
| 75 g/3 oz whole unblanched almonds |
| 50 g/2 oz walnut pieces |
| 5 Tbsp plain flour |
| 1 tsp ground cinnamon |
| ¼ tsp ground coriander |
| ¼ tsp ground cloves |
| ¼ tsp ground nutmeg |
| 225 g/8 oz granulated sugar |
| 3 Tbsp cold water |
| Edible rice paper |
| 2 Tbsp icing sugar, to dust |

Pre-heat oven to 325°F/160°C/Gas mark 3. Cut the rice paper to fit the base of a 20-cm/8-in loose-bottomed tin. Lightly grease the tin, then line with the rice paper.

● Chop the fruit and nuts and put in a mixing bowl with the flour and spices. Put the sugar in a small heavy-bottomed saucepan with the water and heat very gently until the sugar dissolves. Turn up the heat and boil the syrup for 3 to 4 minutes, or until it reaches 220°F/104°C on a sugar thermometer. Pour the syrup over the dry ingredients and mix well.

● Spoon the mixture into the prepared tin and level the top. Bake for 40 minutes. Remove from the oven; it will still be soft, but will firm up as it cools. Leave in the tin for 5 minutes, then loosen the edges with a thin metal spatula and remove from the tin. Allow to cool on the base. When completely cold, remove the base and dust with icing sugar. Cut into very thin slices to serve. Store in an airtight container.

### TIP

If you haven't got a sugar thermometer, boil the syrup to short-thread stage; remove a little syrup in a teaspoon, cool for a minute then press between finger and thumb and pull; it should form a short thread.

# Pine Nut Macaroons

*Preparation time: 25 minutes + cooling* ● *Cooking time: 12 to 15 minutes* ● *Makes: About 24*

**In Italy, pine nut macaroons are often sandwiched together with a little apricot jam – delicious.**

### INGREDIENTS

*3 Tbsp currants*

*3 Tbsp Marsala, or orange juice*

*75 g/3 oz flaked almonds, lightly toasted*

*50 g/2 oz pine nuts, lightly toasted*

*225 g/8 oz caster sugar*

*1 Tbsp plain flour*

*1 egg white*

*¼ tsp almond essence*

*120 g/4 oz pine nuts*

Pre-heat oven to 350°F/175°C/Gas mark 4. Grease or line two baking sheets with non-stick baking parchment.

● In a small bowl combine the currants and Marsala or orange juice and microwave on High for 30 to 60 seconds. Allow to sit until the moisture is absorbed, 3 to 5 minutes. Cool completely.

● In a food processor fitted with a metal blade, process the almonds, pine nuts, sugar and flour until finely ground. Add egg white and almond essence, and process until the mixture forms a dough. Stir in the plumped currants by hand.

● Place the untoasted pine nuts on a plate. Wet your hands, and using a teaspoon of the dough, shape into 2-cm/¾-in balls. Roll balls in pine nuts, pressing lightly to cover completely. Place balls 4 cm/1½-in apart on the baking sheets, flatten slightly to a disc shape.

● Bake until pine nuts are golden, 12 to 15 minutes, rotating the baking sheets halfway through cooking time. Allow to cool slightly, then transfer to wire racks. Store in an airtight container.

# Vanilla Crescents

*Preparation time: 25 minutes + chilling ● Cooking time: 15 minutes ● Makes: 25*

**Forming a horseshoe or crescent shape these "Kipferln" symbolize good luck.**

### INGREDIENTS

| |
|---|
| *25 g/1 oz unblanched almonds* |
| *120 g/4 oz plain flour* |
| *120 g/4 oz unsalted butter, chilled* |
| *2 Tbsp caster sugar* |
| *1 egg yolk* |
| *1 tsp vanilla essence* |
| *120 g/4 oz icing sugar* |

Lightly grease a baking sheet or line with non-stick baking  parchment. Chop the almonds very finely. Sift the flour into a bowl. Cut the butter into pieces and blend it into the flour until the mixture resembles fine breadcrumbs.

● Stir in the chopped almonds and sugar. Mix the egg yolk and vanilla essence together, add to the dry ingredients and mix to a soft dough. Lightly knead on a floured surface until smooth. Wrap in clingfilm and chill in the refrigerator for 20 minutes.

● Pre-heat oven to 350°F/175°C/Gas mark 4. Roll teaspoonfuls of the cookie dough into small crescents and place on the prepared baking sheets. Bake for 15 minutes until pale golden. As soon as you remove the cookies from the oven, thickly dredge with icing sugar. Leave on the baking sheet for 5 minutes, then remove and cool on a wire rack. Store in an airtight container.

### VARIATION

● Coat the cookies with vanilla sugar. Store a vanilla pod in a sealed jar of caster sugar for at least a week. Leave the pod and top up with sugar as it is used.

# Ischl Cookies

*Preparation time: 30 minutes + chilling* ● *Cooking time: 15 minutes* ● *Makes: 12*

**These jam-filled cookies are named after the famous resort in the Austrian Alps.**

## INGREDIENTS

*120 g/4 oz lightly salted butter*

*50 g/2 oz caster sugar*

*1 egg, beaten*

*1 Tbsp ground almonds*

*200 g/7 oz plain flour*

*2 Tbsp cornflour*

*¼ tsp ground cinnamon*

*3 Tbsp raspberry jam*

*3 Tbsp apricot jam*

*3 Tbsp lemon curd*

*1 Tbsp icing sugar*

Lightly grease two baking sheets or line with non-stick baking parchment.

● Beat the butter and sugar until creamy. Gradually add the egg, beating well after each addition, then beat in the ground almonds. Sift over the flour, cornflour and cinnamon and stir in to make a soft dough. Wrap in clingfilm and chill in the refrigerator for 30 minutes.

● Pre-heat oven to 350°F/175°C/Gas mark 4. Roll out on a lightly floured surface to 3 mm/⅛ in thick. Cut the dough into 8-cm/3-in rounds with a plain cutter. Cut a leaf or flower design from the middle of half the squares with a 2.5-cm/1-in cutter. Transfer to the baking sheets. Bake for 15 minutes, until golden. Leave on the baking sheets for 5 minutes, then transfer to a wire rack to cool.

● Warm and sieve the jam. Spread a third of the uncut cookies with each of the jams and the third with lemon curd. Place the cookies with cut-out middles on top, so that the jam or curd shows through. Lightly dust with sifted icing sugar before serving. The cookies should be eaten on the same day they are filled.

# Spanish Churros

*Preparation time: 15 minutes* ● *Cooking time: 10 minutes* ● *Makes: 25*

**These are freshly made and sold as a snack on street stalls throughout Spain to be eaten while you stroll along.**

## INGREDIENTS

*75 g/3 oz slightly salted butter*

*225 ml/8 fl oz water*

*120 g/4 oz plain flour*

*3 Tbsp caster sugar*

*3 eggs*

*Oil for deep-frying*

Put the butter and water in a saucepan and heat gently until melted. Meanwhile, sift the flour and ½ teaspoon of the sugar onto a piece of greaseproof paper.
● Bring the butter and water to a fast boil, then add the sifted flour and sugar all at once. Remove the pan from the heat and beat vigorously. Leave to cool for 5 minutes.
● Lightly beat the eggs and gradually add to the mixture, beating until very smooth and glossy. Spoon the mixture into a piping bag fitted with a 1-cm/½-in star nozzle.
● Half-fill a pan with oil and heat to 375°F/190°C. Pipe five 10-cm/4-in lengths of the mixture at a time into the hot oil. Fry for about 2 minutes, or until golden and crisp. Remove from the oil with slotted spoon and drain on kitchen paper. Repeat until all the mixture is used up. Serve warm or cold, dredged with remaining sugar.

## TIP

If preferred, dust the churros with icing sugar mixed with a little ground cinnamon instead of the caster sugar.

# Parisian Palmiers

*Preparation time: 20 minutes ● Cooking time: 10 minutes ● Makes: 20*

**These light-as-air French puff pastry cookies have a sugary glaze which caramelizes as they cook.**

## INGREDIENTS

*120 g/4 oz caster sugar*

*225 g/8 oz puff pastry, thawed if frozen*

Pre-heat oven to 450°F/230°C/Gas mark 8. Lightly grease two baking sheets or line with non-stick baking parchment.

● Sprinkle half the sugar evenly over the work surface or on a pastry board, then roll out the pastry into a rectangle of about 25 x 30 cm/10 x 12 in. Trim the edges to neaten, then sprinkle with the remaining sugar.

● Roll the two longer sides to the centre to make a double roll. Cut into 5-mm/½-in slices and transfer to the prepared baking sheets, spacing slightly apart. Bake for 10 minutes, or until well-risen, golden-brown and crisp. Remove from the baking sheets and cool on a wire rack.

## VARIATIONS

### Cinnamon Palmiers

● Mix the sugar with 1 teaspoon ground cinnamon before sprinkling.

### Jam Palmiers

● Sandwich together in pairs with 150 ml/5 fl oz double cream, lightly whipped and 3 tablespoons warmed and sieved apricot jam.

### Cheese Palmiers

● Fine grate 50 g/2 oz Gruyère cheese and 50 g/2 oz Parmesan cheese. Mix with 1 teaspoon paprika and use instead of the sugar. Sandwich together in pairs with 25 g/ 1 oz unsalted butter flavoured with 2 teaspoons tomato purée.

# Cigarettes Russes

*Preparation time: 20 minutes* ●
*Cooking time: 4 to 5 minutes per sheet* ● *Makes: 25*

**These crisp cigar-shaped cookies make a delicious
accompaniment to ice creams and mousses.**

### INGREDIENTS

| |
|---|
| *50 g/2 oz unsalted butter* |
| *2 egg whites* |
| *120 g/4 oz caster sugar* |
| *50 g/2 oz plain flour* |
| *½ tsp vanilla essence* |

Pre-heat oven to 375°F/190°C/Gas mark 4. Line a baking sheet with non-stick baking parchment. Melt the butter over a low heat, then leave to cool.

● Whisk the egg whites until stiff peaks form. Gradually add the sugar a tablespoon at a time, whisking between each addition. Sift half the flour over the whisked mixture and trickle the melted butter around the edge. Carefully fold in. Sift the remaining flour over the mixture and fold in with the vanilla essence.

● Drop teaspoonfuls of the mixture onto the prepared baking sheets, spacing well apart. Spread the mixture thinly and evenly to form a circle 10 cm/4 in in diameter. Bake for 5 to 6 minutes, or until golden-brown around the edges. It is best to bake only 3 Cigarettes at a time as they need to be rolled quickly while warm, before the mixture hardens.

● Using a metal spatula, carefully remove the cookies, one at a time from the baking sheet while still hot. Roll immediately around the oiled handle of a wooden spoon. Remove and leave on a wire rack to cool. Repeat with the remaining cookie mixture until used up.

# Fours Poches

*Preparation time: 30 minutes* ● *Cooking time: 15
minutes* ● *Makes: 30*

**These tiny almond treats are perfect for serving with
after-dinner coffee and can be made several days ahead.
In France the word "poche" refers to a piping bag, hence
the name of these cookies.**

### INGREDIENTS

| |
|---|
| *2 egg whites* |
| *120 g/4 oz caster sugar* |
| *150 g/5 oz ground almonds* |
| *¼ tsp almond essence* |
| *Edible rice paper* |
| *Whole hazelnuts, walnut pieces and quartered glacé cherries, to decorate* |

Pre-heat oven to 350°F/175°C/Gas mark 4. Line two baking sheets with rice paper.

● Whisk the egg whites until stiff, then fold in the caster sugar, ground almonds and almond essence.

● Spoon the mixture into a piping bag fitted with a 1-cm/½-in star nozzle and pipe small rosettes onto the rice paper. Decorate each with a hazelnut, walnut or glacé cherry. Bake for 15 minutes, until light golden-brown. Leave on the baking sheets for 2 to 3 minutes, then cool on a wire rack. Remove surplus rice paper when cold. Store in an airtight container.

# Sablés Nantais

*Preparation time: 25 minutes + chilling* ● *Cooking time: 15 minutes* ● *Makes: 25*

**These cookies come from the French region of Nantes. "Sable" is the French word for sand,
and reflects their golden crumbly texture.**

### INGREDIENTS

*120 g/4 oz unsalted butter*

*120 g/4 oz icing sugar*

*1 tsp vanilla essence*

*1 egg, separated*

*1 egg yolk*

*175 g/6 oz plain flour*

*¼ tsp baking powder*

Put the butter in a mixing bowl and beat until soft. Sift over the icing sugar and beat the mixture until light and fluffy. Beat in the egg yolks, one at a time, then beat in the vanilla essence. Sift the flour and baking powder over the butter mixture and mix to a soft dough. Lightly knead on a floured surface for a few seconds until smooth. Wrap in clingfilm and chill in the refrigerator for 1 hour.

● Pre-heat oven to 375°F/190°C/Gas mark 5. Lightly grease two baking sheets or line with non-stick baking parchment.

● Roll out the cookie dough on a floured surface to 5 mm/¼ in thickness and stamp out rounds using a fluted 5-cm/2-in cutter. Transfer to the prepared baking sheets.

● Lightly beat the egg white. Mark criss-cross patterns on top of the cookies with the back of a knife or with a fork. Brush with the egg white, then bake for 15 minutes, until golden-brown. Leave on the baking sheets for 3 minutes, then transfer to a wire rack to cool.

# Rascals

*Preparation time: 30 minutes + chilling* ● *Cooking time: 20 minutes* ● *Makes: 20*

**Known as "Spitzbuben", these Viennese vanilla and lemon cookies are sandwiched together with plum jam.**

### INGREDIENTS

*225 g/8 oz lightly salted butter*

*120 g/4 oz vanilla sugar*

*Grated rind of 1 lemon*

*300 g/10 oz plain flour*

*1 egg, separated*

*1 egg yolk*

*3 Tbsp caster sugar, for sprinkling*

*120 g/4 oz plum jam*

*2 tsp lemon juice*

Lightly grease two baking sheets or line with non-stick baking parchment.

● Beat the butter, vanilla sugar and lemon rind together until mixed. Sift in the flour and stir into the mixture with the egg yolks to make soft dough. Wrap in clingfilm and chill for 30 minutes.

● Pre-heat oven to 325°F/160°C/Gas mark 3. Roll out the dough on a lightly floured surface to a 5 mm/¼ in. Use a 6-cm/2½-in round or star cutter to cut out about 40 cookies. Transfer to the prepared baking sheets, spacing slightly apart. Lightly whisk the egg white and brush over the tops of half the cookies, then sprinkle generously with caster sugar.

● Bake for 20 minutes, until lightly browned. Leave on the baking sheets for 2 to 3 minutes, then transfer to a wire rack to cool.

● Gently heat the plum jam in a pan, then sieve. Use to sandwich the cookies together in pairs with a plain cookie on the bottom and a sugar-dusted one on top.

# Eponges

*Preparation time: 25 minutes* ● *Cooking time: 9 to 10 minutes* ● *Makes: 20*

**"Eponge" is the French word for sponge and is thought to be the name given to these cookies because they look like sea sponges.**

## INGREDIENTS

*2 egg whites*

*2 Tbsp caster sugar*

*50 g/2 oz icing sugar*

*50 g/2 oz ground almonds*

*75 g/3 oz blanched almonds, finely chopped*

*75 g/3 oz seedless raspberry jam*

*1 Tbsp icing sugar, for dusting*

Pre-heat oven to 375°F/190°C/Gas mark 5. Line two baking sheets with non-stick baking parchment.

● Whisk the egg whites until soft peaks form, then gradually add the caster sugar, whisking after each addition until the mixture is stiff and glossy.

● Sift the icing sugar and ground almonds together and fold in. Spoon the mixture into a piping bag fitted with a 1-cm/½-in plain nozzle and pipe small rounds onto the baking sheets, spacing them slightly apart.

● Sprinkle with the chopped almonds and bake for 9 to 10 minutes, until golden. The "éponges" will rise slightly during cooking, and shrink again as they cool. Remove from the baking sheets and cool on a wire rack. When cool, sandwich together in pairs with the jam. Dust with icing sugar before serving. Eponges are best eaten on the day they are made.

# Chrabeli Bread

*Preparation time: 20 minutes + standing* ● *Cooking time: 10 minutes* ● *Makes: 25*

**These crisp and light Mediterranean cookies are usually served with black coffee or eaten as a simple snack.
Before baking they're left on the baking sheet to dry overnight.**

## INGREDIENTS

| |
|---|
| *3 egg whites* |
| *50 g/2 oz icing sugar* |
| *150 g/5 oz plain flour* |
| *4 Tbsp cornflour* |

Put the egg whites in a large mixing bowl. Sift the icing sugar over the egg whites, then whisk until the mixture will hold stiff peaks.

● Sift over the flour and gently fold in until combined, taking care not to over-mix. Cover the bowl with a damp cloth and leave for 1 hour.

● Line two baking sheets with non-stick baking parchment, then lightly dust with the cornflour. Knead the dough on a lightly floured surface for a minute or so until smooth.

● Take walnut-sized pieces of the mixture and shape into ovals. Using scissors, snip three cuts down one side, then place on the prepared sheets, bending the cookies slightly to open up the cuts. Keep dipping your hands in flour when shaping the cookies, to prevent them sticking. Leave uncovered overnight to allow the cookies to dry out.

● The following day, pre-heat oven to 400°F/200°C/Gas mark 6. Bake the cookies for 10 minutes, until very pale brown. Remove from the baking sheets and cool on a wire rack.

# Zitron

*Preparation time: 30 minutes* ● *Cooking time: 10 minutes* ● *Makes: 20*

**These tangy Swiss cookies have a double helping of lemon, in both the filling and icing.**

## INGREDIENTS

*120 g/4 oz plain flour*

*25 g/1 oz self-raising flour*

*75 g/3 oz ground almonds*

*120 g/4 oz lightly salted butter*

*2 Tbsp icing sugar*

*1 egg yolk*

### FILLING

*120 g/4 oz unsalted butter*

*175 g/6 oz icing sugar*

*Grated rind 1 lemon*

### ICING

*175 g/6 oz icing sugar*

*About 4 tsp lemon juice*

*Yellow food colouring*

Pre-heat oven to 350°F/175°C/Gas mark 4. Lightly grease two baking sheets or line with non-stick baking parchment.

● Sift the flours into a bowl. Stir in the ground almonds, then blend in the butter until the mixture resembles fine breadcrumbs. Sift the icing sugar and stir in. Add the egg yolk and mix to a dough.

● Lightly knead the dough for a few seconds, then roll out on a floured surface to 3 mm/⅛ in. Cut into rounds using an 8-cm/3-in plain cutter and transfer to the baking sheets. Bake for 10 minutes, until lightly browned. Leave on the baking sheets for 2 minutes, then transfer to a wire rack to cool.

● For the filling, beat the butter, sifted icing sugar and lemon rind until the mixture is light and fluffy. Use to sandwich the cookies together in pairs.

● For the icing, sift the icing sugar into a bowl and stir in enough lemon juice to make a thick icing. Add a drop of yellow food colouring to make a pale yellow. Use to ice the tops of the cookies. Leave to set before serving.

# Dutch Butter Cookies

*Preparation time: 25 minutes + chilling ● Cooking time: 15 to 20 minutes ● Makes: 30*

**These lemon-scented cookies are known as "Botermopen" and should always
be made with unsalted butter for the best flavour.**

### INGREDIENTS

*175 g/6 oz unsalted butter*

*Grated rind of ½ lemon*

*50 g/2 oz caster sugar*

*50 g/2 oz light brown sugar*

*½ tsp almond or vanilla essence*

*225 g/8 oz plain flour*

*120 g/4 oz demerera sugar*

Beat the butter until creamy, then add the lemon rind, sugars and almond or vanilla essence and beat until light and fluffy. Sift over the flour and stir into the mixture to make a firm dough. Lightly knead on a floured surface for a few seconds until smooth. Divide the dough in half, wrap each piece in clingfilm and chill in the refrigerator for 30 minutes.

● Shape each piece into a roll about 15 cm/6 in long. Sprinkle the demerera sugar over a piece of greaseproof paper and roll the cookies to coat with sugar. Wrap the rolls in clingfilm or foil and chill in the refrigerator for at least 2 hours or overnight.

● Pre-heat oven to 325°F/160°C/Gas mark 3. Cut each roll into 15 slices and space slightly apart on the baking sheets. Bake for 15 to 20 minutes or until light golden and firm. Leave on the baking sheets for 3 minutes, then transfer onto a wire rack to cool.

# Polish Macaroons

*Preparation time: 25 minutes* ● *Cooking time: 15 to 20 minutes* ● *Makes: 16*

**These "Makaroniki" are sprinkled with poppy seeds before baking.
Halved blanched almonds may also be used to decorate these cookies.**

### INGREDIENTS

*75 g/3 oz blanched almonds*

*225 g/8 oz caster sugar*

*2 Tbsp cornflour*

*2 egg whites*

*¼ tsp almond essence, optional*

*1 Tbsp poppy seeds*

*Edible rice paper*

Pre-heat oven to 375°F/190°C/Gas mark 5. Line two baking sheets with rice paper.

● Spread the blanched almonds on a tray and toast for 5 minutes, or until just beginning to brown. Allow to cool, then grind them finely in a nut grinder or food processor.

● Mix together the ground almonds, sugar and cornflour. Lightly whisk the egg whites and add to the dry ingredients, with the almond essence if using, to make a thick paste.

● Spoon the mixture into a piping bag fitted with a plain 1-cm/½-in nozzle. Pipe 16 rounds of the mixture on the prepared baking sheets, spacing well apart. Sprinkle each with a few poppy seeds. Bake for 15 to 20 minutes, or until lightly browned. Leave on the baking sheets for 5 minutes, then remove and cool on a wire rack. Tear away any excess rice paper when cold.

# Lepeshki

*Preparation time: 20 minutes* ●
*Cooking time: 10 minutes* ● *Makes: 20*

**These creamy Russian cookies are made with soured cream rather than butter and sprinkled with flaked almonds before baking.**

### INGREDIENTS

225 g/8 oz self-raising flour

Pinch of salt

120 g/4 oz caster sugar

1 Tbsp ground almonds

1 egg, separated

150 ml/5 fl oz soured cream

½ tsp vanilla essence

50 g/2 oz flaked almonds

Pre-heat oven to 400°F/200°C/Gas mark 6. Lightly grease two baking sheets or line with non-stick baking parchment.

● Sift the flour and salt into a mixing bowl. Stir in the caster sugar and ground almonds. Reserve 1 tablespoon egg white. Mix the rest with the egg yolk, soured cream and vanilla essence. Add to the dry ingredients and mix to a firm dough. Lightly knead on a floured surface until smooth.

● Roll out to 8 mm/⅓ in and stamp into rounds using an 8-cm/3-in cutter. Place on the prepared baking sheets, spacing slightly apart. Brush the tops with the reserved egg white and sprinkle with flaked almonds. Bake for 10 minutes until lightly browned. Leave the cookies on the baking sheets for 5 minutes, then transfer to a wire rack to cool.

# Finnish Fingers

*Preparation time: 25 minutes* ●
*Cooking time: 12 minutes* ● *Makes: 12*

**These golden log-shaped cookies have a crumbly airy texture and a topping of chopped almonds.**

### INGREDIENTS

175 g/6 oz unsalted butter

50 g/2 oz icing sugar

1 tsp vanilla essence

175 g/6 oz plain flour

5 Tbsp cornflour

50 g/2 oz blanched almonds or pistachios, chopped

### FILLING

50 g/2 oz unsalted butter

75 g/3 oz icing sugar

Pre-heat oven to 350°F/175°C/Gas mark 4. Lightly grease a baking sheet or line with non-stick baking parchment.

● Put the butter in a mixing bowl and beat until creamy.

● Sift over the icing sugar, add the vanilla essence and beat until light and fluffy. Sift the flour and cornflour over the butter mixture and fold in.

● Spoon the mixture into a piping bag fitted with a 2-cm/¾-in plain nozzle and pipe 6-cm/2½-in lengths onto the prepared baking sheets, spacing well apart. Sprinkle with the chopped nuts. Bake for 12 minutes, until pale golden-brown. Leave on the baking sheets for 3 to 4 minutes, then remove and cool on a wire rack.

● For the filling, beat the butter until softened. Sift over the icing sugar and beat until light and fluffy. Use to sandwich the cookies together in pairs.

# Danish Piped Cookies

*Preparation time: 30 minutes* ●
*Cooking time: 12 minutes* ● *Makes: 30*

**These classic buttery cookies from Denmark melt in the mouth and are perfect with morning coffee.**

### INGREDIENTS

| |
| --- |
| *225 g/8 oz unsalted butter* |
| *120 g/4 oz caster sugar* |
| *1 egg yolk* |
| *175 g/6 oz plain flour* |
| *50 g/2 oz self-raising flour* |
| *75 g/3 oz ground almonds* |

### GLAZE

| |
| --- |
| *2 Tbsp caster sugar* |
| *2 Tbsp milk* |

Pre-heat oven to 375°F/190°C/Gas mark 5. Lightly grease two baking sheets or line with non-stick baking parchment.

● Beat the butter in a bowl until creamy. Add the caster sugar and mix until blended, then beat in the egg yolk. Sift the plain and self-raising flours over the butter mixture and stir in with the ground almonds.

● Spoon into a piping bag fitted with a 1-cm/½-in star nozzle and pipe scrolls, fingers or whirls as liked onto the prepared baking sheets. Bake for 10 to 12 minutes until pale golden.

● Meanwhile, prepare the glaze. Mix the caster sugar and milk together in a small saucepan and heat gently to dissolve. As soon as you remove the cookies from the oven, brush with the milk glaze. Leave on the baking sheets for 5 minutes, then transfer to a wire rack to cool.

# Scandinavian Slices

*Preparation time: 25 minutes + chilling* ●
*Cooking time: 10 minutes* ● *Makes: 20*

**This dark, spicy cookie mixture is chilled overnight to let the flavours develop.**

### INGREDIENTS

| |
| --- |
| *120 g/4 oz lightly salted butter* |
| *120 g/4 oz caster sugar* |
| *2½ Tbsp golden syrup* |
| *2 tsp honey* |
| *50 g/2 oz flaked almonds* |
| *2 tsp ground cinnamon* |
| *1 tsp ground ginger* |
| *½ tsp ground cardamom* |
| *½ tsp bicarbonate of soda* |
| *1 tsp water* |
| *200 g/7 oz plain flour* |

Put the butter, sugar, syrup and honey in a small pan and heat gently until the butter has melted. Stir in almonds and spices and bring to the boil. Remove from the heat. Mix the bicarbonate and water together and stir into the mixture.

● Sift the flour into a bowl and make a well in the middle. Pour in the melted mixture and mix. Cool, then turn out and knead on a floured surface until smooth. Shape into a block 5 cm/2 in in diameter. Wrap in clingfilm and chill in the refrigerator overnight.

● Pre-heat oven to 350°F/175°C/Gas mark 4. Lightly grease two baking sheets.

● Cut the block into 3-mm/⅛-in slices and place on the baking sheets, slightly spaced. Bake for 10 minutes, until slightly darkened and crisp. Cool on the baking sheets.

# Grated Peach Shortcake

*Preparation time: 20 minutes + chilling* ● *Cooking time: 45 minutes* ● *Makes: 8 wedges*

**It's not the peaches that are grated in this chunky Australian cookie,
but the buttery shortcake that sandwiches it together.**

## INGREDIENTS

*225 g/8 oz lightly salted butter*

*5 Tbsp light brown sugar*

*1 egg*

*1 Tbsp sunflower oil*

*1 tsp vanilla essence*

*400 g/14 oz plain flour*

*50 g/2 oz cornflour*

*2 tsp baking powder*

*50 g/2 oz dried peaches*

*3 Tbsp peach or orange juice*

*120 g/4 oz peach or apricot jam*

Lightly grease and line the base of a round 20-cm/8-in loose-bottomed tin.

● Beat the butter until creamy, then add the light brown sugar and mix until light and fluffy. Beat the egg, oil and vanilla essence together. Gradually add to the butter mixture, beating well between each addition. Sift the flour, cornflour and baking powder. Stir into the butter mixture to make a stiff dough. Knead on a lightly floured surface until smooth. Wrap and chill the dough in the refrigerator for 15 minutes.

● Meanwhile, finely chop the peaches and put in a small saucepan with the fruit juice. Heat gently for 3 to 4 minutes, until the fruit juice is absorbed. Remove from the heat and stir in the jam.

● Pre-heat oven to 300°F/150°C/Gas mark 2. Cut the dough in two and coarsely grate one half into the prepared tin, so that it covers the base evenly. Spoon over the warm peach jam mixture. Grate the rest of the cookie dough evenly over the jam.

● Bake for 45 minutes or until lightly browned. Leave to cool in the tin. Cut the shortcake into wedges to serve.

## VARIATION

**Grated Pineapple Shortcake**

● Substitute crystallized pineapple for the dried peaches, simmer in pineapple juice, and use pineapple instead of peach jam.

# Chunky Macadamia Cookies

*Preparation time: 20 minutes ● Cooking time: 15 minutes ● Makes: About 25*

**Macadamia trees are native to the woodlands of Australia and produce these small white buttery nuts.**

### INGREDIENTS

| |
|---|
| *50 g/2 oz unsalted butter* |
| *50 g/2 oz white vegetable fat* |
| *120 g/4 oz light brown sugar* |
| *1 egg, beaten* |
| *225 g/8 oz plain flour* |
| *½ tsp baking powder* |
| *75 g/3 oz macadamia nuts* |
| *4 Tbsp milk* |

Pre-heat oven to 350°F/175°C/Gas mark 4. Lightly grease two baking sheets or line with non-stick baking parchment.

● Put the butter and white vegetable fat in a mixing bowl and beat until soft. Add the light brown sugar and cream together until light and fluffy. Gradually add the egg, beating well between each addition.

● Sift the flour and baking powder into the bowl and fold into the butter mixture with the nuts and milk to make a firm dough. Place small teaspoonfuls onto the baking sheets, spacing well apart. Bake for 12 to 15 minutes, until light golden-brown. Cool on the baking sheets for 5 minutes, then transfer to a wire rack to cool.

### VARIATION

**Chocolate Macademia Cookies**

● Substitute 50 g/2 oz unsweetened cocoa powder for 50 g/2 oz of the flour.

# Anzacs

*Preparation time: 15 minutes ● Cooking time: 20 minutes ● Makes: 40*

**These well-known Australian cookies were named after the Australian New Zealand Army Corps (ANZAC).**

### INGREDIENTS

| |
|---|
| *175 g/6 oz plain flour* |
| *150 g/5 oz rolled oats* |
| *75 g/3 oz sweetened flaked coconut* |
| *225 g/8 oz dark brown sugar* |
| *120 g/4 oz lightly salted butter* |
| *2 Tbsp honey* |
| *½ tsp bicarbonate of soda* |
| *2 tsp milk* |

Pre-heat oven to 350°F/175°C/Gas mark 4. Lightly grease three baking sheets or line with non-stick baking parchment.

● Sift the flour into a mixing bowl. Add the oats, coconut and sugar and mix well. Make a well in the centre. Put the butter and honey in a small tin and heat gently until melted, stirring occasionally. Remove from the heat. Blend the bicarbonate with the milk and stir into the melted mixture. Pour into the dry ingredients and mix well.

● Drop heaped teaspoonfuls of the mixture onto the baking sheets, spacing them well apart. Bake for 20 minutes, until browned. Leave on the baking sheets for 5 minutes, then transfer to a wire rack to cool.

# Baklava

*Preparation time: 25 minutes* ● *Cooking time: 30 minutes* ● *Makes: 16*

**These layers of filo pastry filled with nuts and soaked in syrup are eaten in the Middle East, Greece and Turkey.**

## INGREDIENTS

*120 g/4 oz chopped mixed nuts such as hazelnuts and almonds*

*120 g/4 oz golden caster sugar*

*1 tsp ground cinnamon*

*75 g/3 oz unsalted butter*

*120 g/4 oz filo pastry, thawed if frozen*

## SYRUP

*200 g/7 oz granulated sugar*

*2 Tbsp lemon juice*

*2 tsp orange-flower or rose-flower water*

Pre-heat oven to 350°F/175°C/Gas mark 4. Lightly brush the sides of a 28 x 18-cm/11 x 7-in shallow tin with oil.

● Put the nuts, sugar and cinnamon in a bowl and mix together. Melt the butter and allow to cool.

● Cut the pastry to fit the tin. Brush the base of the tin with melted butter, then lay a sheet of pastry over the base of the tin. Brush its top with more melted butter and repeat with three more sheets of pastry. Sprinkle over half of the nut mixture. Top with three more sheets of pastry, brushing butter between the layers, then sprinkle over the remaining nut mixture. Continue layering and buttering the filo pastry until it is used up.

● Press down the edges to seal, then mark the top layer into 16 squares or diamonds. Bake for 30 minutes, until a rich golden-brown and crisp.

● While the pastry is in the oven, put the granulated sugar and lemon juice in a small pan. Heat over a very low heat until the sugar has dissolved. Bring to the boil and simmer for 2 minutes. Stir in the orange-flower or rose-flower water. Pour the hot syrup over the pastry as soon as it comes out of the oven. Leave to cool in the tin, then cut into squares or diamonds and remove from the tin.

## TIP

When using filo pastry, cover it with a damp teatowel, to prevent it drying out.

# Jalebi

*Preparation time: 20 minutes* ●
*Cooking time: 20 minutes* ● *Makes: 16-20*

**These Indian batter coils are deep-fried, then soaked in a saffron and cardamom syrup.**

### INGREDIENTS

*225 g/8 oz plain flour*

*8 g/¼ oz easy-blend dried yeast*

*50 ml/2 fl oz plain yoghurt*

*300 ml/10 fl oz warm water*

*Sunflower oil for deep-frying*

### SYRUP

*225 g/8 oz granulated sugar*

*Large pinch of saffron strands*

*6 cardamom pods, lightly crushed*

*300 ml/10 fl oz water*

Sift the flour into a bowl and stir in the easy-blend dried yeast. Make a well in the middle. Add the yoghurt and water and gradually blend in the flour to make a thick batter. Cover the bowl with a teatowel and leave the batter for 2 hours.

● Meanwhile, make the syrup. Put the sugar, saffron and cardamom pods in a pan with the water. Heat gently, stirring occasionally until the sugar dissolves. Bring to the boil and simmer for 1 minute. Strain the syrup into a bowl.

● Half-fill a deep saucepan with oil and heat to 375°F/190°C. Stir the batter, then pour through a basting spoon in a steady stream into the oil to form coils, making 4 or 5 at a time. Deep fry for about 30 seconds, then turn over and continue cooking until deep golden. Remove from the pan and drain on kitchen paper, then immerse in the sugar syrup for 2 to 3 minutes. Repeat with remaining batter and syrup until used up. Serve straight away.

# Coconut Fortune Cookies

*Preparation time: 30 minutes* ●
*Cooking time: 5 minutes* ● *Makes: 36*

**Everyone knows these Chinese cookies. These have a pretty texture provided by a little grated coconut.**

### INGREDIENTS

*2 egg whites*

*50 g/2 oz icing sugar, sifted*

*1 tsp coconut or almond essence*

*25 g/1 oz unsalted butter, melted*

*5 Tbsp plain flour, sifted*

*50 g/2 oz finely shredded coconut, toasted and chopped*

Grease and flour two baking sheets. Using a glass 8 cm/3 in in diameter, mark two circles in diagonal corners of the baking sheet, to allow cookies to spread.

● In a medium bowl, beat the egg whites until foamy. Gradually beat in icing sugar, coconut or almond essence, and melted butter. Fold in the flour until well blended.

● Drop a teaspoonful of batter in the centre of each marked circle and, using the back of a spoon, spread evenly to cover the circle. Sprinkle each cookie with a little toasted coconut.

● Bake one sheet at a time until the edges are lightly browned, about 5 minutes. Remove the baking sheet to a wire rack, and working quickly, use a thin-bladed metal spatula to loosen the edges of the cookie. Set on a board and fold in half, then curve each cookie over the rim of a glass creating the classic shape. Hold for 30 seconds, then place on a wire rack to cool completely. Repeat with the remaining cookies. If the cookies become too firm, return to the oven for 30 seconds.

# Special Cookies for Gifts

Cookies make the perfect gift, especially for those who have everything. These simple food gifts add a personal touch and are the perfect way to show that you care. Here are a variety of gift suggestions ranging from ideas for birthday presents to the perfect hostess gift. There are cookies to congratulate the parents of a new baby, "congratulations" on an engagement and "get well" to cheer up someone who is ill. Often it is hard to know what to take to a party as a little thank you to present to your host or hostess – make cookies and you are onto a sure winner. Why not gift-wrap extra-luxurious cookies and make a contribution to the meal?

## Birthdays

## Family Celebrations

# Romantic Anniversaries

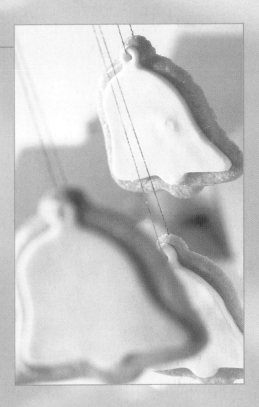

# Special Occasions

# Present Cookies

*Preparation time: 35 minutes ● Cooking time: 15 minutes ● Makes: 11*

**If you can't find number cutters, trace some numbers, cut them out, and use them as a template.**

### INGREDIENTS

*150 g/5 oz plain flour, sifted*

*50 g/2 oz ground almonds*

*120 g/4 oz lightly salted butter, cut into small pieces*

*1 egg yolk*

*120 g/4 oz chopped crystallized pineapple*

### DECORATION

*200 g/7 oz ready-to-roll fondant icing*

*Food colouring*

*1 Tbsp apricot jam, warmed*

Pre-heat oven to 350°F/175°C/Gas mark 4. Grease several baking sheets or line with non-stick baking parchment.

● Place the flour and ground almonds in a mixing bowl and blend in the butter using your fingers until the mixture resembles fine breadcrumbs. Stir in the egg yolk and chopped candied pineapple and using your hands bring all the ingredients together to form a soft dough.

● On a lightly floured surface, roll out the dough to about 5 mm/¼ in thick and stamp out squares using an 8-cm/3-in cutter. Lift on to the baking sheets and re-roll the trimmings as necessary. Prick the squares with a fork. Bake the cookies for 15 minutes or until lightly golden at the edges. Transfer to a wire rack to cool.

● To decorate the cookies, place the icing in a bowl and add a few drops of colouring, knead the icing until soft and smooth. On a surface lightly sprinkled with icing sugar, roll out the icing and stamp out the numbers "2" and "1" to make ten "21s."

● Brush the apricot jam over the surface of each cookie and lay the numbers "21" on each cookie. Cut the trimmings from the icing into thin strips and place over the squares and numbers, to represent lengths of ribbon around a present. Store these cookies in an airtight container.

# Birthday Cake Cookies

*Preparation time: 25 minutes ● Cooking time: 15 minutes ● Makes: 18*

**These cookies are made from all the ingredients you expect to find in a fruit cake, making them a clever birthday gift.**

### INGREDIENTS

*120 g/4 oz lightly salted butter, softened*

*120 g/4 oz packed light brown sugar*

*1 egg, beaten*

*1 Tbsp brandy or dark rum*

*150 g/5 oz plain flour, sifted*

*¼ tsp baking powder*

*50 g/2 oz chopped blanched almonds*

*25 g/1 oz chopped glacé cherries*

*50 g/2 oz candied citrus peel*

*50 g/2 oz sultanas*

*1 Tbsp chopped angelica, optional*

*Icing sugar, for dusting*

Pre-heat oven to 350°F/175°C/Gas mark 4. Grease several baking sheets or line with non-stick baking parchment.

● In a mixing bowl beat together the butter and sugar until light and fluffy. Beat in the egg and brandy. Stir in the flour, baking powder and all the remaining ingredients and mix everything together, until evenly combined.

● Place mounds of the mixture onto the baking sheets and bake for 15 minutes or until golden-brown. Lift onto wire racks to cool. Dust the cookies lightly with icing sugar and store them in an airtight container until needed.

### TIP

The angelica gives good colour to these cookies, but is not essential to the flavour.

# Coconut Meringues

*Preparation time: 30 minutes* ● *Cooking time: 1 hour and 30 minutes* ● *Makes: 20*

**These elegant meringues, dipped in chocolate, would be perfect for a little girl's birthday.**

### INGREDIENTS

| |
| --- |
| *4 egg whites* |
| *Pinch of salt* |
| *225 g/8 oz caster sugar* |
| *75 g/3 oz sweetened flaked coconut* |
| *4 oz plain chocolate* |

Pre-heat oven to 250°F/120°C/Gas mark ½. Line several baking sheets with non-stick baking parchment.

● In a large mixing bowl whisk the egg whites and salt using a hand-held electric mixer until they form stiff peaks. Whisk in the sugar a little at a time until the mixture is glossy but still very stiff. Fold in the coconut.

● Using a piping bag fitted with a medium star nozzle, pipe the meringue mixture into loops to make long shapes on the baking sheets. Bake the meringues for 1 hour and 30 minutes or until they can lift off the paper easily. Store in an airtight container until needed.

● To decorate, melt the chocolate in the microwave or in a bowl over simmering water; cool. Dip one end of each meringue in melted chocolate and leave to set on greaseproof paper.

### TIP

Sandwich the meringues together in pairs with 300 ml/10 fl oz whipped cream for a real treat!

# Cassis Pink Cookies

*Preparation time: 40 minutes* ● *Cooking time: 10 to 15 minutes* ● *Makes: 15*

**These very elegant cookies are only for the grown ups! They are flavoured with crème de cassis liqueur for a distinct taste.**

### INGREDIENTS

*225 g/8 oz plain flour, sifted*

*75 g/3 oz icing sugar*

*150 g/5 oz butter, cut into small pieces*

*25 g/1 oz finely chopped blanched almonds*

*2 Tbsp crème de cassis or kirsch liqueur*

### DECORATION

*50 g/2 oz unsalted butter, softened*

*120 g/4 oz icing sugar, sifted*

*1 Tbsp crème de cassis or kirsch liqueur*

*225 g/8 oz marzipan*

*Pink food colouring*

*1 Tbsp raspberry jam, warmed*

Pre-heat oven to 350°F/175°C/Gas mark 4. Grease several baking sheets or line with non-stick baking parchment.

● Place the flour and icing sugar in a mixing bowl and blend in the butter using your fingers until the mixture resembles fine breadcrumbs. Stir in the chopped almonds and crème de cassis and mix all the ingredients together to a firm dough.

● On a lightly floured surface, roll out the dough to about 5 mm/¼ in thick. Stamp out 30 circles using a 6-cm/2½-in fluted cutter. Re-roll the trimmings as necessary and lift onto the prepared baking sheets.

● Bake the cookies for 10 to 15 minutes or until just beginning to turn golden at the edges. Transfer to a wire rack to cool.

● To decorate the cookies, first make the buttercream icing by beating together the butter and icing sugar in a bowl to give a fluffy consistency. Gradually beat in the crème de cassis. Set aside. Add a few drops of pink colouring to the marzipan in a small bowl and knead until soft and smooth. On a clean surface lightly sprinkled with icing sugar, roll out the marzipan quite thinly and stamp out 15 circles using a 6-cm/2½-in fluted cutter.

● Brush 15 of the cookies with the warmed raspberry jam and place a circle of marzipan on top, this will become the top of the cookies. Using the buttercream as the filling, sandwich the cookies together using the marzipan cookie for the top and the plain cookies for the base.

# Candied Cherry Slices

*Preparation time: 30 minutes + chilling* ●
*Cooking time: 15 to 20 minutes* ● *Makes: 18 slices*

**Make these chunky slices of cookie with lots of sticky glacé cherries and ground almonds for a birthday surprise.**

### INGREDIENTS

*120 g/4 oz butter, softened*

*120g /4 oz caster sugar*

*1 egg yolk*

*150 g/5 oz plain flour, sifted*

*50 g/2 oz ground almonds*

*50 g/2 oz chopped blanched almonds*

*120 g/4 oz glacé cherries, quartered*

In a mixing bowl, beat together the butter and sugar until light and fluffy. Beat in the egg yolk.

● Add the flour, ground almonds, blanched almonds and glacé cherries and using your hands bring the mixture together to form a firm dough. Shape into a 15 x 5-cm/6 x 2-in bar shape. Wrap and chill for 30 minutes. Meanwhile, line several baking sheets with nonstick baking parchment.

● Pre-heat oven to 350°F/175°C/Gas mark 4. Slice the bar into 18 equal slices and lift onto the baking sheets. Bake the cookies for 15 to 20 minutes or until evenly golden. Transfer to a wire rack to cool.

### TIP

Melt 150 g/5 oz of chocolate into a small bowl, dip in one end of the cookie and place on a sheet of waxed paper and leave to set.

# Vanilla Cream Cheese Cut-outs

*Preparation time: 20 minutes + chilling* ●
*Cooking time: 10 to 12 minutes* ● *Makes: 36*

**These tender cookies are prefect with just a simple sugar and nut topping.**

### INGREDIENTS

*120 g/4 oz butter, softened*

*75 g/3 oz cream cheese*

*120 g/4 oz plain flour*

*175 g/6 oz icing sugar*

*1 tsp vanilla essence*

### TOPPING

*1 Tbsp sugar*

*1 tsp ground cinnamon*

*2 Tbsp finely chopped almonds*

*1 egg*

Beat together the butter and sugar in a bowl until creamy. Add the flour, sugar and vanilla essence and mix to form a soft dough. Wrap the dough in clingfilm and refrigerate until firm, about 1 hour.

● Line 2 baking sheets with non-stick baking parchment. On a lightly floured surface roll half the dough to 2-mm/⅛-in thick (keep remaining dough refrigerated). Using a floured 5-cm/2-in cutter, cut out as many rounds as possible. Arrange 2.5 cm/1 in apart on the baking sheets. Repeat with remaining dough and trimmings. Chill.

● Preheat oven to 350°F/175°C/Gas mark 4. For the topping stir together the sugar, cinnamon and almonds. In a separate bowl, lightly beat the egg with 1 tablespoon cold water. Brush the tops of the cookies with the egg and sprinkle with a little of the sugar-nut mixture. Bake for 12 to 15 minutes until golden. Transfer to a wire rack to cool.

# Coffee and Walnut Numbers

*Preparation time: 35 minutes ● Cooking time: 15 minutes ● Makes: 14*

**This coffee flavoured cookie is made even more delicious by being dipped in plain and white chocolate.**

## INGREDIENTS

*1 Tbsp instant coffee*

*1 Tbsp boiling water*

*175 g/6 oz self-raising flour*

*120 g/4 oz butter, cut into small pieces*

*175 g/6 oz caster sugar*

*120/4 oz finely chopped walnuts*

*1 egg yolk*

## DECORATION

*50 g/2 oz white chocolate, broken into pieces*

*50 g/2 oz plain chocolate, broken into pieces*

Preheat the oven to 350°F/175°C/Gas mark 4. Grease several baking sheets or line with non-stick baking parchment.

● Dissolve the instant coffee with the boiling water and allow to cool.

● Place the flour in a mixing bowl and blend in the butter using your fingertips until the mixture resembles fine breadcrumbs. Stir in the sugar, walnuts, egg yolk and cooled coffee and mix together well to form a firm dough.

● On a lightly floured work surface, roll out the dough to about 1-cm/½-in thick and stamp out the numbers "1" and "8" using cutters. Re-roll the trimmings to make 14 pairs of numbers and transfer to the baking sheets. Prick each cookie with a fork.

● Bake the cookies for 15 minutes, or until lightly golden-brown and transfer to a wire rack to cool.

● To decorate the cookies, melt the chocolate by placing each one in a separate bowl. Place each of these bowls over a saucepan of simmering water, stir fequently until the chocolate has melted. Dip the number "8" in the white chocolate and the number "1" in the plain chocolate and place on a piece of baking paper to set. Store these cookies in an airtight container.

# Star Cookies

*Preparation time: 45 minutes ● Cooking time: 10 to 15 minutes ● Makes: 16*

**Say "congratulations" with a crisp vanilla cookie base shaped into a star-shape and then decorated with ready-rolled white fondant icing.**

### INGREDIENTS

*120 g/4 oz lightly salted butter, softened*

*120 g/4 oz caster sugar*

*1 egg, beaten*

*1 tsp vanilla essence*

*225 g/8 oz plain flour, sifted*

### DECORATION

*400 g/14 oz ready-to-roll fondant icing*

*2 Tbsp apricot jam*

Pre-heat oven to 350°F/175°C/Gas mark 4. Grease several baking sheets or line with non-stick baking parchment.

● In a mixing bowl beat together the butter and sugar until pale and fluffy. Beat in the egg and vanilla essence. Add the flour and bring the mixture together to form a soft dough.

● On a lightly floured work surface, roll out the dough to 5 mm/¼ in thick, stamp out 16 stars using a 10-cm/4-in star shaped cutter. Re-roll trimmings and place the cookies on a baking sheet. Bake the cookies for 10 to 15 minutes or until golden-brown. Transfer to a wire rack and leave to cool.

● Knead the icing until soft and smooth. Brush each cookie with warmed apricot jam. Roll out the icing on a work surface lightly sprinkled with icing sugar. Stamp out 16 stars using the same size cookie cutter and press a white star onto each cookie, re-rolling if necessary.

# Pink and White Meringues

*Preparation time: 30 minutes* ● *Cooking time: 1 hour and 30 minutes* ● *Makes: 20*

**These pastel meringues, which are as light as air and melt in the mouth, are ideal for a christening celebration.**

### INGREDIENTS

*4 egg whites*

*Pinch of salt*

*225 g/8 oz caster sugar*

*Red food colouring*

*300 ml/10 fl oz double cream, whipped lightly*

Pre-heat oven to 250°F/120°C/Gas mark ½. Line several baking sheets with non-stick baking paper.

● In a large clean bowl, using a balloon whisk or hand-held electric mixer, whisk together the egg whites and salt until they form stiff peaks. Whisk in the sugar a little at a time, the meringue should start to look glossy. Continue whisking in the sugar until all the sugar has been incorporated and the meringue is thick, shiny and stands in stiff peaks. Transfer half the meringue to another bowl, add a few drops of food colouring to create a pastel pink colour.

● Fill a piping bag with the white meringue mixture, using a 5-mm/¾-in star nozzle and pipe about 20 small whirls on to the baking sheets. Repeat with the pink meringue mixture.

● Bake the meringues for 1 hour and 30 minutes until they are dry and crisp and the swirls can be easily lifted off the paper. Leave to cool completely.

● Just before serving, sandwich the meringues together in pairs with the whipped cream. Store unfilled meringues in an airtight container. Once filled, meringues should be eaten within a few hours.

# Chocolate Oaties

*Preparation time: 20 minutes ● Cooking time: 20 minutes ● Makes: 16*

**These chunky oaty cookies with their chocolate topping will be a great edible birthday gift.**

INGREDIENTS

*50 g/2 oz plain flour, sifted*

*200 g/7 oz rolled oats*

*1 tsp sesame seeds*

*1 tsp baking powder*

*120 g/4 oz lightly salted butter, cut into small pieces*

*120 g/4 oz caster sugar*

*1 egg, beaten*

*175 g/6 oz milk or white chocolate, melted*

Pre-heat oven to 350°F/175°C/Gas mark 4. Grease several baking sheets or line with non-stick baking parchment.

● Place the flour, oats, sesame seeds and baking powder in a mixing bowl. Blend in the butter, caster sugar and beaten egg to make a firm dough. Alternatively, place all these ingredients in a food processor and pulse until the mixture comes away from the sides of the bowl.

● On a lightly floured surface, roll out the dough to 5 mm/¼ in thick. Using an 8-cm/3-in cutter, stamp out 16 rounds. Lift onto the baking sheets. Bake for 20 minutes until golden-brown. Transfer the cookies to a wire rack to cool.

● Spread the top of each cookie with melted chocolate and allow to set.

# Marmalade Moons

*Preparation time: 25 minutes + chilling ● Cooking time: 10 to 12 minutes ● Makes: 20*

**Reward your child after their first day at school with these delicious moon-shaped cookies.**

INGREDIENTS

*175 g/6 oz plain flour, sifted*

*50 g/2 oz ground almonds*

*120 g/4 oz light brown sugar*

*75 g/3 oz butter, cut into small pieces*

*1 egg yolk*

*3 Tbsp orange marmalade*

*Icing sugar, for dusting*

Place the flour, ground almonds and sugar in a mixing bowl and using your fingers blend in the butter until the mixture resembles fine breadcrumbs. Add the egg yolk and marmalade and bring the mixture together to form a soft ball. Wrap and chill for 30 minutes.

● Pre-heat oven to 350°F/175°C/Gas mark 4. Grease several baking sheets or line with non-stick baking parchment.

● On a lightly floured work surface roll out the dough to about 5 mm/¼ in thick. Using a 10-cm/4½-in round cutter, stamp out rounds, then cut away a quarter of each round making a crescent shape. Re-roll the trimmings as necessary and lift onto the baking sheets. Prick the cookies well with a fork.

● Bake the cookies for 10 to 12 minutes or until lightly golden. Transfer to a wire rack to cool. Just before serving, dust the tops with icing sugar. Store in an airtight container.

# Maple Syrup Tuiles

*Preparation time: 25 minutes* ● *Cooking time: 8 to 10 minutes* ● *Makes: 21*

**Store these very delicate Mother's Day cookies in an airtight container.**

### INGREDIENTS

50 g/2 oz lightly salted butter

120 g/4 oz caster sugar

2 Tbsp chopped almonds

3 Tbsp maple syrup

50 g/2 oz plain flour, sifted

Pre-heat oven to 350°F/175°C/Gas mark 4. Line 2 to 3 baking sheets with non-stick baking parchment.

● In a saucepan, gently heat the butter, caster sugar, almonds and maple syrup until the butter has melted. Remove from the heat. Add the flour and mix together until thoroughly blended.

● Spoon four teaspoonfuls of the mixture well apart on the baking sheets, bake for 8 to 10 minutes until bubbly and the cookies have spread to a lacy texture. Remove from the oven, leave to cool for one minute, then lift off with a thin, metal spatula and curl around a rolling pin to mould into tuile shapes.

● Shape the remaining cookies in the same way leave to go cold and crisp. Handle the tuiles very carefully once baked.

### TIP

If the tuiles have hardened before you have shaped them, pop them back in the oven for a few seconds to soften them.

# Shortcake with a Hint of Rose

*Preparation time: 25 minutes* ● *Cooking time: 25 to 30 minutes* ● *Makes: 10*

**These thick rounds of delicate shortbread have been flavoured with rose flower-water.**

### INGREDIENTS

*175 g/6 oz plain flour, sifted*

*75 g/3 oz butter, cut into small pieces*

*5 Tbsp caster sugar*

*1 egg yolk*

*2 Tbsp rose flower-water*

*Demerara sugar, for sprinkling, optional*

Pre-heat oven to 300°F/150°C/Gas mark 2. Grease several baking sheets or line with non-stick baking parchment.

● Place the flour in a mixing bowl and blend in the butter using your fingertips until the mixture resembles fine breadcrumbs. Stir in the sugar, egg yolk and rose flower-water, then bring everything together with your hands to form a soft dough. On a lightly floured surface roll out the dough to about 5 mm/¼ in and using an 8-cm/3-in cutter, stamp out rounds and lift onto the baking sheets and prick with a fork. Repeat as necessary.

● Sprinkle with demerara sugar and bake the cookies for 25 to 30 minutes or until lightly golden. Transfer to a wire rack to cool.

# Poppy Seed Cookies

*Preparation time: 25 minutes + chilling* ● *Cooking time: 10 to 12 minutes* ● *Makes: 36*

**These crisp sweet cookies with a hint of orange are ideal for serving with desserts.**

### INGREDIENTS

*75 g/3 oz plain flour, sifted*

*120 g/4 oz icing sugar*

*120 g/4 oz butter, softened*

*1 egg, beaten*

*1 Tbsp poppy seeds*

*Grated rind of half an orange*

*1 Tbsp honey*

Place the flour and icing sugar into a mixing bowl and blend in the butter using your fingers until the mixture resembles fine breadcrumbs.

● Add the egg, poppy seeds, orange rind and honey and combine all the ingredients into a firm dough. On a lightly floured work surface, roll out the dough to a 23-cm/9-in log, wrap and chill for 30 minutes or up to 2 hours until firm.

● Pre-heat oven to 350°F/175°C/Gas mark 4. Grease several baking sheets or line with non-stick baking parchment.

● Slice the log into about 36 even slices and place them slightly apart on the baking sheets. Bake the cookies for 10 to 12 minutes or until lightly golden. Transfer to a wire rack to cool. These cookies can be frozen for up to a month.

# Orange Flower Cookies

*Preparation time: 35 minutes + chilling* ● *Cooking time: 15 minutes* ● *Makes: 13*

**These pretty cookies, sandwiched together with an orange buttercream are perfect for a Mother's Day tea.**

## INGREDIENTS

175 g/6 oz lightly salted butter, softened

75 g/3 oz icing sugar, sifted

Grated rind of 1 orange

900 g/7 oz plain flour, sifted

50 g/2 oz custard mix or cornflour

½ tsp vanilla essence

### FILLING

75 g/3 oz unsalted butter, softened

175 g/6 oz icing sugar, sifted

1 tsp grated orange rind

2 tsp fresh orange juice

Icing sugar, for dusting

In a mixing bowl beat together the butter and icing sugar until light and fluffy. Stir in the orange rind, flour and custard mix or cornflour and vanilla essence and combine all the ingredients well. Using your hands bring the mixture together to form a soft ball. Wrap and chill for 30 minutes.

● Pre-heat oven to 350°F/175°C/Gas mark 4. Grease several baking sheets or line with non-stick baking parchment.

● On a lightly floured work surface, roll out the dough to about 5 mm/¼ in thick. Using a 5-cm/2-in flower-shaped cutter, stamp out 26 flower shapes or rounds and transfer to the baking sheets. Bake the cookies for 15 minutes, or until lightly golden-brown and transfer to a wire rack to cool.

● To decorate the cookies, in a small bowl beat together the butter and icing sugar until soft and stir in the orange rind and juice for a soft buttercream icing. Sandwich the cookies together with some buttercream and dust with icing sugar before serving. Store these cookies in an airtight container for up to 1 week.

# Chocolate Macaroons

*Preparation time: 25 minutes ● Cooking time: 25 minutes ● Makes: 20*

**Show how much you care, by presenting these classic cookies to your Father on Father's Day.**

## INGREDIENTS

*75 g/3 oz plain chocolate*

*2 egg whites*

*Pinch of salt*

*75 g/3 oz caster sugar*

*120 g/4 oz ground almonds*

*5 glacé cherries, halved*

*1 Tbsp almond pieces*

Pre-heat oven to 300°F/150°/Gas mark 2. Line several baking sheets with non-stick baking parchment. Melt the chocolate in the microwave or in a bowl over simmering water. Allow to cool.

● In a large bowl, whisk the egg whites with the salt until they form stiff peaks. Gradually whisk in the sugar a little at a time. Fold in the ground almonds and cooled melted chocolate and mix well together.

● Place tablespoonfuls, spaced well apart, on the baking sheets and spread into circles about 5 cm/2 in across and decorate half the cookies with cherries and the remainder with almonds. Bake the cookies for 25 minutes or until firm, transfer to a wire rack and leave to cool. Store in an airtight container and eat within one week.

# Coconut Curls

*Preparation time: 25 minutes ● Cooking time: 6 to 8 minutes ● Makes: 18*

**These stunning cookies are ideal to serve with coffee or as an accompaniment to a cream-based dessert.**

## INGREDIENTS

*175 g/6 oz butter*

*5 Tbsp caster sugar*

*3 Tbsp golden syrup*

*75 g/3 oz plain flour, sifted*

*2 Tbsp sweetened flaked coconut*

Pre-heat oven to 375°F/190°C/Gas mark 5. Line 2 to 3 baking sheets with non-stick baking parchment.

● In a saucepan gently heat the butter, sugar and golden syrup until the butter has melted. Remove from the heat. Add the flour and coconut and mix together until well blended.

● Spoon 3 tablespoons of the mixture, well apart, on the baking sheets and spread out to a 5-cm/2-in circle, bake for 6 to 8 minutes until bubbly and the cookies have spread to a lacy texture.

● Remove from the oven, leave to cool for one minute, then lift off with a thin, metal spatula and curl around a rolling pin to mould into a curl. Shape the remaining cookies in the same way. Leave to go cold and crisp.

## TIP

Handle these cookies very carefully once baked.

# Classic Butter Sablés

*Preparation time: 25 minutes + chilling* • *Cooking time: 15 minutes* • *Makes: 20*

**These buttery cookies will be so popular, you will be baking a double batch for the next time.**

## INGREDIENTS

*225 g/8 oz plain flour, sifted*

*Pinch of salt*

*75 g/3 oz icing sugar*

*150 g/5 oz lightly salted butter, cut into small pieces*

*2 egg yolks*

*2 tsp vanilla essence*

*1 egg, beaten, for glazing*

In a mixing bowl place the flour, salt and icing sugar. Blend in the butter, until the mixture resembles fine breadcrumbs, add the egg yolks with the vanilla essence and combine all the ingredients together to form a soft dough. Alternatively, place all the ingredients in a food processor and pulse until the mixture comes away from the sides of the bowl in a soft dough.

● Pre-heat oven to 350°F/175°C/Gas mark 4. Grease or line 2 baking sheets with non-stick baking parchment.

● On a lightly floured work surface, roll out the dough to about 5 mm/¼ in thick. Cut out rounds using a 5-mm/2-in cutter and lift onto the baking sheets. Brush the cookies very carefully with the beaten egg and chill for 30 minutes.

● Brush again with beaten egg, then mark with the back of a fork, across the cookie to make a pattern. Bake the cookies for 15 minutes or until evenly golden. Transfer to a wire rack to cool.

● To assemble the sablés, stack them together in neat bundles and tie with ribbon. Add labels marked with the names of friends or family members to the cookies. Store in an airtight container for up to a week.

# Valentine Cookies

*Preparation time: 30 minutes + chilling* ● *Cooking time: 15 minutes* ● *Makes: 22*

**This two-toned dough creates a stunning effect, guaranteed to impress your Valentine!**

### INGREDIENTS

*175 g/6 oz butter, softened*

*50 g/2 oz icing sugar, sifted*

*250 g/9 oz plain flour, sifted*

*Pink food colouring*

*Granulated sugar, for sprinkling*

In a mixing bowl beat together the butter and icing sugar until light and fluffy. Fold in the flour and bring all the ingredients together using your hands to form a soft dough. Take half the dough and add a few drops of colouring to turn the dough pink. Wrap the two doughs separately and chill for 30 minutes.

● Pre-heat oven to 350°F/175°C/Gas mark 4. Grease several baking sheets or line with non-stick baking parchment.

● On a lightly floured work surface, roll out each dough to about 5 mm/¼ in thick. Using a 5-cm/2-in and 2.5-cm/1-in heart-shaped cutter, stamp out hearts from the dough and lift onto the baking sheets. Re-position the centres to alternate the colours. Sprinkle with the granulated sugar. Bake the cookies for 15 minutes or until lightly golden. Allow to cool on the baking sheets, before transferring to a wire rack to cool completely. Store these cookies in an airtight container.

# Valentine Passion Fruit Swirls

*Preparation time: 30 minutes* ● *Cooking time: 15 minutes* ● *Makes: 26*

**These delicately flavoured cookies are crisp to the touch but have a melt-in-the-mouth buttery taste.**

### INGREDIENTS

| |
| :---: |
| *4 passion fruit* |
| *175 g/6 oz butter, softened* |
| *120 g/4 oz icing sugar* |
| *150 g/5 oz flour, sifted* |
| *Icing sugar, for dusting* |

Scoop out the flesh and seeds from the passion fruit and push through a fine sieve. Using a teaspoon, push the seeds against the side of the sieve to extract as much juice as possible. (You should be able to extract about 4 tablespoons of passion fruit juice, discard the black seeds.)

● Pre-heat oven to 350°F/175°C/Gas mark 4. Grease several baking sheets or line with non-stick baking parchment.

● In a mixing bowl beat together the butter and icing sugar until very soft (this will take about 5 minutes.) Then beat in the passion fruit juice and the flour to give a soft consistency. Using a piping bag fitted with a medium star nozzle, pipe small "s" shapes on the baking sheets, spacing them well apart. Bake the cookies for 15 minutes. Allow to cool slightly on the sheets then transfer to a wire rack to cool completely. Dust with icing sugar before serving. Store in an airtight container.

# Chocolate Initials

*Preparation time: 20 minutes + chilling* ● *Cooking time: 20 minutes* ● *Makes: 18*

**These incredibly crisp chocolate cookies are the perfect choice for decorating with initials.**

## INGREDIENTS

*1 egg, separated*

*120 g/4 oz caster sugar*

*120 g/4 oz plain chocolate, finely grated*

*175 g/6 oz plain flour, sifted*

*2 Tbsp orange juice*

## DECORATION

*50 g/2 oz plain chocolate, melted*

In a mixing bowl whisk the egg white until soft, but not dry and fold in the caster sugar. Stir in the chocolate, flour, egg yolk and orange juice and bring the mixture together with your hands to make a soft dough. Wrap and chill for 30 minutes.

● Pre-heat oven to 350°F/175°C/Gas mark 4. Grease several baking sheets or line with non-stick baking parchment.

● On a lightly floured work surface, roll out the dough to about 5 mm/¼ in thick. Using a 5-cm/2-in round cutter, stamp out the cookies, re-rolling the dough as necessary and transfer onto the baking sheets. Bake the cookies for 15 to 20 minutes, or until crisp. Transfer to a wire rack and leave to cool.

● Decorate the cookies by piping initials with melted chocolate using a paper pastry bag. Leave to set then store in an airtight container.

## TIP

Use a selection of cutters in heart, stars, diamonds and flower shapes.

# Lover's Scroll

*Preparation time: 25 minutes + chilling ● Cooking time: 15 minutes ● Makes: 24*

**These sticky buttery cookies are delicious fresh from the oven.**

### INGREDIENTS

*175 g/6 oz plain flour, sifted*

*120 g/4 oz butter, cut into small pieces*

*50 g/2 oz caster sugar*

*Grated rind of ½ lemon*

*2 Tbsp milk*

### FILLING

*50 g/2 oz butter, softened*

*175 g/6 oz packed light brown sugar*

*Grated rind of ½ lemon*

*1 egg, beaten, for glazing*

*120 g/4 oz mixed dried fruit*

*75 g/3 oz chopped glacé cherries*

Place the flour in a mixing bowl and blend in the butter using your fingers until the mixture resembles fine breadcrumbs. Stir in the sugar, lemon rind and milk and using your hands bring all the ingredients together to form a dough. Wrap and chill for 30 minutes.

● Meanwhile beat the butter and sugar together in a mixing bowl until light and fluffy, then stir in the lemon rind.

● On a lightly floured surface roll out the dough to a 15 x 28-cm/6 x 11-in rectangle. Brush with beaten egg and spread over the butter and sugar mixture, keeping within 1 cm/½ in of the edges. Sprinkle over the mixed dried fruit and glacé cherries and lightly press down.

● Roll up the pastry from one long side to the centre, then roll up the other side so the two rolls meet, brushing a little beaten egg along the point where the rolls meet. Wrap and chill for a further 1 hour.

● Pre-heat the oven to 350°F/175°C/Gas mark 4. Grease and line several baking sheets with non-stick baking paper.

● Using a sharp knife, slice the roll into about 24 even pieces and lift onto the baking sheets. Bake the cookies for 15 minutes or until lightly golden. Allow to cool on the sheets for a minute before transferring to a wire rack to cool completely.

# Pine Nut Horseshoes

*Preparation time: 30 minutes ● Cooking time: 15 minutes ● Makes: 10*

**Coated with sweet and crunchy pine nuts, these cookies say "Good Luck" in an edible way.**

## INGREDIENTS

*75 g/3 oz white chocolate, broken into pieces*

*225 g/8 oz plain flour, sifted*

*120 g/4 oz lightly salted butter, cut into small pieces*

*50 g/2 oz caster sugar*

*75 g/3 oz chopped dried apricots*

*1 egg, beaten, for glazing*

*75 g/3 oz pine nuts*

*Icing sugar, for dusting*

Pre-heat oven to 350°F/175°C/Gas mark 4. Grease several baking sheets or line with non-stick baking parchment.

● First melt the chocolate by placing the pieces of chocolate in a small bowl and put this in double boiler over simmering water, stir frequently until the chocolate has melted. Allow to cool.

● Place the flour in a mixing bowl and blend in the butter using your fingers until the mixture resembles fine breadcrumbs. Stir in the sugar, apricots and cooled chocolate and bring all the ingredients together to a firm dough. On a lightly floured surface divide the dough into 10 equal-sized balls.

● Roll out each ball into about 23-cm/9-in thick sausage shape and curve it in the middle to resemble a horseshoe shape. Lay a single layer of the pine kernels on a large plate.

● Brush each cookie with beaten egg, lift onto the plate and flatten slightly to coat each horseshoe with the pine kernels. Lift onto the prepared baking sheets and bake the cookies for 15 minutes or until lightly golden. Transfer to a wire rack to cool. Just before serving dust with icing sugar.

# Wedding Bells

*Preparation time: 45 minutes* ● *Cooking time: 15 minutes* ● *Makes: 30*

**These cookies contain marzipan in the dough which gives them an almond flavour that goes well with the lemon.**

### INGREDIENTS

*120 g/4 oz white marzipan, cut into small pieces*

*120 g/4 oz lightly salted butter, softened*

*50 g/2 oz caster sugar*

*1 egg yolk*

*Grated rind of 1 lemon*

*150 g/5 oz plain flour, sifted*

### DECORATION

*2 Tbsp apricot jam*

*Yellow food colouring*

*400 g/14 oz ready-to-roll fondant icing*

*Gold ribbon*

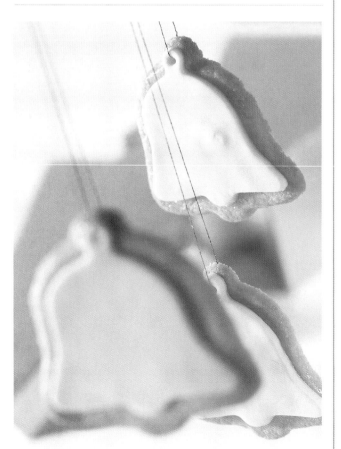

Pre-heat oven to 350°F/175°C/Gas mark 4. Grease several baking sheets or line with non-stick baking parchment.

● In a mixing bowl beat together the marzipan, butter and sugar until light and fluffy. Beat in the egg yolk and lemon rind. Add the flour and bring the mixture together with your hand to form a soft dough. On a lightly floured surface, roll out the dough to 5 mm/¼ in thick and stamp out bells using a 6 cm/2½ in bell-shaped cutter. Re-roll the trimmings and stamp out more bells and place on to the baking sheets. Make a hole at the top of each cookie with a metal skewer (so that you can tie ribbon through the bells when iced).

● Bake the cookies for 10 to 15 minutes or until golden-brown. Transfer to a wire rack and leave to cool. Brush each cookie with warmed apricot jam.

● Add a few drops of yellow colouring to the icing. Knead the icing until soft and smooth. On a surface lightly sprinkled with icing sugar, roll out the icing and stamp out 30 bells using the same bell-shaped cutter, re-rolling as necessary. Press the icing "bell" onto each cookie and re-shape the hole with a metal skewer. Tie ribbon through the holes and pair up the bells.

# Golden Ginger Cookies

*Preparation time: 25 minutes + chilling* ● *Cooking time: 15 minutes* ● *Makes: 16*

**These ginger cookies are deliciously moist but crisp around the edges.**

## INGREDIENTS

125 g/4 oz lightly salted butter, softened

125 g/4 oz light brown sugar

1 egg, beaten

150 g/5 oz plain flour, sifted

2 tsp ground ginger

2 Tbsp crystallized ginger, finely chopped

## DECORATION

6 Tbsp icing sugar, sifted

3 tsp lemon juice

In a mixing bowl beat together the butter and sugar until light and fluffy. Beat in the egg. Add the flour, ground ginger and crystallized ginger and bring the mixture together to form a soft ball. Wrap and chill for 30 minutes.

● Pre-heat oven to 350°F/175°C/Gas mark 4. Grease several baking sheets or line with non-stick baking parchment.

● On a lightly floured surface divide the dough into 16 equal-sized pieces. Roll each piece into a ball and place on the baking sheets. Bake only 6 cookies on each sheet as they will spread during baking. Flatten slightly with a wet fork.

● Bake the cookies for 15 minutes, or until lightly golden at the edges. Allow to cool on the baking sheets before transferring to a wire rack.

● To decorate the cookies, mix the icing sugar with the lemon juice and mix to a thin icing. Using a paper piping bag, drizzle the icing randomly over each cookie and allow to set.

# Cranberry Cookies

*Preparation time: 45 minutes + chilling* ● *Cooking time: 30 minutes* ● *Makes: 16*

**These stunning ruby-coloured cookies are great for special wedding anniversaries.**

## INGREDIENTS

*75 g/3 oz cranberries*

*5 Tbsp caster sugar*

*1 Tbsp water*

*225 g/8 oz plain flour, sifted*

*75 g/3 oz icing sugar, sifted*

*150 g/5 oz slightly salted butter, cut into small pieces*

*Granulated sugar, for sprinkling*

Place the cranberries, sugar and water in a small saucepan and set over a medium heat until the sugar dissolves. Reduce the heat and simmer uncovered for 8 to 10 minutes until the mixture is very thick and jam-like; cool.

● Place the flour and icing sugar in a mixing bowl and blend in the butter using your fingertips until the mixture resembles fine breadcrumbs, add the cooled cranberry sauce mixture and bring all the ingredients together to form a soft ball. Wrap and chill for 30 minutes.

● Pre-heat oven to 350°F/175°C/Gas mark 4. Grease several baking sheets or line with non-stick baking parchment.

● On a lightly floured work surface, roll out the dough to about 5 mm/¼ in thick and stamp out 8-cm/3-in fluted ovals or rounds, re-rolling the dough as necessary; there should be about 16. Transfer to the baking sheets.

● Bake the cookies for 15 minutes or until they are lightly golden at the edges. Transfer to a wire rack to cool. Just before serving sprinkle with granulated sugar.

# Lemon Rings

*Preparation time: 35 minutes ● Cooking time:*
*10 to 15 minutes ● Makes: 16*

**These cookies are sandwiched together with a lemon
butter icing to symbolize wedding rings.**

### INGREDIENTS

25 g/1 oz butter, softened

120 g/4 oz caster sugar

1 egg, beaten

225 g/8 oz self-raising flour

Grated rind of 1 lemon

2 Tbsp lemon juice

### ICING

50 g/2 oz unsalted butter, softened

120 g/4 oz icing sugar

2 tsp lemon juice

1 tsp grated lemon rind

Icing sugar, for dusting

Pre-heat oven to 350°F/175°C/Gas mark 4. Grease several baking sheets.

● In a mixing bowl beat together the butter and sugar until light and fluffy. Beat in the egg. Fold in the flour, lemon rind and lemon juice and mix to a firm dough. On a lightly floured surface roll out the dough to about 5 mm/¼ in thick. Using a 6-cm/2½-in and 2.5-cm/1-in cutter, cut out rings from the dough, carefully removing the central circle, and lift on to the baking sheets. Re-roll the trimmings as necessary. Bake for 10 to 15 minutes. Transfer to a wire rack to cool.

● To decorate the cookies, in a mixing bowl beat together the butter and icing sugar to give a fluffy consistency. Gradually beat in the lemon juice and rind. Sandwich the rings together with the filling and dust with icing sugar before serving.

# Pine Nut Biscotti

*Preparation time: 30 miniutes ● Cooking time:*
*35 to 40 minutes ● Makes: 13*

**Pine nuts and ground cinnamon are used to flavour these
crisp cookies. Serve them with black coffee after a meal.**

### INGREDIENTS

1 egg

7 Tbsp caster sugar

120 g/4 oz plain flour, sifted

½ tsp baking powder

1 tsp ground cinnamon

50 g/2 oz pine nuts

Icing sugar, for dusting

Pre-heat oven to 350°F/175°C/Gas mark 4. Grease a large baking tray or line with non-stick baking parchment.

● In a mixing bowl whisk together the egg and sugar with an electric hand-held mixer until pale and thick (ribbons of mixture should leave a trail from the whisk as you lift it).

● Fold in the flour, baking powder, cinnamon and pine nuts and mix everything together to form a soft dough. Turn out onto a lightly floured work surface and roll into a 23-cm/9-in long log. Transfer onto the prepared baking sheet and flatten the dough until it is about 5 mm/¾ in thick.

● Bake the dough for about 30 minutes or until golden and firm. Leave to cool for about 5 minutes. Transfer to a cutting board and using a serrated bread knife cut the log on the diagonal into 1-cm/½-in thick slices. Lift onto the baking sheet and cook for a further 10 to 15 minutes or until crisp.

● Transfer to a wire rack to cool. Dust with icing sugar and store in an airtight container for up to one week.

# Confetti Cookies

*Preparation time: 50 minutes ● Cooking time: 10 to 12 minutes ● Makes: 35 small cookies*

**These tiny crisp cookies with a delicate hint of lime are decorated with clear icing to resemble confetti.**

## INGREDIENTS

*120 g/4 oz plain flour, sifted*

*1 tsp grated lime rind*

*3 Tbsp icing sugar*

*70 g/2⅓ oz butter, cut into small pieces*

## DECORATION

*125 g/4 oz Icing sugar, sifted*

*1 Tbsp water*

*Blue, yellow and pink food colouring*

Pre-heat oven to 350°F/175°C/Gas mark 4. Grease several baking sheets or line with non-stick baking parchment.

● In a large mixing bowl place the flour, grated lime and icing sugar. Blend in the butter, using your fingertips, until the mixture begins to form together in a soft ball. On a lightly floured surface roll out the dough to 5 mm/ ¼ in thick and using a selection of small cutters, stamp out different shapes. Re-roll the trimmings to make about 35 cookies in all and lift on to the baking sheets. Bake for 10 to 12 minutes or until lightly golden. Transfer the cookies to a wire rack and leave to cool completely.

● To decorate the cookies, mix the icing sugar with sufficient water to form a thin icing and divide into four bowls. Colour the icing blue, yellow and pink, leaving one quarter white. Spread a little icing on each cookie and allow to set. Gift-wrap in coloured cellophane bags to look just like confetti!

# Butter Viennese Fingers

*Preparation time: 25 minutes • Cooking time: 10 to 15 minutes • Makes: 20*

**These cookies look very impressive, they are crisp on the outside but have a melt-in-the-mouth texture.**

## INGREDIENTS

*175 g/6 oz butter, softened*

*3 Tbsp icing sugar, sifted*

*175 g/6 oz plain flour, sifted*

## DECORATION

*50 g/2 oz plain chocolate, broken into pieces*

Pre-heat oven to 350°F/175°/Gas mark 4. Grease several baking sheets or line with non-stick baking parchment.

● In a large mixing bowl beat together the butter and icing sugar until very soft (this will take about 5 minutes), then beat in the flour until thoroughly mixed and a soft consistency.

● Using a piping bag fitted with a medium star nozzle, pipe 8-cm/3-in long finger shapes on the baking sheets, spacing them well apart. Bake the cookies for 10 to 15 minutes or until pale golden. Transfer to a wire rack to cool.

● To decorate the cookies, place the chocolate in a small bowl and put this in a double boiler set over a saucepan of simmering water and stir frequently until the chocolate has melted. Dip the ends of each cookie in the chocolate and allow to set on a piece of greaseproof paper or baking parchment.

# Two-tone Cookies

*Preparation time: 30 minutes + chilling* ●
*Cooking time: 10 to 12 minutes* ● *Makes: 32*

**Once you have mastered the basic technique, have fun creating different cookie patterns.**

### INGREDIENTS

*175 g/6 oz butter, softened*

*75 g/3 oz icing sugar*

*150 g/5 oz plain flour, sifted*

*½ tsp grated lemon rind*

*2 Tbsp unsweetened cocoa powder, sifted*

*1 egg white, for glazing*

In a mixing bowl, beat together the butter and sugar until light and fluffy. Stir in the flour and lemon rind, then combine the ingredients to form a soft ball. Transfer half the mixture to another bowl and stir in the cocoa powder. Wrap separately and chill for 30 minutes.

● Pre-heat oven to 350°F/175°C/Gas mark 4. Grease several baking sheets or line with non-stick baking parchment.

● On a lightly floured work surface divide each dough in half and roll into four sausage shapes about 30 cm/12 in long and 1 cm/½ in wide. Using the egg white, brush the sausage shapes and stack together alternating the colours. Cut the log shape into 32 slices and lift onto the baking sheets. Bake the cookies for 10 to 12 minutes. Transfer to a wire rack to cool completely. Store the cookies in an airtight container.

# Hot Ham and Cheese Triangles

*Preparation time: 25minutes + chilling* ●
*Cooking time: 15 minutes* ● *Makes: 28*

**These cookies have a great colour from the red Leicester cheese and the dried red chilli flakes give the taste buds a kick!**

### INGREDIENTS

*120 g/4 oz plain flour, sifted*

*½ tsp salt*

*½ tsp dried crushed chillies*

*75 g/3 oz butter, cut into small pieces*

*175 g/6 oz grated red Leicester cheese*

*75 g/3 oz ham, finely chopped*

Place the flour, salt and dried chilli flakes in a mixing bowl and using your fingers blend in the butter until the mixture resembles fine breadcrumbs. Stir in the cheese and ham and mix together using your hands to form a dough. Wrap and chill for 30 minutes.

● Pre-heat oven to 375°F/190°C/Gas mark 5. Grease several baking sheets or line with non-stick baking parchment.

● On a lightly floured work surface, roll out the dough about 5 mm/¼ in thick and stamp out squares using a 10-cm/4-in fluted cutter, cut in half to make triangles. Lift onto the baking sheets. Bake the cookies for 15 minutes, or until puffed up and lightly golden-brown. Transfer to a wire rack to cool. Store in an airtight container and eat within one week.

# Lime and Coconut Hearts

*Preparation time: 35 minutes* ● *Cooking time: 15 minutes* ● *Makes: 16*

**Ideal for any journey, the exotic flavours of coconut and lime are reminiscent of the Caribbean.**

### INGREDIENTS

*225 g/8 oz plain flour, sifted*

*50 g/2 oz rice flour*

*175 g/6 oz butter, cut into small pieces*

*50 g/2 oz caster sugar*

*75 g/3 oz unsweetened flaked coconut*

*Grated rind of 1 lime*

*2 Tbsp milk*

### DECORATION

*7 Tbsp icing sugar, sifted*

*3 tsp cold water*

*Grated rind of 1 lime*

Pre-heat oven to 350°F/175°C/Gas mark 4. Grease several baking sheets or line with non-stick baking parchment.

● Place the flour and rice flour in a mixing bowl and add the butter. Blend in the butter using your fingers until the mixture resembles fine breadcrumbs, add the sugar, coconut, lime rind and milk and mix all the ingredients together to form a soft dough.

● On a lightly floured work surface, roll out the dough to about 5 mm/¼ in thick, stamp out hearts using an 8-cm/3-in heart-shaped cutter and lift onto the baking sheets. Bake the cookies for 15 minutes or until they are lightly golden. Transfer to a wire rack to cool.

● To decorate the cookies, mix the icing sugar with the cold water and mix to a thin icing. Fill a paper pastry bag with icing and drizzle it over the cookies, sprinkle with lime rind and allow the icing to set. Store in an airtight container.

# Rosemary and Lime Cookies

*Preparation time: 25 minutes ● Cooking time: 15 to 20 minutes ● Makes: 30*

**The combination of fresh rosemary with lime results in a crisp scented cookie.**

### INGREDIENTS

50 g/2 oz lightly salted butter, softened

120 g/4 oz light brown sugar

1 egg, separated

Grated rind of 1 lime

200 g/7 oz plain flour, sifted

2 Tbsp lime juice

2 tsp finely chopped fresh rosemary

Granulated sugar, for sprinkling

Pre-heat oven to 350°F/175°C/Gas mark 4. Grease several baking sheets or line with non-stick baking parchment.

● In a mixing bowl beat together the butter and sugar until light and fluffy. Beat in the egg yolk and lime rind. Add the flour and begin to work the mixture into a soft dough. Add the lime juice and rosemary and using your hands bring the dough together in a soft ball.

● On a lightly floured surface, roll out the dough to 5 mm/¼ in thick, stamp out diamond shapes using a 8-cm/3-in cutter. Re-roll the trimmings and stamp out more shapes and place on the baking sheets.

● Lightly whisk the egg white in a small bowl, gently brush over the surface of each cookie, then sprinkle with a little granulated sugar. Bake the cookies for 15 to 20 minutes or until lightly golden. Transfer to a wire rack to cool. Store the cookies in an airtight container for up to one week.

# Smiling Faces

*Preparation time: 35 minutes ● Cooking time: 15 minutes ● Makes: 16*

**These coffee-flavoured cookies are great for cheering up a special friend!**

### INGREDIENTS

1 Tbsp instant coffee powder

1 Tbsp hot water

225 g/8 oz plain flour, sifted

75 g/3 oz icing sugar, sifted

150 g/5 oz butter, cut into small pieces

### DECORATION

6 Tbsp icing sugar

3 tsp water

Pre-heat oven to 350°F/175°C/Gas mark 4. Grease several baking sheets or line with non-stick baking parchment.

● Dissolve the coffee in the hot water and leave to cool completely.

● Place the flour and icing sugar in a mixing bowl and blend in the butter using your fingertips until the mixture resembles fine breadcrumbs. Pour in the cooled coffee and bring all the ingredients together to form a soft dough.

● On a lightly floured surface, roll out the dough to about 5 mm/¼ in thick. Using an 8-cm/3-in cutter, stamp out rounds and lift on to the prepared baking sheets, re-rolling the dough as necessary. Prick the cookies with a fork. Bake for about 15 minutes or until crisp. Transfer to a wire rack to cool.

● To decorate, mix the icing sugar with sufficient cold water to make a thin icing. Using a paper pastry bag, pipe smiling faces onto the cookies. Leave to set. Store in an airtight container.

# Pecan Pinwheel Cookies

*Preparation time: 25 minutes + chilling* ● *Cooking time: 20 minutes* ● *Makes: 24*

**A cinnamon cookie base is sprinkled with pecan nuts and orange rind then rolled up and cut into pinwheels.**

## INGREDIENTS

*175 g/6 oz plain flour, sifted*

*1 tsp ground cinnamon*

*120 g/4 oz sugar*

*120 g/4 oz lightly salted butter, cut into small pieces*

*1 Tbsp maple syrup*

## FILLING

*5 Tbsp smooth peanut butter*

*2 Tbsp maple syrup*

*Grated rind of 1 orange*

*50 g/2 oz chopped pecan nuts*

*2 Tbsp maple syrup, optional*

Place the flour, cinnamon and sugar in a mixing bowl and using your fingers blend in the butter until the mixture resembles fine breadcrumbs. Add the maple syrup and mix everything together with your hands to form a soft dough. Wrap and chill for 30 minutes.

● On a lightly floured work surface roll out the dough to a 30 x 8-cm/12 x 7-in rectangle. In a small bowl combine the peanut butter and maple syrup and beat using a wooden spoon until soft enough to spread. Spread this mixture over the rectangle leaving a 2.5-cm/1-in border around the edge of the dough. Sprinkle over the orange rind and pecan nuts. Starting from the long end, roll up the dough tightly into a "sausage" shape. Wrap and chill for 30 minutes.

● Pre-heat oven to 350°F/175°C/Gas mark 4. Grease several baking sheets or line with non-stick baking parchment.

● Using a sharp knife cut the log into 24 equal slices (discarding the first and last slice, which have little filling) and lift onto the baking sheets. Bake the cookies for 20 minutes or until lightly golden. Drizzle with maple syrup to glaze, if liked. Transfer to a wire rack to cool. Store in an airtight container until required.

# Fan-tailed Shortbread

*Preparation time: 25 minutes ● Cooking time: 35 to 40 minutes ● Makes: 8*

**This classic buttery shortbread is very rewarding to make – and a great gift.**

### INGREDIENTS

120 g/4 oz butter, softened

25 g/1 oz caster sugar

75 g/3 oz plain flour, sifted

2 Tbsp rice flour

Pinch of salt

2 Tbsp finely chopped mixed nuts, to sprinkle

Pre-heat oven to 300°F/150°C/Gas mark 2. Grease a baking sheet or line with non-stick baking parchment.

● In a mixing bowl beat together the butter and sugar until light and fluffy. Add the flour, rice flour and salt and mix everything together to form a soft dough. On a lightly floured surface, roll out the dough to form a neat circle about 20 cm/8 in across and 5 mm/¼ in thick.

● Transfer to the prepared baking sheet, then crimp the edges with your fingertips and mark into 8 even wedges with a sharp knife. Prick with a fork, sprinkle with the chopped nuts and bake for about 35 to 40 minutes until lightly golden.

● Leave to cool slightly on the tray before transferring to a wire rack to cool completely. Cut along the scored lines to divide into 8 wedges.

# Sesame Cracker Cookies

*Preparation time: 20 minutes ● Cooking time: 15 minutes ● Makes: 15*

**Serve these savoury cookies with chunks of Cheddar cheese.**

### INGREDIENTS

175 g/6 oz wholemeal flour

50 g/2 oz oat bran

½ tsp salt

1 tsp baking powder

15 g/½ oz caster sugar

2 Tbsp sesame seeds

125 g/4 oz butter, cut into small pieces

1 Tbsp water

Pre-heat oven to 375°F/190°C/Gas mark 5. Grease several baking sheets or line with non-stick baking parchment.

● In a mixing bowl place the wholemeal flour, oat bran, salt, baking powder, sugar and sesame seeds and give a good mix. Blend in the butter, using your fingers, until the mixture resembles fine breadcrumbs. Add sufficient cold water (about 1 tablespoon) and work all the ingredients together into a firm dough.

● On a lightly floured work surface, roll out the dough to about 5 mm/¼ in thick and using an 8-cm/3-in round cutter, stamp out 15 circles and lift onto the baking sheets, re-rolling the dough as necessary. Prick the cookies with a fork. Bake for 15 minutes. Transfer to a wire rack to cool, then store these cookies in an airtight container.

# Coffee Meringue Snails

*Preparation time: 25 minutes* ● *Cooking time: 1 hour and 30 minutes* ● *Makes: 15*

**The addition of coffee to the meringue makes it quite soft when piping but the taste is delicious. Any gardener should see the funny side of making a snail cookie!**

## INGREDIENTS

*1 Tbsp instant coffee powder*

*1 Tbsp boiling water*

*4 egg whites*

*Pinch of salt*

*400 g/14 oz caster sugar*

## DECORATION

*3 Tbsp icing sugar*

*1 tsp water*

*Black food colouring*

Dissolve the coffee in the boiling water in a small jug and leave to go cold. Pre-heat the oven to 250°F/120°C/Gas mark ½. Line several baking sheets with non-stick baking parchment.

● In a large clean bowl, using a balloon whisk or hand-held electric mixer, whisk together the egg whites and salt until they form stiff peaks. Whisk in the sugar a little at a time. The meringue should start to look glossy.

● Continue whisking in the sugar until it has been incorporated and the meringue is thick and shiny and stands in stiff peaks. Fold in the coffee and mix through.

● Fill a piping bag with the meringue, using a 5-mm/¾-in plain nozzle, pipe about 15 "snail" shapes. Bake the meringues for 1 hour and 30 minutes until they are dry and crisp and can be easily lifted off the paper.

● To decorate the snails, mix the icing sugar with the water to form a thin icing. Add a few drops of colouring. Fill a piping bag with the black icing and pipe on eyes and mouths. Store in an airtight container.

# Almond Tiles

*Preparation time: 45 minutes* ● *Cooking time: 4 to 5 minutes per batch* ● *Makes: 30*

**These are one of the most popular French cookies, "tuiles aux amandes", so called because they resemble the curved roof tiles seen all over France.**

### INGREDIENTS

*50 g/2 oz whole blanched almonds, lightly toasted*

*225 g/8 oz sugar*

*3 Tbsp unsalted butter*

*2 egg whites*

*½ tsp almond essence*

*25 g/1 oz flour, sifted*

*75 g/3 oz flaked almonds*

In a food processor fitted with a metal blade, process the toasted almonds with 2 tablespoons of the sugar until finè crumbs form.

● Preheat oven to 400°F/200°C/Gas mark 6. Generously butter 2 baking sheets or line with non-stick baking parchment.

● In a medium bowl beat the butter until creamy, add the sugar and beat until light and fluffy. Gradually beat in the egg whites and almond essence until well blended. Sift over the flour and fold into the butter mixture, then fold in the almond-sugar mixture.

● Begin by working in batches of 4 cookies on each sheet. Drop tablespoonfuls of batter about 15-cm/6-in apart on the baking sheet. With the back of a moistened spoon, spread each mound of batter into very thin 8-cm/3-in rounds. Each round should be transparant. If you make a few holes, the batter will spread and fill them in. Sprinkle tops with flaked almonds.

● Bake, one sheet at a time, until the edges are browned and the centres are just golden, 4 to 5 minutes. Remove baking sheet to a wire rack, working quickly, use a thin-bladed metal spatula to loosen the edge of a hot cookie and transfer to a rolling pin or glass tumbler. Gently press, side down, to shape each cookie. If the cookie becomes too firm to transfer, return to the oven for 30 seconds to soften, the proceed as above. When cool, transfer immediately to airtight containers in single layers. These cookies are very fragile.

# Hazelnut and Nutmeg Cookies

*Preparation time: 30 minutes + chilling* ● *Cooking time: 15 to 18 minutes* ● *Makes: 24*

**The crunchy hazelnuts and spicy nutmeg make these a great treat for morning coffee.**

### INGREDIENTS

*225 g/8 oz lightly salted butter, softened*

*175 g/6 oz caster sugar*

*2 egg yolks*

*1 tsp vanilla essence*

*225 g/8 oz self-raising flour, sifted*

*½ tsp ground nutmeg*

*¾ cup chopped hazelnuts*

*Icing sugar, for dusting, optional*

In a mixing bowl cream together the butter and sugar until light and fluffy. Beat in the egg yolks and vanilla essence, add the flour and nutmeg and mix everything together to form a soft dough. Wrap and chill in the refrigerator for 30 minutes.

● Pre-heat oven to 375°F/190°C/Gas mark 5. Grease several baking sheets or line with non-stick baking parchment.

● On a lightly floured work surface, divide the dough into 24 equal-sized pieces, roll each into a ball and flatten slightly. Place the chopped hazelnuts on a large plate, roll the flattened balls in the chopped hazelnuts and then lift onto the baking sheets spaced well apart. Bake the cookies for 15 to 18 minutes or until lightly golden. Transfer to a wire rack to cool. Dust with icing sugar before serving. Store these cookies in an airtight container.

# Cardamom Crisps

*Preparation time: 25 minutes ● Cooking time: 15 minutes ● Makes: 20*

**These indulgent cookies flavoured with cardamom and ginger are delicious. They will liven up anyone's nightcap.**

### INGREDIENTS

*275 g/9 oz plain flour, sifted*

*½ tsp ground cardamom*

*Pinch of salt*

*120 g/4 oz lightly salted butter, cut into small pieces*

*225 g/8 oz soft brown sugar*

*2 egg yolks*

*2 Tbsp finely chopped stem ginger or ginger preserves*

*Granulated sugar, for sprinkling*

Pre-heat oven to 350°F/175°C/Gas mark 4. Grease several baking sheets or line with non-stick baking parchment.

● In a mixing bowl, place the flour, ground cardamom and salt. Blend in the butter, using your fingers, until the mixture resembles fine bread crumbs, stir in the sugar. Add the egg yolks and mix all the ingredients together to form a soft dough.

● On a lightly floured surface, roll out the dough to 5-mm/¼-in thick. Cut out the cookies using a 6-cm/2½-in shaped cutter, re-rolling the trimmings to make about 20, place on to the baking sheets.

● Sprinkle a little stem ginger or ginger preserves on the top of each cookie. Bake the cookies for 15 minutes or until lightly golden and crisp. Transfer the cookies to a wire rack and leave to cool. Sprinkle with granulated sugar before serving.

### TIP

If using cardamom pods, crack open 7 pods, remove the black seeds and crush with a pestle and mortar.

# Double Chocolate Mint Sandwiches

*Preparation time: 1 hour + chilling* ● *Cooking time: 12 to 16 minutes* ● *Makes: About 24*

**A delicious combination of mint-flavoured white chocolate ganache sandwiched between thin cocoa wafers, glazed with dark chocolate. These cookies are time-consuming to make, but make an excellent presentation gift.**

### INGREDIENTS

*120 g/4 oz plain flour*

*3 Tbsp unsweetened cocoa powder*

*120 g/4 oz butter*

*50 g/2 oz caster sugar*

*1 egg*

*1 tsp mint essence*

### FILLING

*120 ml/4 fl oz whipping cream*

*200 g/7 oz fine-quality white chocolate, chopped*

### GLAZE

*150 g/5 oz plain chocolate, chopped*

*75 g/3 oz butter, cut into pieces*

Sift together the flour and cocoa. In a large bowl, beat the butter until creamy, add the sugar and continue beating until light and fluffy. Beat in the egg and mint essence until blended. Stir in the flour-cocoa mixture until a soft dough forms. Place the dough in clingfilm and refrigerate for 1 to 2 hours until firm.

● Preheat oven to 350°F/175°C/Gas mark 4. Grease 2 baking sheets with non-stick baking parchment.

● On a lightly floured work surface, roll out half the dough to about 2.5 cm/⅛ in thick. Using a 5-cm/2½-in cutter, stamp out as many cookies as possible, re-rolling the dough as necessary and lift onto the baking sheets.

● Bake for 6 to 8 minutes or until the edges are set. Allow to cool and then transfer to a wire rack to cool completely. Repeat with the remaining dough.

● In a medium saucepan over a medium heat, bring the cream to a boil. Remove from the heat and add the white chocoate, stirring constantly until melted. Stir in mint essence and strain into a bowl. Cool until firm.

● Slightly beat white chocolate cream to lighten, then spread a little filling onto half of the cookies, pressing together gently. Allow to set for 24 hours.

● In a small saucepan over a low heat, melt the chocolate and butter for the glaze, stirring until smooth. Remove from the heat. Cool until thickened to spreading consistency, 20 to 30 minutes. Spread a small amount of glaze onto the top of each sandwiched cookie, smoothing tops. Refrigerate until set, 30 minutes or so. Store these cookies in an airtight container, refrigerated, with greaseproof paper between the layers.

# Strawberry Jam Sandwiches

*Preparation time: 25 minutes + chilling ● Cooking time: 8 to 10 minutes ● Makes: About 24*

**Children love strawberry jam sandwiches and these are the perfect cookies to take to a family party.**

## INGREDIENTS

| |
|---|
| *75 g/3 oz blanched almonds* |
| *175 g/6 oz plain flour* |
| *175 g/6 oz lightly salted butter* |
| *225 g/8 oz caster sugar* |
| *1 egg, separated* |
| *Grated rind of 1 lemon* |
| *1 tsp vanilla essence* |
| *½ tsp salt* |
| *50 g/2 oz flaked almonds, chopped* |
| *5 Tbsp strawberry jam* |
| *1 Tbsp lemon juice* |

In a food processor fitted with a metal blade, process the blanched almonds and 15 g/1 oz flour until the mixture becomes very fine. In a separate bowl, beat the butter until creamy, add the sugar and continue beating until light and fluffy. Beat in the egg yolk, lemon rind and vanilla essence until blended. Stir in the almond mixture and add the remaining flour and salt; process until combined. Wrap the dough in clingfilm and refrigerate for 2 hours or overnight, until the dough is firm enough to handle.

● Pre-heat oven to 350°F/175°C/Gas mark 4. Grease or line two baking sheets with non-stick baking parchment.

● On a floured surface, roll half the dough into a 30-cm/12-in square; keep the other half refrigerated. Cut the square crosswise and lengthwise into 6 strips to make 24 squares. Using a 5-mm/¾-in cutter, cut out centres from half the squares.

● Place the squares on baking sheets 1 cm/½ in apart. In a small bowl, whisk the egg white until frothy. Brush the top of cookies only with it and sprinkle with the almonds. Bake until just golden, 8 to 10 minutes. Allow the cookies to cool slightly, then transfer to wire racks to cool completely.

● In a saucepan over a low heat, melt the strawberry jam with the lemon juice. Spoon a little of the glaze over the cookie squares, then top with an almond-topped cookie, pressing the two gently together. Allow the jam to set before serving. These cookies are best eaten as soon as possible after baking as they will begin to go soft if kept for too long.

# Real Vanilla Cookies

*Preparation time: 30 minutes ● Cooking time: 8 to 10 minutes ● Makes: About 24*

**These cookies are a Danish speciality. They use real vanilla seeds from a pod.**

### INGREDIENTS

*225 g/8 oz plain flour*

*2 Tbsp cornflour*

*5 Tbsp caster sugar*

*3 Tbsp finely chopped blanched almonds*

*½ vanilla pod or 1 tsp vanilla essence*

*225 g/8 oz unsalted butter, cut into small pieces*

*1 egg, separated*

*Sugar, for sprinkling*

*Icing sugar, for dusting*

Pre-heat oven to 400°F/200°C/Gas mark 6. Grease two baking sheets, or line with non-stick baking parchment.

● Sift together the flour and cornflour and stir in the sugar and almonds.

● Using a sharp knife, split the vanilla pod and scrape out the seeds. Add to the flour mixture and mix well. (If using vanilla essence, mix with the egg yolk and add later.) Blend the butter into the flour mixture until it resembles breadcrumbs. In a separate bowl, beat the egg yolk (and vanilla essence) and add to the crumb mixture. Knead until a soft dough forms. (If the dough seems a little wet, add a little more flour.)

● Spoon the dough into a large piping bag fitted with a large plain nozzle and pipe "doughnut" shapes 4 cm/1½ in apart on the baking sheets. In a small bowl, beat the egg whites until foamy, then use to brush the shapes. Sprinkle with sugar.

● Bake until lightly golden and set, 8 to 10 minutes. Allow to cool slightly, then, using a metal spatula, transfer to wire racks to cool completely. Dust with icing sugar. Store in an airtight container for up to one week.

# Bitter Chocolate Discs

*Preparation time: 25 minutes* ● *Cooking time: 15 minutes* ● *Makes: 16*

**These cookies have a crumbly melt-in-the-mouth texture with a rich chocolate flavour.**

## INGREDIENTS

*150 g/5 oz butter, softened*

*120 g/4 oz caster sugar*

*225 g/8 oz plain flour, sifted*

*Pinch of salt*

*50 g/2 oz unsweetened cocoa powder, sifted*

## DECORATION

*75 g/3 oz white chocolate, melted*

Pre-heat oven to 350°F/175°C/Gas mark 4. Grease several baking sheets or line with non-stick baking parchment.

● In a mixing bowl beat together the butter and sugar until light and fluffy. Add the flour, salt and cocoa. Using your hands work these ingredients into the butter and sugar mixture until it comes together in a firm dough.

● On a lightly floured surface, roll out the dough to 5 mm/¼ in thick. Using an 8-cm/3-in fluted round cutter, stamp out 16 cookies, re-rolling as necessary and transfer onto the baking sheets. Prick with a fork and bake the cookies for 15 minutes. Cool on a wire rack.

● Decorate the cookies by drizzling freestyle with melted white chocolate using a paper piping bag. Leave on the wire rack until the chocolate icing becomes firm.

# Chocolate Cookies

For many people, this will be their favourite chapter in the book. The appeal of chocolate just cannot be denied, even its Latin name acknowledges this, *Theobroma cacao* means "food of the gods" and who could doubt it. Chocoholics will find reading through these recipes alone will send them on a chocolate high.

When shopping for chocolate, be sure to buy real chocolate and not a synthetic chocolate-flavoured substitute. Different brands of the same type of chocolate can vary in taste, so to avoid disappointment, make sure that the chocolate you cook with tastes the same as the one you most enjoy eating. If you are not sure, then have a nibble before you begin.

The biggest problem will be which recipe to cook first – maybe a purely chocolate cookie, or one with a hint of orange, or perhaps a chocolate cookie with a nutty crunch. One thing is guaranteed, and that is the enjoyment of tasting these rich and sumptuous cookies.

## Lunch-box or Picnic Treats

## Cookies with Crunch

# Afternoon Tea

# Special Occasions

# After-dinner Cookies

# No-cook Peanut Squares

*Preparation time: 30 minutes + chilling ●*
*Cooking time: 5 minutes ● Makes: About 24*

**You do not even have to switch the oven on to make these chocolatey treats.**

## INGREDIENTS

300 ml/10 fl oz golden syrup

225 g/8 oz peanut butter

250 g/9 oz All-Bran breakfast cereal

225 g/8 oz chopped peanuts

200 g/7 oz milk chocolate

Grease or line a shallow 18 x 28-cm/7 x 11-in tin with non-stick baking parchment.

● Mix the syrup and peanut butter together in a large saucepan and cook over a medium heat stirring until the mixture begins to boil. Remove from the heat and stir in the breakfast cereal and chopped peanuts until well blended. Spread the mixture into the baking tin. Press out evenly and chill for 1 hour in the refrigerator.

● Melt the chocolate in a small bowl set over a saucepan of simmering water and spread over the cookie base using a spatula. When set cut into squares and store in an airtight container.

## TIP

All the cookies in this chapter will freeze for up to one month unless otherwise stated.

# Lunch-box Crunchies

*Preparation time: 20 minutes ● Cooking time:*
*15 minutes ● Makes: About 24*

**This is a small crunchy cookie, suitable for a lunch-box or picnic.**

## INGREDIENTS

175 g/6 oz plain flour

50 g/2 oz slightly salted butter, softened

50 g/2 oz light brown sugar

1 egg

75 g/3 oz plain chocolate, chopped

Pre-heat oven to 350°F/175°C/Gas mark 4. Grease two baking sheets or line with non-stick baking parchment.

● Sift the flour into a bowl. Beat together the butter and sugar in a separate bowl. Beat in the egg. Mix the sifted flour into the butter with the chocolate pieces.

● Mould the mixture into 24 pieces. Place on baking sheets and press the top lightly with a fork. Bake for 15 minutes. Leave to cool on the baking sheet. Store in an airtight container.

# Chequerboards

*Preparation time: 25 minutes* ● *Cooking time: 15 to 20 minutes* ● *Makes: About 26*

**These cookies are good fun to make and look great for children's parties.**

## INGREDIENTS

175 g/6 oz butter, softened

200 g/7 oz caster sugar

½ tsp vanilla essence

2 eggs

600 g/1¼ lb plain flour

2 tsp baking powder

1 tsp milk

1½ Tbsp unsweetened cocoa powder, sifted

Divide the butter and sugar evenly between 2 bowls. For the vanilla dough, beat butter and sugar until light and fluffy. Beat in the vanilla essence and one egg. Sift half the flour and baking powder into the bowl. Blend in with a spoon and then work by hand to form a smooth dough.

● Make the chocolate dough in the same way with the remaining butter, sugar and egg, adding milk and sifted cocoa along with the remaining flour and baking powder. Divide each portion of dough into 4 equal pieces.

● On a floured surface roll each piece into a rope 30 cm/12 in long. Place a chocolate rope next to a vanilla one. Place a chocolate one on top of the vanilla rope and a vanilla one on top of the chocolate. Press firmly together to form a square. Wrap in clingfilm. Repeat with the remaining dough. Chill for 1 hour in the refrigerator.

● Pre-heat oven to 350°F/175°C/Gas mark 4. Grease two baking sheets or line with non-stick baking parchment.

● Cut dough into 26 slices and place onto the baking sheets. Bake for 15 to 20 minutes until lightly browned. Transfer to a wire rack to cool. Once completely cool, store in an airtight container.

# Chocolate Crackle-Tops

*Preparation time: 25 minutes + chilling* ● *Cooking time: 10 to 15 minutes* ● *Makes: About 48*

**A simple chocolate cookie which is easy to make and will become a family favourite.**

### INGREDIENTS

*200 g/7 oz plain chocolate, chopped*

*50 g/2 oz slightly salted butter, softened*

*120 g/4 oz caster sugar*

*3 eggs*

*1 tsp vanilla essence*

*175 g/6 oz plain flour*

*25 g/1 oz unsweetened cocoa powder*

*½ tsp baking powder*

*175 g/6 oz icing sugar, for decoration*

Heat the chocolate and butter in a saucepan over a low heat, stirring frequently. Remove from the heat and stir in the sugar. Continue stirring for 2 to 3 minutes until the sugar dissolves. Add the eggs one at a time, beating well. Add the vanilla essence.

● Sift the flour, cocoa, and baking powder into a bowl. Gradually stir into the chocolate mixture in batches, until just blended. Cover dough and refrigerate for 1 hour or until cold.

● Pre-heat oven to 325°F/160°C/Gas mark 3. Grease two baking sheets or line with non-stick baking parchment.

● Place the icing sugar in a small bowl. Using a teaspoon, scoop dough into small balls and between palms of hand, roll into 1-cm/½-in balls. Drop balls one at a time into icing sugar and roll until heavily coated. Remove ball with a slotted spoon and tap against the side of the bowl to remove excess sugar.

● Place the cookies on baking sheets spaced well apart. Bake for 10 to 15 minutes. Leave to cool on baking sheet for 3 minutes then remove to wire cooling rack. Eat within 2 days.

# Oaty Jacks

*Preparation time: 15 minutes ● Cooking time: 25 to 30 minutes ● Makes: 12*

**A perfect lunch-box treat or a substantial afternoon snack. Try dipping them in white chocolate too.**

### INGREDIENTS

*120 g/4 oz slightly salted butter, softened*

*120 g/4 oz light brown sugar*

*200 g/7 oz rolled oats*

*175 g/6 oz plain chocolate*

Pre-heat oven to 325°F/160°C/Gas mark 3. Grease or line a shallow 20 x 20-cm/8 x 8-in tin with non-stick baking parchment.

● Melt the butter over a medium heat in a saucepan, then transfer to a bowl. Stir in the sugar and rolled oats.

● Spoon the mixture into the baking tin and bake for 25 to 30 minutes. Leave to cool in the tin for 5 minutes, then cut into squares.

● Melt the chocolate in a bowl over a saucepan of simmering water. When the oaty jacks are cold, dip each piece into melted chocolate and leave to set on greaseproof paper. Once the chocolate is set, store the cookies in an airtight container.

# Amaretti Drops

*Preparation time: 25 minutes ● Cooking time: 12 to 15 minutes ● Makes: About 15*

**This cookie is light and crispy on the outside, chewy on the inside and ideal as after-dinner treat.**

### INGREDIENTS

*50 g/2 oz amaretti cookies, crushed*

*1 Tbsp unsweetened cocoa powder*

*50 g/2 oz icing sugar*

*2 egg whites*

Pre-heat oven to 350°F/170°C/Gas mark 4. Grease or line a large baking sheet with non-stick paper.

● Place the cookies in a food processor and process briefly to produce coarse crumbs. Place in a bowl and sift in the unsweetened cocoa powder. Stir to blend.

● In a medium bowl beat the egg whites until stiff peaks form. Gradually beat in the icing sugar a tablespoonful at a time. Then add the cookie mixture to the egg whites and fold the two together gently until just blended.

● Place rounded teaspoonfuls of the cookie mixture well apart on the prepared baking sheet and bake for 12 to 15 minutes. Cool the cookies on the baking sheet for about 10 minutes, then remove to a wire rack to cool completely. When cool, store cookies in an airtight container. Not suitable for freezing.

# Apricot and Chocolate Cookies

*Preparation time: 20 minutes* ● *Cooking time: 12 minutes* ● *Makes: About 25*

**A lovely chewy cookie with the unusual but delicious combination of chocolate and apricots.**

### INGREDIENTS

175 g/6 oz butter

120 g/4 oz light brown sugar

1 egg, beaten

175 g/6 oz plain flour

Pinch of salt

1 tsp baking powder

75 g/3 oz chopped ready-to-eat dried apricots

25 g/1 oz chocolate chips

Pre-heat oven to 350°F/175°C/Gas mark 4. Grease two baking sheets or line with non-stick baking parchment.

● Beat the butter and sugar together until smooth and soft. Beat in the egg until fluffy. Sift the flour with the salt and baking powder into the butter mixture. Mix together until thoroughly blended. Beat in the apricots and chocolate chips.

● Roll the mixture into small balls and place well apart on baking sheets. Flatten with the prongs of a fork. Bake for 12 to 14 minutes until golden-brown. While hot, ease off the baking sheets and cool on a wire rack. Once completely cool, store in an airtight container.

# Spiced Rum Chocolate Cookies

*Preparation time: 20 minutes ● Cooking time:*
*10 to 12 minutes ● Makes: About 18*

**A small, dark and spicy cookie which is strictly for the adults.**

### INGREDIENTS

| |
|---|
| *50 g/2 oz light brown sugar* |
| *2 eggs, separated* |
| *175 g/6 oz plain flour* |
| *1 Tbsp unsweetened cocoa powder* |
| *1 tsp ground cinnamon* |
| *1 tsp allspice* |
| *225 g/8 oz caster sugar* |
| *Grated rind of ½ orange* |
| *2 Tbsp dark rum* |

Pre-heat oven to 375°F/190°C/Gas mark 5. Grease two baking sheets or line with non-stick baking parchment.

● Beat together the brown sugar with the egg yolks until light and fluffy. Sift the flour and spices together, then stir in until the mixture resembles breadcrumbs. Whisk the egg whites until they form stiff peaks and then beat in the caster sugar until glossy. Fold into the mixture with the grated orange rind.

● Roll the mixture into walnut-sized pieces, and place on the baking sheets. Bake for 10 to 15 minutes. Brush with rum while still warm, then use a metal spatula to transfer to a wire cooling rack to cool completely. Store in an airtight container.

# Cherry Chocolate Dreams

*Preparation time: 15 minutes ● Cooking time:*
*12 to 15 minutes ● Makes: About 15*

**A winning combination of cherries and chocolate.**

### INGREDIENTS

| |
|---|
| *120 g/4 oz slightly salted butter, softened* |
| *50 g/2 oz caster sugar* |
| *½ tsp vanilla essence* |
| *150 g/5 oz plain flour, sifted* |
| *2 Tbsp finely chopped glacé cherries* |
| *2 Tbsp finely chopped plain chocolate,* |

Pre-heat oven to 375°F/190°C/Gas mark 5. Grease two baking sheets or line with non-stick baking parchment.

● Beat together the butter, sugar and vanilla essence until light and fluffy. Stir in the flour until well combined. Add the cherries and chocolate and mix until blended. Place teaspoonfuls of the mixture on baking sheets.

● Bake for 12 to 15 minutes until lightly golden. Leave to cool for 2 minutes before transferring onto a wire cooling rack. Once cool, store in an airtight container.

### TIP

It is easier to chop glacé cherries if they have first been dipped in flour. Try using floured scissors instead of a knife.

# Chocolate Pinwheels

*Preparation time: 25 minutes + chilling* ● *Cooking time: 8 to 10 minutes* ● *Makes: About 25*

**A good, fun cookie, that is great for children's parties.**

### INGREDIENTS

*120 g/4 oz slightly salted butter, softened*

*50 g/2 oz caster sugar*

*1 egg, beaten*

*1 tsp vanilla essence*

*150 g/5 oz plain flour*

*Pinch of salt*

*25 g/1 oz plain chocolate*

In a large bowl beat together the butter and sugar until light and fluffy. Beat in the egg and vanilla essence until blended. Sift the flour and salt onto the mixture and beat briefly until combined.

● Divide the dough in half and wrap one half in clingfilm. Refrigerate until firm enough to roll. Melt the chocolate in a small bowl set over a saucepan of simmering water. Allow to cool slightly. Add the melted chocolate to remaining dough and mix until completely blended. Wrap chocolate dough in clingfilm and refrigerate until firm enough to roll.

● On a lightly floured surface or between 2 sheets of clingfilm, roll the vanilla dough to a rectangle. Repeat with the chocolate dough, rolling to the same size. If rolling between sheets of film, remove top sheet and place chocolate dough on top of plain dough. Roll up dough, from one short end as tightly as possible. Wrap tightly and refrigerate until very firm.

● Pre-heat oven to 375°F/190°C/Gas mark 5. Grease two baking sheets or line with non-stick baking parchment.

● Using a sharp knife, cut the dough roll into 5-mm/¼-in slices and place well apart onto the baking sheets. Bake for 7 to 10 minutes, until beginning to change colour at the edges. Transfer to a wire rack and once completely cool, store in an airtight container.

### TIP

The initial beating together of the butter and sugar is best done using an electric mixer. Beat for between 1 and 2 minutes, until light and fluffy. Reduce the speed to low to add any dry ingredients.

# Orange Chocolate Cookies

*Preparation time: 20 minutes ● Cooking time: 20 minutes ● Makes: About 18*

**Orange and chocolate are such a good combination. Try these with a cup of coffee at any time of day.**

## INGREDIENTS

*175 g/6 oz plain flour*

*¼ tsp baking powder*

*Pinch of salt*

*1 tsp grated orange rind*

*120 g/4 oz granulated sugar*

*50 g/2 oz light brown sugar*

*120 g/4 oz slightly salted butter, softened*

*1 egg*

*½ tsp orange liqueur, optional*

*120 g/4 oz plain chocolate, coarsely chopped*

Pre-heat oven to 300°F/150°C/Gas mark 2. Grease two baking sheets or line with non-stick baking parchment.

● Sift the flour, baking powder and salt into a bowl. In a large bowl blend the orange rind, sugars and butter together until light and fluffy. Add the egg and orange liqueur if using and beat until light and well combined. Add the flour mixture and chopped chocolate. Mix together with a spoon to combine.

● Drop rounded tablespoons onto the baking sheet spaced 5 cm/2 in apart. Bake for 20 minutes until golden. Transfer cookies to a flat surface to cool completely. Once completely cool, store in an airtight container.

# Mocha Chunk Cookies

*Preparation time: 20 minutes ● Cooking time: 20 minutes ● Makes: About 16*

**A classic chunky style cookie with a rich coffee taste.**

## INGREDIENTS

*150 g/5 oz plain flour*

*2 Tbsp unsweetened cocoa powder*

*¼ tsp baking soda*

*Pinch of salt*

*2 tsp instant coffee powder*

*1 tsp coffee liqueur, optional*

*120 g/4 oz caster sugar*

*50 g/2 oz dark brown sugar*

*120 g/4 oz slightly salted butter, softened*

*1 egg*

*175 g/6 oz plain chocolate, coarsely chopped*

Pre-heat oven to 350°F/175°C/Gas mark 4. Grease 2 baking sheets or line with non-stick baking parchment.

● Into a medium-sized bowl, sift the flour, cocoa, baking soda and salt. In a small bowl dissolve coffee powder in coffee liqueur or hot water and set aside. In a large bowl, mix together the sugars. Add the butter and mix thoroughly until light. Add the eggs and coffee mixture and beat until smooth. Add the flour mixture and the chocolate chunks and mix gently with a spoon until well combined.

● Place rounded tablespoons of the mixture onto the baking sheets spaced 5 cm/2 in apart. Bake for 20 minutes until set. Transfer cookies to a flat surface to cool. Once completely cool, store in an airtight container.

# Chocolate Chip and Raisin Cookies

*Preparation time: 20 minutes ● Cooking time: 18 to 20 minutes ● Makes: About 18*

**A classic cookie which is moist, chewy and delicious.**

### INGREDIENTS

| |
|---|
| 150 g/5 oz plain flour |
| ¼ tsp baking powder |
| 50 g/2 oz light brown sugar |
| 120 g/4 oz caster sugar |
| 120 g/4 oz slightly salted butter, softened |
| 1 egg |
| 1 tsp vanilla essence |
| 150 g/5 oz raisins |
| 120 g/4 oz plain chocolate chips |

Pre-heat oven to 300°F/150°C/Gas mark 2. Grease two baking sheets or line with non-stick baking parchment.

● Combine the flour and baking powder in a medium-sized bowl. Place the sugars in a separate bowl, add the butter, then beat in the sugar until light and fluffy. Add the egg and vanilla essence and mix well. Add the flour mixture, raisins and chocolate and blend well with a spoon.

● Drop rounded tablespoons of the mixture onto the baking sheet spaced 5 cm/2 in apart. Bake for 18 to 20 minutes until lightly golden. Remove cookies to a cool flat surface to cool completely. Store in an airtight container.

# Coconut and Chocolate Crunch

*Preparation time: 20 minutes ● Cooking time: 20 minutes ● Makes: About 28*

**The coconut in these cookies makes them really moist and chewy. This makes a good lunch-box cookie.**

### INGREDIENTS

| |
|---|
| *120 g/4 oz slightly salted butter, softened* |
| *5 Tbsp light brown sugar* |
| *1 egg, beaten* |
| *1 tsp vanilla essence* |
| *120 g/4 oz plain flour* |
| *½ tsp baking powder* |
| *Pinch of salt* |
| *75 g/3 oz shredded coconut* |
| *75 g/3 oz plain chocolate chips* |
| *200 g/7 oz hazelnuts, finely chopped* |

Pre-heat oven to 300°F/150°C/Gas mark 2. Grease two baking sheets or line with non-stick baking parchment.

● In a medium bowl beat together the butter and sugar. Beat in the egg and vanilla essence. Mix thoroughly until light and fluffy. Sift in the flour, baking powder and salt. Stir in the coconut, chocolate and chopped nuts. Mix well with a spoon to combine.

● Drop rounded tablespoons of the cookie dough (spaced well apart) onto the baking sheets. Bake the cookies for 20 minutes until lightly golden, then transfer to a wire rack to cool. Once completely cool, store in an airtight container.

# White Chocolate Cashew Thins

*Preparation time: 20 minutes ● Cooking time: 8 to 10 minutes ● Makes: About 30*

**These cookies are really thin and crunchy. Try eating them with ice cream.**

### INGREDIENTS

| |
|---|
| *50 g/2 oz slightly salted butter, softened* |
| *50 g/2 oz light brown sugar* |
| *3 Tbsp golden syrup* |
| *120 g/4 oz finely chopped salted cashews* |
| *5 Tbsp plain flour* |
| *1 tsp vanilla essence* |
| *175 g/6 oz white chocolate, coarsely chopped* |

Pre-heat oven to 350°F/175°C/Gas mark 4. Grease two baking sheets or line with non-stick baking parchment.

● Melt the butter in a saucepan. Add the brown sugar and golden syrup, then bring to the boil stirring constantly for 3 to 4 minutes until the sugar dissolves. Remove from the heat. Stir in the cashews, flour and vanilla essence.

● Drop half-teaspoon mounds spaced well apart onto the baking sheet. Use the back of a spoon to spread each mound into a circle. Bake for 8 to 10 minutes or until golden-brown. Turn the baking sheet around halfway through cooking. Cool on the baking sheet for 1 minute, then transfer to a wire rack to cool completely.

● Melt the chocolate in a small bowl set over a saucepan of barely simmering water. Dip a fork into the melted chocolate and drizzle over the cookies. Return to cooling rack to set. Once set, store in an airtight container. Not suitable for freezing.

# White Chocolate Chunk and Pecan Cookies

*Preparation time: 20 minutes • Cooking time: 20 minutes • Makes: About 26*

**These cookies are really rich and chocolatey.**

## INGREDIENTS

*250 g/9 oz plain flour, sifted*

*½ tsp baking powder*

*Pinch of salt*

*225 g/8 oz light brown sugar*

*120 g/4 oz caster sugar*

*175 g/6 oz butter, softened*

*2 eggs*

*1 tsp vanilla essence*

*225 g/8 oz pecan nuts, coarsely chopped*

*225 g/8 oz white chocolate, coarsely chopped*

Pre-heat oven to 300°F/150°C/Gas mark 2. Grease two baking sheets or line with non-stick baking parchment.

● Sift the flour, baking powder and salt into a bowl. In a large bowl mix together the sugars and butter until well blended. Add the eggs and vanilla essence and beat until light and fluffy. Add the flour, pecans and white chocolate and mix together with a spoon until combined.

● Drop rounded tablespoons of the mixture onto the greased or lined baking sheets spaced about 5 cm/2 in apart. Bake the cookies for 20 minutes until golden-brown. Transfer to a flat surface to cool. Once completely cool, store in an airtight container.

# Chocolate-dipped Macaroons

*Preparation time: 25 minutes + cooling* ●
*Cooking time: 12 minutes* ● *Makes: About 18*

**These lovely little mounds of coconut dipped in chocolate make a great addition to a special afternoon tea.**

### INGREDIENTS

*200 g/7 oz shredded coconut, unpacked*

*200 g/7 oz chopped blanched almonds*

*150 ml/5 fl oz sweetened condensed milk*

*1 tsp vanilla essence*

*2 egg whites*

*Pinch of salt*

*175 g/6 oz plain chocolate*

Pre-heat oven to 350°F/175°C/Gas mark 4. Line two baking sheets with non-stick baking parchment and brush with oil.

● Place the coconut on one baking sheet and the almonds on another. Toast in the oven for 5 minutes, shaking frequently. Pour onto separate plates to cool.

● Place the condensed milk, vanilla essence, coconut and nuts in a large bowl and mix well to combine. Place the egg whites in a medium bowl and beat until foamy. Add the salt and continue beating until stiff peaks form. Fold egg whites into coconut mixture.

● Drop tablespoonfuls onto the baking sheets. Bake for 12 minutes, or until golden. Place baking sheets on wire racks to cool completely, then peel off the paper.

● Melt the chocolate in a small bowl set in a saucepan of barely simmering water. Dip macaroon bottoms into the melted chocolate then place on greaseproof paper to set. Store in an airtight container. Not suitable for freezing.

# Muesli Chocolate Chip Cookies

*Preparation time: 20 minutes* ● *Cooking time: 15 to 20 minutes* ● *Makes: About 24*

**Choose a muesli that contains your favourite ingredients. These cookies make a substantial lunch-box or picnic treat.**

### INGREDIENTS

*225 g/8 oz plain flour*

*1 tsp ground cinnamon*

*2 tsp baking powder*

*½ tsp bicarbonate of soda*

*Pinch of salt*

*120 g/4 oz slightly salted butter, softened*

*50 g/2 oz caster sugar*

*50 ml/2 fl oz fresh orange juice*

*1 egg*

*150 g/5 oz unsweetened muesli*

*75 g/3 oz milk chocolate chips*

Pre-heat oven to 275°F/140°C/Gas mark 1. Grease two baking sheets or line with non-stick baking parchment.

● Sift the flour, cinnamon, baking powder, bicarbonate and salt into a bowl. In a separate bowl, beat the butter and sugar together until light and fluffy. Gradually beat in the orange juice and egg. Stir in flour mixture and then the muesli and chocolate chips.

● Drop rounded tablespoonfuls spaced 5 cm/2 in apart onto the baking sheets. Flatten a little with the back of a spoon. Bake for 15 to 20 minutes until lightly browned. Cool on the baking sheet for a few minutes, then transfer to a wire rack. Once completely cool, store in an airtight container.

# Chocolate Cream-filled Hearts

*Preparation time: 40 minutes + chilling* ● *Cooking time: 12 to 15 minutes Makes: About 18*

**A special-occasion cookie with a delicious chocolate-fudge filling.**

### INGREDIENTS

*175 g/6 oz slightly salted butter, softened*

*120 g/4 oz icing sugar*

*2 tsp vanilla essence*

*150 g/5 oz plain flour*

### FILLING

*5 Tbsp double cream*

*50 g/2 oz plain chocolate chips*

Beat the butter until soft and fluffy. Add the icing sugar and vanilla essence and beat until smooth. Stir in the flour. Gather dough into 2 balls and flatten into discs. Wrap in clingfilm. Refrigerate for 1 hour until firm.

● Pre-heat oven to 325°F/160°C/Gas mark 3. Grease two baking sheets or line with non-stick baking parchment.

● On a lightly floured surface, roll out the dough to 5 mm/¼ in thick. Cut out 5-cm/2-in hearts with a cutter. Repeat with all of the dough. Place the cookies on baking sheets spaced 2.5 cm/1 in apart. Bake for 12 to 15 minutes until firm. Transfer to a wire rack to cool.

● Place the cream in a small saucepan and warm briefly, add in the chocolate chips and stir until melted. Transfer to a small bowl. Set to one side and allow to cool at room temperature.

● To assemble, spread 1 teaspoon of the chocolate filling on the bottom side of half the cookies. Top with bottom side of another cookie to form a sandwich. Repeat with remaining cookies and cream. These cookies are best eaten soon after filling as they contain fresh cream; however, they may be stored for up to 2 days in an airtight container in the refrigerator.

# Ultimate Chocolate Chip Cookies

*Preparation time: 20 minutes* ● *Cooking time: 18 to 20 minutes* ● *Makes: 10 to 12*

**A huge cookie, the ultimate indulgence, packed with 3 types of chocolate. Make them as large as you dare.**

### INGREDIENTS

| |
|---|
| *175 g/6 oz plain flour* |
| *½ tsp baking powder* |
| *Pinch of salt* |
| *120 g/4 oz slightly salted butter, softened* |
| *120 g/4 oz light brown sugar* |
| *½ Tbsp honey* |
| *1 egg* |
| *1 tsp vanilla essence* |
| *175 g/6 oz plain chocolate, chopped* |
| *75 g/3 oz milk chocolate, chopped* |
| *75 g/3 oz white chocolate, chopped* |

Pre-heat oven to 325°F/160°C/Gas mark 3. Grease two baking sheets or line with non-stick baking parchment.

● Sift the flour, baking powder and salt together into a bowl. Beat together the softened butter and light brown sugar until light and fluffy. Gradually beat in the egg, vanilla essence and honey. Stir in the flour mixture and all of the chocolate. Mix all the ingredients to combine.

● Drop about 2 tablespoonfuls of the dough spaced 5 to 8 cm/2 to 3 in apart on baking sheets. Bake the cookies for 18 to 22 minutes, depending on their size. Transfer them to a wire rack to cool. Once completely cool, store in an airtight container.

# Chocolate Ginger Cookies

*Preparation time: 25 minutes • Cooking time: 18 to 20 minutes • Makes: About 20*

**Ginger preserves give a lovely flavour without the harshness sometimes associated with ground ginger.**

### INGREDIENTS

*120 g/4 oz dark brown sugar*

*50 g/2 oz granulated sugar*

*120 g/4 oz slightly salted butter, softened*

*1 egg*

*1 tsp ginger or golden syrup*

*175 g/6 oz plain flour*

*½ tsp baking powder*

*Pinch of salt*

*50 g/2 oz chocolate chips*

*3 Tbsp ginger preserves*

Pre-heat oven to 300°F/150°C/Gas mark 2. Grease two baking sheets or line with non-stick baking parchment.

In a large bowl blend the sugars together. Add the butter and beat together until light. Add the egg and ginger or golden syrup and mix well. Sift the flour, baking powder and salt into the mixture. Add the chocolate chips and ginger preserves and mix thoroughly with a spoon.

Drop rounded tablespoons onto a baking sheet spaced 5 cm/2 in apart. Bake the cookies for 18 to 20 minutes or until golden-brown. Transfer cookies to a flat surface to allow to cool completely. Store in an airtight container.

# Red, White and Blue Cookies

*Preparation time: 20 minutes • Cooking time: 8 to 10 minutes • Makes: About 36*

**Dried sour cherries and blueberries make a lovely sweet-sour contrast to the sweet white chocolate.**

### INGREDIENTS

*120 g/4 oz plain flour*

*3 Tbsp unsweetened cocoa powder*

*1 tsp baking powder*

*Pinch of salt*

*120 g/4 oz slightly salted butter, softened*

*225 g/8 oz granulated sugar*

*1 egg*

*½ tsp vanilla essence*

*120 g/4 oz white chocolate chips*

*50 g/2 oz chopped dried sour cherries*

*50 g/2 oz dried blueberries*

Pre-heat oven to 350°F/175°C/Gas mark 4. Grease two baking sheets or line with non-stick baking parchment.

Sift the flour, cocoa, baking powder and salt into a medium bowl. Beat together the butter and sugar in a large bowl until light and fluffy. Beat in the egg and vanilla essence until blended. Beat in the flour mixture at low speed until just combined. Stir in the chocolate chips, sour cherries and blueberries.

Drop rounded teaspoonfuls of the dough onto the baking sheets. Bake for 8 to 10 minutes, until just firm. Transfer to a wire rack to cool. Once completely cool, store in airtight container.

# Chocolate Refrigerator Cookies

*Preparation time: 20 minutes + chilling* ● *Cooking time: 10 to 12 minutes* ● *Makes: About 45 in all*

**This dough enables you to bake fresh cookies whenever you want them.**

### INGREDIENTS

150 g/5 oz plain flour

1 tsp baking powder

120 g/4 oz slightly salted butter, softened

50 g/2 oz caster sugar

5 Tbsp finely grated plain chocolate

1 tsp vanilla essence

1 egg, beaten

Sift together the flour and baking powder. Blend in the butter using the fingertips until mixture resembles fine breadcrumbs. Add sugar and chocolate. Mix to form a dough with vanilla essence and beaten egg.

● Shape into a sausage. Transfer to a length of clingfilm. Wrap the film around dough and twist ends. Work backwards and forwards to form a roll about 5 cm/2 in in diameter. Refrigerate for one hour.

● When you are ready to make the cookies, pre-heat oven to 375°F/190°C/Gas mark 4. Grease two baking sheets or line with non-stick baking parchment.

● Cut very thin slices from the dough roll and place well apart onto the baking sheets. Bake for 10 to 12 minutes until pale gold. Cool on a wire cooling rack. The remaining roll can be returned to refrigerator and left for up to a week until required. Alternatively, freeze the dough for up to 1 month. Store the baked cookies in an airtight container.

### TIP

A food processor can be used to blend the butter into the flour.

# Chocolate and Orange Sandwiches

*Preparation time: 45 minutes + chilling ● Cooking time: 8 minutes ● Makes: About 25*

**Orange cream is sandwiched between wafer cookies topped with melted chocolate.**

### INGREDIENTS

*120 g/4 oz plain flour*

*5 Tbsp unsweetened cocoa powder*

*120 g/4 oz slightly salted butter, softened*

*50 g/2 oz caster sugar*

*1 egg*

### FILLING

*120 ml/4 fl oz whipping cream*

*200 g/7 oz white chocolate, chopped*

*1 tsp orange essence or liqueur*

### TOPPING

*150 g/5 oz plain chocolate*

*75 g/3 oz unsalted butter, chopped*

Sift the flour and cocoa into a bowl. In a separate large bowl, beat the butter and sugar together until light and fluffy. Gradually beat in the egg until well combined; stir in the flour–cocoa mixture. Spoon the dough into a piece of clingfilm and shape into a flat disc. Wrap well and refrigerate for 2 hours or overnight until firm.

● Pre-heat oven to 350°F/175°C/Gas mark 4. Grease two baking sheets or line with non-stick baking parchment.

● On a lightly floured surface roll out half of the cookie dough as thin as possible. Using a 5-cm/2-in heart-shaped cutter, cut out as many cookies as possible. Re-roll and cut out trimmings. Bake the cookies for 6 to 8 minutes until set. Cool on a wire rack and then repeat the process with remaining dough.

● Place the whipping cream in a saucepan over a medium heat and bring to the boil. Remove from the heat and add the white chocolate, stirring constantly until melted and smooth. Stir in orange essence or liqueur and pour into a bowl. Cool until firm but not hard, about 1 hour.

● Beat the orange filling with a wooden spoon until smooth. Spread a little filling onto half the cookies and immediately cover with another cookie, pressing together very gently. Repeat with remaining cookies. Allow to set at room temperature.

● Melt the plain chocolate and butter in a small saucepan until smooth. Remove from the heat and cool until thickened slightly, about 20 to 30 minutes. Using a metal spatula, spread a small amount of chocolate onto the top of each cookie. Refrigerate until set. Once set, store in an airtight container in layers separated by greaseproof paper. These cookies are best eaten soon after filling as they contain fresh cream; however, they may be stored for up to 2 days in the refrigerator.

# Chocolate-dipped Orange Shortbread

*Preparation time: 30 minutes* ● *Cooking time: 10 minutes* ● *Makes: About 35*

**These elegant piped cookies make a great addition to a smart afternoon tea.**

## INGREDIENTS

250 g/9 oz plain flour

Pinch of salt

1 tsp baking powder

225 g/8 oz butter, softened

225 g/8 oz granulated sugar

1 egg

1 tsp grated orange rind

120 g/4 oz plain chocolate, chopped

Pre-heat oven to 350°F/175°C/Gas mark 4. Grease two baking sheets or line with non-stick baking parchment.

● Combine the flour, salt and baking powder in a bowl. Beat the butter and sugar in a large bowl until light and fluffy. Beat in the egg and orange rind. Fold in the flour until just combined.

● Spoon the mixture into a piping bag fitted with a large star nozzle. Pipe 4-cm/1½-in swirls, spaced 5 cm/2 in apart onto the baking sheets. Bake 10 to 12 minutes until just beginning to turn light gold around the edges. Transfer to a wire rack to cool completely.

● Melt the chocolate in a small bowl over a saucepan of barely simmering water. Dip the top of each cookie into the melted chocolate. Place cookies on a wire rack to set. Once cool, store in an airtight container.

# Marble Cookies

*Preparation time: 20 minutes • Cooking time: 18 minutes • Makes: About 26*

**A really unusual looking cookie with a rich velvety chocolate taste.**

## INGREDIENTS

| |
|---|
| *250 g/9 oz plain flour* |
| *½ tsp baking powder* |
| *Pinch of salt* |
| *120 g/4 oz light brown sugar* |
| *120 g/4 oz granulated sugar* |
| *120 g/4 oz slightly salted butter, softened* |
| *1 egg* |
| *125 ml/4 fl oz soured cream* |
| *1 tsp vanilla essence* |
| *120 g/4 oz plain chocolate chips* |

Pre-heat oven to 300°F/150°C/Gas mark 2. Grease two baking sheets.

● Sift the flour, baking powder and salt into a bowl. Beat together the butter and sugars in a large bowl until well blended. Add the egg, soured cream and vanilla essence and beat until light and fluffy. Add the flour mixture and blend until just combined.

● Melt the chocolate chips in a bowl set over a saucepan of barely simmering water. Cool chocolate for a few minutes, then pour into the cookie mixture. Using a wooden spoon very lightly fold chocolate into the cookie mixture. Do not mix completely.

● Drop rounded tablespoonfuls of the mixture spaced 5 cm/2 in apart onto the baking sheets. Bake for 20 minutes. Transfer to a flat surface to cool. Once completely cool, store in an airtight container.

# Sesame Chocolate Chewies

*Preparation time: 20 minutes* ●
*Cooking time: 12 minutes* ● *Makes: About 12*

**A thin and crispy cookie great with ice cream.**

### INGREDIENTS

*2 egg whites*

*175 g/6 oz icing sugar*

*3 Tbsp unsweetened cocoa powder*

*2 Tbsp plain flour*

*50 g/2 oz sesame seeds*

Pre-heat oven to 350°F/175°C/Gas mark 4. Line a large baking sheet with non-stick baking parchment.

● Using an electric hand-mixer whisk the egg whites together until frothy. Add the sugar, cocoa and flour to the bowl. Beat slowly firstly to incorporate the ingredients, then increase the speed of the hand mixer and beat until the cookie mixture thickens. Carefully fold in the sesame seeds.

● Place tablespoonfuls of the cookie mixture about 2.5 cm/1 in apart on the baking sheet. Bake the cookies for 12 minutes. Using a spatula, transfer the cookies to a wire rack and leave to cool at room temperature. Once cool, store in an airtight container. Not suitable for freezing.

# Chocolate Pistachio Cookies

*Preparation time: 20 minutes* ● *Cooking time:*
*15 to 20 minutes* ● *Makes: About 12*

**Sweet pistachio nuts are lovely when combined with chocolate in this classic-style cookie.**

### INGREDIENTS

*120 g/4 oz slightly salted butter, softened*

*50 g/2 oz caster sugar*

*½ tsp vanilla essence*

*120 g/4 oz plain flour*

*½ tsp baking powder*

*120 g/4 oz pistachio nuts, coarsely chopped*

*25 g/1 oz plain chocolate, chopped*

Pre-heat oven to 375°F/190°C/Gas mark 5. Grease two baking sheets or line with non-stick baking parchment.

● Beat together the butter, sugar and vanilla essence until light and creamy. Stir in the flour and baking powder, and then mix well. Add nuts and chocolate and mix to combine.

● Drop rounded teaspoonfuls of the mixture 2.5 cm/1 in apart onto the baking sheets. Bake for 15 to 20 minutes. Leave to cool onto the baking sheet for 2 minutes. Transfer to a wire rack to cool completely. Once completely cool, store in an airtight container.

# Chocolate Pockets

*Preparation time: 45 minutes + chilling* ● *Cooking time: 15 minutes* ● *Makes: About 12*

**These little pastry pockets are filled with a melt-in-the-mouth creamy chocolate filling.**

## INGREDIENTS

*175 g/6 oz slightly salted butter, softened*

*25 g/1 oz icing sugar*

*3 Tbsp light brown sugar*

*2 egg yolks*

*1 tsp vanilla essence*

*150 g/5 oz plain flour*

## FILLING

*125 ml/4 fl oz double cream*

*120 g/4 oz plain chocolate chips*

In a medium bowl, beat together the butter and sugars until well biended. Add the egg yolks and vanilla essence and beat well until light and fluffy. Add the flour and stir until combined. Gather into a ball and flatten to a disc. Place between 2 sheets of clingfilm and refrigerate for 1 hour.

● Meanwhile, heat the cream until just hot but not boiling. Remove pan from the heat and add the chocolate chips and stir well until melted.

● Pre-heat oven to 325°F/160°C/Gas mark 3. Grease two baking sheets or line with non-stick baking parchment.

● On a lightly floured surface, roll out half of the dough to 5 mm/¼ in thick. Cut out circles using a 5-cm/2-in round cutter. Place on baking sheets spaced 2.5 cm/ 1 in apart.

● Repeat with the remaining dough but set circles aside. Drop 1 teaspoon of the chocolate filling in the centre of each circle onto the baking sheet, and then top with another circle. Use a fork to press down and seal the edges of the pockets. Bake for 15 minutes or until golden-brown on the top. Transfer cookies with a spatula to a wire rack to cool. Once cool, store in an airtight container in a cool place. Not suitable for freezing.

# Chocolate-frosted Heart Cookies

*Preparation time: 1 hour + chilling* ● *Cooking time: 8 to 10 minutes* ● *Makes: About 45*

**Decorate these little cookies with sugar strands, sugar crystals, or silver and gold dragées, depending on the occasion.**

### INGREDIENTS

*120 g/4 oz slightly salted butter, softened*

*50 g/2 oz brown sugar*

*3 Tbsp treacle*

*1 tsp ground ginger*

*1 tsp ground cinnamon*

*½ tsp ground cloves*

*1 tsp bicarbonate of soda*

*1 egg, beaten*

*450 g/1 lb plain flour*

### DECORATION

*120 g/4 oz icing sugar*

*2 Tbsp unsweetened cocoa powder*

*1 egg white*

*Sugar strands or dragées to decorate*

Pre-heat oven to 325°F/160°C/Gas mark 3. Grease two baking sheets or line with non-stick baking parchment.

● Cut the butter into pieces and place in a large bowl. Place the sugar, treacle and spices in a saucepan and bring to the boil. Add the bicarbonate and pour into the bowl with the butter. Stir until butter has melted, then stir in the egg. Sift in the flour and mix until thoroughly combined. Chill the dough until firm enough to roll out.

● Roll out on a lightly floured surface to 5 mm/¼ in thick. Cut into heart shapes with an 8-cm/3-in cutter. Place onto the baking sheets and bake in batches for 8 to 10 minutes. Transfer to a wire rack to cool completely.

● Sift the icing sugar and cocoa into a bowl. Beat in the egg white and continue beating until soft peak consistency is reached. Spoon the icing onto the cookies to cover then decorate with sugar strands or dragées. Return the cookies to wire rack to set. Once set, store in an airtight container.

# Monkey Puzzles

*Preparation time: 45 minutes* ● *Cooking time: 10 minutes* ● *Makes: About 14*

**The cookies are really rich and chocolatey, great with a cup of coffee.**

### INGREDIENTS

*50 g/2 oz plain flour*

*1½ Tbsp unsweetened cocoa powder*

*¼ tsp baking powder*

*75 g/3 oz slightly salted butter, softened*

*6 Tbsp golden syrup*

*25 g/1 oz bran flakes, coarsely crushed*

*175 g/6 oz plain chocolate, roughly chopped*

Pre-heat oven to 350°F/175°C/Gas mark 4. Grease two baking sheets or line with non-stick baking parchment.

● Sift the flour, cocoa and baking powder into a bowl. Beat together the butter and syrup until soft. Stir in the flour mixture until combined. Blend in the bran flakes.

● Place spoonfuls of the mixture spaced apart onto the baking sheets. Bake for 10 minutes. Transfer to a wire rack to cool.

● Melt the chocolate in a bowl set over a saucepan of barely simmering water. When the cookies are completely cold, spread spoonfuls of the melted chocolate over the surface of the cookies then return to the wire rack to allow the chocolate to set. Once set, store in an airtight container.

### TIP

Decorate these cookies with white chocolate, if liked. Melt it as above and drizzle over the cookies.

# Chocolate-dipped Cinnamon Meringues

*Preparation time: 30 minutes + cooling* ● *Cooking time: 1 hour 15 minutes* ● *Makes: About 36*

**These delicate little meringues are easy to make and are great for a special occasion.**

## INGREDIENTS

*2 egg whites*

*¼ tsp cream of tartar*

*Pinch of salt*

*120 g/4 oz caster sugar*

*½ tsp vanilla essence*

*3 Tbsp unsweetened cocoa powder*

*¼ tsp ground cinnamon*

*120 g/4 oz plain chocolate, roughly chopped*

Pre-heat oven to 225°F/110°C/Gas mark ¼. Line two cookie sheets with foil.

● Beat the egg whites in a large mixing bowl with a hand-held electric mixer until foamy. Add the cream of tartar and salt and continue to beat until soft peaks form. Gradually beat in the sugar, 1 tablespoon at a time, then continue to beat until stiff.

● Gently fold in the vanilla essence, cocoa and cinnamon with a large spoon until just blended. Spoon the meringue mixture into a large piping bag fitted with a large star nozzle. Pipe into 8-cm/3-in lengths onto the baking sheets. Bake for 1 hour 15 minutes. Turn off oven and leave meringues in the oven to cool for 1½ hours or preferably overnight.

● Melt the chocolate in a bowl over a saucepan of barely simmering water. Gently peel the meringues away from the foil. Dip the tip of each meringue into the melted chocolate. Transfer the meringues to a wire rack and let stand until chocolate is set. Once set, store the meringues in an airtight container.

# Chocolate Wafers

*Preparation time: 20 minutes* • *Cooking time: 15 minutes* • *Makes: About 28*

**These nutty thins are great served with ice cream.**

## INGREDIENTS

120 g/4 oz slightly salted butter, softened

50 g/2 oz caster sugar

125 ml/4 fl oz golden syrup

1 egg

½ tsp vanilla essence

120 g/4 oz plain flour

1 Tbsp unsweetened cocoa powder

¼ tsp bicarbonate of soda

75 g/3 oz chopped mixed nuts

Pre-heat oven to 350°F/175°C/Gas mark 4. Line two baking sheets with non-stick baking parchment.

● Beat the butter, sugar and syrup together until light and fluffy. Thoroughly beat in the egg and vanilla essence. Sift the flour, cocoa and bicarbonate onto the butter mixture. Lightly stir into the mixture with the chopped mixed nuts.

● Place walnut-sized spoonfuls spaced 5 cm/2 in apart onto the baking sheets. Bake for 15 minutes. Lift from the baking sheet with a thin metal spatula and lay over a lightly oiled rolling pin to produce a curved shape. Leave to cool on the rolling pin for a few minutes before transferring to a wire rack to cool completely. Once completely cool, store in an airtight container.

# Almond and Chocolate Clusters

*Preparation time: 25 minutes* ● *Cooking time: 15 minutes* ● *Makes: About 22*

**A light nutty cookie which you can either dip in or drizzle with chocolate.**

## INGREDIENTS

120 g/4 oz slightly salted butter, softened

150 g/5 oz sugar

1 egg

½ tsp almond essence

50 g/2 oz ground almonds

120 g/4 oz flaked almonds

150 g/5 oz plain flour

### TOPPING

50 ml/2 fl oz double cream

120 g/4 oz plain chocolate chips

2 tsp golden syrup

Pre-heat oven to 350°F/175°C/Gas mark 4. Grease two baking sheets or line with non-stick baking parchment.

● Beat together the butter and sugar until well blended. Add the egg and almond essence and beat until light and fluffy. Add the ground almonds and flour then stir until just combined. Form dough into walnut-sized balls and roll in the flaked almonds, pressing down slightly to coat each ball thoroughly.

● Place the balls onto the baking sheets spaced 5 cm/2 in apart. Bake for 15 minutes. Transfer cookies to a cool flat surface covered with greaseproof paper.

● Meanwhile, heat the cream, but do not allow to boil. Remove from the heat and stir in the chocolate chips and golden syrup. Cover and allow to stand for 10 minutes. Mix glaze gently with a wooden spoon until smooth.

● When cookies are cool, drizzle patterns on them with the warm chocolate or dip half of each cookie into the chocolate. Return the cookies to the greaseproof paper and place in the refrigerator until set. Once set, store in an airtight container. These cookies are best eaten soon after decorating as they contain fresh cream; however, they may be stored for up to 2 days in the refrigerator.

# Hazelnut Chocolate Crescents

*Preparation time: 30 minutes + chilling* ● *Cooking time: 15 to 20 minutes* ● *Makes: 24*

**These delicious nutty shortbread crescents can be dipped in or drizzled with chocolate.**

### INGREDIENTS

*75 g/3 oz hazelnuts, unskinned*

*50 g/2 oz plain chocolate, coarsely chopped*

*4 Tbsp granulated sugar*

*120 g/4 oz plain flour*

*Pinch of salt*

*200 g/7 oz slightly salted butter*

Pre-heat oven to 350°F/175°C/Gas mark 4. Spread the hazelnuts on a baking sheet. Toast for 12 to 15 minutes until lightly browned. Leave to cool completely.

● Melt half the chocolate in a small bowl over a saucepan of barely simmering water. Remove and set aside to cool.

● Process the nuts and 1 tablespoon of sugar in a food processor until fine, do not overprocess. Transfer to a medium bowl with the flour and salt. Beat the butter and remaining sugar until light and fluffy. Beat in the melted chocolate and the nut mixture and mix well to combine. Cover and refrigerate for 2 hours.

● Pre-heat oven to 350°F/175°C/Gas mark 4. Grease 2 baking sheets or line with non-stick baking parchment.

● Shape teaspoonfuls of the dough into crescents and place onto the baking sheets spaced 5 cm/2 in apart. Bake for 15 to 20 minutes. Transfer to a wire rack to cool completely.

● Melt the remaining chocolate in a bowl set over a saucepan of barely simmering water. Remove from the heat. Dip one end of the cookie into the chocolate or drizzle the surface with a thin stream of chocolate. Return to wire rack and allow chocolate to set. Once set, store the cookies in airtight containers. Not suitable for freezing.

# Strawberry Cocoa Sandwich Stars

*Preparation time: 1 hour + chilling ● Cooking time: 8 to 10 minutes ● Makes: About 20*

**This makes a lovely special-occasion cookie.**

## INGREDIENTS

200 g/7 oz plain flour

3 Tbsp unsweetened cocoa powder

1½ tsp baking powder

½ tsp ground cinnamon

Pinch of salt

175 g/6 oz lightly salted butter

120 g/4 oz caster sugar

50 g/2 oz light brown sugar

1 egg, beaten

2 tsp vanilla essence

Grated rind of 1 lemon

## FILLING

225 g/8 oz strawberry jam

1 Tbsp lemon juice

1 Tbsp caster sugar

Icing sugar, for dusting

Sift the flour, cocoa, baking powder, cinnamon and salt. In a separate bowl, beat together the butter and sugars until light and creamy. Gradually beat in the egg, vanilla essence and lemon rind until well combined. Scrape the dough onto a piece of clingfilm, cover with another sheet and press the dough into a disc. Refrigerate until firm enough to roll.

● Grease two baking sheets or line with non-stick baking parchment.

● On a lightly floured surface roll out half of the dough to 3 mm/⅛ in thick. Refrigerate remaining dough. Using a 9-cm/3½-in star-shaped cutter, cut out an even number of cookies. Using a 2.5-cm/1-in or 4-cm/1½-in star-shaped cutter, cut out the centre of half of the cookies. Arrange cookies on baking sheets spaced 2.5 cm/1 in apart. Cover and refrigerate for 15 minutes.

● Pre-heat oven to 350°F/175°C/Gas mark 4.

● Bake cookies for 8 to 10 minutes. Cool onto the baking sheets for a couple of minutes then transfer to wire rack to cool completely. Repeat with remaining dough.

● Place the strawberry jam, sugar and lemon juice in a small pan. Heat gently until runny. Sieve into a small bowl and allow to cool. Spread about 1 teaspoon of the strawberry mixture on each whole biscuit star to within 1 cm/½ in of the edge. Arrange cut out biscuit stars on a wire cooling rack. Dust liberally with icing sugar. Carefully place cut out tops over whole stars, gently pressing together. Allow cookies to set for 1 hour at room temperature. Once set, store in an airtight container. Not suitable for freezing.

# Chocolate and Chilli Cookies

*Preparation time: 20 minutes • Cooking time: 10 to 12 minutes • Makes: About 20*

**An unusual but fantastic combination.**

### INGREDIENTS

120 g/4 oz butter

25 g/1 oz caster sugar

50 g/2 oz dark brown sugar

1 egg, beaten

½ tsp vanilla essence

120 g/4 oz plain flour

½ tsp baking powder

½ to 1 tsp dried chilli flakes

75 g/3 oz plain chocolate chips

Pre-heat oven to 350°F/175°C/Gas mark 4. Grease two baking sheets or line with non-stick baking parchment.

● Beat the butter and sugar together in a medium bowl, until light and fluffy. Gradually add the egg and vanilla essence and beat well. Stir the flour, baking powder and chilli flakes into the butter mixture and mix well to combine. Stir in the chocolate chips.

● Drop teaspoonfuls spaced 2.5 cm/1 in apart onto the baking sheets. Bake for 10 to 12 minutes. Remove with a spatula and place on a flat surface to cool. Once completely cool, store cookies in an airtight container.

# Chocolate Viennese Whirls

*Preparation time: 25 minutes • Cooking time: 20 minutes • Makes: About 20*

**A rich and attractive cookie, great for a smart afternoon tea party.**

### INGREDIENTS

175 g/6 oz butter

50 g/2 oz icing sugar

175 g/6 oz plain flour

½ tsp vanilla essence

10 glacé cherries, halved

175 g/6 oz plain chocolate, coarsely chopped

Pre-heat oven to 325°F/160°C/Gas mark 3. Grease two baking sheets or line with non-stick baking parchment.

● Beat together the butter and sugar until light and fluffy. Sift the flour into the bowl, add the vanilla and mix well to combine.

● Spoon the mixture into a piping bag fitted with a large star-shaped nozzle. Pipe flat whirls onto the baking sheets. Put half a cherry on each one. Bake for 20 minutes until just golden. Leave to cool onto the baking sheet for 5 minutes then transfer to a wire rack to cool completely.

● Meanwhile, melt the chocolate in a small bowl set over a saucepan of simmering water. When the cookies are cold, dip into the melted chocolate. Return to the wire rack until the chocolate has completely set, then store in an airtight container.

# Crunchy Chocolate Chip Cookies

*Preparation time: 15 minutes* • *Cooking time: 10 to 12 minutes* • *Makes: About 20*

**A cookie jar classic with a twist, crisp on the outside and chewy on the inside.**

### INGREDIENTS

*120 g/4 oz slightly salted butter, softened*

*50 g/2 oz caster sugar*

*5 Tbsp dark brown sugar*

*1 egg, beaten*

*½ tsp vanilla essence*

*120 g/4 oz plain flour*

*½ tsp baking powder*

*175 g/6 oz chocolate bar containing crisped rice, chopped*

Pre-heat oven to 350°F/175°C/Gas mark 4. Grease two baking sheets or line with non-stick baking parchment.

● Beat the butter and sugar together in a medium bowl, until light and fluffy. Gradually add the egg and vanilla essence and beat well. Stir the flour and baking powder into the butter mixture and mix well to combine. Stir in the chocolate chunks.

● Drop teaspoons spaced 2.5 cm/1 in apart onto the baking sheets. Bake for 10 to 12 minutes. Remove with a spatula and place on a flat surface to cool. Once completely cool, store cookies in an airtight container.

### TIP

Other flavoured chocolates could be substituted. Dark chocolate orange is particularly good, so is rum and raisin, and mint-flavoured chocolates that contain small pieces of crunchy mint are great too. The chunks should be left quite large to get the maximum effect from their flavours.

# Raspberry and White Chocolate Cookies

*Preparation time: 20 minutes* ● *Cooking time: 20 minutes* ● *Makes: About 16*

**A sweet and fruity cookie, great served with vanilla ice cream.**

## INGREDIENTS

*175 g/6 oz plain flour*

*¼ tsp bicarbonate of soda*

*Pinch of salt*

*75 g/3 oz caster sugar*

*120 g/4 oz slightly salted butter, softened*

*1 Tbsp beaten egg*

*5 Tbsp sieved raspberry jam*

*175 g/6 oz white chocolate, coarsely chopped*

Pre-heat oven to 300°F/150°C/Gas mark 2. Grease two baking sheets.

● Sift the flour, baking soda and salt and set aside. Beat together the sugar and butter until light and fluffy. Beat in the egg and then the raspberry jam. Add the flour mixture and white chocolate chunks and mix to combine.

● Drop tablespoonfuls onto the baking sheets spaced 5 cm/2 in apart. Bake for 20 minutes. Transfer to a cool surface. When cold, store in an airtight container.

# Chocolate Fudge Cookies

*Preparation time: 20 minutes* ● *Cooking time: 18 to 20 minutes* ● *Makes: About 28*

**These cookies have a pure chocolate taste and a really smooth texture.**

### INGREDIENTS

| |
|---|
| *175 g/6 oz plain chocolate, finely chopped* |
| *175 g/6 oz plain flour* |
| *3 Tbsp unsweetened cocoa powder* |
| *½ tsp baking powder* |
| *Pinch of salt* |
| *120 g/4 oz slightly salted butter, softened* |
| *225 g/8 oz dark brown sugar* |
| *2 eggs* |
| *1 tsp vanilla essence* |
| *75 g/3 oz white chocolate, coarsely chopped* |

Pre-heat oven to 300°F/150°C/Gas mark 2. Grease two baking sheets.

● Melt the chocolate in a bowl set over a saucepan of simmering water. Set aside to cool slightly.

● Sift the flour, cocoa, bicarbonate and salt and set aside. In a separate bowl, beat the butter and sugar together until light and fluffy. Beat in the eggs and vanilla essence until well blended. Mix in the cooled chocolate and fold in the flour until just combined.

● Drop rounded tablespoonfuls of the dough spaced 5 cm/2 in apart onto the baking sheet. Bake for 18 to 20 minutes. Cool the cookies on the sheet for one minute then transfer to a wire rack to cool completely.

● Melt the white chocolate as above. Dip a fork into the melted chocolate and drizzle over the cookies. Leave to set and store in an airtight container.

# Chocolate Mint Cookies

*Preparation time: 20 minutes* ● *Cooking time: 20 minutes* ● *Makes: About 18*

**A nice cookie to enjoy after dinner.**

### INGREDIENTS

| |
|---|
| *175 g/6 oz plain flour* |
| *¼ tsp baking powder* |
| *Pinch of salt* |
| *3 Tbsp unsweetened cocoa powder* |
| *5 Tbsp light brown sugar* |
| *3 Tbsp granulated sugar* |
| *120 g/4 oz slightly salted butter, softened* |
| *1 egg* |
| *1 tsp peppermint essence* |
| *⅔ cup semi-sweet chocolate chips* |

Pre-heat oven to 300°F/150°C/Gas mark 2. Grease two baking sheets or line with non-stick baking parchment.

● Sift the flour, baking powder, salt and cocoa into a bowl and set aside. In a separate bowl, beat together the sugars and butter until light. Beat in the eggs and peppermint essence until thoroughly blended. Add the flour mixture and chocolate chips, mix well to combine. Do not over-mix.

● Drop rounded tablespoonfuls of the mixture onto the baking sheets spaced 4 cm/1½ in apart. Bake 20 minutes apart. Bake 20 minutes until lightly golden. Transfer to a cool flat surface. When completely cool, store in an airtight container.

# Chocolate Rugelach

*Preparation time: 45 minutes + chilling* ● *Cooking time: 20 minutes* ● *Makes: About 60*

**A traditional Jewish cookie much loved by children.**

## INGREDIENTS

225 g/8 oz strong white flour

Pinch of salt

120 g/4 oz slightly salted butter, softened

120 g/4 oz cream cheese

50 ml/2 fl oz soured cream

3 Tbsp caster sugar

1 egg, separated

150 g/5 oz apricot jam

75 g/3 oz plain chocolate, finely chopped

2 Tbsp caster sugar

Sift the flour and salt into a large bowl. Place the flour with the butter, cream cheese, soured cream, sugar and egg yolk in a food processor. Process until a soft dough forms. Shape dough into a ball and flatten into a disc. Wrap in clingfilm and refrigerate for 1 to 2 hours.

● Pre-heat oven to 350°F/175°C/Gas mark 4. Grease two baking sheets or line with non-stick baking parchment.

● On a lightly floured surface roll out one quarter of the dough to 3 mm/⅛ in thick. Using a plate as a guide, cut the dough into a 25- to 28-cm/10- to 11-in round. Spread with 3 tablespoons of apricot jam, leaving a small border around the edge. Sprinkle with the chopped chocolate.

● Cut this round into 12 equal-sized wedges. Starting the widest end, roll up each wedge like a Swiss roll. Place on the baking sheet spaced 2.5 cm/1 in apart. Beat the egg white with 1 tablespoon of water, and brush each roll with a little of the egg and water. Sprinkle each roll with a little sugar. Repeat with remaining dough.

● Bake until puffed and golden-brown. Turn the baking sheet around halfway through cooking. Cool onto the baking sheet for a few minutes then transfer to a wire cooling rack to cool completely.

# Chocolate Crescents

*Preparation time: 20 minutes* ● *Cooking time: 15 minutes* ● *Makes: About 30*

**Dusted with plenty of sugar, these make a great cookie.**

## INGREDIENTS

*225 g/8 oz plain flour*

*3 Tbsp unsweetened cocoa powder*

*120 g/4 oz slightly salted butter, softened*

*200 g/7 oz caster sugar*

*1 tsp vanilla essence*

*1 egg*

*Icing sugar, for decorating*

Pre-heat oven to 325°F/160°C/Gas mark 3. Grease two baking sheets or line with non-stick baking parchment.

● Combine the flour and cocoa in a small bowl. In a medium bowl, beat together the butter and sugar until creamy. Add the vanilla and egg and beat well until light and fluffy. Fold in the flour–cocoa mixture until just blended.

● Shape a tablespoonful of the mixture into an 8-cm/3-in long log. Bend into a crescent shape. Repeat with remaining dough. Place onto the baking sheets, spaced 2.5 cm/1 in apart. Bake for 15 minutes. Cool onto the baking sheet and then transfer to a wire rack. While still warm, roll the cookies in icing sugar to coat. Once completely cool, store in an airtight container. Freeze for up to 1 month without the icing sugar.

# Children's Cookies

This part of the book has some creative ideas to make your snacks a bit more fun and they have all been specially written for children to make. Some of them are ideal to take in lunch boxes, like the cheesy ones, for example. Others are more for parties, such as the Chocolate Octopuses or the Snakes, and some are for when you just feel hungry.

I like making cookies because they are quick and easy, and most people eat them. If I make a batch of cookies on Monday I know that they will be gone by Friday. They are great to share – sometimes I take some Chocolate Chip Cookies to school and give them to my friends. I made cookies for the teachers at Christmas too and put them in pretty china bowls.

If you are quite slow at cooking (like me) or you don't have an electric mixer, then do not pre-heat the oven immediately – wait for a bit! Good Luck.

Katherine Gray, aged 11.

## After-school Snacks

## Cookies for Special Friends

# Birthday Parties

# Lunch-Box Favourites

# Alphabet Cookies

*Preparation time: 30 minutes* ●
*Cooking time: 20 minutes* ● *Makes: 25*

**These cookies have a full lemon flavour which melts in the mouth.**

### INGREDIENTS

50 g/2 oz butter, softened

5 Tbsp caster sugar

1 egg yolk

175 g/6 oz plain flour, sifted

½ tsp baking powder

2 Tbsp lemon juice

Grated rind of ½ lemon

1 Tbsp milk

Icing sugar, for dredging

Pre-heat oven to 325°F/160°C/Gas mark 3. Grease two baking sheets or line with non-stick baking parchment.

● In a mixing bowl, beat together the butter and caster sugar until pale and fluffy, add the egg yolk, flour, baking powder, lemon juice and lemon rind, then blend together.

● Add the milk and mix to a firm dough using your hands so that the dough comes together in a soft ball. Turn the dough out on to a lightly floured work surface and divide into about 25 equal-sized pieces. Roll each piece into a sausage shape with your hands and make letters of the alphabet, twisting the dough and trimming with a small knife if needed.

● Place the cookies on to the baking sheets and bake for 15 to 20 minutes. Lift them on to a wire rack to cool completely before dusting with icing sugar. Store in an airtight container for up to 1 week.

# Teddy Bear Cookies

*Preparation time: 35 minutes* ●
*Cooking time: 10 to 12 minutes* ● *Makes: 26*

**These cookies are made with a spicy dough, you can use any other similar-sized cutter if you like.**

### INGREDIENTS

175 g/6 oz plain flour, sifted

½ tsp baking powder

1 tsp ground ginger

½ tsp ground cinnamon

120 g/4 oz icing sugar

150 g/5 oz butter, cut into small pieces

½ tsp vanilla essence

1 Tbsp water

### DECORATION

120 g/4 oz icing sugar

1 Tbsp water

Pre-heat oven to 375°F/190°C/Gas mark 5. Grease several baking sheets or line with non-stick baking parchment.

● Place the flour, baking powder, ground ginger, ground cinnamon and icing sugar in a bowl and combine. Blend in the butter using your fingertips, add the vanilla essence and 1 Tbsp cold water and, using your hands, bring together in a soft ball.

● Roll out the dough to about 5 mm/¼ in thick. Using an 8-cm/3-in teddy bear cutter, stamp out shapes and lift them on to the baking sheets, spacing well apart. Gather up the remaining dough and roll it out again and cut into more shapes. Bake for 10 to 12 minutes or until evenly golden. Transfer to a wire rack to cool.

● To decorate, mix the icing sugar with sufficient cold water to form a thin icing. Using a piping bag, pipe on the faces and patterns.

# Balloon Cookies

*Preparation time: 40 minutes + chilling* • *Cooking time: 20 minutes* • *Makes: 16*

**These cookies are thick and crunchy, and you can really taste the coconut and orange flavours.**

## INGREDIENTS

*50 g/2 oz butter, softened*

*120 g/4 oz caster sugar*

*1 egg, beaten*

*250 g/9 oz self-raising flour*

*75 g/3 oz sweetened flaked coconut*

*Grated rind of 1 orange*

## DECORATION

*120 g/4 oz icing sugar, sifted*

*1 Tbsp water*

*Food colourings*

*Coloured ribbon*

In a mixing bowl beat together the butter and sugar until pale and fluffy. Beat in the egg, sift in the flour and add the coconut and orange rind. Mix all the ingredients together with your hands, until they come together in a soft ball. Chill the dough in clingfilm in the refrigerator for 30 minutes.

● Pre-heat oven to 325°F/160°C/Gas mark 3. Grease two baking sheets or line with non-stick baking parchment.

● On a lightly floured working surface, roll out the dough. Keep the dough quite thick when rolling out, if cracks appear gather up the dough, sprinkle more flour on the work surface and try again. Using a 6-cm/2½-in round cutter, cut out the cookies and lift on to the baking sheets. Using a metal skewer, make a hole at the top of each cookie for the ribbon. Bake the cookies for 15 to 20 minutes or until lightly golden. As soon as they come out of the oven re-shape the holes with a skewer. Lift them on to a wire rack to cool.

● To decorate the cookies, mix the icing sugar with sufficient water to form a thin icing. Divide into four bowls and colour each one using a few drops of food colouring. Spread different colours onto each cookie and when the icing has set, tie ribbons through the holes.

# Big White Chocolate and Apricot Cookies

*Preparation time: 5 minutes* ● *Cooking time: 12 to 15 minutes* ● *Makes: 12*

**These chewy cookies contain pieces of apricot that give a really juicy texture as well as pieces of chocolate.**

## INGREDIENTS

120 g/4 oz butter, softened

120 g/4 oz light brown sugar

1 egg, beaten

200 g/7 oz self-raising flour

75 g/3 oz white chocolate chips, or white chocolate, chopped

50 g/2 oz milk or plain chocolate chips

50 g/2 oz dried apricots, chopped

Pre-heat oven to 375°F/190°C/Gas mark 5. Grease two baking sheets or line with non-stick baking parchment.

● In a mixing bowl, beat together the butter and sugar until light and fluffy. Beat in the egg. Sift in the flour, both types of chocolate chips and apricots, then stir everything together, until evenly mixed.

● Place mounds of the mixture onto the baking sheets, spaced well apart to allow for spreading. Bake the cookies for 12 to 15 minutes or until golden-brown. Lift onto wire racks to cool. These cookies are best eaten on the day they are baked, but once the cookies are completely cold, they may be stored in an airtight container.

# Sunflower Cookies

*Preparation time: 35 minutes ● Cooking time: 15 to 20 minutes ● Makes: 10*

**These happy sunflowers will brighten up your day. The cookies taste great too, with crunchy sunflower seeds mixed into the cookie dough.**

### INGREDIENTS

*75 g/3 oz butter, softened*

*5 Tbsp caster sugar*

*120 g/4 oz plain flour, sifted*

*1 egg, beaten*

*3 Tbsp sunflower seeds*

*2 Tbsp lemon juice*

### DECORATION

*6 Tbsp icing sugar, sifted*

*4 tsp water*

*Yellow and orange food colourings*

Pre-heat oven to 350°F/175°C/Gas mark 4. Grease several baking sheets or line with non-stick baking parchment.

● In a mixing bowl beat together the butter and sugar until pale and fluffy. Add the flour, then the egg, sunflower seeds and lemon juice and mix everything together to combine.

● Using two teaspoons, place mounds of dough on the baking sheet about 10 cm/4 in apart to allow for the cookies to spread, and flatten slightly with a wet knife. Bake the cookies for 15 to 20 minutes or until lightly golden around the edges. Lift them on to a wire rack to cool. If your rounds are not even after cooking, don't worry, they will still make good faces.

● To decorate the sunflowers, mix the icing sugar with sufficient cold water to form a thin icing, colour half yellow and half orange. Using piping bags, pipe on a happy face and then pipe a pattern around each face.

# Lemon-scented Peanut Butter Cookies

*Preparation time: 25 minutes + chilling*
*Cooking time: 15 minutes ● Makes: 20*

**These popular cookies with their nutty taste will be enjoyed not only by children but adults as well.**

### INGREDIENTS

*120 g/4 oz butter, softened*

*225 g/8 oz caster sugar*

*125 g/4 oz chunky peanut butter*

*1 egg, beaten*

*150 g/5 oz plain flour, sifted*

*½ tsp baking powder*

*50 g/2 oz unsalted natural peanuts, chopped*

*1 tsp grated lemon rind*

*Demerera sugar, for sprinkling*

In a bowl beat together the butter and sugar until light and fluffy, add the peanut butter and beat again. Add the egg, a little at a time until it is mixed in, stir in the flour, baking powder, peanuts and lemon rind and bring together to form a soft ball. Wrap the dough in clingfilm and chill in the refrigerator for 30 minutes.

● Pre-heat oven to 375°F/190°C/Gas mark 5. Grease several baking sheets or line with non-stick baking parchment.

● On a lightly floured surface, divide the dough into 20 equal pieces and shape them into a ball. Lift on to the baking sheets, spacing them apart. Using the back of a fork flatten the balls slightly.

● Sprinkle with a little demerera sugar and bake for 15 minutes or until golden. Transfer to a wire rack to cool.

# Strawberry Cookies

*Preparation time: 35 minutes + chilling ●*
*Cooking time: 15 minutes ● Makes: 12*

**Have fun decorating these strawberries, you can choose any coloured icing and pattern you like.**

### INGREDIENTS

*175 g/6 oz plain flour, sifted*

*75 g/3 oz butter, cut into small pieces*

*200 g/7 oz caster sugar*

*3 Tbsp strawberry jam*

### DECORATION

*7 Tbsp icing sugar*

*About 3 tsp water*

*Green food colouring*

Place the flour in a mixing bowl and blend in the butter using your fingertips until the mixture resembles fine breadcrumbs. Stir in the sugar and strawberry jam and mix together with your hands to form a soft ball. Wrap in clingfilm and chill in the refrigerator for 30 minutes.

● Pre-heat oven to 350°F/175°C/Gas mark 4. Grease several baking sheets or line with non-stick baking parchment. Roll out the dough to about 5 mm/¼ in. Using a 9-cm/3½-in cutter, stamp out hearts and lift onto the baking sheets. Gather up the remaining dough and roll it out again and cut out more shapes. With the trimmings, roll tiny balls into sausage shapes and attach these to the top of the hearts to look like the strawberry stalk.

● Bake the cookies for 15 minutes or until lightly golden at the edges. Transfer to a wire rack to cool.

● To decorate, mix the icing sugar with sufficient water to form a thin icing, add a few drops of green colouring. Using a piping bag, pipe on little dots of icing to look like a strawberry. Store in an airtight container.

# Stars and Moons

*Preparation time: 40 minutes* ● *Cooking time: 15 minutes* ● *Makes: 20*

**These delicious cookies are really buttery, with a crisp coconut texture.**

### INGREDIENTS

*120 g/4 oz butter, softened*

*120 g/4 oz caster sugar*

*175 g/6 oz plain flour, sifted*

*50 g/2 oz sweetened flaked coconut*

*2 Tbsp milk*

### DECORATION

*6 Tbsp icing sugar, sifted*

*About 4 tsp water*

Pre-heat oven to 350°F/175°C/Gas mark 4. Grease two baking sheets or line with non-stick baking parchment.

● In a mixing bowl, beat together the butter and sugar until pale and fluffy. Add the flour to the mixture then add the coconut and milk; mix well. Using your hands bring the dough together to form a soft ball.

● Turn the dough out on to a lightly floured work surface and roll out to 5 mm/¼ in thick. Using a large star cutter, cut out shapes. To make the moon shape cut out rounds with an 9-cm/3½-in round cutter, cut away one-quarter of the round with the cutter to leave a crescent shape. Gather up the left-over dough, roll it out again and cut out more shapes. Lift the cookies on to the baking sheets. Bake the cookies for 15 to 20 minutes or until lightly golden and crisp, then lift them on to a wire rack to cool.

● To decorate the cookies, mix the icing sugar with sufficient water to form a thin icing. Fill a piping bag with the icing and pipe patterns onto the cookies.

# Tutti Frutti Faces

*Preparation time: 35 minutes* ● *Cooking time: 15 minutes* ● *Makes: 10*

**Adding glacé cherries to this recipe makes these cookies really tasty as well as pretty.**

### INGREDIENTS

*50 g/2 oz soft tub margarine*

*75 g/3 oz caster sugar*

*1 egg, beaten*

*200 g/7 oz plain flour, sifted*

*50 g/2 oz multi-coloured glacé cherries, chopped*

### DECORATION

*5 Tbsp icing sugar, sifted*

*3–4 tsp water*

*Food colourings*

Pre-heat oven to 350°F/175°C/Gas mark 4. Grease several baking sheets or line with non-stick baking parchment.

● In a mixing bowl beat together the margarine and sugar until pale and fluffy. Beat in the egg. Stir in the flour and chopped cherries and mix everything together. Use your hands to bring the dough together to form a soft ball.

● Turn the dough out onto a lightly floured work surface and roll out to 5 mm/¼ in. Using a large 9-cm/3½-in round cutter, cut out your shapes. Gather up the left-over dough, roll it out again and cut out more shapes and lift the cookies onto the baking sheets. Bake the cookies for 15 minutes or until golden. Lift them onto a wire rack to cool.

● To decorate the faces, mix the icing sugar with 3 to 4 teaspoons of cold water to make a thin icing. Divide the icing into three bowls and colour one blue, one pink and one yellow. Fill piping bags with the icing and pipe carefully onto the cookies to make different faces.

# Wholesome Hearts

*Preparation time: 25 minutes* ● *Cooking time: 20 minutes* ● *Makes: 10 Large cookies*

**These cookies are full of good things, so no extra icing is needed.**

### INGREDIENTS

*120 g/4 oz butter, softened*

*120 g/4 oz caster sugar*

*1 egg, beaten*

*1 tsp vanilla essence*

*225 g/8 oz self-raising flour, sifted*

*150 g/5 oz rolled oats*

*50 g/2 oz sweetened flaked coconut, plus 2 Tbsp extra for sprinkling*

Pre-heat oven to 350°F/175°C/Gas mark 4. Grease several baking sheets or line with non-stick baking parchment.

● In a mixing bowl, beat together the butter and sugar until pale and fluffy. Beat in the egg with the vanilla essence, followed by the flour. Mix well. Stir in the rolled oats and 50 g/2 oz coconut and knead the mixture with your hands to form a soft ball.

● Turn the dough out onto a lightly floured work surface and roll out to 5 mm/¼ in thick. Using a heart cutter, cut out your shapes and lift the cookies onto the baking sheets. Gather up the left-over dough, roll it out again, and cut more shapes. Sprinkle each with the remaining coconut. Bake for 20 minutes or until lightly golden. Lift them on to a wire rack to cool.

# Apple Cookies

*Preparation time: 35 minutes + chilling* ●
*Cooking time: 18 to 20 minutes* ● *Makes: 10*

**Using apple sauce in these cookies creates a smooth texture as well as sweetness.**

### INGREDIENTS

225 g/8 oz plain all-purpose flour, sifted

75 g/3 oz icing sugar

150 g/5 oz butter, cut into small pieces

3 Tbsp apple sauce

### DECORATION

7 Tbsp icing sugar

3 tsp cold water

Green food colouring

Place the flour and icing sugar in a mixing bowl and blend in the butter using your fingertips until the mixture resembles fine breadcrumbs. Add the apple sauce and bring the mixture together in a soft ball. Wrap in clingfilm and chill in the refrigerator for 30 minutes.

● Pre-heat oven to 350°F/175°C/Gas mark 4. Grease several baking sheets or line with non-stick baking parchment.

● On a lightly floured surface, roll out the dough to about 5 mm/¼ in thick. Using a 9-cm/3½-in cutter, stamp out rounds and lift onto the baking sheets. Roll out the remaining dough again and cut out more shapes. Roll the trimmings into sausage shapes and attach these to the top of the circles to look like stalks.

● Bake the cookies for about 18 to 20 minutes or until golden at the edges. Transfer to a wire rack.

● To decorate, mix the icing sugar with water to form a thin icing, and add a few drops of colouring. Using a piping bag, decorate each apple with eyes and mouths.

# Butterflies

*Preparation time: 25 minutes + chilling* ●
*Cooking time: 15 minutes* ● *Makes: 20*

**These cookies are made by mixing melted chocolate through the dough, creating a marbled effect.**

### INGREDIENTS

75 g/3 oz milk chocolate, broken into pieces

120 g/4 oz butter, softened

120 g/4 oz caster sugar

1 egg, beaten

175 g/6 oz plain flour, sifted

Icing sugar, for dusting

Ask an adult to help you place a saucepan of water to boil on the hob. When the water is simmering, place the chocolate in a heatproof bowl on top of the saucepan, gently melt the chocolate, stirring until smooth. Remove from the heat and allow to cool.

● In a mixing bowl, beat together the butter and sugar until light and fluffy. Beat in the egg. Stir in the flour and combine all the ingredients to form a soft ball. Add the chocolate and gently stir through to give a marbled effect. Wrap the dough in clingfilm and chill in the refrigerator for 30 minutes.

● Pre-heat oven to 350°F/175°C/Gas mark 4. Grease several baking sheets or line with non-stick baking parchment.

● On a lightly floured surface, roll out the dough to about 5 mm/¼ in. Using an 8-cm/3-in butterfly cutter, stamp out shapes and lift onto the baking sheets. Roll out the remaining dough again and cut out more shapes.

● Bake the cookies for 15 minutes or until evenly golden-brown. Transfer to a wire rack to cool. Just before eating dust with icing sugar.

# Wiggly Sheep

*Preparation time: 30 minutes* ● *Cooking time: 15 minutes* ● *Makes: 18*

**This lemon shortbread is delicious, so bake double the quantity!**

## INGREDIENTS

150 g/5 oz butter, softened

75 g/3 oz icing sugar

225 g/8 oz plain flour, sifted

Grated rind of 1 lemon

1 Tbsp milk

## DECORATION

5 Tbsp sugar, sifted

3–4 tsp water

Pre-heat oven to 350°F/175°C/Gas mark 4. Grease several baking sheets or line with non-stick baking parchment.

● In a mixing bowl beat together the butter and icing sugar until pale and fluffy. Stir in the flour, then add the lemon rind and milk. Mix everything together to form a soft dough using your hands.

● On a lightly floured work surface, roll out the dough to 5 mm/¼-in. Using your cutter, cut out your shapes and lift the cookies onto the baking sheets. Gather up the left-over dough, roll it out again and cut out more shapes. Bake the cookies for 15 minutes or until lightly golden. Lift them on to a wire rack to cool.

● To decorate the sheep, mix the icing sugar with sufficient cold water to make a thin icing. Fill a piping bag with the icing and pipe it in a wiggly pattern, onto the body of the sheep.

# Ice-cream Cone Cookie

*Preparation time: 40 minutes* ● *Cooking time: 15 minutes* ● *Makes: 18*

**Decorate these cookies with your favourite coloured icing to look like real ice-cream cones with different toppings!**

## INGREDIENTS

*175 g/6 oz plain flour, sifted*

*120 g/4 oz butter, cut into small pieces*

*120 g/4 oz caster sugar*

*50 g/2 oz dried apricots, chopped*

*Grated rind of ½ orange*

*2 Tbsp orange juice*

## DECORATION

*7 Tbsp icing sugar*

*About 3 tsp water*

*Yellow or other food colouring*

Pre-heat oven to 350°F/175°C/Gas mark 4. Grease several baking sheets or line with non-stick baking parchment.

● Place the flour in a mixing bowl and blend in the butter using your fingers, until the mixture resembles fine breadcrumbs. Stir in the sugar, apricot, orange rind and orange juice and mix everything together, bring the mixture together in a soft ball using your hands. Then on a lightly floured surface roll out the dough to about 5 mm/¼ in.

● Using a 10-cm/4-in heart cutter, stamp out hearts, gather up the left over dough, roll it out again and cut out more hearts. Cut each heart in half lengthways and lift onto the baking sheets. Using the back of a knife, mark a line halfway across the top of the cookie, then below make criss-cross lines to resemble the cone. Bake the cookies for 15 minutes or until golden-brown. Lift onto a wire rack to cool.

● To decorate the cookies, mix the icing sugar with about 3 teaspoons of cold water to form a thin icing, add a few drops of yellow or other food colouring. Using a piping bag, pipe the icing onto the cookies to decorate. Allow to set.

# Cheese Fish Sticks

*Preparation time: 30 minutes + chilling* ●
*Cooking time: 20 minutes* ● *Makes: 16*

**These crunchy cookies, coated in crushed cornflakes, are cut into bars to look like savoury fish sticks!**

### INGREDIENTS

*150 g/5 oz plain flour, sifted*

*150 g/5 oz butter, cut into small pieces*

*150 g/5 oz mature Cheddar cheese, grated*

*50 g/2 oz tinned sweetcorn, drained and dried on kitchen paper*

*25 g/1 oz cornflakes, crushed*

*1 egg, beaten*

Place the flour in a mixing bowl and blend in the butter using your fingertips until the mixture resembles fine breadcrumbs. Stir in the cheese and corn and bring the mixture together in a soft ball using your hands. Wrap in clingfilm and chill for 30 minutes.

● Pre-heat oven to 375°F/190°C/Gas mark 5. Grease several baking sheets or line with non-stick baking parchment.

● On a lightly floured surface, roll out the dough to a 23 x 18-cm/9 x 7-in rectangle. Cut in half widthways, then cut each half of dough into 8 equal bars. Place the crushed cornflakes on a large plate. Dip each cookie in beaten egg, then coat well by pressing each bar down on to the crushed cornflakes. Lift onto the prepared baking sheets. Bake the cookies for 15 to 20 minutes, until evenly golden and crisp. Transfer to a wire rack to cool. These cookies are best eaten the day they are made.

# Ladybird Cookies

*Preparation time: 25 minutes* ●
*Cooking time: 20 minutes* ● *Makes: 8*

**These savoury cookies get their colour from tomato purée, which also adds to their flavour.**

### INGREDIENTS

*120 g/4 oz plain flour, sifted*

*120 g/4 oz butter, cut into small pieces*

*50 g/2 oz mature Cheddar cheese, grated*

*1 Tbsp tomato purée*

*About 50 g/2 oz currants*

Pre-heat oven to 375°F/190°C/Gas mark 5. Grease several baking sheets or line with non-stick baking parchment.

● Place the flour in a mixing bowl and blend in the butter using your fingertips until the mixture resembles fine breadcrumbs. Stir in the cheese with the tomato purée and bring the mixture together in a soft ball using your hands. On a lightly floured surface, divide into 8.

● Roll each piece into a ball using the palms of your hands, then flatten to an 8-cm/3-in oval shape and lift onto the baking sheets. Using the back of a knife mark a line down the centre of the oval to make the body of the ladybirds.

● Using 4 currants for each half of one ladybird, press down well into the dough to look like spots and repeat. Bake for 20 minutes or until evenly golden. Transfer to a wire rack to cool. Eat these cookies on the same day.

# Noughts and Crosses

*Preparation time: 30 minutes + chilling* ● *Cooking time 10 to 15 minutes* ● *Makes: 24*

**Have fun with these two coloured cookies and see who can win!**

## INGREDIENTS

| |
| --- |
| *120 g/4 oz butter, softened* |
| *120 g/4 oz caster sugar* |
| *1 egg, beaten* |
| *225 g/8 oz plain flour* |
| *¼ tsp baking powder* |
| *Grated rind of 1 orange* |
| *2 Tbsp unsweetened cocoa powder, sifted* |

In a mixing bowl, beat the butter and sugar together until pale and fluffy. Beat in the egg. Sift in the flour with the baking powder and stir in the grated orange rind. Mix everything together to form a soft dough.

● Divide the mixture in half, to one half fold in the cocoa powder thoroughly, so you are left with two mixtures. Chill the dough separately in clingfilm in the refrigerator for 30 minutes.

● Pre-heat oven to 375°F/190°C/Gas mark 5. Grease two baking sheets or line with non-stick baking parchment. On a lightly floured surface, roll out the chocolate dough and using a 6-cm/2½-in round cutter, stamp out rounds, then using a 4-cm/1½-in round cutter place in the middle of the cookie to create another circle, this becoming the "zero". Re-roll the dough to make 12 "zeros".

● Roll out the orange dough on a lightly floured surface and, using a cutter or a sharp knife, cut out 12 crosses and lift onto the baking sheets. Bake the cookies for 15 minutes or until lightly golden and crisp. Lift the cookies onto a wire rack to cool. Store in an airtight container for up to 1 week.

# Chocolate Chip Cookies

*Preparation time: 25 minutes ● Cooking time: 12 minutes ● Makes: 18*

**These chocolate chip cookies are so easy to make; they are chewy and full of chocolate chunks in every mouth-watering bite.**

### INGREDIENTS

*120 g/4 oz butter, softened*

*150 g/5 oz light brown sugar*

*1 egg, beaten*

*120 g/4 oz plain flour, sifted*

*½ tsp bicarbonate of soda*

*1 tsp vanilla essence*

*50 g/2 oz plain chocolate or white chocolate chips*

Pre-heat oven to 375°F/190°C/GAs mark 5. Grease two baking sheets or line with non-stick baking parchment.

● In a mixing bowl, beat together the butter and sugar until light and fluffy. Beat in the egg. Mix together the flour and bicarbonate. Add to the mixture with the vanilla essence and stir together well. Add the chocolate chips and stir them in until evenly spread.

● Spoon mounds of the mixture onto the baking sheets, leaving big spaces between each cookie for spreading. Bake the cookies for 10 to 12 minutes or until golden brown. Lift onto wire racks to cool.

# Jewelled Cookie Bars

*Preparation time: 25 minutes plus 4 hours to set (up to 24 hours)* ● *Makes:16 bars*

**This a really easy recipe for children to use when they start cooking by themselves
as these cookies do not require baking.**

## INGREDIENTS

*300 g/10 oz milk or plain chocolate*

*250 g/9 oz digestive biscuits*

*50 g/2 oz multi-coloured candied cherries, chopped*

*50 g/2 oz raisins*

*50 g/2 oz dried apricots, chopped*

*50 g/2 oz white chocolate chips*

*50 g/2 oz flaked almonds*

Line a 23 x 23-cm/9 x 9-in shallow tin with non-stick baking parchment.

● Under adult supervision, melt the chocolate over a pan of simmering water. Break the chocolate into pieces and place in a heatproof bowl and sit on top of the saucepan. Gently melt the chocolate, stirring until smooth.

● Using your fingers break up the digestives into tiny pieces and place in a large mixing bowl. Keeping some of the remaining ingredients aside for the top of the cookies, add the remaining ingredients to the crushed digestives. Add the melted chocolate and mix well.

● Press the mixture into the tin, level the surface and sprinkle on the remaining ingredients and press gently down to set. Leave the tin in the refrigerator for 4 hours or overnight until it sets hard. Turn out of the tin onto a chopping board and cut into bars.

# Mushroom Cookies

*Preparation time: 35 minutes* ● *Cooking time: 20 minutes* ● *Makes: 16*

**The stalks of these mushrooms are made from ready-made marzipan, with a chocolate macaroon for the top!**

### INGREDIENTS

*Edible rice paper*

*75 g/3 oz icing sugar*

*3 Tbsp ground almonds*

*2 tsp unsweetened cocoa powder*

*1 egg white*

*1½ tsp caster sugar*

*300 g/10 oz white marzipan*

### DECORATION

*Pink food colouring*

*3 Tbsp icing sugar*

*2 tsp water*

Pre-heat oven to 350°F/175°C/Gas mark 4. Line a baking sheet with a sheet of rice paper.

● Sift the icing sugar, ground almonds and cocoa together in a small bowl. In another mixing bowl, whisk the egg white until it forms soft peaks, then whisk in the caster sugar. Fold in the sifted ingredients until combined.

● Spoon 16 small dots onto the rice paper, spaced well apart. Bake for 20 minutes or until firm and cracking has appeared on the top of each cookie. Leave to go cold on the baking sheet, then neaten the edges of each cookie by trimming away the unwanted rice paper.

● Divide the marzipan into 17 equal-sized pieces. On a lightly floured work surface, roll 16 balls into a pear-shaped stalk. Colour the remaining ball with the pink food colouring to make 16 small noses. To decorate the mushrooms, mix the icing sugar with sufficient cold water to form a thin icing and fill a piping bag. Squeeze a small dot of icing on the underside of each cookie and press on top of the marzipan stalk to complete the mushroom. Eyes and mouths can be pressed into the marzipan using the back of a sharp knife. Pipe a small dot of icing to attach the nose.

# Chocolate Button Cookies

*Preparation time: 30 minutes + chilling* ●
*Cooking time: 15 minutes* ● *Makes: 13*

**These brightly coloured cookies bring enjoyment to any play time!**

## INGREDIENTS

*6 Tbsp soft tub margarine*

*120 g/4 oz light brown sugar*

*1 egg, beaten*

*175 g/6 oz self-raising flour, sifted*

*1 tsp ground cinnamon*

*2 packets chocolate milk buttons*

In a mixing bowl, beat together the margarine and sugar until pale and fluffy. Beat in the egg and stir in the flour and ground cinnamon. Knead the mixture together with your hands until it comes together in a soft ball. Chill the dough in clingfilm in the refrigerator for 30 minutes.

● Pre-heat oven to 350°F/175°C/Gas mark 4. Grease two baking sheets or line with non-stick baking parchment.

● Roll out the dough on a lightly floured surface, adding more flour if it begins to stick. Using an 8-cm/3-in oval or round cutter, stamp out the cookies. Gather up the left-over dough, roll it out again and cut out more shapes and lift on to baking sheets. Lightly press the chocolate buttons into the dough to decorate the egg shape. Bake the cookies for 15 minutes. Lift the cookies on to a wire rack to cool completely, then store them in an airtight container.

# Love Hearts

*Preparation time: 40 minutes + chilling* ●
*Cooking time: 15 minutes* ● *Makes: 16*

**Choose your favourite colours to decorate these heart-shaped cookies.**

## INGREDIENTS

*75 g/3 oz butter, softened*

*150 g/5 oz caster sugar*

*1 egg, beaten*

*175 g/6 oz plain flour, sifted*

*Grated rind of 1 lemon*

## DECORATION

*120 g/4 oz icing sugar*

*1 Tbsp water*

*Pink, green and yellow food colouring*

In a mixing bowl beat together the butter and sugar until light and fluffy. Beat in the egg. Stir in the flour and lemon rind and using your hands bring the mixture together in a soft ball. Wrap the dough in clingfilm and chill in the refrigerator for 30 minutes.

● Pre-heat oven to 350°F/175°C/Gas mark 4. Grease several baking sheets.

● On a lightly floured surface roll out the dough to about 5 mm/¼ in. Using an 8-cm/3-in heart cutter, stamp out hearts and lift onto the baking sheets. Gather up the remaining dough and roll it out again and cut out more shapes. Bake the cookies for 15 minutes or until lightly golden at the edges.

● To decorate the cookies, mix the icing sugar with sufficient water to form a thin icing. Transfer some of the icing to two other bowls and add drops of food colouring to each bowl. Spread each cookie with different coloured icings and allow to set.

# Peppermint Rings

*Preparation time: 30 minutes + chilling* ● *Cooking time: 15 minutes* ● *Makes: 20*

**These cookies are for anyone who enjoys mint, they have peppermint essence in the dough with a mint-flavoured boiled sweet in the centre.**

## INGREDIENTS

*175 g/6 oz plain flour, sifted*

*50 g/2 oz icing sugar*

*120 g/4 oz lightly salted butter, cut into small pieces*

*1 tsp peppermint essence*

*1 Tbsp water*

*20 sparkling clear mint sweets*

Place the flour and icing sugar in a large mixing bowl and blend in the butter until the mixture resembles fine breadcrumbs. Add the peppermint essence and water, using your hands bring the mixture together to form a dough. Wrap the dough in a plastic bag and chill in the refrigerator for 30 minutes or so.

● Line several baking sheets with non-stick baking parchment.

● On a lightly floured work surface, roll out the dough to about 5-mm/¼-inch thick, using a 6-cm/2½-in round cutter, stamp out the middle of each cookie. Unwrap the sweets and place in the gaps. Re-roll the trimmings and cut out more shapes. Chill the cookies in the refrigerator for 15 minutes.

● Pre-heat oven to 350°F/175°C/Gas mark 4. Bake the cookies for 15 minutes or until lightly golden. Allow to cool on the baking sheets and for the sweets to harden, before lifting onto a wire rack to cool. Store in an airtight container.

# Flower Cookies

*Preparation time: 40 minutes* ●
*Cooking time: 15 minutes* ● *Makes: 20*

**The children will love these cookies as they contain little pieces of chocolate buttons in the cooked dough.**

### INGREDIENTS

*175 g/6 oz plain flour, sifted*

*120 g/4 oz butter, cut into small pieces*

*120 g/4 oz caster sugar*

*3 Tbsp chocolate buttons, broken into small pieces*

*2 Tbsp milk*

### DECORATION

*7 Tbsp icing sugar*

*About 3 tsp water*

*Yellow and pink food colourings*

Pre-heat oven to 350°F/175°C/Gas mark 4. Grease several baking sheets.

● Place the flour in a mixing bowl and blend in the butter using your fingers until the mixture resembles fine breadcrumbs. Stir in the sugar, chocolate buttons and milk and bring the mixture together in a soft ball using your hands. On a lightly floured surface, roll out the dough to about 5 mm/¼ in.

● Using a 6-cm/2½-in fluted cutter, cut out your shapes and lift the cookies onto the baking sheets. Gather up the left-over dough, roll it out again and cut more shapes. Bake for 15 minutes. Transfer to a wire rack to cool.

● To decorate the flowers, mix the icing sugar with the water and mix to a thin icing. Transfer half the icing to another bowl, add a few drops of yellow colouring to one bowl and pink colouring to the other bowl.

● Using piping bags, pipe it carefully onto the flowers to make patterns. Allow to set.

# Golden Circles

*Preparation time: 25 minutes + chilling* ●
*Cooking time: 15 to 20 minutes* ● *Makes: 18*

**Crisp cookies with a hint of cheese and sesame seed will make the perfect snack.**

### INGREDIENTS

*120 g/4 oz plain flour, sifted*

*1 tsp dried mixed herbs*

*75 g/3 oz butter, cut into small pieces*

*120 g/4 oz mature Cheddar cheese, grated*

*1 egg, beaten*

*3 Tbsp sesame seeds*

Place the flour in a mixing bowl with the dried mixed herbs and blend in the butter using your fingertips until the mixture resembles fine breadcrumbs. Add the cheese and bring the mixture together in a soft ball using your hands. On a lightly floured surface, shape the dough into a 23 x 2.5-cm/9 x 1-in log shape. Wrap in clingfilm and chill in the refrigerator for 30 minutes.

● Brush the log shaped dough with beaten egg, place the sesame seeds on a large plate and roll the dough in the sesame seeds until they evenly coat the log. Chill in the refrigerator for 15 minutes.

● Pre-heat oven to 375°F/190°C/Gas mark 5. Grease several baking sheets or line with non-stick baking parchment.

● Cut the dough into 18 equal slices and lift onto the baking sheets. Bake the cookies for 15 to 20 minutes or until golden and crisp. Transfer to a wire rack to cool. These cookies are best eaten on the day they are made.

# Mouse Cookies

*Preparation time: 30 minutes ●*
*Cooking time: 20 minutes ● Makes: 14*

**These cheeky little "mice" are flavoured with cinnamon. If you like, you can dust them with extra cinnamon and icing sugar after they have come out of the oven!**

### INGREDIENTS

*175 g/6 oz plain flour, sifted*

*1 tsp ground cinnamon*

*120 g/4 oz butter, cut into small pieces*

*120 g/4 oz caster sugar*

*2 Tbsp milk*

### DECORATION

*7 currants, halved*

*Ground cinnamon, for dusting*

*Icing sugar, for dusting*

Pre-heat oven to 350°F/175°C/Gas mark 4. Grease several baking sheets or line with non-stick baking parchment.

● Place the flour and ground cinnamon in a bowl and blend in the butter using your fingertips to form fine breadcrumbs. Add the sugar and milk and using your hands bring together to form a soft dough.

● Divide the dough into 16 equal-sized pieces. Roll 14 pieces into balls using the palms of your hands, then flatten one side to look like the nose of a mouse.

● Divide the remaining 2 balls into 14 little balls and roll each one to a long sausage shape for the tail. Using a little water, attach each tail to the back of the mice. Position the currants to look like eyes then, using a pair of small scissors, snip into the dough to look like ears. Lift the mice onto the baking sheets.

● Bake the cookies for 20 minutes. Lift onto a wire rack to cool. Dust with a little cinnamon and icing sugar.

# Chicks

*Preparation time: 25 minutes ● Cooking time: 1 hour*
*30 minutes ● Makes: 30*

**These cookies are made with meringue. If you do not want to use a piping bag, make small blobs with teaspoons, they will be just as fun.**

### INGREDIENTS

*3 egg whites*

*Pinch of salt*

*200 g/7 oz caster sugar*

### DECORATION

*25 g/1 oz marzipan*

*Yellow food colouring*

*3 Tbsp icing sugar, sifted*

*2 tsp water*

Pre-heat oven to 250°F/120°C/Gas mark ½. Line several baking sheets with non-stick baking parchment.

● In a mixing bowl, whisk the egg whites with the salt until they form soft peaks. Whisk in the sugar, a little at a time, until the mixture is very thick and glossy. If you are using a piping bag, fit it with a plain nozzle and pipe the meringue into small circles. Lift up and pipe a smaller circle to create a head. Allow a little space in between each chick.

● Bake the chicks for 1 hour and 30 minutes, until crisp and dried out so that the meringue lifts off the paper easily. Meanwhile, in a small bowl, colour the marzipan yellow and shape into 60 small balls for the eyes and 30 bigger balls for the beak shape.

● Mix the icing sugar with sufficient water to form a thin icing and using a piping bag, pipe little dots on each chick and place the eyes and beak in place. These meringues store well in an airtight container, if there are any left over!

# Children's Name Cookies

*Preparation time: 40 minutes + chilling ● Cooking time: 15 minutes ● Makes: 15*

**Using a banana-flavoured pudding mix in these cookies gives them a real banana boost.
Try using other flavours if you prefer.**

### INGREDIENTS

*6 Tbsp soft tub margarine*

*5 Tbsp caster sugar*

*1 egg, beaten*

*175 g/6 oz self-raising flour, sifted*

*¼ cup banana-flavoured pudding mix*

### DECORATION

*150 g/5 oz icing sugar, sifted*

*2 Tbsp water*

*Pink and blue food colouring*

In a mixing bowl, beat together the margarine and sugar until pale and fluffy. Beat in the egg, add the flour and banana pudding mix. Knead the mixture together with your hands until it comes together in a soft ball. Chill the dough in clingfilm in the refrigerator for 30 minutes.

● Pre-heat oven to 350°F/175°C/Gas mark 4. Grease two baking sheets or line with non-stick baking parchment.

● Sprinkle some flour on the work surface and a rolling pin. Roll out the dough to about 5 mm/¼ in. Using a 6-cm/2½-in square cutter, cut out your cookies and lift onto the baking sheets. Gather up the left-over dough, roll it out again and cut out more shapes. Bake the cookies for 15 minutes or until golden then lift them onto a wire rack to cool.

● To decorate the squares, mix the icing sugar with sufficient water to form a thin icing. Keeping about 3 tablespoons of the icing in the bowl, place the remaining icing in two bowls and colour one pink and one blue. Fill piping bags with the icings, pipe your favourite boys' names with the blue icing on half the cookies and use the pink icing to pipe girls' names onto the cookies. Use the white icing to make a border around the names. Eat on the day iced.

# Chocolate Octopus

*Preparation time: 35 minutes + chilling ● Cooking time: 20 minutes ● Makes: 2 giant cookies*

**This recipe makes two giant octopuses, if you prefer you can make lots of little ones!**

### INGREDIENTS

50 g/2 oz soft tub margarine

120 g/4 oz caster sugar

1 egg, beaten

220 g/7 oz plain flour

2 Tbsp unsweetened cocoa powder

### DECORATION

3 Tbsp icing sugar, sifted

2 tsp water

4 chocolate buttons or chocolate chips

In a mixing bowl beat together the margarine and sugar until pale and fluffy. Add the egg. Sift together the flour and cocoa and mix everything together. Using your hands, bring the dough together until it forms a ball. Chill the dough in clingfilm in the refrigerator for 30 minutes.

● Pre-heat oven to 325°F/160°C/Gas mark 3. Grease two baking sheets or line with non-stick baking parchment. Divide the dough roughly in half to make two bodies for the octopus. Shape into a large oval and then cut five or six strips halfway up the oval to make the tentacles, push the dough apart and curl the edges of the strips. Transfer onto a baking sheet and make the second octopus. Bake the cookies for 20 minutes or until crisp, lift the two cookies on to wire racks to cool.

● To decorate mix the icing sugar with sufficient water and mix to a thin icing. Using a piping bag pipe around the body with the icing and pipe eyes on each octopus and top with the candies. Allow the icing to set.

# Treasure Coins

*Preparation time: 30 minutes ●*
*Cooking time: 25 minutes ● Makes: 24*

**Small discs of vanilla shortbread are encrusted with glacé cherries, candied citrus peel and nuts to make these delicious edible coins.**

### INGREDIENTS

*175 g/6 oz plain flour, sifted*

*120 g/4 oz caster sugar*

*120 g/4 oz butter, cut into small pieces*

*2 tsp vanilla essence*

*50 g/2 oz candied citrus peel*

*12 glacé cherries, halved*

*24 whole blanched hazelnuts*

Pre-heat oven to 350°F/175°C/Gas mark 4. Grease two baking sheets or line with non-stick baking parchment.

● Place the flour and sugar in a mixing bowl. Blend in the butter using your fingertips until the mixture resembles fine breadcrumbs, add the vanilla essence and, using your hands, bring the mixture together in a soft ball.

● On a lightly floured surface, roll out the dough to about 5 mm/¼ in. Using a 5-cm/2-in round cutter, stamp out rounds and lift onto the baking sheets. Gather up the remaining dough and roll it out again and cut out more shapes.

● Press a little bit of candied citrus peel onto each cookie, then add half a cherry to each cookie, followed by a hazelnut. Bake the cookies for 25 minutes or until pale golden at the edges. Transfer to a wire rack to cool. Store these cookies in an airtight container and eat within one week.

# Mandarin Flying Saucers

*Preparation time: 30 minutes + chilling ●*
*Cooking time: 15 to 20 minutes ● Makes: 10*

**The tinned mandarins used in these cookies make for a great flavour and colour.**

### INGREDIENTS

*175 g/6 oz plain flour, sifted*

*120 g/4 oz icing sugar*

*150 g/5 oz lightly salted butter, cut into small pieces*

*Grated rind of 1 orange*

*50 g/2 oz tinned mandarin segments, drained and dried*

### DECORATION

*7 Tbsp icing sugar*

*About 3 tsp reserved mandarin juice or water*

*Few mandarin segments, chopped*

Place the flour and icing sugar in a bowl, blend in the butter using your fingertips until the mixture resembles fine breadcrumbs. Add the orange rind and mandarin segments, chopped, and, using your hands, bring together in a soft ball. Wrap in clingfilm and chill in the refrigerator for 30 minutes.

● Pre-heat oven to 350°F/175°C/Gas mark 4. Grease several baking sheets or line with non-stick baking parchment. Roll out the dough to about 5 mm/¼ in. Using a 10-cm/4-in round cutter, stamp out rounds and lift onto the baking sheets. Gather up the remaining dough and roll it out again and cut out more rounds.

● Bake the cookies for 15 to 20 minutes or until just golden at the edges. Transfer to a wire rack to cool.

● To decorate, mix the icing sugar with sufficient juice or water to form a thin icing. Place a dollop of icing on each cookie and top with mandarin pieces.

# Chocolate Snakes

*Preparation time: 30 minutes* ● *Cooking time: 15 minutes* ● *Makes: 8*

**These crunchy chocolate cookies are fun to make. Glazing them with egg white and sugar makes all the difference.**

## INGREDIENTS

*4 Tbsp soft tub margarine*

*50 g/2 oz caster sugar*

*1 egg, separated*

*120 g/4 oz plain flour*

*¼ tsp baking powder*

*2 Tbsp unsweetened cocoa powder, sifted*

*1 Tbsp milk*

### DECORATION

*4 currants, halved*

*Granulated sugar, for sprinkling*

Pre-heat oven to 375°F/190°C/Gas mark 5. Grease two baking sheets or line with non-stick baking parchment.

● In a mixing bowl beat together the margarine and sugar until pale and fluffy. Add the egg yolk. Sift together the flour, baking powder and unsweetened cocoa powder then add with the milk and mix thoroughly. The dough should come together in a soft ball.

● Turn the dough out onto a lightly floured work surface and divide into 8 equal-sized pieces. Roll each piece into a long sausage shape with your hands. Then make a spiral pattern with one piece of dough and overlap as you wind the dough up and around. Add 2 pieces of currants to make the eyes and place onto the baking sheets. Repeat with the remaining shapes.

● In a small bowl lightly beat the egg white and then, using a pastry brush, glaze the snakes all over and sprinkle with sugar. Bake for 15 minutes. Lift onto a wire rack to cool. Store in an airtight container.

# Fishies

*Preparation time: 25 minutes + chilling* ● *Cooking time: 10 to 15 minutes* ● *Makes: 40 small cookies*

**Adding candied peel to this creamed mixture gives these cookies a really fruity texture.**

## INGREDIENTS

| |
|---|
| 75 g/3 oz butter, softened or soft tub margarine |
| 150 g/5 oz caster sugar |
| 1 egg, beaten |
| 175 g/6 oz plain flour, sifted |
| 6 Tbsp candied citrus peel |
| Grated rind of ½ lemon |

In a mixing bowl beat together the butter or margarine and sugar until light and fluffy. Beat in the egg. Stir in the flour, then stir in the candied citrus peel and lemon rind. Using your hands, bring the mixture together to form a soft dough. Wrap in clingfilm and chill in the refrigerator for 20 minutes.

● Pre-heat oven to 350°F/175°C/Gas mark 4. Grease two baking sheets or line with non-stick baking parchment.

● On a lightly floured surface roll out the dough to 5 mm/¼ in. Using a cutter, cut out as many fish shapes as possible (the exact number will depend on the size of your cutter) and lift onto the baking sheets. Gather up the remaining dough and roll it out again and cut out more fish shapes.

● Using the back of a teaspoon, decorate the fish with scales and make an eye with a metal skewer. Bake the cookies for 10 to 12 minutes until golden and crisp. Lift onto a wire rack to cool. Store in an airtight container.

# Gingerbread Selection

*Preparation time: 40 minutes + chilling* ● *Cooking time: 8 to 10 minutes* ● *Makes: 24*

**These cookies are just as good as traditional gingerbread but with currants in the mixture.
You can use any cookie cutter you like.**

## INGREDIENTS

*50 g/2 oz soft brown sugar*

*3 Tbsp golden syrup*

*½ tsp ground cinnamon*

*½ tsp ground ginger*

*25 g/1 oz butter*

*225 g/8 oz plain flour, sifted*

*1 tsp baking powder*

*1 egg, beaten*

*50 g/2 oz currants, chopped*

## DECORATION

*5 Tbsp icing sugar, sifted*

*About 4 tsp water*

*Green food colouring*

Grease two baking sheets or line with non-stick baking parchment. Ask an adult to help you dissolve the sugar, syrup, spices and butter together in a saucepan. Stir over a low heat until they have melted.

● Sift the flour and baking powder into a mixing bowl add the syrup mixture, beaten egg and currants. Mix everything together, then knead the mixture into a ball using your hands. Chill the dough in clingfilm in the refrigerator for 30 minutes.

● Pre-heat oven to 325°F/160°C/Gas mark 3. Sprinkle some flour on the work surface and rolling pin. Roll out the dough thinly to about 5 mm/¼ in. Using the cutters, cut out your shapes and lift the cookies onto baking sheets. Gather up the left-over dough, roll it out again and cut out more shapes. Bake the cookies for 8 to 10 minutes or until golden-brown then lift them on to a wire rack to cool.

● To decorate the gingerbread selection, mix the icing sugar with sufficient water to make a thin icing and add a few drops of green colouring. Using a piping bag, pipe onto the cookies and decorate.

# Jam Heart Cookies

*Preparation time: 30 minutes + chilling* ● *Cooking time: 20 minutes* ● *Makes: 12*

**Who can resist a crisp cookie base filled with lots of strawberry jam.
Use a different flavoured jam if you prefer.**

### INGREDIENTS

*175 g/6 oz plain flour, sifted*

*50 g/2 oz ground almonds*

*120 g/4 oz butter, softened*

*50 g/2 oz caster sugar*

*2 Tbsp milk*

*1 egg, beaten*

*4 Tbsp strawberry jam*

Place the flour and ground almonds in a mixing bowl, blend in the butter until the mixture resembles fine breadcrumbs. Stir in the sugar and milk and, using your hands, work the mixture together to form a dough. Wrap in clingfilm and chill in the refrigerator for 20 minutes.

● Pre-heat oven to 350°F/175°C/Gas mark 4. Grease two baking sheets or line with non-stick baking parchment.

● On a lightly floured surface, roll out the dough and cut out 8-cm/3-in hearts with a cutter. Place 12 of these heart cookies onto the baking sheets and prick with a fork. Cut out a heart shape from the centre of the remaining hearts, using a 5-cm/2-in heart cutter. Gather up the remaining dough and roll it out again and cut out more 5-cm/2-in hearts so you have 12 "lids" for the cookies.

● Using a pastry brush, apply the beaten egg to the large heart cookies. Top with a heart lid and seal around the edges. Brush the whole cookie with more beaten egg. Bake the cookies for 20 minutes or until golden. Lift onto a wire rack to cool.

● Once the cookies have cooled spoon the jam onto each cookie keeping within the heart shape in the centre.

# Orange Carrot Shortbread

*Preparation time: 35 minutes* ● *Cooking time: 15 to 20 minutes* ● *Makes: 16*

**A rich, buttery shortbread flavoured with orange rind, with a drop of food colouring.
See how many people take a second look!**

## INGREDIENTS

150 g/5 oz butter, softened

5 Tbsp caster sugar

225 g/8 oz plain flour, sifted

Grated rind of 2 oranges

2 Tbsp orange juice

Few drops orange food colouring, optional

Pre-heat oven to 325°F/160°C/Gas mark 3. Grease two baking sheets or line with non-stick baking parchment.

● In a mixing bowl beat together the butter and sugar until light and fluffy. Add all the remaining ingredients and begin to mix well. Using your hands bring the mixture together to form a soft dough.

● On a lightly floured work surface, divide the dough into 16 equal pieces. Roll each piece of dough into a ball using the palms of your hands. Roll backwards and forwards so that one end begins to get thinner and you produce a carrot shape. Repeat with the remaining dough and lift onto the baking sheets. Using the back of a knife lightly score marks all over the carrots.

● Bake the cookies for 15 to 20 minutes or until lightly golden at the edges. Allow to cool slightly before lifting onto a wire rack.

## TIP

If you prefer, cut the shortbread into your favourite shape.

# Poppy Seed Pinwheels

*Preparation time: 25 minutes + chilling* ●
*Cooking time: 15 to 20 minutes* ● *Makes: About 20*

**These crunchy cookies are sweet and sticky from the jam which oozes out during baking. We've used apricot, but you can use your favourite flavour of jam.**

## INGREDIENTS

| |
|---|
| *120 g/4 oz butter, softened* |
| *50 g/2 oz caster sugar* |
| *175 g/6 oz plain flour, sifted* |
| *2 Tbsp milk* |
| *4 Tbsp apricot jam* |
| *1½ Tbsp poppy seeds* |

In a mixing bowl beat together the butter and sugar until light and fluffy. Stir in the flour and milk. Using your hands, bring the mixture together to form a dough. Wrap in clingfilm and chill for 30 minutes.

● Pre-heat oven to 350°F/175°C/Gas mark 4. Line two baking sheets with non-stick baking parchment.

● On a lightly floured surface, roll out the dough to a 30 x 18-cm/12 x 7-in rectangle. Place the apricot jam in a small bowl and stir well with a wooden spoon so it becomes easier to spread. Spoon onto the dough and spread out evenly, sprinkle with poppy seeds.

● Starting from the longest edge, begin to roll up the dough tightly into a large sausage shape. Very carefully slice the dough so you have 20 even slices, lift onto the baking sheets. Bake the cookies for 15 to 20 minutes or until they are lightly golden. Allow to cool slightly on the sheets before lifting onto a wire rack to cool.

# Number Cookies

*Preparation time: 25 minutes + chilling* ●
*Cooking time: 10 to 15 minutes* ● *Makes: 40*

**These cookies are made with an orange dough, half of it flavoured with cocoa powder to create these two colours.**

## INGREDIENTS

| |
|---|
| *175 g/6 oz butter, softened* |
| *5 Tbsp caster sugar* |
| *250 g/9 oz plain flour, sifted* |
| *½ tsp grated orange rind* |
| *2 Tbsp unsweetened cocoa powder, sifted* |

In a mixing bowl beat together the butter and sugar until light and fluffy. Add the flour and orange rind and combine all the ingredients together in a soft ball. Transfer half the mixture to another bowl and fold in the cocoa powder until evenly mixed. Wrap the doughs separately in clingfilm and chill in the refrigerator for 30 minutes.

● Pre-heat oven to 350°F/175°C/Gas mark 4. Grease several baking sheets or line with non-stick baking parchment.

● On a lightly floured surface, roll out the chocolate dough to about 5 mm/¼ in and stamp out numbers. Lift onto the baking sheets. Gather up the remaining dough and roll it out again and cut out more numbers. Repeat with the orange dough.

● Bake the cookies for 10 to 15 minutes or until golden at the edges. Lift onto a wire rack to cool. Store in an airtight container.

# Apple Cheese Cookies

*Preparation time: 20 minutes ●*
*Cooking time: 20 minutes ● Makes: 16*

**These savoury cookies have a hint of sweetness from the chopped apple.**

## INGREDIENTS

150 g/5 oz self-raising flour

Pinch of salt

120 g/4 oz butter, cut into small pieces

120 g/4 oz mature Cheddar cheese, grated

1 apple, cored and finely chopped

Pre-heat oven to 350°F/175°C/Gas mark 4. Grease and line several baking sheets with non-stick baking parchment.

● Place the flour and salt in a mixing bowl and blend in the butter using your fingertips until the mixture resembles fine breadcrumbs. Stir in the cheese and chopped apple and, using your hands, bring all the ingredients together to form a soft ball.

● On a lightly floured surface divide the dough into 16 equal-sized pieces and roll into balls using the palms of your hands and lift onto the baking sheets. Flatten slightly with the back of a fork.

● Bake the cookies for 20 minutes or until evenly golden-brown. Transfer to a wire rack to cool. These cookies are best eaten on the day they are made.

# Clock Cookies

*Preparation time: 35 minutes + chilling ●*
*Cooking time: 15 to 20 minutes ● Makes: 10*

**These cookies are flavoured with sultanas and cut into circles to make big clock faces. Pipe the icing to show a different time on each cookie!**

## INGREDIENTS

6 Tbsp soft tub margarine

150 g/5 oz caster sugar

1 egg, beaten

175 g/6 oz plain flour, sifted

50 g/2 oz sultanas

## DECORATION

120 g/4 oz icing sugar

About 1 Tbsp cold water

In a mixing bowl beat together the margarine and sugar until light and fluffy. Beat in the egg. Stir in the flour and sultanas and, using your hands, bring all the mixture together in a soft ball. Wrap the dough in clingfilm and chill in the refrigerator for 30 minutes.

● Pre-heat oven to 350°F/175°C/Gas mark 4. Grease several baking sheets.

● On a lightly floured surface roll out the dough to about 5 mm/¼-in. Using a 10-cm/4-in round cutter, stamp out rounds and lift onto the baking sheets. Gather up the remaining dough and roll it again and cut out more shapes. Bake the cookies for 15 to 20 minutes or until evenly golden. Transfer to a wire rack to cool.

● To decorate the "clocks", mix the icing sugar with about 1 tablespoon of cold water to form a thin icing. Using a piping bag, pipe the numbers 12, 3, 6 and 9 on to the circles in the correct clock positions. Then pipe an "hour" hand and "minute" hand to show a different time on each cookie. Leave to set.

# Fruit Segments

*Preparation time: 25 minutes* ● *Cooking time: 15 minutes* ● *Makes: 16*

**These look just like a segment of fruit and they are full of citrus flavours.**

## INGREDIENTS

120 g/4 oz butter, softened

5 Tbsp caster sugar

1 egg, separated

200 g/7 oz plain flour, sifted

Grated rind of 1 lemon

Grated rind of 1 orange

2 Tbsp orange juice

Granulated sugar, for sprinkling

Pre-heat oven to 350°F/175°C/Gas mark 4. Grease two baking sheets or line with non-stick baking parchment.

● In a mixing bowl, beat together the butter and sugar until pale and fluffy. Beat in the egg yolk. Stir in the flour, grated rinds and orange juice and mix everything together. Using your hands bring the dough together to form a ball.

● Turn the dough out on to a lightly floured work surface and roll out to 5 mm/¼ in. Using a 9-cm/3½-in round cutter, cut out rounds, then cut each circle in half to make the segments. Gather up the left-over dough and roll it out again and cut out more circles. Lift the cookies onto the baking sheets and, using the back of a small knife, score marks across each segment.

● In a small bowl, whisk the egg white lightly with a fork and, using a pastry brush, glaze each cookie then sprinkle with a little extra sugar. Bake the cookies for 15 minutes or until lightly golden and crisp. Lift them onto a wire rack to cool. When cold store them in an airtight container.

# Cookies for Special Diets

Some people believe that being on a special diet puts an end to treats such as cookies. However, this need not be the case. This chapter is full of recipes specially created for those with specific dietary requirements. These cookies are so delicious that they will become firm favourites with the whole family.

Many of the recipes retain butter as the suggested fat because butter really does give the cookies a richness of flavour. However, margarine can be substituted for the butter, but be aware that the trans fats found in hard margarines are saturated like those in butter. Trans fats behave like saturated fats, increasing the risk of heart disease. Reduced and low-fat spreads have a high water content so cannot be substituted for butter. The butter content is kept as low as possible in these recipes and inventive techniques using prunes and apple sauce are used in some recipes to reduce the need for fat.

## High Fibre

*Increasing fibre is one of the basic tenets of healthy eating.*

# Reduced Fat

*Being placed on a low-cholesterol diet does not have to mean total denial of cookies as these recipes show.*

# Gluten-Free/Wheat-Free/Healthy

# Coconut Crisps

*Preparation time: 10 minutes ● Cooking time:*
*15 minutes ● Makes: About 20*

**These deliciously light, crisp cookies are quick and easy
to make and simply melt in the mouth.**

### INGREDIENTS

*120 g/4 oz lightly salted butter*

*1 heaped Tbsp golden syrup*

*50 g/2 oz demerara sugar*

*150 g/5 oz rolled oats*

*75 g/3 oz sweetened flaked coconut*

*120 g/4 oz plain flour*

*1 tsp bicarbonate of soda*

*1 tsp hot water*

Pre-heat oven to 350°F/175°C/Gas mark 4. Grease
or line two baking sheets with non-stick baking
parchment.

● Place the butter, syrup and sugar in a large saucepan.
Heat the mixture gently until the butter has melted and
the sugar dissolved. Stir in the rolled oats and flour and
mix well. Dissolve the bicarbonate in the hot water and
stir into the mixture. Allow to cool slightly.

● Roll heaped teaspoonfuls of the mixture into balls the
size of a walnut. Then place on the baking sheets
allowing plenty of space for the mixture to spread. Bake
for 15 minutes or until evenly browned. Leave to cool
slightly, then use a thin metal spatula to transfer to a
wire rack to cool completely. Store for up to 1 week in
an airtight container.

# Wholemeal Shortbread

*Preparation time: 15 minutes + chilling ●*
*Cooking time: 15 minutes ● Makes: About 15*

**The fibre content of these shortbread cookies is
increased by substituting half the plain flour
with wholemeal.**

### INGREDIENTS

*50 g/2 oz plain flour*

*Pinch of salt*

*50 g/2 oz plain wholemeal flour*

*5 Tbsp ground rice*

*120 g/4 oz lightly salted butter*

*25 g/1 oz icing sugar*

Sift the plain flour and salt together and stir in the
wholemeal flour and ground rice.

● Beat the butter and sugar until light and fluffy. Mix in
the dry ingredients. When the mixture resembles
breadcrumbs, gather the dough together with your
hands and turn onto a clean work surface. Knead lightly
until it forms a ball then roll into a sausage shape, about
5 cm/2 in in diameter. Wrap in clingfilm and chill in the
refrigerator for at least 1 hour or until firm.

● Pre-heat oven to 375°F/190°C/Gas mark 5. Grease or
line two baking sheets with non-stick baking parchment.

● Using a sharp knife slice the dough into 8-mm/⅓-in
thick slices. Transfer to the baking sheets and bake for
15 minutes. Allow to cool slightly then, using a thin
metal spatula, transfer to a wire rack to cool completely.
Store in an airtight container for up to 1 week.

# Peanut and Raisin Cookies

*Preparation time: 15 minutes + cooling* ● *Cooking time: 15 minutes* ● *Makes: About 20*

**Diets which contain a daily intake of peanuts, peanut butter or peanut oil may help protect against heart disease.**

### INGREDIENTS

120 g/4 oz lightly salted butter, melted

75 g/3 oz caster sugar

1 egg, beaten

5 tsp baking powder

200 g/7 oz crunchy peanut butter

5 Tbsp plain flour

50 g/2 oz wholemeal flour

150 g/5 oz raisins

Pre-heat oven to 375°F/190°C/Gas mark 5. Grease or line two baking sheets.

● Place all the ingredients except the raisins into a bowl and beat together until well blended. Stir in the raisins. Spoon heaping teaspoonfuls of the mixture onto baking sheets spaced well apart to allow the mixture to spread. Bake for 15 to 20 minutes or until brown around the edges.

● Leave to cool slightly, then using a thin metal spatula, transfer to a wire rack to cool completely. Store for up to 1 week, in an airtight container.

# Banana and Date Cookies

*Preparation time: 15 minutes ● Cooking time: 15 to 20 minutes ● Makes: About 15*

**Bananas are an excellent source of fibre and potassium and are rich in vitamin B6.**

### INGREDIENTS

| |
|---|
| *120 g/4 oz lightly salted butter or margarine* |
| *5 Tbsp caster sugar* |
| *1 egg, beaten* |
| *75 g/3 oz plain flour* |
| *1 tsp baking powder* |
| *50 g/2 oz plain wholemeal flour* |
| *50 g/2 oz roughly chopped dried banana chips* |
| *200 g/7 oz roughly chopped dates* |

Pre-heat oven to 375°F/190°C/Gas mark 5. Grease or line two baking sheets with non-stick baking parchment.

● Beat together the butter and sugar until light and fluffy. Beat in the egg. Sift the plain flour and baking powder into a bowl. Stir in the wholemeal flour, banana chips and dates.

● With floured hands, roll the dough into balls the size of walnuts. Place on baking sheets, allowing enough space for the mixture to spread. Bake for 15 to 20 minutes or until brown around the edges. Allow to cool slightly, then use a thin, metal spatula, to transfer to a wire rack to cool completely. Store for up to 1 week in an airtight container.

# Caribbean Lime Cookies

*Preparation time: 15 minutes ● Cooking time: 15 to 20 minutes ● Makes: About 15*

**Dried tropical fruits are readily available and make a good alternative to dried apricots.**

### INGREDIENTS

| |
|---|
| *120 g/4 oz lightly salted butter* |
| *75 g/3 oz caster sugar* |
| *1 egg, beaten* |
| *75 g/3 oz plain flour* |
| *1 level tsp baking powder* |
| *50 g/2 oz wholemeal flour* |
| *75 g/3 oz chopped dried mango* |
| *75 g/3 oz sweetened flaked coconut* |
| *Grated rind of 2 limes* |

Pre-heat oven to 375°F/190°C/Gas mark 5. Grease or line two baking sheets with non-stick baking parchment.

● Beat together the butter and sugar until soft. Beat in the egg. Sift the plain flour and the baking powder into a bowl. Stir in the wholemeal flour, mango, coconut and grated lime rind.

● With floured hands roll the dough into balls the size of walnuts. Place on the baking sheets, allowing enough space for the mixture to spread. Bake in the oven for 15 to 20 minutes or until brown around the edges. Allow to cool slightly, then use a thin metal spatula to transfer to a wire rack to cool completely. Store for up to 1 week in an airtight container.

# Apricot and Almond Cookies

*Preparation time: 15 minutes + cooling* ● *Cooking time: 15 minutes* ● *Makes: 15 to 20*

**Dried apricots provide good amounts of betacarotene, potassium and soluble fibre.
They are also a useful source of iron.**

### INGREDIENTS

120 g/4 oz lightly salted butter

5 Tbsp caster sugar

1 egg, beaten

75 g/3 oz plain flour

1 tsp baking powder

75 g/3 oz wholemeal flour

50 g/2 oz roughly chopped ready-to-eat dried apricots

75 g/3 oz flaked almonds

1 tsp almond essence

Pre-heat oven to 375°F/190°C/Gas mark 5. Grease or line two baking sheets with non-stick baking parchment.

● Beat together the butter and sugar until soft. Beat in the egg. Sift the plain flour together with the baking powder in a bowl. Stir in the wholemeal flour, apricots, almonds and almond essence.

● With floured hands roll the dough into balls the size of walnuts. Place on the baking sheets, allowing enough space for the mixture to spread. Bake for 15 to 20 minutes or until brown around the edges. Allow to cool slightly, then transfer to a wire rack to cool completely. Store for up to 1 week in an airtight container.

# Sesame Oat Crisps

*Preparation time: 10 minutes* ● *Cooking time: 15 minutes* ● *Makes: About 20*

**Sesame seeds are a good source of calcium and vitamin E and add a delicious nutty flavour to these cookies.**

## INGREDIENTS

*120 g/4 oz lightly salted butter*

*1¼ Tbsp golden syrup*

*120 g/4 oz demerera sugar*

*75 g/3 oz rolled oats*

*5 Tbsp sesame seeds*

*120 g/4 oz plain flour*

*1 tsp bicarbonate of soda*

*1 tsp hot water*

Pre-heat oven to 350°F/175°C/Gas mark 4. Grease or line two baking sheets.

● Place butter, syrup and sugar in a large saucepan. Heat the mixture gently until the butter has melted and the sugar dissolved. Stir in rolled oats, sesame seeds and flour and mix well. Dissolve the bicarbonate in the hot water and stir into the mixture. Leave to cool slightly.

● Roll heaped teaspoonfuls of the mixture into balls the size of walnuts. Place on the baking sheets allowing plenty of space for the mixture to spread as it bakes. Bake for 15 minutes or until evenly browned. Remove from the oven and allow to cool slightly, then using a thin metal spatula transfer to a wire rack to cool completely. Store for up to 1 week in an airtight container.

# Ginger Thins

*Preparation time: 10 minutes ● Cooking time: 7 minutes ● Makes: About 10*

**These cookies contain just 1.3g fat each. Serve them with frozen yogurt or reduced-fat ice cream.**

### INGREDIENTS

| |
|---|
| *15 g/½ oz unsalted butter* |
| *1 Tbsp icing sugar* |
| *3 Tbsp golden syrup* |
| *2 Tbsp plain flour* |
| *1 level tsp ground ginger* |
| *Pinch of salt* |

Pre-heat oven to 375°F/190°C/Gas mark 5. Grease or line two baking sheets with non-stick baking parchment.

● Place the butter, icing sugar and syrup in a small saucepan and heat gently until the sugar has dissolved. Remove from the heat and leave to cool slightly.

● Sift together the flour, ginger and salt and stir into the butter mixture.

● Place small spoonfuls of the mixture on to the prepared baking sheets, allowing plenty of space for the mixture to spread. Bake for 7 minutes or until golden brown. Allow the cookies to cool on the tray for about 30 seconds. Using a thin, metal spatula carefully lift the cookies off the baking sheet and while they are still warm and pliable, shape them over a rolling pin or tall glass. Once set, transfer to a wire rack to cool completely. Store for up to 1 week in an airtight container.

# Treacle Cookies

*Preparation time: 10 minutes ● Cooking time: 20 minutes ● Makes: About 15*

**These cookies contain just 1.7g fat. Oatmeal is rich in soluble fibre, which can help reduce high blood cholesterol levels.**

### INGREDIENTS

| |
|---|
| *120 g/4 oz self-raising flour* |
| *50 g/2 oz fine oatmeal* |
| *3 Tbsp caster sugar* |
| *3 Tbsp treacle* |
| *50 g/2 oz lightly salted butter* |
| *2 Tbsp skimmed milk* |

Pre-heat oven to 375°F/190°C/Gas mark 5. Grease or line two baking sheets with non-stick baking parchment.

● Mix all the dry ingredients in a bowl. Place the butter and treacle in a small saucepan and heat gently until the butter has melted. Pour the treacle mixture onto the dry ingredients, add the milk and mix to make smooth dough.

● Knead the dough on a lightly floured surface then roll out to about 8 mm/⅓ in thick. Using a 5-cm/2-in round cutter, cut out the cookies and transfer to baking sheet. Using a sharp knife make shallow cuts across the surface and bake for 20 minutes or until firm to the touch. Transfer to a wire rack to cool. Store for up to 1 week in an airtight container.

# Lemon and Poppy Seed Cookies

*Preparation time: 15 minutes* ● *Cooking time: 15 to 20 minutes* ● *Makes: About 36*

**Poppy seeds give these healthy gluten-free cookies an added crunch.**

### INGREDIENTS

| |
| --- |
| *120 g/4 oz lightly salted butter or margarine* |
| *120 g/4 oz caster sugar* |
| *1 egg, beaten* |
| *175 g/6 oz gluten-free flour* |
| *Grated rind of 2 lemons* |
| *2 Tbsp poppy seeds* |

Pre-heat oven to 350°F/175°C/Gas mark 4. Grease or line two baking sheets.

● Beat together the butter and sugar until light and fluffy. Gradually beat in the egg. Add in the gluten-free flour, lemon rind and poppy seeds and mix well.

● On a lightly floured surface roll out the dough to 5 mm/¼ in thick. Using a 5-cm/2-in round cutter, cut out the cookies and transfer to the baking sheets and bake for 15 to 20 minutes. Cool slightly on the baking sheets then, using a thin metal spatula carefully transfer to a wire rack to cool completely.

# Sour Cherry and Orange Oatmeal Cookies

*Preparation time: 15 minutes ● Cooking time: 15 to 20 minutes ● Makes: 15 to 20*

**Oats are an excellent source of soluble fibre which can help reduce high blood cholesterol levels, thereby lessening the risk of heart disease.**

### INGREDIENTS

120 g/4 oz plain flour

½ tsp bicarbonate of soda

½ tsp baking powder

½ tsp salt

120 g/4 oz unsalted butter

225 g/8 oz dark brown sugar

1 egg, beaten

1 tsp vanilla essence

1 Tbsp milk

Grated rind of 1 large orange

175 g/6 oz rolled oats

50 g/2 oz roughly chopped sour cherries

Pre-heat oven to 350°F/175°C/Gas mark 4. Grease or line two baking sheets.

● Sift together the flour, bicarbonate, baking powder and salt. Beat together the butter and sugar. Gradually add the egg, vanilla essence and milk and beat until smooth. Stir in the sifted ingredients and mix well. Stir in the grated orange rind, oats and sour cherries.

● Scoop up balls of dough with a tablespoon and place them spaced well apart on the baking sheets to allow the mixture to spread. Bake for 15 to 20 minutes or until just brown. Remove from the oven and leave to cool slightly then, using a thin metal spatula, transfer to a wire rack to cool completely. Store for up to 1 week in an airtight container.

# Low-Fat Chocolate Brownies

*Preparation time: 15 minutes ● Cooking time: 50 to 60 minutes ● Makes: 9*

**These brownies contain a fraction of the fat used in traditional brownies.**

### INGREDIENTS

225 g/8 oz ready-to-eat prunes

3 Tbsp water

120 g/4 oz plain chocolate

3 egg whites

225 g/8 oz light brown sugar

1 tsp salt

1 tsp vanilla essence

50 g/2 oz plain flour, sifted

25 g/1 oz pecan nuts, chopped

Pre-heat oven to 350°F/175°C/Gas mark 4. Grease and line the base of an 20 x 20-cm/8 x 8-in shallow cake tin with non-stick baking parchment.

● Using a blender, blend the prunes with the water until they make a smooth purée. Break the chocolate into a bowl and place over a saucepan of simmering water. Stir occasionally until the chocolate has melted. Remove from the heat and set aside to cool slightly.

● In a bowl mix together the prune purée, melted chocolate, egg whites, sugar, salt and vanilla essence. Fold in the sifted flour.

● Spread the mixture into the prepared tin, sprinkle with pecans and bake for about 50 to 60 minutes or until firm to the touch. Leave in the tin to cool completely. Store, covered in the tin, for 3 days.

# Muesli Cookies

*Preparation time: 10 minutes ● Cooking time: 15 to 20 minutes ● Makes: About 15*

**Muesli is high in fibre and rich in vitamins.**

### INGREDIENTS

120 g/4 oz lightly salted butter or margarine

5 Tbsp demerara sugar

1 egg, beaten

120 g/4 oz sugar-free muesli

50 g/2 oz wholemeal flour

1¼ tsp baking powder

Pre-heat oven to 375°F/190°C/Gas mark 5. Grease or line two baking sheets with non-stick baking parchment.

● Beat together the butter and sugar until light and fluffy. Gradually beat in the egg. Stir in the muesli and flour and mix well. Roll into balls the size of a walnut and place on the baking sheets, allowing space for the cookies to spread. Using the palm of your hand flatten the cookies slightly.

● Bake the cookies for 15 to 20 minutes. Allow to cool slightly on the baking sheets then use a thin metal spatula to transfer to a wire rack to cool completely. Store in an airtight container.

# Wheat-free Fruit and Oat Bars

*Preparation time: 10 minutes ● Cooking time: 30 to 35 minutes ● Makes: 9*

**Sunflower seeds are a rich source of vitamin E, the B vitamins thiamin and niacin and the mineral zinc.**

### INGREDIENTS

*120 g/4 oz unsalted butter or margarine*

*50 g/2 oz light brown sugar*

*1 Tbsp golden syrup*

*50 g/2 oz rolled oats*

*25 g/1 oz sultanas*

*25 g/1 oz roughly chopped ready-to-eat dried apricots*

*6 Tbsp sunflower seeds*

Pre-heat oven to 350°F/175°C/Gas mark 4. Lightly grease and base-line a shallow 20 x 20-cm/ 8 x 8-in baking tin.

● Heat the butter, sugar and syrup in a saucepan until dissolved. Remove from the heat, add the remaining ingredients and mix well. Spoon the mixture into the prepared tin, level the surface and bake in the oven for about 30 minutes or until golden brown.

● Leave to cool for 5 minutes in the tin, then cut into 9 pieces. When the cookies are completely cold, transfer to an airtight container.

# Simple Macaroons

*Preparation time: 10 minutes ● Cooking time: 25 minutes ● Makes: About 24*

**These classic cookies use no flour whatsoever so are gluten-free and wheat-free. They are low in fat too.**

### INGREDIENTS

| |
|---|
| *1 egg white* |
| *175 g/6 oz ground almonds* |
| *120 g/4 oz icing sugar, sifted* |
| *12 blanched almonds, split in half* |

Pre-heat oven to 300°F/150°C/Gas mark 2. Line two baking sheets with non-stick baking parchment.

● Whisk the egg whites in a bowl until stiff but not dry. Gently fold in the icing sugar and almonds until the mixture becomes a sticky dough.

● Spoon walnut-sized balls of mixture onto the baking sheets leaving plenty of space in between. Press half an almond onto the top of each macaroon. Bake for about 25 minutes; the outer crust should be golden and the inside soft. Transfer to a wire rack to cool. Store for up to 1 week in an airtight container.

# Apple and Raisin Cookies

*Preparation time: 15 minutes ● Cooking time: 15 to 20 minutes ● Makes: 16 to 18*

**Apple sauce has been used to replace some of the fat in these cookies.**

### INGREDIENTS

| |
|---|
| *50 g/2 oz lightly salted butter or margarine* |
| *120 g/4 oz caster sugar* |
| *125 ml/4 fl oz unsweetened apple sauce* |
| *1 egg yolk* |
| *150 g/5 oz plain flour* |
| *120 g/4 oz rolled oats* |
| *½ tsp bicarbonate of soda* |
| *½ tsp baking powder* |
| *40 g/1½ oz raisins* |
| *25 g/1 oz chopped walnuts* |

Pre-heat oven to 375°F/190°C/Gas mark 5. Line two baking sheets with non-stick baking parchment.

● Beat together the butter and sugar until light and fluffy. Beat in the apple sauce and egg yolk. Add the flour, oats, bicarbonate, baking powder, raisins and walnuts and beat to make a soft dough.

● With lightly floured hands roll the mixture into balls the size of a walnut and place on the baking sheets, allowing space for the cookies to spread. Using the palm of your hand flatten the cookies slightly and bake for 15 to 20 minutes until set. Allow to cool slightly on the baking sheet, then transfer to a wire rack to cool. Store for up to 1 week in an airtight container.

# Cookies for Festive Occasions

Cookies are treats and treats are for enjoying on special occasions. It is no wonder that there are cookies associated with specific festivities throughout the world. The very best ingredients are always reserved for these special times, so the cookies are packed with dried fruit, nuts and exotic spices. In America and some other countries special cookies are baked for Christmas, Valentine's Day and Easter.

Children love being involved in the preparation for these events, so have them help make the cookies and maybe decorate some too. Their childish cookies will have a special appeal and would make a lovely, personalized gift.

## Christmas

*The rich scent of warm cinnamon and spice is one of the first smells of Christmas. Some recipes can be cooked in advance and frozen.*

## Thanksgiving

*An important holiday in the American calendar. Try some of these delicious cookies as an autumn treat.*

# National Holidays

*Cookies can be baked to serve as part of National Holiday celebrations.
Ice them according to the relevant flag colours!*

# Passover and Hanukkah

*Home-baked treats are an essential part of Jewish holidays.*

# Valentine's Day

*These cookies are perfect gifts for loved ones. They are light and airy,
pink and fancy – and fun to make.*

# Saints' Days and Special Days

*Many saints and even some poets have a special day with accompanying
customs and traditional foods. The following are just a few.*

# Cinnamon Jelly Bean Trees

*Preparation time: 30 minutes ● Cooking time: 15 minutes ● Makes: About 20*

**These crisp cinnamon Christmas cookies are decorated with jelly beans.**

### INGREDIENTS

*120 g/4 oz unsalted butter*

*50 g/2 oz caster sugar*

*150 g/5 oz plain flour*

*½ tsp ground cinnamon*

*5 Tbsp rice flour*

### ICING

*25 g/1 oz icing sugar*

*1 tsp lemon juice*

*2 small packets small jelly beans*

Pre-heat oven to 350°F/170°C/Gas mark 4. Line two large baking sheets with non-stick baking parchment.

● Beat the butter in a bowl until soft, then gradually mix in the sugar. Stir in the flour, cinnamon and rice flour until well mixed, then knead lightly. Roll out on a lightly floured surface to 5 mm/¼ in. Cut out twenty 8-cm/3-in tree shapes. Lift onto the baking sheets, spacing slightly apart.

● Bake for 15 minutes, until golden. Leave on the baking sheets for a few minutes, then remove and cool on wire racks. Sift the icing sugar into a small bowl and stir in the lemon juice to make a smooth icing. Dip the bases of the jelly beans into the icing and stick onto the trees. Leave to set.

### VARIATION

● Substitute 50 g/2 oz unsweetened cocoa powder for the same amount of flour and omit the cinnamon.

# Spiced Christmas Cookies

*Preparation time: 30 minutes ● Cooking time: 15 minutes ● Makes: About 20*

**With their crunchy, sugary topping and warm spicy flavouring, these cookies are
good with mulled wine.**

## INGREDIENTS

*120 g/4 oz unsalted butter, softened*

*5 Tbsp light brown sugar*

*1 egg, separated*

*150 g/5 oz plain flour, sifted*

*1 tsp ground cinnamon*

*½ tsp ground ginger*

*¼ tsp freshly grated nutmeg*

*¼ tsp ground cloves*

*2 Tbsp granulated sugar*

Pre-heat oven to 350°F/170°C/Gas mark 4. Line two baking sheets with non-stick baking parchment.
● Beat the butter and sugar together until light and fluffy. Reserve 2 teaspoons egg white. Add the remaining white and yolk to the mixture and mix well. Stir in the flour and spices to make a soft dough. Wrap in clingfilm and chill in the refrigerator for 1 hour.
● Roll out the dough to about 5 mm/¼ in on a lightly floured surface. Cut into Christmas shapes with floured 6-cm/2½-in cutters.
● Transfer the cookies to baking sheets. Brush with the reserved egg white and sprinkle with sugar. Bake for 10 to 12 minutes. Leave for 1 or 2 minutes before lifting off the baking sheets and cooling on wire racks.

## TIP

If you want to hang the cookies on the Christmas tree, make a small hole in each with a skewer before baking to allow a ribbon to be threaded through.

# Tipsy Christmas Puddings

*Preparation time: 30 minutes* ●
*Cooking time: 15 minutes* ● *Makes: About 20*

**These spice and fruit cookies are half-coated in a rich
rum icing to look like Christmas puddings.**

### INGREDIENTS

*120 g/4 oz lightly salted butter*

*120 g/4 oz dark brown sugar*

*2 egg yolks*

*225 g/8 oz plain flour*

*½ tsp ground mixed spice*

*25 g/1 oz glacé cherries, chopped*

*50 g/2 oz dried mixed fruit*

### ICING

*120 g/4 oz icing sugar*

*2 tsp white rum or lemon juice*

*1–2 tsp hot water*

*Glacé cherries and angelica, to decorate*

Pre-heat oven to 350°F/175°C/Gas mark 4. Lightly
grease two baking sheets.

● Beat the butter and sugar until light and fluffy. Add
the egg yolks and mix. Work in the flour with the mixed
spice, cherries and mixed fruit to make a firm dough.
Lightly knead, then roll out on a lightly floured surface
to 5 mm/¼ in. Cut into rounds, using a plain 6-cm/2¾-
in cutter. Transfer to baking sheets.

● Bake for about 15 minutes, until lightly browned.
Then transfer to wire racks to cool.

● Sift the icing sugar into a bowl. Stir in enough rum or
lemon juice to make a thick icing. Ice the top half of
each cookie and decorate with a piece of glacé cherry
and angelica.

# Stained-glass Windows

*Preparation time: 45 minutes* ●
*Cooking time: 8 to 10 minutes* ● *Makes: About 20*

**These cookies look wonderful hanging on the Christmas
tree with light shining through.**

### INGREDIENTS

*225 g/8 oz plain flour*

*150 g/5 oz lightly salted butter*

*200 g/7 oz caster sugar*

*Grated rind of 1 orange*

*1 egg yolk*

*Boiled sweets, preferably clear with bright colours*

Pre-heat oven to 375°F/190°C/Gas mark 5. Line two
large baking sheets with non-stick baking
parchment.

● Sift the flour into a bowl. Blend in the butter until the
mixture resembles breadcrumbs. Stir in the sugar and
orange rind. Add the egg yolk and mix to a dough.

● Knead on a lightly floured surface for a few seconds,
then roll out to 3mm/⅛ in. With floured cutters, cut out
various Christmas shapes. Cut out the centres leaving a
border at least 5 mm/¼ in all round. Cut a hole in each
to hold a ribbon. Transfer to the baking sheets.

● Put the boiled sweets into plastic bags and coarsely
crush with a rolling pin. Sprinkle the crushed sweets
into the cut-out centres of the cookies. Bake for 8 to 10
minutes, until the cookies are golden and the sweets
have melted. Leave to cool completely on the baking
sheets. Thread ribbon through the holes in the top of
the cookies. Eat within 10 days.

# Snowballs

*Preparation time: 35 minutes* ● *Cooking time: 18 minutes* ● *Makes: About 12*

**These little coconut cookies are sandwiched together in pairs, then coated in more coconut to look like snowballs.**

## INGREDIENTS

*175 g/6 oz lightly salted butter*

*225 g/8 oz caster sugar*

*2 egg yolks*

*375 g/12 oz plain flour*

*½ tsp bicarbonate of soda*

*75 g/3 oz sweetened flaked coconut*

*2 Tbsp milk*

## DECORATION

*120 g/4 oz white chocolate*

*225 g/8 oz apricot jam*

*250 g/9 oz sweetened flaked coconut*

*Icing sugar, to dust (optional)*

Pre-heat oven to 375°F/190°C/Gas mark 5. Lightly grease two baking sheets or line with non-stick baking parchment.

● Beat the butter and sugar together until light and fluffy. Add the egg yolks and beat well. Sift the flour and bicarbonate together, then work into the butter mixture, with the sweetened flaked coconut and milk. Divide the mixture into 24 pieces and shape into balls. Place on the baking sheets, allowing 4 cm/1½ in for them to spread. Bake for 18 to 20 minutes, or until golden-brown. Remove from the baking sheets and cool on a wire rack.

● Break the white chocolate into squares and put in a small bowl over a pan of near-boiling water. Stir occasionally until melted. Dip one cookie into the chocolate and sandwich together with a second cookie to make 12 pairs. Leave to set for 20 minutes.

● Heat the apricot jam in a small pan until melted, then sift. Brush over the cookies, then roll in the sweetened flaked coconut to coat. If desired, pile up the snowballs on a plate and lightly dust with icing sugar before serving.

# White Chocolate Slices

*Preparation time: 30 minutes ● Cook time: 40 minutes ● Makes: 14*

**These slices are covered in coconut that looks like snow, to give them a really festive feel.**

## INGREDIENTS

*50 g/2 oz dates, stoned*

*Grated rind and juice of 2 oranges*

*50 g/2 oz lightly salted butter*

*120 g/4 oz light brown sugar*

*1 egg, beaten*

*50 mg/2 oz self-raising flour*

*120 g/4 oz plain flour*

## TOPPING

*5 Tbsp clear runny honey*

*175 g/6 oz sweetened flaked coconut*

*2 eggs, beaten*

*2 Tbsp sweetened flaked coconut, for sprinkling*

Pre-heat oven to 350°F/175°C/Gas mark 4. Grease and line an 18 x 28-cm/7 x 11-in shallow tin with non-stick parchment.

● Put the dates, orange rind and orange juice into a small pan and heat gently for about 15 minutes, until soft and pulpy. Leave to cool.

● Beat the butter and sugar together until mixed. Gradually add the egg, beating between each addition. Sift the flours together and stir into the mixture. Spread over the base of the prepared tin.

● Spread the date mixture over the base. For the topping, combine the honey, coconut and eggs. Spread evenly over the date mixture. Bake for 40 minutes until pale golden. Leave to cool in the tin then cut into slices. Sprinkle with the coconut flakes and serve.

# Cherry Garlands

*Preparation time: 40 minutes* ●
*Cooking time: 15 to 20 minutes* ● *Makes: About 20*

**These pretty piped cookies are decorated with glacé cherries and angelica.**

### INGREDIENTS

| |
|---|
| 50 g/2 oz icing sugar |
| 225 g/8 oz soft tub margarine |
| 225 g/8 oz plain flour |
| 50 g/2 oz cornflour |
| ½ tsp almond essence |
| 25 g/1 oz glacé cherries, very finely chopped |
| Glacé cherries and angelica, for decorating |
| 1 Tbsp icing sugar, for dredging |

Pre-heat oven to 375°F. Lightly grease two baking sheets or line with non-stick baking parchment.

● Sift the icing sugar into a bowl. Add the margarine and cream together until light and fluffy. Sift the flour and cornflour together and beat into the mixture with the almond essence and the chopped glacé cherries.

● Spoon half the mixture into a piping bag fitted with a 5-mm/½-in star nozzle. Pipe 5-cm/2-in rings onto the baking sheet, spacing apart. Decorate each cookie with quartered glacé cherries and pieces of angelica. Bake for 15 to 20 minutes until pale golden. Leave on the baking sheets for a few minutes, then transfer to a wire rack and allow to cool. Dredge with icing sugar before serving. Store cooled cookies in an airtight container with greaseproof paper between the layers.

# Walnut Macaroons

*Preparation time: 20 minutes* ● *Cooking time: 15 to 20 minutes* ● *Makes: About 20*

**Classic macaroons are made with ground almonds, but here walnuts are used instead. Lightly toasting the nuts before grinding intensifies their flavour. Try a batch using hazelnuts or a mixture of almonds and walnuts.**

### INGREDIENTS

| |
|---|
| 120 g/4 oz walnut pieces |
| 120 g/4 oz caster sugar |
| 1 egg white |
| Edible rice paper |
| 1 Tbsp caster sugar, for sprinkling |

Pre-heat oven to 350°F/175°C/Gas mark 4. Put the walnuts on a baking sheet and toast for 10 minutes, until lightly browned. Leave to cool then put in a food processor and process until finely ground.

● Mix the ground walnuts with the sugar and enough egg white to make a fairly stiff paste. Spoon into a piping bag fitted with a 5-mm/½-in plain nozzle and pipe small rounds onto a baking sheet lined with rice paper, spacing slightly apart.

● Lightly sprinkle the cookies with caster sugar. Bake for 15 to 20 minutes, until lightly browned. Transfer to a wire rack and carefully remove excess rice paper when the cookies are completely cool. Store in an airtight container.

# Rum-glazed Wreaths

*Preparation time: 35 minutes* ● *Cooking time: 15 minutes* ● *Makes: About 16*

**These cookies look impressive, but are very simple to make.**

### INGREDIENTS

*75 g/3 oz lightly salted butter*

*5 Tbsp light brown sugar*

*175 g/6 oz plain flour*

*½ tsp vanilla essence*

*1 Tbsp milk*

### RUM GLAZE

*120 g/4 oz icing sugar*

*4 tsp dark rum, orange-flavoured liqueur or lemon juice*

Pre-heat oven to 375°F/190°C/Gas mark 5. Lightly grease the base of two baking sheets or line them with non-stick baking parchment.

● Beat the butter and sugar until light and fluffy. Sift the flour and work into the mixture along with the vanilla essence and milk. On a floured surface, lightly knead the dough for a few seconds.

● Divide the dough into 16 pieces, then divide each piece into 8, and roll into balls. Arrange the balls in rings on the baking sheets, touching each other. Bake for 15 minutes until golden. Leave the balls to cool on the baking sheets.

● For the glaze, sift the icing sugar into a bowl and stir in the rum, orange liqueur or lemon juice. Brush over the cookies and leave to set on a wire rack before serving.

# Sugar and Spice Stars

*Preparation time: 10 minutes* ●
*Cooking time: 12 to 15 minutes* ● *Makes: About 12*

**These crisp spicy cookies are given a festive finish with a dusting of icing sugar and cinnamon.**

INGREDIENTS

*50 g/2 oz unsalted butter*

*50 g/2 oz caster sugar*

*Grated rind of ½ lemon*

*½ egg, beaten*

*5 Tbsp ground almonds*

*120 g/4 oz plain flour*

*½ tsp mixed spice*

*3 Tbsp raspberry jam*

*2 Tbsp icing sugar, for dusting*

*½ tsp ground cinnamon, for dusting*

Pre-heat oven to 350°F/175°C/Gas mark 4. Lightly grease two baking sheets or line with non-stick baking parchment.

● Beat the butter, sugar and lemon rind together until light and fluffy. Add the egg, a little at a time, beating well after each addition. Stir in the ground almonds, then sift in the flour and spice and mix to a dough. Lightly knead for a few seconds, then wrap in clingfilm and chill in the refrigerator for 30 minutes.

● Roll out the dough to about 3 mm/⅛ in on a lightly floured surface. Using a floured 8-cm/3-in star-shaped cutter, cut out 20 cookies and transfer to the baking sheets.

● Bake for 10 minutes, or until golden. Transfer to a wire rack to cool. Warm the raspberry jam and use to sandwich the cookies together in pairs. Dust with icing sugar, then with ground cinnamon before serving.

# Winter Logs

*Preparation time: 35 minutes* ●
*Cooking time: 12 minutes* ● *Makes: About 35*

**Dipping these meltingly light chocolate cookies in chocolate makes them twice as nice.**

INGREDIENTS

*175 g/6 oz unsalted butter, softened*

*5 Tbsp icing sugar*

*½ tsp vanilla essence*

*150 g/5 oz plain flour*

*25 g/1 oz unsweetened cocoa powder*

*5 Tbsp cornflour*

*125 g/4 oz plain chocolate*

*1 Tbsp icing sugar, for dusting*

Pre-heat oven to 350°F/175 °C/Gas mark 4. Line two baking sheets with non-stick baking parchment.

● Beat the butter, sugar and vanilla essence together until light and fluffy. Sift the flour, cocoa powder and cornflour together and fold in.

● Spoon the mixture into a piping bag fitted with a 1-cm/½-in star nozzle. Pipe 6-cm/2½-in lengths onto the baking sheets, spacing well apart. Bake the logs for 12 minutes, then remove from the baking sheets and transfer to wire racks to cool.

● Melt the chocolate in a bowl over a pan of near-boiling water. Dip both ends of the logs into the chocolate and leave to set on non-stick baking parchment. Dust with icing sugar before serving.

# Maple Moons

*Preparation time: 25 minutes + chilling* ● *Cooking time: 10 minutes* ● *Makes: 40*

**Use real maple syrup in these cookies; its taste is vastly superior to synthetic flavourings.**

### INGREDIENTS

*75 g/3 oz lightly salted butter*

*3 Tbsp light brown sugar*

*3 Tbsp maple syrup*

*1 egg yolk*

*120 g/4 oz plain flour*

*50 g/2 oz self-raising flour*

Lightly grease two baking sheets or line with non-stick baking parchment.

● Beat together the butter and sugar until light and fluffy. Beat in the maple syrup and egg yolk. Sift the flours together and work into the mixture to make a soft dough. Wrap the dough in clingfilm and then chill for 2 hours until firm.

● Pre-heat oven to 350°F/175°C/Gas mark 4.

● Roll out the dough on a lightly floured surface to 3 mm/⅛ in. Cut out moon shapes using a 6-cm/2½-in cutter and place on the baking sheets. Bake for 10 minutes, until golden-brown. Leave on the baking sheets for a few minutes to harden, then transfer to a wire rack and leave to cool.

### VARIATION

● Sandwich the moons together in pairs with coffee buttercream. Dissolve 2 teaspoons instant coffee powder in 2 teaspoons near-boiling water. Cream with 120 g/ 4 oz unsalted butter and 4 tablespoons sifted icing sugar until light and fluffy. Chill in the refrigerator for 15 minutes to firm slightly before serving.

# Catherine Wheels

*Preparation time: 40 minutes + chilling* ● *Cooking time: 10 to 12 minutes* ● *Makes: 40*

**Whirls of orange and chocolate dough make these cookies doubly delicious.**

### INGREDIENTS

*120 g/4 oz lightly salted butter*

*120 g/4 oz caster sugar*

*2 eggs, beaten*

*Grated rind of 1 orange*

*375 g/12 oz plain flour*

*25 g/1 oz unsweetened cocoa powder*

Lightly grease two baking sheets or line with non-stick baking parchment.

● Beat the butter and sugar until very light and fluffy. Divide the butter mixture in two. Work 200 g/7 oz flour and the orange rind into one half of the butter mixture and the remaining flour and the unsweetened cocoa powder into the other. Lightly knead each piece of dough for a few minutes.

● Roll out on a lightly floured surface to a rectangle measuring 25 x 15 cm/10 x 6 in. Lift the sheet of chocolate dough on top of the orange, then roll up like a Swiss roll. Wrap in clingfilm and chill for 2 hours.

● Pre-heat oven to 400°F/200°C/Gas mark 6.

● Cut the roll into 5-mm/¼-in slices and put on the baking sheets. Bake for 10 to 12 minutes, until darkened. Leave to cool on the baking sheets for a few minutes, then remove and cool on a wire rack.

### VARIATION

● For liquorice and vanilla wheels, omit the orange rind and add 1 teaspoon vanilla essence to one half of the dough and omit the unsweetened cocoa powder and add an extra 25 g/1 oz plain flour and 1 teaspoon black liquorice flavouring and colouring to the other half.

# Praline Sparklers

*Preparation time: 50 minutes ● Cooking time: 20 minutes ● Makes: 14*

**Sandwich these short almond cookies together in pairs with a creamy coffee filling,
then sprinkle with crushed praline, for the ultimate cookie.**

## INGREDIENTS

*150 g/5 oz plain flour*

*75 g/3 oz ground almonds*

*120 g/4 oz lightly salted butter*

*1 Tbsp icing sugar*

*1 egg yolk*

### FILLING AND TOPPING

*2 Tbsp plain flour*

*2 Tbsp caster sugar*

*1 egg yolk*

*3 Tbsp milk*

*3 Tbsp icing sugar*

*50 g/2 oz unsalted butter*

*1 tsp coffee essence*

### PRALINE

*120 g/4 oz granulated sugar*

*5 Tbsp flaked almonds*

Pre-heat oven to 350°F/175°C/Gas mark 4. Lightly grease two baking sheets or line with non-stick baking parchment.

● Sift the flour into a bowl. Stir in the ground almonds, then blend in the butter until the mixture resembles breadcrumbs. Sift the icing sugar and stir in. Add the egg yolk and mix to a dough.

● Lightly knead for a few seconds, then roll out on a lightly floured surface to 3 mm/⅛ in. Cut into rounds using a 6-cm/2½-in plain or fluted cutter. Place on the baking sheets. Bake for 10 minutes, until lightly browned. Transfer to a wire rack to cool.

● For the filling, put the flour and sugar in a small saucepan. Gradually blend in the egg yolk and milk to make a smooth paste. Bring to the boil and cook for 1 to 2 minutes until thick, stirring all the time. Leave to cool. Sift the icing sugar into a bowl. Add the butter and beat until light. Add the coffee essence and mix well. Beat in the cooled custard, a little at a time. Chill in the refrigerator for 30 minutes.

● For the praline, put the sugar and 2 tablespoons water in a heavy-bottomed saucepan and heat gently until the sugar has completely dissolved. Bring to the boil and cook until a rich golden-brown. Add the nuts and pour onto an oiled baking sheet. Leave until cold, then crush the praline coarsely.

● Sandwich pairs of cookies together with the coffee cream. Spread the top cookie with coffee cream and sprinkle with crushed praline.

# Vanilla Fudge Crumbles

*Preparation time: 30 minutes + chilling* • *Cooking time: 12 minutes* • *Makes: About 20*

**Chunks of creamy fudge contrast beautifully with the crunchy texture of these substantial cookies.**

## INGREDIENTS

*75 g/3 oz vanilla fudge*

*225 g/8 oz plain flour*

*½ tsp bicarbonate of soda*

*120 g/4 oz unsalted butter*

*120 g/4 oz light brown sugar*

*1 egg*

*1 tsp vanilla essence*

*Icing sugar, for dusting*

Pre-heat oven to 375°F/190°C/Gas mark 5. Lightly grease two baking sheets or line with non-stick baking parchment.

● Finely chop the fudge. Sift the flour and bicarbonate into a bowl. Blend in the butter until the mixture resembles fine breadcrumbs. Stir in the sugar. Mix the egg and vanilla essence together and add to the dry ingredients with the chopped fudge. Mix to a firm dough.

● Turn out onto a lightly floured surface and shape into a cylinder 23 cm/9 in long. Wrap and chill in the refrigerator for 30 minutes. Cut into 20 slices and put the slices on the baking sheets, spaced slightly apart.

● Bake for 12 minutes, until golden-brown. Leave on the baking sheets for 5 minutes, then transfer to a wire rack to cool. Lightly dust with icing sugar before serving.

## VARIATIONS

● Try different flavoured fudges in the cookies for a change; chocolate, coffee or rum and raisin fudge all taste delicious.

# Triple Ginger Cookies

*Preparation time: 30 minutes + chilling* ●
*Cooking time: 10 minutes* ● *Makes: About 36*

**These festive cookies are packed with ginger – ground, crystallized and fresh – not for the faint-hearted.**

### INGREDIENTS

| |
|---|
| 250 g/9 oz plain flour |
| 1 Tbsp ground ginger |
| 2 Tbsp bicarbonate of soda |
| ½ tsp salt |
| 175 g/6 oz unsalted butter, softened |
| 200 g/7 oz dark brown sugar |
| 6 Tbsp treacle |
| 1 egg |
| 2 Tbsp finely chopped root ginger |
| 50 g/2 oz chopped crystallized ginger, plus extra for decoration |

Into a medium bowl, sift together the flour, ground ginger, bicarbonate and salt.

● In a large bowl, beat the butter until soft, beat in the sugar until the mixture is light and fluffy. Beat in the treacle and egg until combined. Stir in the flour-spice mixture followed by the fresh and crystallized ginger.

● Form the dough into a ball, wrap in clingfilm and refrigerate for 2 to 3 hours, or overnight until chilled.

● Pre-heat oven to 350°F/175°C/Gas mark 4. Grease or line two baking sheets.

● Using a tablespoon to scoop up the mixture, form into 5-mm/½-in balls. Place 5 cm/2 in apart on baking sheets and press a few pieces of crystallized ginger into each. Bake until golden-brown, about 10 minutes. Leave the cookies to cool for 2 minutes, then transfer to wire racks to cool completely. Store in an airtight container.

# Kourambiedes

*Preparation time: 25 minutes + chilling* ●
*Cooking time: 15 to 20 minutes* ● *Makes: About 30*

**These rich, tender almond cookies are served at all festive occasions in Greece. At Christmas a whole clove is often buried in the cookies to symbolize the gifts the three wise men brought to the Christ child.**

### INGREDIENTS

| |
|---|
| 50 g/2 oz blanched almonds, lightly toasted and cooled |
| 225 g/8 oz unsalted butter |
| 2 Tbsp icing sugar |
| ¼ tsp salt |
| 1 small egg yolk |
| 1 Tbsp brandy or orange-flavoured liqueur |
| 225 g/8 oz plain flour |
| Icing sugar, for dusting |

In a food processor fitted with a metal blade, process the cooled toasted almonds until very fine crumbs are formed.

● In a medium bowl, beat the butter until soft, beat in the sugar until the mixture becomes light and fluffy. Beat in the salt, egg yolk and brandy until combined. Stir in the flour and ground almonds until a soft dough forms. Refrigerate, covered, until firm, about 1 hour.

● Pre-heat oven to 450°F/230°C/Gas mark 8.

● Use a tablespoon to scoop out dough, and form into 2.5-cm/1-in balls. Place on ungreased baking sheets, and bake until set and just golden, about 15 to 20 minutes. Allow to cool slightly, then transfer the cookies onto wire racks to cool completely. Dust with icing sugar. Store in an airtight container.

# Cookie Canes

*Preparation time: 20 minutes + chilling ●*
*Cooking time: 15 to 17 minutes ● Makes: About 24*

**This dough can be shaped into canes or Christmas
wreaths, then tinted whatever colour you like.**

### INGREDIENTS

225 g/8 oz unsalted butter, softened

175 g/6 oz icing sugar

½ tsp vanilla essence

¼ tsp peppermint essence

300 g/10 oz plain flour, sifted

¼ tsp salt

¼ tsp red food colouring, optional

50 g/2 oz crushed peppermint sweets

In a large bowl, beat the butter until soft, beat in the
sugar until the mixture becomes light and fluffy. Beat
in the egg, vanilla and peppermint essences until
combined. Stir in the flour and salt until well-blended.
● Place half the dough in clingfilm and seal. Add food
colouring and crushed peppermint sweets to the
remaining dough and beat until mixed. Wrap in
clingfilm and refrigerate both doughs for 1 hour.
● Pre-heat oven to 350°F/175°C/Gas mark 4. Grease two
baking sheets or line with non-stick baking parchment.
● To form canes, use a teaspoon to scoop out a piece of
plain dough then roll into a 10-cm/4-in long log shape.
Repeat with the red-coloured dough. Twist the two logs
together, and bend the top end to form into a cane
shape. Set canes 5 cm/2 in apart on baking sheets.
● Bake until firm, about 8 to 10 minutes; do not allow
to brown. Cool for a few minutes then place on wire
racks to cool completely. Store in an airtight container.

# Brandied Shortbread

*Preparation time: 25 minutes ●*
*Cooking time: 25 minutes ● Makes: 8 wedges*

**This buttery brandy-flavoured shortbread is enhanced
by the addition of rice flour, giving it a lighter and
crunchier texture.**

### INGREDIENTS

120 g/4 oz unsalted butter, softened

120 g/4 oz caster sugar

1 Tbsp brandy

Few drops brandy essence

120 g/4 oz plain flour

5 Tbsp fine rice flour

4 Tbsp glacé cherries

Few pieces angelica

1 Tbsp caster sugar, for sprinkling

Pre-heat oven to 350°F/175°C/Gas mark 4. Beat the
butter in a mixing bowl, then gradually add the
sugar, brandy and brandy essence. Add the flour and rice
flour and stir with a thin metal spatula until blended.
● Press the mixture into an 18-cm/7-in round shallow
tin with a removable base and level the top. Prick all
over with a fork. Mark into eight equal wedges and
decorate each with glacé cherries and angelica. Sprinkle
the wedges with caster sugar and bake for 25 minutes,
or until pale golden.
● While the shortbread is still hot, carefully remove
from the tin, but leave on the base. Cut into eight
wedges, as marked, but do not separate the pieces, or
they will dry out. Transfer to a wire rack to cool. Stored
in an airtight tin or wrapped in foil, the shortbread will
keep for up to a week.

# Cranberry and Orange Clusters

*Preparation time: 20 minutes* ●
*Cooking time: 15 minutes* ● *Makes: 20*

**The tartness of dried cranberries adds a certain bite to these soft-textured drop cookies.**

### INGREDIENTS

| |
|---|
| *120 g/4 oz unsalted butter* |
| *120 g/4 oz caster sugar* |
| *Grated rind of 1 orange* |
| *1 egg* |
| *120 g/4 oz rolled oats* |
| *50 g/2 oz dried cranberries* |
| *150 g/5 oz plain flour* |
| *½ tsp baking powder* |

Pre-heat oven to 350°F/175°C/Gas mark 4. Lightly grease two baking sheets or line with non-stick baking parchment.

● Beat the butter, sugar and orange rind in a bowl until creamy. Gradually add the egg, beating well between each addition. Stir in the oats and cranberries. Sift the flour and baking powder into the bowl and mix until evenly combined.

● Place small tablespoons of the mixture on the prepared baking sheets, spacing them well apart. Flatten slightly with the back of a fork. Bake for 15 minutes until risen and light golden-brown. Leave on the baking sheets for 5 minutes, then transfer to a wire rack to cool. The cookies will still be soft when you take them out of the oven, but will become firm as they cool.

# Pumpkin Fingers

*Preparation time: 30 minutes* ●
*Cooking time: 50 minutes* ● *Makes: 18*

**These buttery shortbread fingers with a pumpkin topping could be served for a Thanksgiving or Halloween party.**

### INGREDIENTS

| |
|---|
| *120 g/4 oz plain flour* |
| *50 g/2 oz icing sugar* |
| *50 g/2 oz unsalted butter* |
| *1 egg yolk* |

### TOPPING

| |
|---|
| *120 g/4 oz cooked pumpkin* |
| *225 ml/8 fl oz single cream* |
| *2 eggs, beaten* |
| *225 g/8 oz light brown sugar* |
| *1 tsp ground cinnamon* |
| *1 Tbsp icing sugar, for dusting* |

Pre-heat oven to 350°F/175°C/Gas mark 4. Grease a shallow 18 x 28-cm/7 x 11-in tin and line with non-stick baking parchment.

● Sift the flour and icing sugar into a bowl. Blend in the butter until the mixture resembles fine breadcrumbs. Add the egg yolk and mix to a dough. Lightly knead on a floured surface until smooth, then press into the base of the tin. Prick all over with a fork, then bake for 10 minutes, until golden.

● For the filling, sieve the cooked pumpkin to make a smooth purée. Stir in the cream, eggs, sugar and cinnamon. Pour over the base and bake for 40 to 45 minutes more, or until a skewer inserted into the middle comes out clean.

● Leave to cool in the tin, then cut into 18 fingers. Remove from the tin and lightly dust with icing sugar before serving.

# Sticky Toffee Apple Treats

*Preparation time: 25 minutes* ● *Cooking time: 10 minutes* ● *Makes: 20*

**These autumn cookies are packed with chunks of apple and drizzled with toffee icing.**

### INGREDIENTS

*120 g/4 oz lightly salted butter*

*120 g/4 oz light brown sugar*

*1 egg, beaten*

*200 g/7 oz self-raising flour*

*Pinch of salt*

*120 g/4 oz dried apples, chopped*

### ICING

*50 g/2 oz butter*

*5 Tbsp light brown sugar*

*3 Tbsp milk*

*75 g/3 oz icing sugar*

Pre-heat oven to 375°F/190°C/Gas mark 5. Lightly grease two baking sheets or line with non-stick baking parchment.

● Beat the butter and sugar until light and fluffy. Gradually add the egg, beating well each time. Sift the flour and salt into the mixture and mix in the apples.

● Place heaped teaspoonfuls of the mixture onto the prepared baking sheets, spacing well apart to allow the cookies to spread. Bake for 10 minutes or until just golden-brown. Leave on the baking sheets for 3 minutes, then remove and cool on a wire rack.

● For the toffee icing, melt the butter over a gentle heat. Add the brown sugar and milk and stir gently until dissolved. Boil for 1 minute. Remove from the heat, then sift the icing sugar and beat in. Spoon into a piping bag while still warm, snip off the end and drizzle over the cookies. Ice the cookies quickly before the icing cools and starts to harden. Leave the icing to set.

# Shooting Stars

*Preparation time: 40 minutes* ● *Cooking time: 10 to 12 minutes* ● *Makes: 30*

**Cut these cookies into stars of several sizes and sprinkle with coloured sugar crystals before baking, for a sparkling effect.**

## INGREDIENTS

*120 g/4 oz lightly salted butter*

*120 g/4 oz caster sugar*

*Grated rind of 1 lemon*

*1 egg, beaten*

*250 g/9 oz plain flour*

*25 g/1 oz cornflour*

*½ tsp vanilla essence*

*3 Tbsp coloured sugar crystals*

Pre-heat oven to 350°F/175°C/Gas mark 4. Lightly grease two baking sheets or line with non-stick baking parchment.

● Beat the butter, sugar and lemon rind until pale and fluffy. Gradually add the egg, beating after each addition.

● Sift the flour and cornflour together and blend into the butter mixture with the vanilla essence. Lightly knead for a few seconds until smooth. Roll out on a floured surface to 1 cm/¼ in thick, then cut into large and small star shapes using 6-cm/2½-in, 4-cm/1½-in and 2.5-cm/1-in floured cutters. Place on the prepared baking sheets, separating the largest stars.

● Sprinkle with sugar crystals, then press them down gently. Bake the smaller cookies for 10 minutes and the larger ones for 12 minutes. Cool on the baking sheets for 3 minutes, then transfer to a wire rack to cool.

# Celebration Cookies

*Preparation time: 35 minutes* ● *Cooking time: 15 minutes* ● *Makes: 8*

**These traditional all-American giant cookies are drizzled with icing in the colours of the flag – red, white, and blue. Vary the icing colours to suit your own flag.**

### INGREDIENTS

*50 g/2 oz lightly salted butter*

*120 g/4 oz white vegetable fat*

*5 Tbsp light brown sugar*

*1 egg, beaten*

*½ tsp vanilla essence*

*150 g/5 oz self-raising flour*

### ICING

*120 g/4 oz icing sugar*

*1 Tbsp hot water*

*Red and blue food colouring*

Pre-heat oven to 375°F/190°C/Gas mark 5. Lightly grease two baking sheets or line with non-stick baking parchment.

● Beat the butter, white vegetable fat and sugar together until light and fluffy. Gradually add the egg and vanilla essence, beating well between each addition. Sift the flour and stir into the mixture.

● Drop tablespoonfuls of the mixture onto the baking sheets, spacing well apart. Flatten to about 2 cm/¾ in thick. Bake for 15 minutes until golden. Leave on the baking sheets for 2 to 3 minutes, then remove and cool on a wire rack.

● Sift the icing sugar into a bowl and stir in enough water to make a thick piping consistency. Divide the icing into three. Leave one white, colour one red, and one blue. Spoon into separate piping bags, snip off the ends and drizzle over the cookies. Leave to set before serving.

### TIP

Unbaked, the cookie mixture will keep in a sealed container in the refrigerator for up to a week. The cookies are best eaten on the day they are iced.

# Coffee Meringues

*Preparation time: 20 minutes* ●
*Cooking time: 2 hours* ● *Makes: 50*

**Light as air crisp meringues with just a hint of coffee, are
dipped in smooth chocolate for bite-sized treats.**

### INGREDIENTS

4 egg whites

225 g/8 oz caster sugar

1 tsp coffee essence

225 g/8 oz plain chocolate

Pre-heat oven to 275°F/140°C/Gas mark 1. Lightly
grease two baking sheets or line with non-stick
baking parchment.

● Put the egg whites and sugar into a large bowl over a
pan of very hot water and whisk until stiff and shiny,
making sure that the water does not boil, or the mixture
will get too hot. Remove the bowl from the heat, add the
coffee essence and continue whisking until the mixture
will hold stiff peaks.

● Spoon the mixture into a piping bag fitted with a
large star nozzle and pipe swirls of meringue on the
baking sheets. Bake for 2 hours or until completely
dried out, switching the baking sheets around halfway
through cooking. Allow the meringues to cool on the
baking sheets.

● Melt the chocolate in a bowl over very hot water. Dip
the base of the meringues into the chocolate and leave
to set on greaseproof paper before serving, or if
prefered, sandwich the meringues together in pairs.

# Cinnamon Balls

*Preparation time: 20 minutes* ●
*Cooking time: 25 to 30 minutes* ● *Makes: About 20*

**These are very popular Passover cookies,
as they contain no flour.**

### INGREDIENTS

225 g/8 oz blanched and ground almonds, walnuts, or pecan nuts

250 g/7 oz caster sugar

2 Tbsp ground cinnamon

2 egg whites

¼ tsp cream of tartar

200 g/7 oz icing sugar

Pre-heat oven to 325°F/160°C/Gas mark 3. Grease
or line two baking sheets with non-stick baking
parchment.

● In a medium bowl, combine the nuts, half the sugar,
and half the cinnamon. In a separate bowl, beat the egg
whites until foamy. Add the cream of tartar, and
continue beating until soft peaks form. Gradually add
the remaining sugar, a tablespoon at a time, beating well
after each addition, until the whites are stiff and glossy.
Gently fold in the nut mixture.

● With moistened hands, shape mixture into walnut-
size balls. Place on baking sheets 2.5 cm/1 in apart. Bake
until set and golden, 25 to 30 minutes, turning baking
sheets halfway through cooking. Allow the cookies to
cool slightly.

● Combine the icing sugar and remaining cinnamon.
Roll each warm cinnamon ball in the mixture to coat
completely, then set on a wire rack to cool. Roll balls in
the cinnamon-sugar again when cold. Store in an
airtight container.

# Hanukkah Sugar Cookies

*Preparation time: 45 minutes + chilling* ● *Cooking time: 20 to 24 minutes* ● *Makes: About 40*

**Search out some unusual cutters for this special joyous holiday, or make your own
Jewish star template from a piece of cardboard.**

### INGREDIENTS

*250 g/9 oz plain flour*

*½ tsp baking powder*

*½ tsp salt*

*175 g/6 oz unsalted butter, softened*

*200 g/7 oz caster sugar*

*1 egg, beaten*

*Grated rind of 1 lemon*

*1 Tbsp lemon juice*

*1 tsp vanilla essence*

*½ tsp lemon essence*

### ICING

*450 g/1 lb icing sugar*

*2–3 Tbsp milk*

*1 Tbsp lemon juice*

*Blue food colouring*

Into a medium bowl, sift together the flour, baking powder and salt. In a large bowl beat the butter, until creamy, then add the sugar and beat until light and fluffy. Gradually beat in the egg, lemon rind and juice, vanilla and lemon essences until well blended. Little by little add the flour mixture until a soft dough forms.

Wrap in clingfilm and refrigerate for several hours or overnight until firm enough to roll (the dough can be made up to 2 days ahead).

● Pre-heat oven to 350°F/175°C/Gas mark 4. Grease or line two baking sheets with non-stick baking parchment.

● On a lightly floured surface, roll out half the dough to 5 mm/¼ in thick (keep the remaining dough refrigerated). Using a floured cutter or template, cut out as many shapes as possible. Place 2.5 cm/1 in apart on the baking sheets. Bake until golden, 10 to 12 minutes. Allow the cookies to cool slightly, then transfer to wire racks to cool completely. Repeat with remaining dough.

● In a medium bowl, sift the icing sugar. Stir in 2 tablespoons of milk and the lemon juice, adding a little more milk if the mixture is too thick. Spoon half of the icing into a separate bowl and add a few drops of food colouring mixing to the desired shade. Spoon the icings into two piping bags and pipe designs or decorations onto each cookie shape. Leave icing to set for 2 hours. Store in an airtight container with a layer of greaseproof paper between each of the cookie layers.

# Sweethearts

*Preparation time: 45 minutes* ● *Cooking time: 10 minutes* ● *Makes: 20*

**Use gingerbread men and women cutters to make these cute cookies with tiny hearts.**

## INGREDIENTS

| | |
|---|---|
| 1 Tbsp golden syrup | 1 egg yolk |
| 50 g/2 oz butter | 50 g/2 oz pink or red boiled sweets |
| 50 g/2 oz caster sugar | ICING |
| 225 g/8 oz plain flour | 225 g/8 oz icing sugar |
| ½ tsp bicarbonate of soda | 1 egg white |
| 3 Tbsp milk | ¼ tsp lemon juice |

Pre-heat oven to 350°F/175°C/Gas mark 4. Line two baking sheets with non-stick baking parchment.

● Put the syrup, butter and sugar in a small saucepan and heat gently until melted, stirring occasionally. Remove from the heat and leave to cool for 2 to 3 minutes. Sift the flour and bicarbonate into a mixing bowl and make a well in the middle. Pour in the syrup mixture, milk and egg yolk. Mix to form a soft smooth dough.

● Roll out the warm dough between two sheets of non-stick baking parchment or clingfilm until 3 mm/⅛ in thick. Cut into men and women using 8-cm/3-in cutters. Transfer to the baking sheets. Cut a small heart shape from the centre of each.

● Roughly crush the boiled sweets and sprinkle about a quarter of a candy in each cutout section. Bake for 10 minutes, until lightly browned and firm. Leave to cool on the baking sheets.

● Sift the icing sugar twice. Put the egg white in a bowl and whisk lightly. Gradually beat in enough icing sugar until the mixture stands in soft peaks and is a pipeable consistency. Spoon into a piping bag fitted with a very fine nozzle and pipe faces, buttons and bows on the people. Leave to set.

# Honeyed Hearts

*Preparation time: 20 minutes + chilling ●*
*Cooking time: 15 minutes ● Makes: 30*

**These honey cookies with a crunchy sugar topping will melt even the hardest heart.**

### INGREDIENTS

| |
|---|
| *75 g/3 oz lightly salted butter* |
| *120 g/4 oz caster sugar* |
| *1 Tbsp set honey* |
| *1 egg, beaten* |
| *175 g/6 oz plain flour* |
| *2 Tbsp cornflour* |
| *1 Tbsp egg white* |
| *2 Tbsp brown sugar crystals* |

Pre-heat oven to 350°F/175°C/Gas mark 4. Lightly grease two baking sheets or line with non-stick baking parchment.

● Beat the butter, sugar and honey until very soft, light and fluffy. Gradually add the egg. Sift the flour and cornflour together and work into the butter mixture to make a soft dough. Lightly knead on a floured surface for a few seconds until smooth, then wrap in clingfilm and chill in the refrigerator for 30 minutes.

● Roll out on a lightly floured surface to a thickness of 5 mm/¼ in. Cut into heart shapes using a floured 5-cm/2-in cutter. Place on the baking sheets, spacing slightly apart. Brush the cookies with egg white and sprinkle each with a few sugar crystals. Bake for 15 minutes, or until lightly browned. Leave the cookies on the baking sheets for 2 to 3 minutes, then remove and cool on a wire rack.

# Rose Petal Cookies

*Preparation time: 25 minutes + chilling ●*
*Cooking time: 10 minutes ● Makes: 16*

**Make these fragrant cookies using red or yellow perfumed rose petals.**

### INGREDIENTS

| |
|---|
| *250 g/9 oz plain flour* |
| *120 g/4 oz icing sugar* |
| *200 g/7 oz unsalted butter* |
| *Petals of 2 roses* |

Lightly grease two baking sheets or line with non-stick baking parchment. Sift the flour and icing sugar into a bowl. Blend in the butter until the mixture resembles fine breadcrumbs.

● Snip the rose petals into small pieces with scissors and stir into the mixture. Continue to blend with your fingers until a dough forms. Lightly knead for a few seconds on a floured surface until smooth. Roll the dough into a cylinder about 20 cm/8 in long. Wrap in clingfilm and chill in the refrigerator for 1 hour.

● Pre-heat oven to 325°F/160°C/Gas mark 3. Cut the dough into 1-cm/½-in slices and arrange on the baking sheets, spacing slightly apart. Bake for 8 to 10 minutes until light golden-brown. Leave on the baking sheets for 2 minutes, then remove and cool on a wire rack.

### TIP

Make sure you use unsprayed freshly picked roses for these cookies.

# Lovers' Knots

*Preparation time: 45 minutes + chilling* ●
*Cooking time: 10 minutes* ● *Makes: 20*

**Rich, dark and handsome, chocolate dough is twisted into knots, then dipped into yet more chocolate.**

### INGREDIENTS

| |
|---|
| *50 g/2 oz unsweetened cocoa powder* |
| *2 Tbsp boiling water* |
| *1 tsp vanilla essence* |
| *120 g/4 oz lightly salted butter* |
| *120 g/4 oz icing sugar* |
| *1 egg, beaten* |
| *225 g/8 oz plain flour* |
| *375 g/12 oz plain chocolate* |

Lightly grease two baking sheets or line with non-stick baking parchment. Sift the unsweetened cocoa powder into a small bowl and pour on the boiling water. Stir to form a smooth paste, then stir in the vanilla essence.

● Beat the butter and sugar until light and fluffy. Gradually add the egg, beating well after each addition. Beat in the cocoa mixture until well mixed. Sift the flour and work into the mixture to make a soft dough. Wrap in clingfilm and chill for 1 hour.

● Pre-heat oven to 325°F/160°C/Gas mark 3. Divide the dough into 20 pieces. Roll each piece into a sausage shape about 15 cm/6 in long, then tie in a loose knot, tucking the ends under. Arrange on the prepared baking sheets and bake for 10 minutes until firm. Allow to cool on the sheets.

● Break the chocolate into pieces and melt, stirring, in a double boiler. Coat the knots, one at a time, with the chocolate. Leave to set on a wire rack.

# Soft Centres

*Preparation time: 25 minutes + chilling* ●
*Cooking time: 10 minutes* ● *Makes: 20*

**A crisp coffee case conceals a melted chocolate centre. Serve these cookies freshly baked while still warm.**

### INGREDIENTS

| |
|---|
| *150 g/5 oz unsalted butter* |
| *200 g/7 oz caster sugar* |
| *2 tsp coffee essence* |
| *1 egg yolk* |
| *300 g/10 oz self-raising flour* |
| *50 g/2 oz plain chocolate* |
| *50 g/2 oz white chocolate* |
| *1 Tbsp unsweetened cocoa powder, for dusting* |

Lightly grease a large baking sheet or line with non-stick baking parchment. Beat the butter and sugar until light and fluffy. Beat in the coffee essence and egg yolk. Sift the flour into the bowl and mix to a firm dough. Wrap and chill in the refrigerator for 20 minutes.

● Pre-heat oven to 350°F/175°C/Gas mark 4.

● Roll out about a third of the dough on a lightly floured surface to 3 mm/⅛ in thick and cut out 20 circles with a 5-cm/2-in cutter. Transfer to the prepared baking sheet. Place a square of chocolate in the middle of each circle. Roll out the remaining dough and cut out 20 circles with a 6-cm/2½-in cutter. Lay these over the chocolate-topped bases, pressing the edges together to seal and enclose the filling.

● Bake for 10 minutes, until darkened and risen. Leave on the baking sheets for 5 minutes, then remove and cool on a wire rack. Dust with cocoa powder before serving.

# Shamrocks

*Preparation time: 25 minutes + chilling* ● *Cooking time: 15 minutes* ● *Makes: 20*

**The shamrock is the emblem of Ireland is and these cookies are ideal to serve on St Patrick's day.**

### INGREDIENTS

*50 g/2 oz mint-flavoured chocolate sticks*

*175 g/6 oz butter*

*225 g/8 oz caster sugar*

*1 egg*

*375 g/12 oz plain flour*

### ICING

*225 g/8 oz icing sugar*

*¼ tsp peppermint essence*

*2 Tbsp hot water*

*Green food colouring*

Lightly grease two baking sheets or line with non-stick baking parchment. Finely chop the mint-flavoured chocolate sticks. Beat the butter and sugar until light and fluffy. Gradually add the egg, beating well after each addition. Sift the flour into the bowl, add the chocolate pieces, and mix to a soft dough. Lightly knead for a few seconds until smooth, then wrap in clingfilm and chill in the refrigerator for 30 minutes.

● Pre-heat oven to 350°F/175°C/Gas mark 4. Roll out the dough on a lightly floured surface until 5 mm/¼ in thick and cut into shamrock shapes with a 6-cm/2½-in cutter. Transfer to the baking sheets. Bake for 15 minutes, until light golden-brown. Leave on the baking sheets for 2 to 3 minutes, then remove and cool on a wire rack.

● Sift the icing sugar into a bowl. Add the peppermint essence and enough water to make a thick icing. Stir in a drop of green food colouring. Use to ice the cookies. Leave the icing to set before serving.

# Sedgemoor Easter Biscuits

*Preparation time: 15 minutes* ● *Cooking time: 20 minutes* ● *Makes: 16*

**Legend has it that when the Duke of Monmouth was fleeing the Battle of Sedgemoor, he fell into a ditch. A local woman thought he was an unfortunate peasant down on his luck and baked him these cookies.**

### INGREDIENTS

*225 g/8 oz plain flour*

*1 tsp ground cinnamon*

*120 g/4 oz lightly salted butter*

*120 g/4 oz caster sugar*

*50 g/2 oz currants*

*1 egg, beaten*

*2 Tbsp brandy*

*1 Tbsp milk*

*1 Tbsp granulated sugar, for sprinkling*

Pre-heat oven to 350°F/175 °C/Gas mark 4. Lightly grease two baking sheets or line with non-stick baking parchment.

● Sift the flour and cinnamon into a bowl and blend in the butter until the mixture resembles breadcrumbs. Stir in the sugar and currants. Mix the egg, brandy and milk together and stir into the dry mixture to produce a soft dropping consistency.

● Drop tablespoonfuls of the mixture onto the baking sheet and sprinkle with granulated sugar. Bake for 20 minutes, until lightly browned and firm. Leave on the baking sheets for a few minutes, then remove and cool on a wire rack.

### VARIATION

Mixed dried fruit or quartered glacé cherries can be added to the mixture instead of currants.

# Iced Easter Ovals

*Preparation time: 25 minutes ● Cooking time: 15 minutes ● Makes: 20*

**These chocolate chip cookies with pastel ribbon and bow icing make great Easter treats.**

## INGREDIENTS

*50 g/2 oz butter*

*225 g/8 oz caster sugar*

*1 egg, beaten*

*375 g/12 oz plain flour*

*2 Tbsp cornflour*

*5 Tbsp plain chocolate chips*

### ICING

*225 g/8 oz icing sugar*

*2 Tbsp hot water*

*Pink, green and yellow food colouring*

Pre-heat oven to 350°F/175°C/Gas mark 4. Lightly grease two baking sheets or line with non-stick baking parchment.

● Beat the butter and sugar until light and fluffy. Gradually add the egg. Sift the flour with the cornflour and work into the butter mixture with the chocolate chips to make a stiff dough. Lightly knead the dough for a few seconds until smooth.

● Roll out on a floured surface to a thickness of 5 mm/¼ in. Cut into 20 ovals with a plain or fluted 8-cm/3-in oval cutter. Bake in the oven for 15 minutes, until light golden-brown. Leave to cool on the baking sheets for a few minutes, then cool on a wire rack.

● For the icing, sift the icing sugar into a bowl and stir in enough hot water to make a smooth frosting. Divide the icing into three and colour one pale pink, one pale green and one yellow. Spoon into piping bags, snip off the ends and pipe a ribbon and bow design on each cookie. Leave to set before serving.

# Maypole Twists

*Preparation time: 40 minutes + chilling* ● *Cooking time: 10 minutes* ● *Makes: 12*

**Strands of dough, one coated in coloured sugar crystals are twisted together to make these cookies.**

## INGREDIENTS

*225 g/8 oz plain flour*

*1 tsp baking powder*

*120 g/4 oz unsalted butter*

*120 g/4 oz caster sugar*

*Grated rind of 1 lemon*

*1 Tbsp lemon juice*

*1 egg, beaten*

*2 Tbsp yellow and orange sugar crystals*

Line two baking sheets with non-stick baking parchment. Sift the flour and baking powder into a bowl. Blend in the butter until the mixture resembles fine breadcrumbs. Stir in the sugar and lemon rind. Add the lemon juice and beaten egg and mix to a soft dough. Lightly knead for a few seconds until smooth. Wrap in clingfilm and chill in the refrigerator for 30 minutes.

● Pre-heat oven to 350°F/175°C/Gas mark 4. Divide the dough into 24 pieces. Roll each into a 10-cm/4-in length, then roll 12 of the lengths in the sugar crystals. Place 2 lengths side by side, one sugar-coated and one plain, and press the top ends together. Twist the two lengths together, pressing the ends to join again at the finish and trimming.

● Place on the prepared baking sheets, spacing slightly apart, and bake for 10 minutes until light golden-brown. Leave on the baking sheets for 2 minutes, then remove and cool on a wire rack.

## VARIATION

● If preferred the twists can be glazed with a lemon icing instead of using the sugar crystals. Sift 120 g/4 oz icing sugar into a bowl. Stir in 5 teaspoons lemon juice to make a thin icing. Lightly brush over the twists while still warm. Leave the cookies to cool and the icing to set before serving.

# Cattern Cakes

*Preparation time: 25 minutes* ●
*Cooking time: 10 minutes* ● *Makes: 15*

**These cookies were served on November 25 in honour of St Catherine, martyred in AD 310, who gave her name to the Catherine Wheel firework. She became the protector of unmarried girls who would crown her statue with a wreath of greenery in the hope of finding a husband.**

### INGREDIENTS

120 g/4 oz lightly salted butter

120 g/4 oz caster sugar

1 egg, beaten

225 g/8 oz plain flour

¼ tsp baking powder

½ tsp ground cinnamon

½ cup ground almonds

2 Tbsp currants

1 Tbsp caraway seeds

4 Tbsp seedless raspberry jam

Pre-heat oven to 350°F/175°C/Gas mark 4. Lightly grease two baking sheets or line with non-stick baking parchment.

● Beat the butter and sugar together, then gradually add the egg, beating between each addition. Sift the flour, baking powder and cinnamon into the bowl and stir into the mixture with the ground almonds, currants and caraway seeds to make a dough. Lightly knead on a floured surface until smooth. Roll out the dough into a 25 x 30-cm/10 x 12-in rectangle.

● Warm the jam in a small pan until runny and thinly brush over the dough. Roll up from one of the long sides like a Swiss roll and cut into 5-mm/¾-in thick slices. Arrange on the baking sheets, spacing slightly apart and bake for 10 minutes. Leave on the baking sheets for 5 minutes, then transfer to a wire rack to cool.

# Honey and Oat Bites

*Preparation time: 20 minutes* ●
*Cooking time: 20 minutes* ● *Makes: 30*

**Use the thicker whole rolled oats for these substantial cookies with their crisp edges and slightly chewy centres.**

### INGREDIENTS

2 Tbsp set honey

175 g/6 oz lightly salted butter

120 g/4 oz caster sugar

150 g/5 oz rolled oats

75 g/3 oz sweetened flaked coconut

150 g/5 oz plain flour

1 tsp bicarbonate of soda

1 Tbsp hot water

Pre-heat oven to 325°F/160°C/Gas mark 3. Lightly grease two baking sheets or line with non-stick baking parchment.

● Put the honey, butter and sugar in a small pan and heat gently until the butter has melted and the sugar dissolved. Remove from the heat and stir in the oats, coconut and flour. Blend the bicarbonate with the water, add to the mixture, and stir well.

● Shape the mixture into 30 balls and place on the baking sheets, spacing well apart. Bake for 20 minutes until golden-brown. Leave on the trays for 10 minutes, then transfer to a wire rack to cool.

# Whisky and Ginger Shortbreads

*Preparation time: 30 minutes* ● *Cooking time: 40 minutes* ● *Makes: 16*

**Join the celebrations with these special shortbread fingers.**

## INGREDIENTS

| |
|---|
| *225 g/8 oz unsalted butter* |
| *120 g/4 oz caster sugar* |
| *2 egg yolks* |
| *1 Tbsp golden syrup* |
| *1 Tbsp whisky* |
| *375 g/12 oz plain flour* |
| *½ tsp baking powder* |
| *50 g/2 oz finely chopped stem ginger* |
| *2 Tbsp milk* |
| *25 g/1 oz flaked almonds* |
| *2 Tbsp caster sugar, for sprinkling* |

Pre-heat oven to 325°F/160°C/Gas mark 3. Then lightly grease an 18 x 28-cm/7 x 11 x ¾-in tin. Put the butter, sugar, egg yolks, golden syrup and whisky into a mixing bowl and beat together until light and creamy. Sift the flour and baking powder into the bowl and mix together to make a soft dough.

● Lightly knead for a few seconds on a floured surface until smooth, then divide into 2 equal pieces. Roll out each piece to the size of the tin. Transfer one piece to the tin, pressing it firmly into the edges. Sprinkle the chopped stem ginger over, then cover with the second piece of shortbread and press down firmly. Brush the top with milk, then sprinkle with flaked almonds and caster sugar.

● Bake for 40 minutes or until light golden. Leave for 5 minutes, then score into 16 fingers. Cool in the tin and cut into fingers to serve.

# Fruit Cookies

This chapter is full of unusual cookies using the wide range of fruit now on the market. Everyday fruit, such as apples, oranges and bananas, make an appearance along with exotic star fruits and papayas. Some recipes use fresh fruit, but many more exploit the rich, intense flavours of dried fruit. A number of cookies contrast the sharp flavour of fruit with the sweetness of the cookie with stunning effect.

There are several bar cookies in this section that would be excellent in lunch boxes and many of the chunky fruit cookies would travel well. Next time you plan a hike or take a trip to the beach, make up a batch of cookies to nibble when hunger pangs strike.

## Quick Bites

## Combined Flavours

# Fruity Treats

# Fresh and Dried Fruits

# Date and Cinnamon Cookies

*Preparation time: 15 minutes + chilling*
*Cooking time: 15 to 18 minutes • Makes: About 30*

**Dates are soft and chewy and keep these cookies really moist.**

### INGREDIENTS

225 g/8 oz butter, softened

200 g/7 oz light brown sugar

3 Tbsp golden syrup

2 eggs, beaten

375 g/12 oz plain flour

1 tsp ground cinnamon

225 g/8 oz chopped dates

Put butter, sugar and golden syrup in a bowl. Beat until light and fluffy. Gradually add the eggs; mix well between additions. Sift in the flour and cinnamon; mix well. Stir in the dates. Chill for 2 hours.

● Pre-heat oven to 350°F/175°C/Gas mark 4. Grease two baking sheets or line with non-stick baking parchment.

● Roll teaspoons of the mixture into balls and flatten slightly. Arrange on the baking sheets at least 5 cm/2 in apart and bake for 15 to 18 minutes. Leave to cool for 5 minutes then transfer to wire racks to cool completely. Store in an airtight container.

# Orange and Cardamom Thins

*Preparation time: 40 minutes + chilling*
*Cooking time: 12 minutes • Makes: About 20 filled cookies*

**These are delicate sandwich cookies, but they are also great fun for kids to make.**

### INGREDIENTS

120 g/4 oz butter, softened

200 g/7 oz caster sugar

2 medium eggs, beaten

Grated rind of 1 large orange

120 g/4 oz plain flour

2 tsp ground cardamom

### FILLING

150 g/5 oz icing sugar

50 g/2 oz butter, softened

1 Tbsp orange juice

Put the butter and sugar in a bowl and beat until light and fluffy. Gradually beat in the eggs and orange rind. Sift in the flour and ground cardamom and mix well. Form into a ball and chill for 30 minutes.

● Meanwhile, beat together the filling ingredients, adding the orange juice gradually.

● Pre-heat oven to 375°F/190°C/Gas mark 5. Grease two baking sheets or line with non-stick baking parchment.

● Roll out the dough thinly and stamp out 5-cm/2-in rounds using a straight-edged cutter. Place the cookies on the baking sheets spaced about 2.5 cm/1 in apart. Bake for about 12 minutes until golden. Cool for 5 minutes on the sheet then transfer to wire racks to cool completely.

● Sandwich the cookies with a little filling and serve.

# Cherry Rings

*Preparation time: 40 minutes + chilling* ● *Cooking time: 20 minutes* ● *Makes: About 30*

**These are crisp cookies with a soft cherry topping.**

## INGREDIENTS

200 g/7 oz butter, softened

120 g/4 oz caster sugar

200 g/7 oz light brown sugar

1 tsp vanilla essence

300g/10 oz plain flour

120 g/4 oz dried cherries, roughly chopped

### GLAZE

1 small egg, beaten

3 tsp milk

2 tsp caster sugar

Put the butter, sugars and vanilla essence in a mixing bowl and beat with an electric mixer until light and fluffy. Sift in the flour, mix well, form into a soft dough and chill for 30 minutes in the refrigerator.

● Pre-heat oven to 325°F/160°C/Gas mark 3. Grease two large baking sheets or line with non-stick baking parchment.

● Mix the glaze ingredients together.

● Dust work surface with flour and roll out dough to 1 cm/½ in. Stamp out 6-cm/2½-in rounds with a fluted cutter. Then, cut out the centre with a 1-cm/½-in cutter. Transfer to the baking sheets and brush with the glaze. Decorate with the cherries, covering the entire surface.

● Bake for about 20 minutes until light brown. Cool for 5 minutes then transfer to wire racks to cool completely. Store in an airtight container.

## VARIATION

● Substitute 125 g/4 oz of dried blueberries for the cherries.

# The Ultimate Banana Cookies

*Preparation time: 15 minutes + chilling* ● *Cooking time: 18 to 20 minutes* ● *Makes: About 35*

**You simply can't fit any more bananas into these banana-coconut cookies!**

## INGREDIENTS

175 g/6 oz butter, softened

120 g/4 oz caster sugar

120 g/4 oz soft brown sugar

1 egg, beaten

3 medium bananas, mashed

1 tsp vanilla essence

250 g/9 oz plain flour

1 tsp baking powder

175 g/6 oz dried banana chips, broken up

50 g/2 oz desiccated coconut

Put the butter and sugars in a bowl and beat until light and fluffy. Gradually beat in the egg ensuring each addition is well incorporated. Stir in the mashed bananas and vanilla essence. Sift in the flour and baking powder. Then stir in the banana chips and coconut. Chill for at least 2 hours in the refrigerator.

● Pre-heat oven to 375°F/190°C/Gas mark 5. Grease two baking sheets or line with non-stick baking parchment.

● Take tablespoons of the mixture and roll into balls. Flatten slightly then place on the baking sheets at least 5 cm/2 in apart. Bake for 18 to 20 minutes until golden. Chill for 5 minutes then transfer to wire cooling racks. Store in an airtight container.

# Spicy Mixed Fruit Bars

*Preparation time: 30 minutes* ● *Cooking time: 40 minutes* ● *Makes: 12 bars*

**These are substantial bars of moist fruit and coconut, well worth the effort.**

INGREDIENTS

TOPPING

*75 g/3 oz finely chopped dried apricots*

*40 g/1½ oz sultanas*

*75 g/3 oz finely chopped dried peaches*

*75 g/3 oz dried blueberries*

*3 Tbsp brandy*

*3 eggs, beaten*

*120 g/4 oz light brown sugar*

*50 g/2 oz plain flour*

*1 tsp baking powder*

*50 g/2 oz desiccated coconut*

BASE

*120 g/4 oz butter, softened*

*5 Tbsp caster sugar*

*150 g/5 oz plain flour*

*1 tsp ground ginger*

*1 tsp ground cinnamon*

Put the apricots, sultanas, peaches and blueberries in a bowl and add the brandy. Leave to soak for 20 minutes.

● Pre-heat oven to 350°F/1175°C/Gas mark 4. Grease and line the base of a 32.5 x 23-cm/13 x 9-in tin with non-stick baking parchment.

● Prepare the base. Place the butter and sugar in a bowl and beat until light and fluffy. Sift in the flour, ginger and cinnamon and mix to a dough. Spread over the base of the tin and bake for 8 to 10 minutes.

● While the base is cooking, finish making the topping. Beat the eggs and sugar together for about 5 minutes until thick and creamy. Sift in the flour and baking powder. Stir in the coconut and soaked fruit. Pour over the baked base and bake for a further 30 to 35 minutes until firm to the touch. Cool in the tin before cutting into 12 bars. Store in an airtight container.

# Cranberry and Orange Cookies

*Preparation time: 20 minutes + chilling* ● *Cooking time: 15 to 17 minutes* ● *Makes: About 35*

**Use dried blueberries if cranberries are unavailable.**

## INGREDIENTS

*225 g/8 oz butter, softened*

*200 g/7 oz caster sugar*

*200 g/7 oz light brown sugar*

*2 eggs, beaten*

*Grated rind of 1 orange*

*250 g/9 oz plain flour*

*1 tsp salt*

*1 tsp baking powder*

*150 g/5 oz whole dried cranberries*

Beat butter and sugars together until soft and creamy. Gradually beat in the eggs and orange rind. The mixture may look as if it is curdling, but it will be fine when cooked. Sift in flour, salt and baking powder and mix to combine. Add the cranberries and mix well. Chill the mixture for at least one hour in the refrigerator.

● Pre-heat oven to 350°F/175°C/Gas mark 4. Grease two large baking sheets or line with non-stick baking parchment.

● Roll tablespoons of the mixture into balls and place on the baking sheets at least 8 cm/3 in apart. Flatten slightly with the back of a spoon. Bake for 15 to 17 minutes until golden. Leave to cool for 5 minutes then transfer to wire racks to cool completely. Store in an airtight container.

## TIP

Dried apricots, papayas, mangoes or peaches also work well in these cookies.

# Lemon and Lime Thins

*Preparation time: 15 minutes + chilling ● Cooking time: 15 to 18 minutes ● Makes: About 20*

**The frosted lemon rind garnish is an effective way to decorate simple cookies.**

## INGREDIENTS

| |
|---|
| *2 lemons* |
| *1 lime* |
| *120 g/4 oz butter, softened* |
| *5 Tbsp caster sugar* |
| *150 g/5 oz plain flour* |
| *1 egg white* |
| *Icing sugar, for decorating* |

Pare the rind from one lemon and place in a bowl. Grate the rind from the lime and other lemon into a separate bowl and squeeze 2 tablespoons of juice from the lemon.

● Put butter, 3 tablespoons of the sugar and grated rinds in a bowl and beat until light and fluffy. Add lemon juice gradually. Sift in the flour and mix to a soft dough. Place on a piece of greaseproof paper and form into a log. Chill for one hour.

● Meanwhile, place the lemon rind in a pan of boiling water for one minute. Drain and pat dry. Lightly beat the egg white until frothy. Dip the rind into the egg white then into the remaining sugar to frost. Leave to dry on greaseproof paper.

● Pre-heat oven to 350°F/175°C/Gas mark 4. Grease two baking sheets or line with non-stick baking parchment.

● Slice the dough log into 1-cm/½-in slices and place on the baking sheets. Bake for 15 to 18 minutes. Leave to cool for 5 minutes then transfer to wire cooling racks. Top with the frosted rind and dust lightly with icing sugar to serve, if liked.

# Strawberry Pinwheels

*Preparation time: 35 minutes + chilling* ● *Cooking time: 11 to 13 minutes* ● *Makes: About 16*

**Adults and children alike will have great fun making these festive cookies.**

### INGREDIENTS

*120 g/4 oz butter, softened*

*1 Tbsp caster sugar*

*1 tsp vanilla essence*

*200 g/7 oz plain flour*

*3 Tbsp strawberry jam*

Put butter, sugar and vanilla in a bowl and beat until light and creamy. Sift in the flour. Mix to a dough by hand then chill for 30 minutes.

● Pre-heat oven to 350°F/175°C/Gas mark 4. Grease two baking sheets or line with non-stick baking parchment.

● Roll out half the dough on a piece of floured greaseproof paper to a 25-cm/10-in square. Trim to these dimensions. Cut into 16 equal-sized squares with a blunt knife or fluted pastry cutter. Cut a 2.5-cm/1-in slice from each corner towards the centre. If the dough sticks to the knife dip it in flour.

● Put half a teaspoon of jam into the centre of each cookie. Fold over every other corner to the centre to form a pinwheel, lightly sticking the dough to the jam. Transfer to the baking sheets and bake for 11 to 13 minutes.

● Cool for 5 minutes on the baking sheets then transfer to wire cooling racks. Store in an airtight container.

# Tropical Papaya Drops

*Preparation time: 20 minutes + cooling* ● *Cooking time: 15 to 18 minutes* ● *Makes: About 30 drops*

**Dried papaya has a more intense flavour than fresh, so a little gives a strong flavour.**

## INGREDIENTS

*200 g/7 oz plain flour*

*1 tsp baking powder*

*1 Tbsp caster sugar*

*120 g/4 oz  finely chopped dried papaya*

*120 g/4 oz butter*

*6 Tbsp golden syrup*

*1 tsp vanilla essence*

Pre-heat oven to 350°F/175°C/Gas mark 4. Grease two baking sheets or line with non-stick baking parchment.

● Sift the flour and baking powder into a large bowl. Stir in the sugar and chopped papaya and make a well in the centre. Put the butter, golden syrup and vanilla essence in a small saucepan and stir over a gentle heat until the butter has melted. Pour into the dry ingredients and mix to a soft dough. Cool for 10 minutes.

● Take teaspoons of the mixture and roll into balls. Place on the baking sheets at least 5 cm/2 in apart and flatten slightly with the back of a spoon. Bake for 15 to 18 minutes. Cool for 5 minutes, then transfer to wire cooling racks. Store in an airtight container.

## VARIATION

Try using a combination of mango and papaya for truly tropical cookie treats.

# Cherry and Vanilla Squares

*Preparation time: 20 minutes* ●
*Cooking time: 30 to 35 minutes* ● *Makes: 16*

**Use dried Morello or sour cherries, rather than glacé cherries for these moist squares.**

### INGREDIENTS

| |
|---|
| *150 g/5 oz plain flour* |
| *5 Tbsp icing sugar* |
| *200 g/7 oz cold butter* |
| *2 tsp vanilla essence* |
| *120 g/4 oz dried cherries* |

Pre-heat oven to 350°F/175°C/Gas mark 4. Grease or line a 20 x 20-cm/8 x 8-in tin with non-stick baking parchment.

● Sift flour and icing sugar together into a bowl. Add the butter and vanilla essence and blend in with your fingertips until the mixture resembles coarse breadcrumbs. Stir in the cherries and form into a soft dough.

● Transfer to the tin and press to fit. Bake for 30 to 35 minutes. Leave to cool then cut into 16 bars. Store, covered, in the tin or in an airtight container.

### TIP

For extra flavour and glaze, brush the cooked dough with cherry or strawberry jam when it comes out of the oven.

# Banana and Cointreau Temptations

*Preparation time: 20 minutes + chilling* ●
*Cooking time: 15 to18 minutes* ● *Makes: About 30*

**Cointreau is delicately flavoured with orange, which is the perfect partner for bananas.**

### INGREDIENTS

| |
|---|
| *200 g/7 oz dried banana chips* |
| *225 g/8 oz butter, softened* |
| *200 g/7 oz caster sugar* |
| *200 g/7 oz light brown sugar* |
| *2 eggs, beaten* |
| *2 Tbsp Cointreau* |
| *250 g/9 oz plain flour* |
| *1 tsp salt* |
| *1 tsp baking powder* |

Place the banana chips in a bag and crush with a rolling pin or wooden spoon to break them up.

● Beat together butter and sugars until soft and creamy. Gradually beat in eggs and Cointreau. Sift in flour, salt and baking powder and mix to combine. Add bananas and mix well. Chill for one hour in the refrigerator.

● Pre-heat oven to 350°F/175°C/Gas mark 4. Grease two large baking sheets or line with non-stick baking parchment.

● Roll tablespoons of the mixture into balls and place on the baking sheets at least 8 cm/3 in apart. Flatten slightly with the back of a spoon. Bake for 15 to 18 minutes until golden.

● Leave to cool for 5 minutes then transfer to wire racks to cool completely. Store in an airtight container.

# Carrot and Date Drops

*Preparation time: 15 minutes + chilling* ● *Cooking time: 10 to 12 minutes* ● *Makes: About 25*

**These are unusual, delicious, and moist – maybe more like a cake than a cookie.**

## INGREDIENTS

| |
| --- |
| *120 g/4 oz butter, softened* |
| *125 g/4 oz light brown sugar* |
| *1 egg, beaten* |
| *75 g/3 oz plain flour* |
| *1 tsp baking powder* |
| *1 tsp salt* |
| *1 tsp ground nutmeg* |
| *½ tsp ground ginger* |
| *75 g/3 oz grated carrot* |
| *120 g/4 oz chopped dates* |

Put butter and sugar in a bowl and beat until light and fluffy. Gradually beat in the egg. Sift in the flour, baking powder, salt, nutmeg and ginger and stir until combined. Then stir in the carrots and dates. Chill for at least 2 hours.

● Pre-heat oven to 375°F/190°C/Gas mark 4. Grease two baking sheets or line with non-stick baking parchment.

● Take small tablespoons of the mixture and roll into balls, then flatten slightly. Place at least 5 cm/2 in apart on the baking sheets and bake for 10 to 12 minutes. Cool for 5 minutes on the baking sheets then transfer to wire racks to cool completely. Store the drops in an airtight container.

# Passionfruit Shortbread

*Preparation time: 25 minutes + chilling* ● *Cooking time: 20 minutes* ● *Makes: About 20*

**Passion fruit pulp contains masses of small seeds that are left in the dough for an added crunch.**

### INGREDIENTS

*175 g/6 oz butter, softened*

*50 g/2 oz caster sugar*

*175 g/6 oz plain flour*

*50 g/2 oz cornflour*

*Pulp of 3 passion fruit*

*Icing sugar, for decorating, optional*

Put butter and sugar in a bowl and beat until light and fluffy. Sift in the flour and cornflour and mix to a dough by hand. Stir in the passion fruit pulp.

● Transfer to a piece of greaseproof paper and form the dough into a log shape. Chill for at least one hour in the refrigerator.

● Pre-heat oven to 350°F/175°C/Gas mark 4. Grease two baking sheets or line with non-stick baking parchment.

● Cut 5-mm/½-in slices from the log and place on the baking sheets. Bake for about 20 minutes until golden-brown. Cool for 5 minutes on the baking sheets then transfer to wire racks to cool completely. Dust with icing sugar to serve, if liked. Store in an airtight container and eat within 4 days.

# Pineapple Drops

*Preparation time: 20 minutes + chilling* •
*Cooking time: 15 minutes* • *Makes: About 30*

**These are very sweet cookies.**

### INGREDIENTS

*225 g/8 oz butter, softened*

*200 g/7 oz caster sugar*

*200 g/7 oz light brown sugar*

*2 eggs, beaten*

*2 Tbsp honey*

*250 g/9 oz plain flour*

*1 tsp salt*

*1 tsp baking powder*

*120 g/4 oz chopped dried pineapple*

Beat together butter and sugars until light and fluffy. Gradually beat in the egg and honey. The mixture may look as if it is curdling, but it will be fine when cooked. Sift in flour, salt and baking powder and mix to combine. Add pineapple and mix well. Chill the mixture for at least one hour in the refrigerator.

● Pre-heat oven to 350°F/175°C/Gas mark 4. Grease two large baking sheets or line with non-stick baking parchment.

● Roll heaped teaspoons of the mixture into balls and place on the baking sheets at least 8 cm/3 in apart. Flatten slightly with the back of a spoon. Bake for 15 minutes until golden. Leave to cool for 5 minutes on the sheets then transfer the cookies to wire racks to cool completely. Store in an airtight container.

# Dried Mango and Ginger Delights

*Preparation time: 20 minutes* •
*Cooking time: 15 minutes* • *Makes: About 40*

**Using cream cheese makes this cookie dough really soft and pliable.**

### INGREDIENTS

*75 g/3 oz butter, softened*

*100 g/3½ oz full-fat soft cheese, softened*

*200 g/7 oz caster sugar*

*1 tsp baking powder*

*1 egg, beaten*

*1 Tbsp ginger preserve or stem ginger syrup*

*(from the stem ginger jar)*

*250 g/9 oz plain flour*

*120 g/4 oz finely chopped dried mango*

*2 tsp finely chopped stem ginger*

Put butter and cream cheese in a bowl and beat for 30 seconds. Add sugar and beat until light and fluffy. Add the baking powder, egg and ginger preserve or syrup and beat again. Sift in the flour and beat for 30 seconds.

● Stir in the mango and ginger and form the mixture into a soft dough. Form into a ball, wrap in clingfilm and chill for 30 minutes in the refrigerator.

● Pre-heat oven to 350°F/175°C/Gas mark 4. Grease two baking sheets or line with non-stick baking parchment.

● Roll out dough to about 8 mm/⅓ in thick and stamp out shapes with cutters. Re-roll as necessary. Transfer to the baking sheets and bake for about 15 minutes until lightly golden. Chill for 5 minutes on the baking sheets then transfer to wire cooling racks to cool completely. Store the cookies in an airtight container.

# Honeyed Apricot Cookies

*Preparation time: 15 minutes + chilling* ●
*Cooking time: 15 minutes* ● *Makes: About 30*

**If you can find honeyed apricots, use these and omit the honey from this recipe.**

INGREDIENTS

225 g/8 oz butter, softened

200 g/7 oz caster sugar

200 g/7 oz light brown sugar

2 eggs, beaten

2 Tbsp honey

1 tsp ground ginger

250 g/9 oz plain flour

1 tsp salt

1 tsp baking powder

225 g/8 oz chopped apricots

Beat together butter and sugars until soft and creamy. Gradually beat in the eggs and honey. The mixture may look as if it is curdling, but it will be fine when cooked. Sift in ginger, flour, salt and baking powder and mix to combine. Add the diced apricots and mix well. Chill the mixture for at least one hour in the refrigerator.

● Pre-heat oven to 350°F/175°C/Gas mark 4. Grease two large baking sheets or line with non-stick baking parchment.

● Roll tablespoons of the mixture into balls and place on the baking sheets at least 8 cm/3 in apart. Flatten slightly with the back of a spoon. Bake for 15 minutes until golden. Leave to cool on the sheets for 5 minutes on the sheets then transfer to wire racks to cool completely. Store in an airtight container.

# Prune and Grapefruit Marmalade Drops

*Preparation time: 15 minutes + chilling* ●
*Cooking time: 15 to 17 minutes* ● *Makes: About 30*

**These are quite dry, chunky cookies.**

INGREDIENTS

225 g/8 oz butter, softened

200 g/7 oz light brown sugar

2 Tbsp golden syrup

2 eggs, beaten

4 Tbsp grapefruit marmalade

300 g/10 oz plain flour

1 tsp salt

1 tsp baking powder

125 g/4 oz chopped, stoned prunes

Icing sugar, optional

Put the butter, sugar and syrup in a bowl and beat until light and fluffy. Gradually beat in eggs and grapefruit marmalade. It may look as if it is curdling, but it will be fine when cooked. Sift in flour, salt and baking powder and mix to combine. Add prunes and mix well. Chill for one hour in the refrigerator.

● Pre-heat oven to 350°F/175°C/Gas mark 4. Grease two large baking sheets or line with non-stick baking parchment.

● Roll tablespoons of the mixture into balls, then flatten between your palms. Place on the baking sheets at least 2.5 cm/1 in apart. Bake for 15 to 17 minutes until golden. Leave to cool for 5 minutes then transfer to wire racks to cool completely.

● Dust lightly with icing sugar to serve, if liked. Store in an airtight container.

# Cherry Chocolate Cookies

*Preparation time: 20 minutes + chilling* ●
*Cooking time: 15 to 18 minutes* ● *Makes: About 18*

**Cherries and chocolate are a classic combination.**

## INGREDIENTS

| |
|---|
| *150 g/5 oz butter* |
| *200 g/7 oz caster sugar* |
| *1 egg yolk* |
| *200 g/7 oz plain flour* |
| *120 g/4 oz coarsely chopped glacé cherries* |
| *75 g/3 oz plain chocolate chips* |

Put butter and sugar in a bowl and mix well until light and fluffy. Add the egg yolk and beat. Sift in flour and mix well then stir in the cherries and chocolate chips. Chill for at least 2 hours.

● Pre-heat oven to 375°F/190°C/Gas mark 5. Grease two baking sheets or line with non-stick baking parchment.

● Take tablespoons of the mixture and roll into balls, then flatten slightly. Place onto the baking sheets at least 2.5 cm/1 in apart. Bake for 15 to 18 minutes. Cool for 5 minutes on the baking sheets then transfer to wire racks to cool completely. Store in an airtight container.

# Dried Fruit and Brazil Nut Cookies

*Preparation time: 20 minutes + chilling* ●
*Cooking time: 17 minutes* ● *Makes: About 35*

**Soft fruit and crunchy nuts give you everything you desire from a cookie.**

## INGREDIENTS

| |
|---|
| *225 g/8 oz butter, softened* |
| *200 g/7 oz caster sugar* |
| *200 g/7 oz light brown sugar* |
| *2 eggs, beaten* |
| *250 g/9 oz plain flour* |
| *1 tsp salt* |
| *1 tsp baking powder* |
| *75 g/3 oz chopped dried fruit salad* |
| *75 g/3 oz chopped Brazil nuts* |

Beat together the butter and sugars until soft and creamy. Gradually beat in the eggs. The mixture may look as if it is curdling, but it will be fine when cooked. Sift in flour, salt and baking powder and mix to combine. Add the fruit salad and Brazil nuts and mix together well. Chill the mixture for at least one hour in the refrigerator.

● Pre-heat oven to 350°F/175°C/Gas mark 4. Grease two large baking sheets or line with non-stick baking parchment.

● Roll tablespoons of the mixture into balls and place on the baking sheets at least 8 cm/3 in apart. Flatten slightly with the back of a spoon. Bake for 15 to 17 minutes until golden. Leave to cool for 5 minutes then transfer to wire racks to cool completely. Store in an airtight container.

# Exotic Fruit and Coconut Treats

*Preparation time: 20 minutes + chilling* ● *Cooking time: 15 to 18 minutes* ● *Makes: About 30*

**Look for packets of assorted tropical fruits, or experiment with your own combinations.**

### INGREDIENTS

*225 g/8 oz butter, softened*

*200 g/7 oz caster sugar*

*200 g/7 oz light brown sugar*

*2 eggs, beaten*

*Grated rind of 1 orange*

*250 g/9 oz plain flour*

*1 tsp salt*

*1 tsp baking powder*

*120 g/4 oz chopped mixed tropical dried fruit or fruit salad*

*225 g/8 oz desiccated coconut*

Beat together butter and sugars until soft and creamy. Gradually beat in the eggs and orange rind. The mixture may look as if it is curdling, but it will be fine when cooked. Sift in flour, salt and baking powder and mix to combine. Add tropical fruits and coconut and mix well. Chill the mixture for at least one hour in the refrigerator.

● Pre-heat oven to 350°F/175°C/Gas mark 4. Grease two large baking sheets or line with non-stick baking parchment.

● Roll tablespoons of the mixture into balls and place on the baking sheets at least 8 cm/3 in apart. Flatten slightly with the back of a spoon. Bake for 15 to 18 minutes until golden. Leave to cool for 5 minutes then cool on wire racks. Store in an airtight container.

# Tangerine Fingers

*Preparation time: 30 minutes + chilling ● Cooking time: 40 to 45 minutes ● Makes: About 30*

**Scrumptious shortbread with a tangy tangerine orange topping.**

## INGREDIENTS

### BASE

*225 g/8 oz butter*

*5 Tbsp caster sugar*

*Grated rind of 1 tangerine*

*225 g/8 oz plain flour*

*50 g/2 oz cornflour*

### TOPPING

*Grated rind of 2 tangerines*

*3 Tbsp freshly squeezed tangerine juice*

*225 g/8 oz caster sugar*

*3 eggs, beaten*

*75 g/3 oz plain flour*

*½ tsp baking powder*

Grease a 23 x 32.5-cm/9 x 13-in tin or line with non-stick baking parchment.

● Put butter, sugar and tangerine rind in a bowl and beat together until light and fluffy. Sift in flour and cornflour; mix well then form into a soft dough. Press into the prepared tin and smooth with a knife. Chill for 30 minutes in the refrigerator.

● Pre-heat oven to 350°F/175°C/Gas mark 4.

● Bake for 15 to 20 minutes until lightly golden. Remove from the oven, leaving the oven switched on.

● Beat together the tangerine rind, sugar and eggs until creamy. Sift in the flour and baking powder and fold in. Beat in the tangerine juice. Pour over the shortbread and bake for a further 25 minutes. Cool in the tin. Cut into 30 bars. Dust with icing sugar to serve, if liked.

# Banana Chocolate Squares

*Preparation time: 30 minutes* ● *Cooking time: 25 to 30 minutes* ● *Makes: 18*

**These delicious cookies are like shortbread with a dark and white chocolate topping.**

## INGREDIENTS

*200 g/7 oz plain flour*

*Pinch salt*

*8 tsp cornflour*

*50 g/2 oz caster sugar*

*175 g/6 oz cold butter, chopped*

*75 g/3 oz dried banana chips, roughly chopped*

*75 g/3 oz plain chocolate chips*

*75 g/3 oz white chocolate chips*

Pre-heat oven to 350°F/175°C/Gas mark 4. Grease and line a shallow 28 x 18-cm/11 x 7-in tin with non-stick baking parchment.

● Sift flour, salt and cornflour into a bowl then stir in the sugar. Add the butter and blend in with your fingertips until it resembles coarse breadcrumbs. Stir in the banana chips and form into a soft dough.

● Roll out to just under the size of the tin. Transfer to the tin and press to fit. Bake for 25 to 30 minutes until lightly browned. Leave to cool for a few minutes then mark out 18 squares (3 rows of 6 squares across). Cool in the tin.

● Cut the squares out of the tin and place on a sheet of greaseproof paper. Melt the dark and white chocolate in 2 separate bowls in the microwave or in a bowl over a saucepan of simmering water. Pipe lines of plain and white chocolate over each square. Leave to set before serving. Store in an airtight container.

## TIP

If you do not have a piping bag, place the chocolate into one corner of a small plastic bag, snip off the end and drizzle lines over each cookie.

# Cranberry and White Chocolate Cookies

*Preparation time: 30 minutes + chilling* ● *Cooking time: 15 to 20 minutes* ● *Makes: About 30*

**Dried cranberries are not as tart as fresh ones and these cookies are made even sweeter by the addition of chocolate.**

### INGREDIENTS

225 g/8 oz butter, softened

200 g/7 oz caster sugar

200 g/7 oz light brown sugar

2 eggs, beaten

250 g/9 oz plain flour

1 tsp salt

1 tsp baking powder

120 g/4 oz dried cranberries

175 g/6 oz white chocolate chips, or white chocolate, chopped

Beat together butter and sugars until soft and creamy. Gradually beat in the eggs. The mixture may look as if it is curdling, but it will be fine when cooked. Sift in flour, salt and baking powder and mix to combine. Add cranberries and 75 g/3 oz of the white chocolate chips and mix well. Chill the mixture for at least one hour in the refrigerator.

● Pre-heat oven to 350°F/175°C/Gas mark 4. Grease two large baking sheets or line with non-stick baking parchment.

● Roll tablespoons of the mixture into balls and place on the baking sheets at least 8 cm/3 in apart. Flatten slightly with the back of a spoon. Bake for 15 to 20 minutes until golden.

● Leave to cool for 5 minutes then transfer to wire racks to cool completely. Melt the white chocolate and drizzle it over the cookies. Leave to cool before serving. Store in an airtight container.

# Mixed Fruit Squares

*Preparation time: 20 minutes* ● *Cooking time: 60 to 70 minutes* ● *Makes: 16*

**These are moist, spongy squares baked just like a cake. Each square is packed with fruit.**

### INGREDIENTS

120 g/4 oz butter, softened

200 g/7 oz caster sugar

1 tsp vanilla essence

2 medium eggs, beaten

125 ml/4 fl oz milk

175 g/6 oz plain flour

600 g/1¼ lb dried and fresh mixed fruit (see Tip)

2 Tbsp raw sugar

Pre-heat oven to 350°F/175°C/Gas mark 4. Grease and line an 18 x 18-cm/7 x 7-in square tin with non-stick baking parchment.

● Put butter, sugar, vanilla essence and eggs in a bowl and beat together for 2 minutes. Beat in the milk, then sift in the flour and mix until smooth.

● Pour half the batter into the prepared tin then scatter over half the mixed fruit. Spoon over the remaining mixture, smooth with a blunt knife and scatter over the remaining fruit and the raw sugar.

● Bake for 60 to 70 minutes until the cake is cooked through. To test if the cake is cooked, insert a skewer into the centre of the cake and leave it for 5 seconds. When the skewer is removed it should be dry with no soggy cake mixture attached. Cool in the tin for 10 minutes, then cut into 16 squares.

### TIP

Just about any mixed fruit can be used in this recipe. Try apricots, blueberries, dried banana chips, pineapple, or mango, depending on seasonal availability.

# Truly Blueberry Cookies

*Preparation time: 20 minutes + chilling* ● *Cooking time: 15 to 18 minutes* ● *Makes: About 30*

**Macerating (soaking) the blueberries in orange and brandy makes the cookies even moister and more delicious. Omit the brandy and increase the orange juice if you want to make these cookies for children.**

### INGREDIENTS

*120 g/4 oz dried blueberries*

*4 Tbsp orange juice*

*2 Tbsp brandy*

*225 g/8 oz butter, softened*

*200 g/7 oz caster sugar*

*200 g/7 oz light brown sugar*

*2 eggs, beaten*

*250 g/9 oz plain flour*

*1 tsp baking powder*

Place blueberries, orange juice and brandy in a small pan and simmer for 5 minutes. Remove from the heat and leave to cool. Beat together butter and sugars until soft and creamy. Gradually beat in eggs. The mixture may look as if it is curdling, but it will be fine when cooked.

● Sift in flour and baking powder and mix to combine. Strain the blueberries, discarding any liquid, and add to cookie mixture. Mix well. Chill the mixture for at least one hour in the refrigerator.

● Pre-heat oven to 350°F/175°C/Gas mark 4. Grease two large baking sheets or line with non-stick baking parchment.

● Roll tablespoons of the mixture into balls and place on the baking sheets at least 8 cm/3 in apart. Flatten slightly with the back of a spoon. Bake for 15 to 18 minutes until golden. Leave to cool for 5 minutes then transfer to wire racks to cool completely.

● Store in an airtight container.

# Pear Flapjacks

*Preparation time: 15 minutes* ● *Cooking time: 20 to 25 minutes* ● *Makes: About 16*

**Dried pears make these flapjacks deliciously moist.**

### INGREDIENTS

*120 g/4 oz butter*

*200 g/7 oz soft brown sugar*

*2 Tbsp golden syrup*

*425 g/15 oz rolled oats*

*120 g/4 oz chopped dried pears*

*75 g/3 oz currants*

Pre-heat oven to 375°F/190°C/Gas mark 5. Lightly grease a shallow 28 x 18-cm/11 x 7-in tin.

● Put butter, sugar and golden syrup in a pan and cook over a gentle heat until the butter has melted. Combine the dry ingredients and add to the pan; stir well.

● Spoon into the prepared tin and press down with the back of a spoon. Bake for 20 to 25 minutes until lightly golden. Cool for 5 minutes in the tin then mark into 6 bars; leave to cool completely in the tin. Store in an airtight container.

# Glacé Cherry Florentines

*Preparation time: 20 minutes* ● *Cooking time: 8 to 10 minutes* ● *Makes: About 12*

**This is the best recipe to use when you want a quick, but impressive cookie.**

## INGREDIENTS

*50 g/2 oz lightly salted butter*

*2 Tbsp golden syrup*

*50 g/2 oz caster sugar*

*75 g/3 oz plain flour*

*75 g/3 oz finely chopped glacé cherries*

*Grated rind of 1 orange*

Pre-heat oven to 350°F/175°C/Gas mark 4. Grease two large baking sheets or line with non-stick baking parchment.

● Put the butter, golden syrup and sugar in a saucepan over a medium heat and stir until the sugar dissolves. Remove from the heat and cool for 5 minutes, stirring. Sift in the flour, then mix in the cherries and orange rind.

● Drop heaped teaspoons onto the baking sheets, at least 8 cm/3 in apart. Shape into neat rounds. Bake for 8 to 10 minutes. Re-shape into rounds while hot, if necessary. Cool for 5 minutes, then transfer to wire racks to cool completely. Store in an airtight container.

325

# Candied Peel and Dark Chocolate Squares

*Preparation time: 45 minutes* ● *Cooking time: 30 to 35 minutes* ● *Makes: 24*

**For a special occasion these bitter treats are perfect. Make up a batch and place in a gift box to take to a dinner party.**

### INGREDIENTS

*250 g/9 oz plain flour*

*50 g/2 oz caster sugar*

*175 g/6 oz cold butter, diced*

*75 g/3 oz chopped candied peel*

*4 squares (25 g/1 oz each) good-quality plain chocolate*

Pre-heat oven to 350°F/175°C/Gas mark 4. Grease and line the base of a shallow 28 x 18-cm/11 x 7-in pan.

● Sift flour into a bowl and stir in the sugar. Add the butter and blend in with your fingertips until the mixture resembles coarse breadcrumbs. Stir in 50 g/2 oz of the mixed peel and form into a soft dough.

● Roll out to just under the size of the tin. Transfer to the tin and press to fit. Prick all over with a fork. Bake for 25 to 30 minutes until lightly browned. Cool for 5 minutes then mark into 24 bars. Cool in the tin.

● Melt chocolate in a microwave or in a glass bowl over a saucepan of simmering water. Cut dough into the squares and remove from the tin. Dip each bar into the chocolate to coat the top and sides and place on greaseproof paper. While the chocolate is still warm, sprinkle over a few pieces of candied peel. Leave to harden before serving. Store in an airtight container between layers of greaseproof paper.

# Apricot Wheels

*Preparation time: 40 minutes + chilling ● Cooking time: 10 to 12 minutes ● Makes: About 40*

**These wheels are cut from a log of dough filled with a sweet apricot filling.**

### INGREDIENTS

### FILLING

*150 g/5 oz dried apricots, finely chopped (see Tip)*

*120 g/4 oz caster sugar*

*1 tsp ground nutmeg*

*125 ml/4 fl oz orange juice*

### DOUGH

*175 g/6 oz butter, softened*

*200 g/7 oz light brown sugar*

*1 medium egg, beaten*

*1 tsp almond essence*

*375 g/12 oz plain flour*

*1 tsp baking powder*

Place all the filling ingredients in a small saucepan and bring to the boil. Simmer for 3 minutes until most of the orange juice has evaporated and the mixture is thick. Set aside and cool.

● Put the butter and sugar in a bowl and mix until light and fluffy. Gradually add the egg; mixing well between each addition. Stir in the almond essence. Sift in the flour and baking powder and form into a dough. Wrap in clingfilm and chill for at least 30 minutes.

● Divide the dough in half, then place one half on a piece of floured greaseproof paper. Roll out the dough on the paper to a 20 x 25-cm/8 x 10-in rectangle. Slide a thin, metal spatula between the paper and the dough so that it does not stick to the paper when rolled up. Cover dough with half the filling and roll up from a long side using the paper to help you roll. Rewrap in clingfilm and chill for about 20 minutes. Repeat with remaining dough and filling.

● Pre-heat oven to 350°F/175°C/Gas mark 4. Grease two baking sheets or line with non-stick baking parchment.

● Cut 1-cm/½-in slices from the log and place on the baking sheets. Bake for 10 to 12 minutes. Cool on baking sheets for 5 minutes then transfer to wire cooling racks. Store in an airtight container.

### TIP

It's important to chop the apricots finely, otherwise it will be difficult to roll up the dough.

# Rum and Raisin Cookies

*Preparation time: 20 minutes + chilling ●*
*Cooking time: 15 to 17 minutes ● Makes: About 35*

**The traditional combination of rum and raisins is perfect for cookies as it makes them moist and chewy.**

### INGREDIENTS

225 g/8 oz butter, softened

200 g/7 oz caster sugar

200 g/7 oz light brown sugar

1 egg, beaten

3 Tbsp rum

250 g/9 oz plain flour

1 tsp salt

1 tsp baking powder

150 g/5 oz seedless raisins

Beat together the butter and sugars until soft and creamy. Gradually beat in the egg and rum. The mixture may look as if it is curdling, but it will be fine when cooked. Sift in the flour, salt and baking powder and mix to combine. Add the raisins and mix well. Chill for at least one hour in the refrigerator.

● Pre-heat oven to 350°F/175°C/Gas mark 4. Grease two large baking sheets or line with non-stick baking parchment.

● Roll tablespoons of the mixture into balls and place on the baking sheets at least 8 cm/3 in apart. Flatten slightly with the back of a spoon. Bake for 15 to 17 minutes until golden. Leave to cool for 5 minutes then transfer to wire racks to cool completely. Store in an airtight container.

# Brandy and Fresh Apple Cookies

*Preparation time: 20 minutes ●*
*Cooking time: 15 minutes ● Makes: About 10 to 12*

**Fresh apples add texture and a sweet flavour.**

### INGREDIENTS

75 g/3 oz grated apple

1 Tbsp lemon juice

50 g/2 oz butter

2 Tbsp golden syrup

50 g/2 oz caster sugar

2 Tbsp brandy

50 g/2 oz plain flour

50 g/2 oz chopped almonds

Pre-heat oven to 350°F/175°C/Gas mark 4. Grease two large baking sheets or line with non-stick baking parchment.

● Squeeze the grated apples in your hand to essence the juice. Discard the juice then toss the apple in the lemon juice to coat.

● Put butter, golden syrup, sugar and brandy in a saucepan over a medium heat and stir until the sugar dissolves. Remove from the heat and cool for 5 minutes, stirring frequently. Sift in the flour, then stir in the almonds and apple. Mix well.

● Drop heaped teaspoons onto the baking sheets, at least 8 cm/3 in apart. Shape them into neat rounds. Bake for about 15 minutes. Cool for 5 minutes, then transfer to wire racks to cool completely. Store in an airtight container.

# Pineapple Crumble Cookies

*Preparation time: 30 minutes + chilling* ● *Cooking time: 20 to 25 minutes* ● *Makes: About 24*

**These cookies are different as they have a pineapple crumble on top of sweet cookie bases.**

## INGREDIENTS

120 g/4 oz butter

3 Tbsp caster sugar

1 tsp vanilla essence

150 g/5 oz plain flour

75 g/3 oz ground almonds

1 egg yolk

### CRUMBLE TOPPING

120 g/4 oz plain flour

50 g/2 oz caster sugar

50 g/2 oz cold butter, chopped

120 g/4 oz dried pineapple, finely chopped

Grease two large baking sheets or line with non-stick baking parchment.

● Put the butter and sugar in a bowl and beat until light and fluffy. Stir in the vanilla essence. Sift in flour then stir in the ground almonds. Mix to a soft dough. Chill for 30 minutes in the refrigerator.

● Dust the work surface with a little flour, then roll out the dough to about 8 mm/⅓-in thick. Stamp out 3-inch rounds with a cutter, re-rolling and stamping out the trimmings. Place the cookies on the baking sheets and chill for at least 30 minutes in the refrigerator.

● Meanwhile, combine the flour and sugar for the topping. Add the butter and mix with your fingertips to the consistency of coarse breadcrumbs. Stir in the chopped pineapple.

● Pre-heat oven to 325°F/160°C/Gas mark 3.

● Brush the cookies with the egg yolk then sprinkle a little crumble onto each. Bake cookies for 20 to 25 minutes until lightly golden. Leave to cool slightly, then transfer to wire racks to cool completely. Store in an airtight container.

# Star Fruit Cookies

*Preparation time: 20 minutes + chilling* •
*Cooking time: 15 to 17 minutes* • *Makes: About 35*

**Dried star fruit has a slightly perfumed flavour and make these most unusual cookies really special.**

## INGREDIENTS

225 g/8 oz butter, softened

200 g/7 oz caster sugar

200 g/7 oz light brown sugar

2 eggs, beaten

Grated rind of 1 lemon

250 g/9 oz plain flour

1 tsp salt

1 tsp baking powder

375 g/12 oz dried star fruit, roughly chopped

Beat together the butter and sugars until soft and creamy. Gradually beat in the eggs and lemon rind. The mixture may look as if it is curdling, but it will be fine when cooked. Sift in the flour, salt and baking powder and mix to combine. Stir in the chopped star fruit and mix well. Chill the mixture for at least one hour in the refrigerator.

● Pre-heat oven to 350°F/175°C/Gas mark 4. Grease two large baking sheets or line with non-stick paper.

● Roll tablespoons of the mixture into balls and place on the baking sheets at least 8 cm/3 in apart. Flatten slightly with the back of a spoon. Bake for 15 to 17 minutes until golden. Leave to cool for 5 minutes then transfer to wire racks to cool completely. Store in an airtight container.

## TIP

Dried star fruit is quite difficult to find. Look for it in health shops and good-quality specialized shops.

# Peach and Cherry Thins

*Preparation time: 15 minutes* •
*Cooking time: 10 minutes* • *Makes: About 10*

**These cookies are packed full of fruit with just a little dough to hold them together.**

## INGREDIENTS

50 g/2 oz butter

2 Tbsp golden syrup

50 g/2 oz caster sugar

75 g/3 oz plain flour

50 g/2 oz chopped dried peaches

75 g/3 oz dried Morello or sour cherries

Pre-heat oven to 350°F/175°C/Gas mark 4. Grease two large baking sheets or line with non-stick baking parchment.

● Put butter, golden syrup and sugar in a saucepan over a medium heat and stir until the sugar dissolves. Remove from the heat and cool for 5 minutes, stirring frequently. Stir in the flour, followed by the dried peaches and cherries. Mix well.

● Drop heaped teaspoons onto the baking sheets, at least 4 cm/1½ in apart. Shape them into neat rounds. Bake for about 10 minutes. Re-shape into rounds while hot, if necessary. Cool for 5 minutes, then transfer to wire racks to cool. Store in an airtight container.

# Pineapple and Ginger Cookies

*Preparation time: 15 minutes + chilling* ● *Cooking time: 15 to 17 minutes* ● *Makes: About 25*

**Chewy cookies with a hint of ginger.**

## INGREDIENTS

*225 g/8 oz butter, softened*

*200 g/7 oz light brown sugar*

*200 g/7 oz caster sugar*

*2 eggs, beaten*

*1 Tbsp finely chopped stem ginger or ginger preserve*

*3 tsp stem ginger syrup (from the stem ginger jar) or golden syrup*

*250 g/9 oz plain flour*

*1 tsp baking powder*

*1 tsp salt*

*120 g/4 oz diced dried pineapple*

Put the butter and sugars in a bowl and beat together until pale and creamy. Gradually beat in the eggs, stem ginger and ginger syrup. Do not worry if the mixture looks as if it is curdling, it will be fine when cooked. Sift in the flour, baking powder and salt and mix. Stir in the pineapple and mix well. Chill for at least one hour in the refrigerator.

● Pre-heat oven to 350°F/175°C/Gas mark 4. Grease two baking sheets or line with non-stick baking parchment.

● Roll tablespoons of the mixture into balls and place onto the baking sheets, at least 8 cm/3 in apart. Flatten with the back of a spoon. Bake for 15 to 17 minutes until golden, but still soft. Cool for 5 minutes on the baking sheets then transfer to wire cooling racks. Store in an airtight container.

# Winter Fruit Cookies

*Preparation time: 20 minutes + chilling* ●
*Cooking time: 15 to 17 minutes* ● *Makes: About 30*

**These cookies are full of the flavour of Christmas as they are packed with the dried fruit associated with the festive season.**

### INGREDIENTS

225 g/8 oz butter, softened

200 g/7 oz caster sugar

200 g/7 oz light brown sugar

2 eggs, beaten

250 g/9 oz plain flour

1 tsp salt

1 tsp baking powder

75 g/3 oz chopped dates

75 g/3 oz dried cherries

75 g/3 oz diced candied citrus peel

12 whole glacé cherries, halved

Put the butter and sugars in a bowl and beat until light and fluffy. Gradually beat in the eggs. The mixture may look as if it is curdling but it will be fine when cooked. Sift in the flour, salt and baking powder and mix. Add dates, cherries and candied peel and mix well. Chill for 1 hour in the refrigerator.

● Pre-heat oven to 350°F/175°C/Gas mark 4. Grease two large baking sheets or line with non-stick baking paper.

● Roll tablespoons of the mixture into balls and place on the baking sheets at least 8 cm/3 in apart. Flatten slightly between your palms and push half a cherry into the centre of each cookie. Bake for 15 to 17 minutes until golden. Leave to cool for 5 minutes then transfer to wire racks to cool completely. Store in an airtight container.

# Dried Pear and Walnut Wheaties

*Preparation time: 15 minutes + chilling* ●
*Cooking time: 15 to 17 minutes* ● *Makes: About 30*

**The wholemeal flour gives the cookies a really rich flavour.**

### INGREDIENTS

225 g/8 oz butter, softened

200 g/7 oz light brown sugar

200 g/7 oz caster sugar

2 eggs, beaten

1 tsp vanilla essence

250 g/9 oz wholemeal flour

1 tsp baking powder

1 tsp salt

120 g/4 oz finely chopped dried pears

120 g/4 oz chopped walnut pieces

Put the butter and sugars in a bowl and beat together until pale and creamy. Gradually beat in the eggs and vanilla essence. Do not worry if the mixture looks as if it is curdling, it will be fine when cooked. Sift in the flour, baking powder and salt and mix. Stir in the pears and walnuts and mix well. Chill for at least one hour in the refrigerator.

● Pre-heat oven to 350°F/175°C/Gas mark 4. Grease two baking sheets or line with non-stick baking parchment.

● Roll tablespoons of the mixture into balls and place onto the baking sheets, at least 8 cm/3 in apart. Flatten with the back of a spoon. Bake for 15 to 17 minutes until golden, but still soft. Cool for 5 minutes on the baking sheets then transfer to wire cooling racks. Store in an airtight container.

# Nut Cookies

Nuts are a central feature in many of the most successful cookies. They add an additional crunch to already crunchy cookies or a contrasting bite to soft, chewy cookies. Some cookies substitute ground nuts for flour, giving the resulting cookies a rich, dense flavour. The subtle flavours and textures of almonds, macadamia, pecan and cashew nuts, for instance, can be used on their own or in clever combinations that enhance each to best advantage. Combined with fragrant spices or delectable chocolate, nut-based cookies are simply wonderful.

Anyone who loves nutty cookies will be pleased to learn that the latest health findings are in favour of nuts. Nuts are high in proteins, monounsaturated fats, (the same fats found in olive oil), and polyunsaturated fats (which help lower cholesterol levels), and masses of micronutrients including vitamin E and folic acid. Of course, these cookies still contain butter and sugar so it's not all good news, but eaten in moderation they make a truly satisfying treat.

## Traditional Classics

## Family Favourites

# Clever Combinations

# Exotic Delights

# Almond Brittle Cookies

*Preparation time: 25 minutes + chilling ●*
*Cooking time: 15 to 20 minutes ● Makes: About 20*

**Almond brittle is unusual, yet simple to make.**

INGREDIENTS

ALMOND BRITTLE

*150 g/5 oz blanched almonds*

*50 g/2 oz caster sugar*

COOKIE DOUGH

*225 g/8 oz butter, softened*

*225 g/8 oz caster sugar*

*2 eggs, beaten*

*225 g/8 oz plain flour*

*1 tsp baking powder*

*1 tsp salt*

For the almond brittle, pre-heat oven to 425°F/220°C/Gas mark 7. Place almonds on a baking sheet and toast for 3 to 4 minutes. Melt sugar in a small saucepan over a medium heat without stirring. Add the almonds, mix, then remove from the heat. Quickly spread onto a baking sheet and cool. Chop.

● To make the cookies, put the butter and sugars in a bowl and beat until pale and creamy. Gradually beat in the eggs. Sift in flour, baking powder and salt; mix well. Stir in the almond brittle and mix. Chill for 1 hour.

● Pre-heat oven to 350°F/175°C/Gas mark 4. Grease or line two baking sheets.

● Drop teaspoons of the mixture onto the baking sheets, at least 8 cm/3 in apart. Flatten with the back of a spoon. Bake for 15 to 18 minutes until golden. Cool for 5 minutes then transfer to wire racks. Store in an airtight container.

# PistachioDrops

*Preparation time: 20 minutes + chilling ●*
*Cooking time: 15 to 18 minutes ● Makes: About 25*

**The green of the pistachios gives these cookies an exotic appeal.**

INGREDIENTS

*225 g/8 oz butter, softened*

*175 g/6 oz caster sugar*

*175 g/6 oz light brown sugar*

*2 eggs, beaten*

*250 g/9 oz plain flour*

*1 tsp salt*

*1 tsp baking powder*

*175 g/6 oz chopped unsalted, pistachios*

*1 tsp vanilla essence*

Beat together butter and sugars until soft and creamy. Gradually beat in eggs. The mixture may look as if it is curdling, but it will be fine when cooked. Sift in flour, salt and baking powder; mix to combine. Stir in pistachios and vanilla essence. Chill mixture for at least 1 hour in the refrigerator.

● Pre-heat oven to 350°F/175°C/Gas mark 4. Grease two baking sheets or line with non-stick baking parchment.

● Roll tablespoons of the mixture into balls and place on the sheets at least 8 cm/3 in apart. Flatten slightly with the back of a spoon. Bake for 15 to 18 minutes until golden. Leave to cool for 5 minutes then transfer to wire racks to cool. Store in an airtight container for up to 1 week.

# Almond and Ginger Hearts

*Preparation time: 30 minutes + chilling* ● *Cooking time: 20 to 25 minutes* ● *Makes: About 24*

**These delicate hearts are perfect for afternoon tea.**

### INGREDIENTS

120 g/4 oz butter

3 Tbsp caster sugar

150 g/5 oz plain flour, plus extra for rolling

75 g/3 oz ground almonds

2 tsp finely chopped stem ginger or ginger preserve

2 tsp stem ginger syrup (from the stem ginger jar) or golden syrup

Icing sugar, for serving, optional

Grease two baking sheets or line with non-stick baking parchment.

● Put the butter and sugar in a bowl and beat until light and fluffy. Sift in flour then stir in almonds, stem ginger or ginger preserve and syrup. Mix to a soft dough. Chill for 30 minutes.

● Roll out dough on a floured surface to a thickness of about 8 mm/⅓ in. Stamp out heart shapes with a pastry cutter, re-rolling and stamping out the trimmings. Transfer to the baking sheets and chill for at least 30 minutes in the refrigerator.

● Pre-heat oven to 325°F/160°C/Gas mark 3. Bake cookies for 20 to 25 minutes until lightly golden. Transfer to wire racks to cool. Dust with icing sugar to serve, if liked. Store in an airtight container for up to 1 week.

# Peanut Butter Cookies

*Preparation time: 30 minutes + chilling ●*
*Cooking time: 15 to 20 minutes ● Makes: About 20*

**These are really chunky, perfect for lunch boxes and picnics.**

INGREDIENTS

*75 g/3 oz butter, softened*

*5 Tbsp crunchy peanut butter*

*5 Tbsp dark brown sugar*

*120 g/4 oz caster sugar*

*1 egg, beaten*

*150 g/5 oz plain flour*

*1 tsp baking powder*

Put the butter, peanut butter and sugars in a bowl and beat until light and fluffy. Gradually beat in the egg. Don't worry if it looks as if it is curdling, it will be fine once cooked. Sift in the flour and baking powder. Chill mixture for 1 hour.

● Pre-heat oven to 350°F/175°C/Gas mark 4. Grease two baking sheets or line with non-stick baking parchment.

● Place spoonfuls of the dough onto the baking sheets at least 8 cm/3 in apart. Flatten slightly with the back of a spoon. Bake for 15 to 20 minutes until golden. Cool for 5 minutes on the baking sheet then transfer to wire racks to cool. Store in an airtight container for up to 1 week.

# Pecan and Cinnamon Cookies

*Preparation time: 20 minutes + chilling ●*
*Cooking time: 12 to 15 minutes ● Makes: 25*

**Pecans and cinnamon are an excellent combination.**

INGREDIENTS

*225 g/8 oz butter, softened*

*200 g/7 oz caster sugar*

*200 g/7 oz light brown sugar*

*2 eggs, beaten*

*250 g/9 oz plain flour*

*1 tsp salt*

*2 tsp ground cinnamon*

*1 tsp baking powder*

*225 g/8 oz chopped pecan nuts*

Beat together butter and sugars in a bowl until soft and creamy. Gradually beat in eggs. The mixture may look as if it is curdling, but it will be fine when cooked. Sift in flour, salt, ground cinnamon and baking powder and mix to combine. Stir in pecans and ground cinnamon. Chill mixture for at least 1 hour in the refrigerator.

● Pre-heat oven to 350°F/175°C/Gas mark 4. Grease two baking sheets or line with non-stick baking parchment.

● Roll tablespoons of the mixture into balls and place on the sheets at least 8 cm/3 in apart. Flatten slightly with the back of a spoon. Bake for 12 to 15 minutes until golden. Leave to cool for 5 minutes then transfer to wire racks to cool. Store in an airtight container for up to 1 week.

# White Chocolate and Macadamia Nut Treats

*Preparation time: 15 minutes + chilling* ● *Cooking time: 10 to 15 minutes* ● *Makes: About 20*

**You can really get your teeth into these chunky cookies.**

## INGREDIENTS

*225 g/8 oz butter, softened*

*200 g/7 oz caster sugar*

*200 g/7 oz light brown sugar*

*2 eggs, beaten*

*250 g/9 oz plain flour*

*1 tsp salt*

*1 tsp baking powder*

*120 g/4 oz chopped macadamia nuts*

*125 g/4 oz white chocolate chips*

Beat together butter and sugars until soft and creamy. Gradually beat in eggs. The mixture may look as if it is curdling, but it will be fine when cooked. Sift in flour, salt and baking powder; mix to combine. Add macadamia nuts and white chocolate chips and mix together well. Chill mixture for at least 1 hour in the refrigerator.

● Pre-heat oven to 350°F/175°C/Gas mark 4. Grease two baking sheets or line with non-stick baking parchment.

● Roll tablespoons of the mixture into balls and place on the sheets at least 8 cm/3 in apart. Flatten slightly with the back of a spoon. Bake for 10 to 15 minutes until golden. Leave to cool for 5 minutes then transfer to wire racks to cool. Store in an airtight container for up to 1 week.

# Walnut Crescents

*Preparation time: 30 minutes + chilling* ● *Cooking time: 20 to 25 minutes* ● *Makes: About 25*

**These cookies are light, crumbly and nutty.**

## INGREDIENTS

120 g/4 oz butter

3 Tbsp caster sugar

150 g/5 oz plain flour

50 g/2 oz finely chopped walnuts

Put the butter and sugar in a bowl and beat until light and fluffy. Sift in the flour then stir in the walnuts. Mix to form a soft dough. Chill the dough for 30 minutes in the refrigerator.

● Grease two baking sheets or line with non-stick baking parchment. Dust work surface with a little flour, then roll out dough to a thickness of about 8 mm/⅓ in. Stamp out crescent shapes with a cutter, re-rolling and stamping out the trimmings. Transfer to the baking sheets and chill for a further 30 minutes.

● Pre-heat oven to 325°F/160°C/Gas mark 3. Bake cookies for 20 to 25 minutes until lightly golden. Transfer to wire racks to cool. Store in an airtight container for up to 1 week.

# Hazelnut and Orange Cookies

*Preparation time: 20 minutes + chilling* ●
*Cooking time: 18 to 20 minutes* ● *Makes: 40*

**The combination of hazelnut and orange works really well in these cut-out cookies. Use Christmas cutters and serve over the festive season.**

### INGREDIENTS

*225 g/8 oz butter, softened*

*120 g/4 oz caster sugar*

*120 g/4 oz light brown sugar*

*300 g/10 oz plain flour, plus extra for rolling*

*150 g/5 oz chopped hazelnuts*

*Grated rind of 1 orange*

Put the butter and sugars in a mixing bowl and beat with an electric beater until light and fluffy. Sift in the flour and mix to a dough. Stir in the chopped hazelnuts and orange rind. Mix well. Chill for 30 minutes.

● Pre-heat oven to 325°F/160°C/Gas mark 3. Grease two baking sheets or line with non-stick baking parchment.

● Dust work surface with flour and roll out dough to 5 mm/½ in thick. Stamp out 5-cm/2-in rounds with a cutter. Transfer to the baking sheets. Bake for 18 to 20 minutes until golden. Cool for 5 minutes then transfer to wire racks to cool. Store in an airtight container.

# Pine Nut and Peach Chews

*Preparation time: 20 minutes + chilling* ●
*Cooking time: 12 to 15 minutes* ● *Makes: About 25*

**The crystallized peaches in these cookies give them a great chewy texture.**

### INGREDIENTS

*225 g/8 oz butter, softened*

*200 g/7 oz light brown sugar*

*200 g/7 oz caster sugar*

*2 eggs, beaten*

*225 g/8 oz plain flour*

*1 tsp baking powder*

*1 tsp salt*

*150 g/5 oz pine nuts*

*75 g/3 oz crystallized peaches, roughly chopped*

Put the butter and sugars in a bowl and beat together until pale and creamy. Gradually beat in the eggs. Don't worry if the mixture looks as if it is curdling, it will be fine when cooked. Sift in flour, baking powder and salt; stir to combine. Stir in the pine nuts and glacé peaches and mix well. Chill for 1 hour.

● Pre-heat oven to 350°F/175°C/Gas mark 4. Grease two baking sheets or line with non-stick baking parchment.

● Roll tablespoons of the mixture into balls and place onto the baking sheets, at least 8 cm/3 in apart. Flatten with the back of a spoon. Bake for 12 to 15 minutes until golden, but still soft. Cool for 5 minutes on the baking sheets then transfer to wire racks. Store in an airtight container for up to 1 week.

# Pecan and Chocolate Pebbles

*Preparation time: 30 minutes* ● *Cooking time: 10 to 12 minutes* ● *Makes: 15*

**These are very rich meringue-style cookies that look just like beach pebbles!
They are filled with a delicious chocolate ganache.**

## INGREDIENTS

*175 g/6 oz pecan nuts*

*250 g/9 oz caster sugar*

*3 egg whites*

*1 tsp vanilla essence*

### GANACHE FILLING

*200 g/7 oz good-quality plain chocolate, broken up*

*25 g/1 oz unsalted butter*

*50 ml/2 fl oz double cream*

Pre-heat oven to 325°F/160°C/Gas mark 3. Grease two baking sheets or line with non-stick baking parchment.

● Place pecans in a food processor and grind until finely chopped but not into a paste. Add 225 g/8 oz of the sugar and grind for 10 seconds more.

● Beat the egg whites until stiff peaks form. Beat in the remaining sugar a little at a time, beating well after each addition. Beat in the vanilla essence. Gradually beat in the pecan mixture a little at a time until it is all incorporated.

● Fit a piping bag with a 5-mm/½-in nozzle and fill with the mixture. Pipe 5-cm/2-in fingers about 2.5 cm/ 1 in apart on the baking sheets. Bake for 10 to 12 minutes until pale golden. Leave to cool completely on the baking sheets before adding the ganache.

● To make the ganache, melt the chocolate in a bowl in the microwave or in a double boiler over simmering water. Heat the butter and cream in a small saucepan, add to the chocolate and stir until smooth and glossy. Cool, stirring occasionally, until a spreadable consistency is reached. Carefully spread half the fingers with the ganache and sandwich with another finger. Because these cookies contain fresh cream they should be eaten on the day they are made.

# Coconut and Chocolate Swirls

*Preparation time: 40 minutes + chilling* ● *Cooking time: 10 to 15 minutes* ● *Makes: About 25*

**These are very delicate pinwheel cookies, ideal for a child's party.**

### INGREDIENTS

120 g/4 oz butter, softened

150 g/5 oz light brown sugar

120 g/4 oz plain flour

50 g/2 oz unsweetened cocoa powder

½ tsp salt

½ tsp baking powder

### COCONUT FILLING

2 heaped Tbsp apricot jam

75 g/3 oz sweetened flaked coconut

Beat butter and sugar together in a bowl until light and fluffy. Sift in flour, cocoa powder, salt and baking powder. Gradually mix to a soft dough using your fingertips. Roll out on a piece of greaseproof paper to a 23 x 25-cm/9 x 10-in rectangle, cutting the dough to shape. Do not flour the greaseproof paper as it will change the colour of the dough. Carefully slide a thin metal spatula under the dough to release it from the paper, but leave it on the paper.

● Gently warm the jam then brush all over the cookie dough. Sprinkle over the coconut, patting it into the jam. Roll up the dough from a long side using the paper to help, but ensuring that it does not go inside the rolled dough. Do not allow the dough to crack. If it does, gently warm a knife and seal the crack. Roll up in the paper and chill for at least 30 minutes.

● Pre-heat oven to 350°F/175°C/Gas mark 4. Grease or line a baking sheet with non-stick baking parchment.

● Allow the rolled dough to sit at room temperature for 5 minutes then, using a thin-bladed knife, cut the log into 5-mm/½-in slices and place on the baking sheet. Bake for 10 to 15 minutes. Cool for 5 minutes then transfer to wire racks to cool. Store in an airtight container for up to 1 week.

# Toasted Cashew and Raisin Cookies

*Preparation time: 20 minutes + chilling* ●
*Cooking time: 12 to 15 minutes* ● *Makes: About 20*

**Toasting the cashews makes them crisper, so the cookies are crunchier.**

### INGREDIENTS

| |
|---|
| 150 g/5 oz cashew nuts |
| 120 g/4 oz butter, softened |
| 150 g/5 oz light brown sugar |
| 1 egg, beaten |
| 2 tsp almond essence |
| 120 g/4 oz plain flour |
| 2 tsp baking powder |
| 1 tsp salt |
| 175 g/6 oz raisins |

Pre-heat oven to 375°F/190°C/Gas mark 5. Place cashew nuts on a baking sheet and toast for 5 minutes. Cool then roughly chop.

● Put butter and sugars in a bowl and beat until light and fluffy. Beat in the egg and almond essence. Sift in the flour, baking powder and salt; mix well. Add the chopped cashew nuts and raisins. Mix to a dough. Chill for 30 minutes if the dough is really soft.

● Pre-heat oven to 350°F/175°C/Gas mark 4. Grease two baking sheets or line with non-stick baking parchment.

● Drop heaped teaspoons of the mixture onto the sheets at least 5 cm/2 in apart and flatten slightly. Bake for 12 to 15 minutes until lightly golden. Cool for 5 minutes on the baking sheets then transfer to wire racks. Store in an airtight container for up to 1 week.

# Orange and Macadamia Half Moons

*Preparation time: 30 minutes + chilling* ●
*Cooking time: 20 to 25 minutes* ● *Makes: 25*

**Orange flower-water gives the cookies a subtle orange flavour.**

### INGREDIENTS

| |
|---|
| 120 g/4 oz butter, softened |
| 3 Tbsp caster sugar |
| 175 g/6 oz plain flour, plus extra for rolling |
| 75 g/3 oz chopped macadamia nuts |
| 1 Tbsp orange flower-water |
| 75 g/3 oz good-quality plain chocolate, broken up |

Grease two baking sheets or line with non-stick baking parchment.

● Put the butter and sugar in a bowl and beat until light and fluffy. Sift in flour, then stir in macadamia nuts and orange flower-water. Mix to a soft dough. Chill for 30 minutes.

● Dust work surface with a little flour, then roll out dough to about 8 mm/⅓ in thick. Stamp out half-moon shapes with a cutter, re-rolling and stamping out the trimmings. Transfer to the baking sheets and chill for at least 30 minutes in the refrigerator.

● Pre-heat oven to 325°F/160°C/Gas mark 3. Bake cookies for 20 to 25 minutes until golden. Cool on wire racks.

● Meanwhile, melt the chocolate in a bowl in the microwave or in a double boiler over simmering water. Once the cookies have cooled, dip one half into the melted chocolate. Place on greaseproof paper to set. Store in an airtight container, but eat within a day or two.

# Banoffee Squares

*Preparation time: 35 minutes + chilling* ● *Cooking time: 35 minutes* ● *Makes: 24*

**These cookies are packed with dried banana chips and topped with a rich
toffee and pecan sauce – truly scrumptious!**

### INGREDIENTS

### BANANA BASE

*120 g/4 oz butter, softened*

*120 g/4 oz caster sugar*

*1 medium egg, beaten*

*175 g/6 oz plain flour*

*½ tsp baking powder*

*75 g/3 oz dried banana chips*

### PECAN TOPPING

*50 g/2 oz unsalted butter*

*200 g/7 oz light brown sugar*

*50 ml/2 fl oz double cream*

*125 ml/4 fl oz golden syrup*

*150 g/5 oz roughly chopped pecan nuts*

Grease and line the base and sides of a 28 x 20-cm/11 x 8-in baking tin with non-stick baking parchment.

● Put the butter and sugar in a bowl and beat until light and fluffy. Beat in the egg. Sift in the flour and baking powder and mix well. Stir the banana chips into the mixture. Spoon the mixture into the tin, spreading it evenly. This takes a little time and is easiest with a small spatula or round-bladed knife. Chill for 30 minutes.

● Pre-heat oven to 375°F/190°C/Gas mark 5. Cover dough with a piece of greaseproof paper and bake for 5 minutes. Remove paper and bake for a further 5 minutes. Cool while making the topping. (Leave the oven turned on.)

● To make the topping, put the butter, sugar, cream and golden syrup in a saucepan and melt gently over a low heat until the sugar dissolves, stirring frequently. Boil hard for 1 minute. Remove from the heat and stir in the pecans. Pour over the baked crust and bake for a further 10 minutes until the top is bubbling. Leave to cool completely in the tin on a wire rack.

● Run a knife around the edges, between the tin and the paper and lift out onto a board. Cut into 24 pieces, 6 across and 4 down. Store in an airtight container for up to 1 week.

# Walnut and Banana Cookies

*Preparation time: 20 minutes + chilling* ● *Cooking time: 10 to 15 minutes* ● *Makes: 25*

**These cookies are quite sweet, with a soft consistency.**

## INGREDIENTS

175 g/6 oz butter, softened

200 g/7 oz light brown sugar

200 g/7 oz caster sugar

2 large ripe bananas, mashed

300 g/10 oz plain flour

1 tsp salt

1 tsp baking powder

120 g/4 oz chopped walnuts

Put the butter and sugars in a bowl and beat until light and fluffy. Mix in the bananas. Sift in the flour, salt and baking powder and mix well. Stir in the walnuts. Chill for about 2 hours.

● Pre-heat oven to 350°F/175°C/Gas mark 4. Grease two baking sheets or line with non-stick baking parchment.

● Drop heaped teaspoons of the mixture onto the baking sheets and flatten with the back of a spoon. Bake for 10 to 15 minutes until golden. Cool for 5 minutes on the baking sheets then transfer to wire racks. Store in an airtight container for up to 1 week.

# Pistachio and Orange Thins

*Preparation time: 30 minutes + chilling* ● *Cooking time: 15 minutes* ● *Makes: About 25*

**Look out for shelled pistachios which will save you lots of time shelling them!**

## INGREDIENTS

*120 g/4 oz butter, softened*

*3 Tbsp caster sugar*

*3 Tbsp light brown sugar*

*3 Tbsp Grand Marnier*

*175 g/6 oz plain flour*

*50 g/2 oz shelled, unsalted pistachios*

Put butter and sugars in a mixing bowl and beat until pale and creamy. Beat in Grand Marnier. Sift in the flour and mix to a firm dough. Transfer to a piece of greaseproof paper and roll into a log 5 cm/2 in in diameter. Chill for 30 minutes.

● Meanwhile, grind or finely chop the pistachios and transfer to a sheet of greaseproof paper. Roll log in the pistachios several times, ensuring the whole log is covered in nuts. Rewrap in the greaseproof paper and chill for a further 30 minutes.

● Pre-heat oven to 325°F/160°C/Gas mark 3. Grease two baking sheets or line with non-stick baking parchment.

● Cut the log into 8-mm/⅓-in thick slices and place on the baking sheets 5 cm/2 in apart. Bake for 15 minutes. Cool for 5 minutes then transfer to wire racks to cool. Store in an airtight container for up to 1 week.

# Chunky Pine Nut and Lemon Cookies

*Preparation time: 15 minutes + chilling* ● *Cooking time: 10 to 15 minutes* ● *Makes: 20*

**Toasting pine nuts brings out their flavour and gives them a slightly smoky taste.**

## INGREDIENTS

### COOKIES

| |
|---|
| 200 g/7 oz pine nuts |
| 120 g/4 oz butter, softened |
| 200 g/7 oz light brown sugar |
| 200 g/7 oz caster sugar |
| 2 eggs, beaten |
| Grated rind of 1 lemon |
| 250 g/9 oz plain flour |
| 1 tsp baking powder |
| 1 tsp salt |

### GLAZE (OPTIONAL)

| |
|---|
| 5 Tbsp granulated sugar |
| 2 Tbsp water |
| 1 Tbsp lemon juice |
| Grated rind of 1 lemon |

Pre-heat oven to 375°F/190°C/Gas mark 5. Place pine nuts on a baking sheet and toast for 5 minutes. Cool.

● Put the butter and sugars in a bowl and beat together until pale and creamy. Gradually beat in the eggs. Don't worry if the mixture looks as if it is curdling, it will be fine when cooked. Stir in the lemon rind. Sift in flour, baking powder and salt and mix. Stir in the nuts and mix well. Chill for 1 hour.

● Pre-heat oven to 350°F/175°C/Gas mark 4. Line two baking sheets with non-stick baking parchment.

● Roll tablespoons of the mixture into balls and place onto the baking sheets at least 8 cm/3 in apart. Flatten with the back of a spoon. Bake for 10 to 15 minutes until golden, but still soft. Cool for 5 minutes on the baking sheets then transfer to wire racks.

● If making the glaze, gently dissolve the sugar in the water and lemon juice. Boil for 5 minutes. Remove from the heat and stir in the lemon rind. Cool then drizzle a little over each cookie. Eat within a day or two, otherwise the cookies will go soft due to the glaze.

### TIP

For a special occasion, omit 1 tablespoon of the water and stir in 1 tablespoon of liqueur into the glaze once it has cooled.

# Coffee Brazil Cookies

*Preparation time: 30 minutes + chilling*
*Cooking time: 15 to 20 minutes • Makes: About 25*

**These elegant cookies are subtly flavoured with coffee.**

### INGREDIENTS

*1 Tbsp strong instant coffee granules*

*2 Tbsp boiling water*

*50 g/2 oz Brazil nuts*

*120 g/4 oz butter, softened*

*50 g/2 oz light brown sugar*

*175 g/6 oz plain flour, plus extra for dusting*

Dissolve the coffee in the boiling water and cool. Put the Brazil nuts in a food processor and finely grind, but take care not to grind to a paste.

● Place butter and sugar in a mixing bowl and beat together until light and fluffy. Beat in the coffee, then sift in the flour. Stir in the ground Brazil nuts and mix to a stiff dough. Chill for at least 30 minutes.

● Grease two baking sheets or line with non-stick baking parchment. Dust work surface with flour and roll out the dough to 8 mm/⅓ in thick. Stamp out shapes using cookie cutters, re-rolling and stamping out the trimmings. Transfer to the baking sheets and chill for about 15 minutes.

● Pre-heat oven to 350°F/175°C/Gas mark 4. Bake for 15 to 20 minutes. Cool for 5 minutes then transfer to wire racks. Store in an airtight container for up to 1 week.

# Coconut and Walnut Cookies

*Preparation time: 15 minutes + chilling*
*Cooking time: 12 minutes • Makes: About 40*

**The coconut gives these cookies a delicious chewy texture.**

### INGREDIENTS

*225 g/8 oz butter, softened*

*225 g/8 oz granulated sugar*

*2 eggs, beaten*

*1 tsp vanilla essence*

*225 g/8 oz plain flour*

*1 tsp baking powder*

*1 tsp salt*

*120 g/4 oz sweetened flaked coconut*

*About 75 g/3 oz walnut halves*

Put butter and sugar in a bowl and beat until pale and creamy. Gradually add the eggs and vanilla essence. Sift in the flour, baking powder and salt and stir in the sweetened flaked coconut. Divide the dough into two pieces, transfer to two pieces of greaseproof paper and form each piece into a log about 5 cm/2 in in diameter. Chill for at least 2 hours and preferably overnight.

● Pre-heat oven to 350°F/175°C/Gas mark 4. Grease two baking sheets or line with non-stick baking parchment.

● Unwrap one log and slice into 5-mm/½ in slices. Transfer to the baking sheets and press a walnut half into the centre of each cookie. Bake for about 12 minutes until lightly golden around the edges. Cool for 5 minutes then transfer to wire cooling racks. Repeat with the second log. Store in an airtight container for up to 1 week.

# Hazelnut and Cinnamon Rounds with Vanilla Glaze

*Preparation time: 25 minutes + chilling* ●
*Cooking time: 15 minutes* ● *Makes: About 40*

**Have fun with these cookies stamping out all different shapes and sizes.**

### INGREDIENTS

120 g/4 oz butter, softened

3 Tbsp caster sugar

120 g/4 oz plain flour

2 tsp ground cinnamon

175 g/6 oz ground hazelnuts

### GLAZE

75 g/3 oz icing sugar, sifted

1 tsp vanilla essence

2–3 tsp water

Put butter and sugar in a bowl and beat until light and creamy. Sift in the flour and cinnamon, then stir in the ground hazelnuts. Mix to a dough. Transfer to non-stick baking parchment and roll into a log about 5 cm/2 in in diameter. Chill for 2 hours.

● Grease two baking sheets or line with non-stick baking parchment. Cut 8-mm/⅓-in slices from the log. Transfer to the baking sheets.

● Pre-heat oven to 350°F/175°C/Gas mark 4. Bake cookies for 15 minutes until lightly browned. Cool for 5 minutes on the sheets then transfer to wire racks.

● To make the glaze, place the icing sugar and vanilla essence in a small bowl and add sufficient water to make a pourable icing. Drizzle over the cookies. Allow glaze to set before serving.

# Double Almond Cookies

*Preparation time: 15 minutes + chilling* ●
*Cooking time: 15 to 17 minutes* ● *Makes: About 30*

**If you like almonds, you'll love these cookies! You simply couldn't fit any more almonds in the batter.**

### INGREDIENTS

225 g/8 oz butter, softened

200 g/7 oz caster sugar

200 g/7 oz light brown sugar

2 large eggs, beaten

225 g/8 oz plain flour

1 tsp salt

1 tsp baking powder

175 g/6 oz chopped blanched almonds

125 g/4 oz flaked almonds

Beat together butter and sugars until soft and creamy. Gradually beat in the eggs. The mixture may look as if it is curdling, but it will be fine when cooked. Sift in flour, salt and baking powder and mix to combine. Add all the almonds and mix well. Chill mixture for at least 1 hour in the refrigerator.

● Pre-heat oven to 350°F/175°C/Gas mark 4. Line two large baking sheets with non-stick baking parchment.

● Roll tablespoons of the mixture into balls and place on the baking sheets at least 8 cm/3 in apart. Flatten slightly with the back of a spoon. Bake for about 15 to 17 minutes until golden. Leave to cool for five minutes then transfer to wire racks to cool. Store in an airtight container.

# Drizzled Chocolate and Brazil Nut Cookies

*Preparation time: 35 minutes + chilling* ● *Cooking time: 10 to 15 minutes* ● *Makes: About 25*

**The swirled chocolate makes these cookies a bit special.**

## INGREDIENTS

225 g/8 oz butter, softened

200 g/4 oz light brown sugar

200 g/7 oz caster sugar

2 eggs, beaten

250 g/9 oz plain flour

1 tsp baking powder

1 tsp salt

120 g/4 oz finely chopped Brazil nuts

50 g/2 oz plain chocolate, chopped

Put the butter and sugars in a bowl and beat together until pale and creamy. Gradually beat in the eggs. Don't worry if the mixture looks as if it is curdling, it will be fine when cooked. Sift in flour, baking powder and salt and mix. Stir in the Brazil nuts and mix well. Chill for 1 hour.

● Pre-heat oven to 350°F/175°C/Gas mark 4. Grease two baking sheets or line with non-stick baking parchment.

● Roll tablespoons of the mixture into balls and place onto the baking sheets, at least 8 cm/3 in apart to allow for speading. Flatten with the back of a spoon. Bake for 10 to 15 minutes until golden, but still soft. Cool for 5 minutes on the baking sheets then transfer to wire cooling racks.

● Melt the chocolate in a microwave or in a bowl over a pan of simmering water. Using a teaspoon, drizzle the chocolate over the cookies. Allow to set before serving. Best eaten on the day they are made, but may be stored in an airtight container.

# Pistachio and Apricot Cookies

*Preparation time: 25 minutes + chilling* ● *Cooking time: 15 to 20 minutes* ● *Makes: 20*

**These are very buttery cookies and need a little care in cooking.**

### INGREDIENTS

175 g/6 oz butter, softened

150 g/5 oz caster sugar

2 medium egg yolks

Grated rind of 1 orange

1 tsp vanilla essence

175 g/6 oz plain flour

3 Tbsp shelled pistachios, finely chopped

3 Tbsp apricot jam

Place butter and sugar in a bowl and beat until pale and fluffy. Beat in the egg yolks, orange rind and vanilla essence. Sift in the flour and mix to a soft dough. Chill for at least 1 hour.

● Pre-heat oven to 350°F/175°C/Gas mark 4. Grease two baking sheets or line with non-stick baking parchment.

● Roll tablespoons of the dough into balls then flatten between your palms. Place on the baking sheets, at least 2.5 cm/1 in apart. Bake for 15 to 20 minutes.

● Meanwhile, place the pistachios in a food processor and finely grind. Take care not to over-grind them, otherwise a paste will form. Warm the jam or preserve over low heat until melted. As soon as the cookies come out of the oven, brush with the melted jam and sprinkle with the nuts. Cool for 5 minutes then transfer to wire racks. Store in airtight containers.

### TIP

If you don't have a food processor, chop the nuts finely by hand or buy them ready-chopped.

# Flaky Chocolate and Peanut Cookies

*Preparation time: 15 minutes + chilling*
*Cooking time: 10 to 15 minutes • Makes: 25*

**Chocolate flakes in the dough give these cookies a crazy speckled appearance.**

### INGREDIENTS

*75 g/3 oz blanched, unsalted peanuts, finely chopped*

*225 g/8 oz butter, softened*

*200 g/7 oz light brown sugar*

*200 g/7 oz caster sugar*

*2 eggs, beaten*

*250 g/9 oz plain flour*

*1 tsp baking powder*

*1 tsp salt*

*50 g/2 oz chocolate flakes*

Pre-heat oven to 375°F/190°C/Gas mark 5. Place peanuts on a baking sheet and toast for 5 to 8 minutes. Cool.

● Put the butter and sugars in a bowl and beat together until pale and creamy. Gradually beat in the eggs. Don't worry if the mixture looks as if it is curdling, it will be fine when cooked. Sift in flour, baking powder and salt and mix. Stir in the peanuts and chocolate flakes and mix well. Chill for 1 hour.

● Pre-heat oven to 350°F/175°C/Gas mark 4. Grease two baking sheets or line with non-stick baking parchment.

● Roll tablespoons of the mixture into balls and place onto the baking sheets, at least 8 cm/3 in apart. Flatten with the back of a spoon. Bake for 10 to 15 minutes until golden, but still soft. Cool for 5 minutes on the baking sheets then transfer to wire racks.

# Coffee and Walnut Cookies

*Preparation time: 20 minutes + chilling*
*Cooking time: 15 to 18 minutes • Makes: 35*

**Chocolate-covered coffee beans give you the best of both worlds with their combination of flavours.**

### INGREDIENTS

*225 g/8 oz butter, softened*

*200 g/4 oz light brown sugar*

*200 g/7 oz caster sugar*

*2 eggs, beaten*

*250 g/9 oz plain flour*

*1 tsp baking powder*

*125 g/4 oz finely chopped walnuts*

*75 g/3 oz chocolate-covered coffee beans, finely chopped (see tip)*

Put the butter and sugar in a bowl and beat until light and fluffy. Gradually beat in the eggs. Don't worry if the mixture looks as if it is curdling, it will be fine when cooked. Sift in flour and baking powder and mix. Stir in the walnuts and chocolate-covered coffee beans and mix well. Chill for 1 hour.

● Pre-heat oven to 350°F/175°C/Gas mark 4. Grease two baking sheets or line with non-stick baking parchment.

● Roll tablespoons of the mixture into balls and place onto the baking sheets, at least 8 cm/3 in apart. Flatten with the back of a spoon. Bake for 15 to 18 minutes until golden, but still soft. Cool for 5 minutes on the baking sheets then transfer to wire racks. Store in an airtight container for up to 1 week.

### TIP

You can find chocolate-covered coffee beans in good supermarkets or gourmet food shops.

# Almond and Orange Sandwich Cookies

*Preparation time: 35 to 40 minutes* ● *Cooking time: 10 minutes* ● *Makes: About 15*

**Crunchy almond cookies sandwiched together with an orange buttercream filling.**

### INGREDIENTS

*150 g/5 oz plain flour*

*1 tsp baking powder*

*1 Tbsp caster sugar*

*75 g/3 oz ground almonds*

*120 g/4 oz butter*

*125 ml/4 fl oz golden syrup*

### FILLING

*50 g/2 oz unsalted butter, softened*

*120 g/4 oz icing sugar*

*Grated rind of 1 orange*

*1 Tbsp orange juice*

Pre-heat oven to 375°F/190°C/Gas mark 5. Grease two baking sheets or line with non-stick baking parchment.

● Sift the flour and baking powder into a large bowl. Stir in the sugar and ground almonds and make a well in the centre. Put the butter and golden syrup in a small saucepan and stir over a gentle heat until the butter has melted. Pour into the dry ingredients and mix to a soft dough. Cool slightly.

● Take teaspoons of the mixture and roll into balls. Place on the baking sheets at least 5 cm/2 in apart and flatten slightly with the back of a spoon. Bake for 10 minutes. Cool for 5 minutes then transfer to wire racks.

● To make the filling, beat the butter until very soft and creamy, then gradually beat in the icing sugar. Slowly beat in the orange rind and juice. Leave it to harden slightly, then use to sandwich the cookies together. These cookies are best eaten soon after filling but may be stored in an airtight container.

# Coconut and Lime Crunchies

*Preparation time: 20 minutes + chilling* ●
*Cooking time: 7 minutes* ● *Makes: About 12*

**These are light and crispy cookies with a hint of tangy lime.**

### INGREDIENTS

*75 g/3 oz sweetened flaked coconut*

*120 g/4 oz butter, softened*

*50 g/2 oz caster sugar*

*Pinch of salt*

*Grated rind of 1 lime*

*1 Tbsp fresh lime juice*

Heat a frying pan over a medium to high heat. Add sweetened flaked coconut a little at a time and dry fry for about 30 seconds, stirring continuously until lightly golden. Transfer to a mixing bowl.

● In a separate bowl beat the butter and sugar together until pale and fluffy. Beat in salt, lime rind and lime juice. Stir in toasted coconut and form a soft dough. Cover and chill for at least 2 hours.

● Pre-heat oven to 375°F/190°C/Gas mark 5. Grease two baking sheets or line with non-stick baking parchment.

● Take teaspoons of the mixture, roll into balls then squash flat. Place on baking sheets at least 2.5 cm/1 in apart. Bake for about 7 minutes. Cool on the baking sheets. Store in an airtight container for up to 1 week.

### TIP

Toasting coconut before using it really improves the flavour and gives it a chewy texture.

# Crunchy Nut Cookies

*Preparation time: 15 minutes + chilling* ●
*Cooking time: 10 to 15 minutes* ● *Makes: 30*

**Crunchy nut cereals are great for adding to cookie dough because they already contain nuts and the cereal makes the cookies really crunchy.**

### INGREDIENTS

*225 g/8 oz butter, softened*

*200 g/7 oz light brown sugar*

*200 g/7 oz caster sugar*

*2 eggs, beaten*

*250 g/9 oz plain flour*

*1 tsp baking powder*

*1 tsp salt*

*70 g/2½ oz crunchy nut cereal*

Put the butter and sugars in a bowl and beat together until pale and creamy. Gradually beat in the eggs. Don't worry if the mixture looks as if it is curdling it will be fine when cooked. Sift in flour, baking powder and salt; fold into the mixture. Stir in the crunchy nut cereal and mix well. Chill for 1 hour.

● Pre-heat oven to 350°F/175°C/Gas mark 4. Grease two baking sheets or line with non-stick baking parchment.

● Roll tablespoons of the mixture into balls and place onto the baking sheets, at least 8 cm/3 in apart. Flatten with the back of a spoon. Bake for 10 to 15 minutes until golden, but still soft. Cool for 5 minutes on the baking sheets then transfer to wire racks. Store in an airtight container for up to 1 week.

# Double Ginger Pecan Cookies

*Preparation time: 20 minutes* ●
*Cooking time: 12 minutes* ● *Makes: 25*

**These cookies are for real ginger lovers. They contain both ground ginger and stem or preserved ginger.**

INGREDIENTS

*200 g/7 oz plain flour*

*1 tsp baking powder*

*2 tsp ground ginger*

*1 Tbsp caster sugar*

*75 g/3 oz chopped pecan nuts*

*120 g/4 oz butter*

*125 ml/4 fl oz golden syrup*

*1 Tbsp finely chopped stem ginger or ginger preserve*

*2 tsp stem ginger syrup (from the stem ginger jar)*

*or additional golden syrup*

Pre-heat oven to 375°F/190°C/Gas mark 5. Grease two baking sheets or line with non-stick baking parchment.

● Sift the flour, baking powder and ground ginger into a large bowl. Stir in the sugar and pecans and make a well in the centre.

● Put butter, syrup, stem ginger and stem ginger syrup, if using, in a small saucepan and stir over a gentle heat until the butter has melted. Pour into the dry ingredients and mix to a soft dough. Cool for 10 minutes.

● Take teaspoons of the mixture and roll into balls. Place on the baking sheets at least 5 cm/2 in apart and flatten slightly with the back of a spoon. Bake for 15 to 20 minutes until golden. Cool for 5 minutes then transfer to wire racks. Store in an airtight container for up to 1 week.

# Pistachio and Mint Creams

*Preparation time: 30 minutes + chilling* ● *Cooking time: 10 to 15 minutes* ● *Makes: About 20*

**Delicate pistachio cookies sandwiched together with a rich, dark chocolate and mint ganache**

INGREDIENTS

*75 g/3 oz pistachios*

*120 g/4 oz butter, softened*

*3 Tbsp caster sugar*

*150 g/5 oz plain flour*

MINT GANACHE

*25 g/1 oz butter*

*125 g/4 oz plain chocolate*

*1 tsp peppermint essence*

*2 Tbsp whipping cream, at room temperature*

Put pistachios in a food processor and finely grind. Put butter and sugar in a bowl and beat until light and fluffy. Sift in the flour, add the ground pistachios, and mix to a dough. Scrape onto a piece of greaseproof paper and form into a log 5 cm/2 in in diameter. Chill for 1 hour.

● Pre-heat oven to 350°F/175°C/Gas mark 4. Grease two baking sheets or line with non-stick baking parchment.

● Slice 5-mm/½-in thick cookies from the dough and put on baking sheets 2.5 cm/1 in apart. Bake for 10 to 15 minutes. Cool, then transfer to wire racks.

● To make the ganache, place the butter, chocolate and peppermint essence and cream in a double boiler over simmering water. Stir until melted and smooth. Remove from the heat and cool for 5 minutes. Then stir until thick. Spread over the base of half the cookies and gently stick to the base of the remaining cookies. These are best eaten on the day they are made.

# Chocolate and Hazelnut Treats

*Preparation time: 25 minutes* ●
*Cooking time: 10 to 15 minutes* ●
*Makes: 30 double cookies*

**These are deliciously crumbly and you get twice the amount of cookie!**

### INGREDIENTS

*225 g/8 oz butter, softened*

*200 g/7 oz light brown sugar*

*200 g/7 oz caster sugar*

*2 eggs, beaten*

*250 g/9 oz plain flour*

*1 tsp baking powder*

*1 tsp salt*

*175 g/6 oz chopped hazelnuts*

*175 g/6 oz chocolate and hazelnut spread*

Put the butter and sugars in a bowl and beat together until pale and creamy. Gradually beat in the eggs. Don't worry if the mixture looks as if it is curdling, it will be fine when cooked. Sift in flour, baking powder and salt and mix. Stir in the hazelnuts and mix well. Chill for 1 hour.

● Pre-heat oven to 350°F/175°C/Gas mark 4. Grease two baking sheets or line with non-stick baking parchment.

● Roll level teaspoons of the mixture into balls and place onto the baking sheets, at least 5 cm/2 in apart. Flatten with the back of a spoon. Bake for 10 to 15 minutes until golden, but still soft. Cool for 5 minutes on the sheets then transfer to wire cooling racks. Once cooled, sandwich together with the chocolate spread. Best eaten soon after filling but may be stored in an airtight container.

# Mixed Nut and Cherry Cookies

*Preparation time: 30 minutes + chilling* ●
*Cooking time: 13 to 15 minutes* ● *Makes: About 30*

**Any combination of nuts can be used, or buy a packet of ready-mixed nuts.**

### INGREDIENTS

*225 g/8 oz butter, softened*

*120 g/4 oz light brown sugar*

*200 g/7 oz caster sugar*

*2 eggs, beaten*

*250 g/9 oz plain flour*

*1 tsp baking powder*

*1 tsp salt*

*120 g/4 oz finely chopped mixed nuts*

*125 g/4 oz dried Morello or sour cherries*

Put the butter and sugars in a bowl and beat together until pale and creamy. Gradually beat in the eggs. Don't worry if the mixture looks as if it is curdling, it will be fine when cooked. Sift in flour and baking powder and mix. Stir in the chopped nuts and dried cherries mix well. Chill for 1 hour.

● Pre-heat oven to 350°F/175°C/Gas mark 4. Grease two baking sheets or line with non-stick baking parchment.

● Roll tablespoons of the mixture into balls and place onto the baking sheets, at least 8 cm/3 in apart. Flatten with the back of a spoon. Bake for 13 to 15 minutes until golden, but still soft. Cool for 5 minutes on the sheets then transfer to wire cooling racks.

● These cookies are best eaten on the day they are made, but may be stored in an airtight container.

# Pecan and Marshmallow Munchies

*Preparation time: 15 minutes + chilling ●*
*Cooking time: 12 to 15 minutes ● Makes: About 25*

**These chewy cookies are simply irresistible! The marshmallows melt in little patches of each cookie giving an unexpected change of flavour.**

## INGREDIENTS

175 g/6 oz butter, softened

50 g/2 oz light brown sugar

200 g/7 oz caster sugar

2 eggs, beaten

3 Tbsp clear runny honey

250 g/9 oz plain flour

1 tsp baking powder

1 tsp salt

120 g/4 oz finely chopped pecan nuts

120 g/4 oz mini marshmallows

Put the butter and sugars in a bowl and beat together until pale and creamy. Gradually beat in the eggs and honey. Sift in flour, baking powder and salt; mix well. Stir in the pecans and marshmallows until well combined. Chill for at least 1 hour.

● Pre-heat oven to 350°F/175°C/Gas mark 4. Grease two baking sheets or line with non-stick baking parchment.

● Roll tablespoons of the mixture into balls and place onto the baking sheets, at least 8 cm/3 in apart. Flatten with the back of a spoon. Bake for 12 to 15 minutes until golden, but still soft. Cool for 5 minutes on the baking sheets then transfer to wire racks. Store in an airtight container for up to 1 week.

# Walnut and Marmalade Cookies

*Preparation time: 15 minutes + chilling ●*
*Cooking time: 15 to 18 minutes ● Makes: About 30*

**Adding marmalade to cookies gives them a toffee-like flavour and texture.**

## INGREDIENTS

225 g/8 oz butter, softened

200 g/7 oz light brown sugar

200 g/7 oz caster sugar

2 eggs, beaten

3 Tbsp orange marmalade

250 g/9 oz plain flour

1 tsp baking powder

1 tsp salt

120 g/4 oz finely chopped walnuts

Put the butter and sugars in a bowl and beat together until pale and creamy. Gradually beat in the eggs and marmalade. Don't worry if the mixture looks as if it is curdling, it will be fine when cooked. Sift in flour, baking powder and salt and mix. Stir in the walnuts and mix well. Chill for 1 hour.

● Pre-heat oven to 350F/175°C/Gas mark 4. Grease two baking sheets or line with non-stick baking parchment.

● Roll tablespoons of the mixture into balls and place onto the baking sheets, at least 8 cm/3 in apart. Flatten with the back of a spoon. Bake for 15 to 18 minutes until golden, but still soft. Cool for 5 minutes on the baking sheets then transfer to wire racks. Store in an airtight container for up to 1 week.

# Walnut and Carrot Cookies

*Preparation time: 30 minutes + chilling* ●
*Cooking time: 10 to 12 minutes* ● *Makes: About 20*

**Carrots have a sweet flavour and make the perfect match for walnuts.**

### INGREDIENTS

175 g/6 oz butter, softened

250 g/9 oz caster sugar

2 eggs, beaten

150 g/5 oz chopped walnuts

50 g/2 oz grated carrot

400 g/14 oz plain flour

1 tsp baking powder

Put butter and sugar in a mixing bowl and beat until pale and fluffy. Gradually beat in the eggs. Don't worry if the mixture looks as if it is curdling, it will be fine once cooked. Stir in the walnuts and grated carrot. Sift in the flour and baking powder and form into a dough. Chill for 1 hour.

● Pre-heat oven to 350°F/175°C/Gas mark 4. Grease two baking sheets or line with non-stick baking parchment.

● Take tablespoonfuls of the dough and form into balls. Place on the baking sheets at least 2.5 cm/1 in apart and flatten with the back of a spoon. Bake for 10 to 12 minutes. Cool on the baking sheets. Store the cookies in an airtight container.

# Syrupy Macadamia Nut Cookies

*Preparation time: 30 minutes + chilling* ●
*Cooking time: 20 minutes* ● *Makes: About 16*

**Macadamia nuts are very rich so not many are required to give a strong, nutty flavour.**

### INGREDIENTS

120 g/4 oz butter, softened

150 g/5 oz light brown sugar

4 tsp golden syrup

1 medium egg yolk

1 Tbsp orange juice

175 g/6 oz plain flour

½ tsp baking powder

120 g/4 oz macadamia nuts, roughly chopped

50 g/2 oz white chocolate chips

Put butter and sugar in a bowl and beat until pale and fluffy. Beat in the golden syrup, egg yolk and orange juice. Sift in the flour and baking powder; mix well. Stir in the macadamia nuts and mix to a soft dough.

● Press into a greased 20-cm/8-in square tin and chill for 30 minutes.

● Pre-heat oven to 350°F/175°C/Gas mark 4. Bake the mixture for about 20 minutes until cooked through.

● Meanwhile, melt the chocolate in a microwave or in a double boiler over simmering water. Drizzle the baked dough with the chocolate. Allow to harden before slicing into 16 squares. Store in an airtight container for up to 1 week.

# Macadamia Chocolate Bars

*Preparation time: 35 minutes* •
*Cooking time: 25 minutes* • *Makes: 21*

**The easy way to make a chocolate topping – just use whole bars of chocolate and let them melt over the warm cookie dough!**

### INGREDIENTS

*175 g/6 oz butter, softened*

*120 g/4 oz caster sugar*

*3 Tbsp milk*

*1 tsp almond essence*

*175 g/6 oz plain flour*

*Pinch of salt*

*120 g/4 oz macadamia nuts, roughly chopped*

*300 g/10 oz good-quality milk or plain chocolate bars*

Pre-heat oven to 350°F/175°C/Gas mark 4. Grease and base line a 32.5 x 23-cm/13 x 9-in baking tin.
● Put the butter and sugar in a bowl and beat until light and fluffy. Beat in the milk and almond essence. Sift in the flour and salt and form into a dough. Add half the nuts and mix well. Spread into the prepared tin and bake for 20 to 25 minutes until lightly browned around the edges.
● As soon as it is out of the oven, cover with the chocolate bars, then return to the oven for 2 minutes. Once out of the oven leave for 1 minute to let the chocolate melt. Once melted spread the chocolate evenly over the baked dough. Scatter over the remaining nuts and leave to cool completely. Cut into 21 bars, 7 across and 3 down. Store in an airtight container for up to 1 week.

# Hazelnut and Treacle Cookies

*Preparation time: 15 minutes + chilling* •
*Cooking time: 15 minutes* • *Makes: About 25*

**Some of the sugar is replaced by treacle in this drop cookie. It makes the cookies rich, rather than intensely sweet.**

### INGREDIENTS

*175 g/6 oz butter, softened*

*200 g/7 oz light brown sugar*

*3 Tbsp treacle*

*1 egg, beaten*

*250 g/9 oz plain flour*

*1 tsp baking powder*

*1 tsp grated nutmeg*

*1 tsp salt*

*120 g/4 oz chopped hazelnuts*

Put the butter and sugar in a bowl and beat until light and fluffy. Gradually beat in the treacle and egg. Sift in the flour, baking powder, nutmeg and salt; then mix. Stir in the nuts and form into a dough. Chill for at least 1 hour or overnight.
● Pre-heat oven to 350°F/175°C/Gas mark 4. Grease two baking sheets or line with non-stick baking parchment.
● Take heaped teaspoons of the dough, form into balls and flatten slightly between your palms. Place on the baking sheets at least 5 cm/2 in apart and bake for 15 minutes. Cool for 5 minutes and then transfer to wire racks.

# Coconut Macaroons

*Preparation time: 10 minutes • Cooking time: 20 minutes • Makes: 20*

**These are so simple to make, you'll never buy shop-bought macaroons again!**

### INGREDIENTS

| |
|---|
| *4 egg whites* |
| *4 tsp cornflour* |
| *225 g/8 oz caster sugar* |
| *225 g/8 oz sweetened flaked coconut* |
| *20 whole blanched almonds* |
| *Edible rice paper, optional* |

Pre-heat oven to 350°F/175°C/Gas mark 4. Grease two baking sheets or line with rice paper or non-stick baking parchment.

● Beat the egg whites until foamy but not holding their shape. Stir in the remaining ingredients and mix well. Place 2 teaspoons of the mixture on the baking sheets about 5 cm/2 in in diameter, spaced well apart. Flatten slightly and place an almond in the centre of each.

● Bake for 20 minutes until just turning golden. Cool on the baking sheets. If using rice paper, tear from around each macaroon once cooled.

# Coconut and Rum Cookies

*Preparation time: 30 minutes + chilling* ● *Cooking time: 15 to 20 minutes* ● *Makes: About 20*

**These are delicate, crisp and crumbly cookies.**

### INGREDIENTS

*120 g/4 oz sweetened flaked coconut*

*225 g/8 oz butter, softened*

*200 g/7 oz light brown sugar*

*2 Tbsp dark rum*

*200 g/7 oz plain flour*

*Pinch of salt*

*50 g/2 oz chopped flaked almonds*

Heat a frying pan over high heat. Add half the coconut and dry-fry for about 30 seconds, stirring continuously until lightly golden. Place in a bowl and repeat with remaining coconut.

● Place the butter and sugar in a separate bowl and beat until light and fluffy. Beat in the rum. Sift in the flour and salt and mix well. Stir in the almonds and half the toasted coconut; mix well. Lightly flour the work surface and knead dough until soft.

● Divide mixture in two. Place each piece in a piece of greaseproof paper and shape each into a log about 5 cm/2 in in diameter and wrap each piece in greaseproof paper. Chill for at least 2 hours or overnight.

● Pre-heat oven to 350°F/175°C/Gas mark 4. Grease two baking sheets or line with non-stick baking parchment.

● Cut dough into 5-mm/½-in slices and arrange on the baking sheets at least 5 cm/2 in apart. Cook for 15 to 20 minutes until very lightly browned. As soon as the cookies are out of the oven, sprinkle over the remaining toasted coconut. Cool for 5 minutes on the baking sheets then transfer to wire racks. Store in an airtight container for up to 1 week.

# Mocha Mixed Nut Drops

*Preparation time: 30 minutes + chilling* ●
*Cooking time: 15 minutes* ● *Makes: About 25*

**Nuts, coffee and chocolate – there is something for everyone in these delicate cookies.**

### INGREDIENTS

*1 Tbsp strong instant coffee granules*

*2 Tbsp boiling water*

*120 g/4 oz butter*

*3 Tbsp caster sugar*

*150 g/5 oz plain flour*

*50 g/2 oz mixed nuts*

Dissolve the coffee granules in the boiling water and leave to cool.

● Put the butter and sugar in a bowl and beat until light and fluffy. Add the cooled coffee. Sift in the flour, then stir in the mixed nuts. Mix to a soft dough, then transfer to greaseproof paper and roll into a fat log, about 5 cm/2 in in diameter. Chill for 1 hour.

● Pre-heat oven to 325°F/175°C/Gas mark 2. Grease two baking sheets or line with non-stick baking parchment.

● Using a sharp knife, cut 2-cm/¾-in slices off the log and transfer to the baking sheets. If you have time, chill for a further 30 minutes in the refrigerator. Bake for about 15 minutes until lightly golden. Cool for 5 minutes then transfer to wire racks. Store in an airtight container for up to 1 week.

# Brazil and Orange Chocolate Treats

*Preparation time: 15 minutes + chilling* ●
*Cooking time: 10 to 15 minutes* ● *Makes: About 30*

**This is the best type of cookie for a quick, scrumptious snack – rich and chewy.**

### INGREDIENTS

*225 g/8 oz butter, softened*

*200 g/7 oz caster sugar*

*200 g/7 oz light brown sugar*

*2 eggs, beaten*

*250 g/9 oz plain flour*

*1 tsp salt*

*1 tsp baking powder*

*150 g/5 oz chopped Brazil nuts*

*150 g/5 oz orange-flavoured chocolate, chopped*

Beat together butter and sugars until soft and creamy. Gradually beat in the eggs. The mixture may look as if it is curdling, but it will be fine when cooked. Sift in flour, salt and baking powder and mix to combine. Stir in Brazil nuts and chocolate until combined. Chill mixture for at least 1 hour in the refrigerator.

● Pre-heat oven to 350°F/175°C/Gas mark 4. Line two large baking sheets with non-stick baking parchment.

● Roll tablespoons of the mixture into balls and place on the baking sheets at least 8 cm/3 in apart. Flatten slightly with the back of a spoon. Bake for 10 to 15 minutes until golden. Leave to cool for 5 minutes then transfer to wire racks to cool. Store in an airtight container.

# Almond and Ginger Florentines

*Preparation time: 20 minutes* ●
*Cooking time: 10 minutes* ● *Makes: About 10*

**Delicious tangy nut cookies are ideal as a gift.**

## INGREDIENTS

50 g/2 oz butter

2 Tbsp golden syrup

50 g/2 oz caster sugar

3 Tbsp plain flour

½ tsp ground ginger

50 g/2 oz chopped almonds

5 Tbsp flaked almonds

5 Tbsp chopped crystallized ginger

Grated rind of 1 lemon

50 g/2 oz good-quality plain chocolate

50 g/2 oz good-quality white chocolate

Pre-heat oven to 350°F/175°C/Gas mark 4. Grease two baking sheets.

● Put butter, golden syrup and sugar in a saucepan over medium heat and stir until the sugar dissolves. Remove from the heat and cool for 5 minutes, stirring. Sift in the flour and ground ginger, then stir in the almonds, crystallized ginger and lemon rind. Drop heaped teaspoons onto the baking sheets at least 8 cm/3 in apart. Shape into neat rounds. Bake for about 10 minutes. Cool for 5 minutes, then transfer to wire racks to cool.

● Melt the dark and white chocolates in two separate bowls in a microwave or over pans of simmering water. Spread the base of each Florentine with either dark or white chocolate then run a fork over the chocolate. Leave upside down to cool.

# Cheddar and Peanut Cookies

*Preparation time: 20 minutes + chilling* ●
*Cooking time: 15 to 17 minutes* ● *Makes: About 30*

**This savory cookie is great for lunch boxes or a quick snack.**

## INGREDIENTS

250 g/9 oz grated Cheddar cheese

175 g/6 oz butter, diced

125 ml/4 fl oz milk

150 g/5 oz plain flour

Pinch of salt

1 tsp baking powder

125 g/4 oz salted peanuts, chopped

About 20 whole salted peanuts

Combine all the ingredients, except the whole peanuts in a large bowl and mix with your fingers until a dough is formed. Chill for 30 minutes.

● Pre-heat oven to 350°F/175°C/Gas mark 4. Grease two baking sheets or line with non-stick baking parchment.

● Take heaped teaspoons of the mixture, roll into balls then flatten slightly. Place on the sheets at least 5 cm/ 2 in apart and press a whole peanut into each cookie. Bake for about 15 to 17 minutes until golden-brown. Cool on the baking sheets and serve warm or cold.

# Bar Cookies

A cross between a cookie and a cake, bar cookies make a satisfying treat. This selection includes some old favourites as well as some new ideas that draw on the new ingredients on the market. There is even a short-cut recipe for making delicious brownies in the microwave. So whether you're making bar cookies as a dessert, or to pack in a lunch box, whether you want them crispy or crunchy, healthy or indulgent, you'll find plenty of inspiration in this chapter.

## Old Favourites

## Special Treats

# Quick Bites

# Portable Snacks

# Grasmere Gingerbread

*Preparation time: 20 minutes* ●
*Cooking time: 30 minutes* ● *Makes: 16 pieces*

**Grasmere, one of the prettiest lakes in the English Lake District, is famous for a ginger shortbread. The gingerbread shop in Grasmere jealously guards its recipe but this family recipe is as good, if not better!**

## INGREDIENTS

*225 g/8 oz plain flour*

*1½ teaspoons ground ginger*

*120 g/4 oz lightly salted butter*

*200 g/7 oz light brown sugar*

*1 Tbsp golden syrup*

*1 Tbsp chopped candied orange peel or candied citrus peel*

*1 Tbsp chopped crystallized ginger*

Pre-heat oven to 350°F/175°C/Gas mark 4. Grease and base-line an 18 x 28-cm/7 x 11-in shallow tin and line with waxed paper or nonstick baking parchment.

● Beat the butter, sugar and golden syrup until light and well blended. Beat in the remaining ingredients and press into the prepared tin.

● Bake for 25 to 30 minutes or until pale golden. Cut into 16 pieces while still hot but leave in the tin to cool. Store in an airtight container.

## TIP

Try to find candied orange peel rather than candied citrus peel as the flavour and texture is superior.

# Coconut and Prune Triangles

*Preparation time: 30 minutes* ●
*Cooking time: 35 to 40 minutes* ● *Makes: 18 triangles*

**This recipe is a delicious mixture of basic store cupboard ingredients.**

## INGREDIENTS

*50 g/2 oz stoned prunes*

*Juice and rind of 1 lemon*

*4 Tbsp water*

*1 Tbsp sugar*

*50 g/2 oz wholemeal flour*

*¼ tsp baking powder*

*120 g/4 oz plain flour*

*6 Tbsp soft tub margarine*

*200 g/7 oz soft brown sugar*

*1 egg, beaten*

## TOPPING

*225 g/8 oz sweetened flaked coconut*

*4 Tbsp clear/runny honey*

*2 eggs*

Pre-heat oven to 350°F/175°C/Gas mark 4. Grease and base line an 18 x 28-cm/7 x 11-in shallow tin.

● Chop the prunes and place in a pan with the lemon rind and juice, water and sugar. Cook until soft.

● Sift the two flours and baking powder, retaining the bran. Beat the margarine and sugar and beat in the egg. Work in the flours to form a dough and press into the pan. Spread the prune mixture over the dough.

● Beat the remaining 2 eggs, then beat in the honey and stir in the coconut. Spread over the prune mixture.

● Bake for 30 to 35 minutes or until golden-brown. Cool in the tin, then cut into squares and across into triangles.

# Double Pear Treats

*Preparation time: 1 hour ● Cooking time: 40 to 45 minutes ● Makes: 15 pieces*

**Double Pear Treats are delicious served hot with cream or yoghurt as a dessert. Or store them in an airtight container and eat cold whenever you feel like spoiling yourself.**

### INGREDIENTS

### BASIC SHORTBREAD

*75 g/3 oz plain flour*

*50 g/2 oz lightly salted butter*

*25 g/1 oz caster sugar*

### BASIC TOPPING

*50 g/2 oz lightly salted butter or margarine*

*50 g/2 oz soft brown sugar*

*1 egg, beaten*

*50 g/2 oz wholewheat flour*

*1½ tsp baking powder*

*¼ tsp mixed spice*

*¼ tsp nutmeg*

*Grated rind of ½ orange*

*1 Tbsp milk*

### FILLING

*3 pear halves from a tin of pears in natural juice*

*4 dried pear halves*

*2 Tbsp plain chocolate chips*

To make the shortbread, pre-heat oven to 350°F/175°C/Gas mark 4. Grease a 20-cm/8-in square tin and line with non-stick baking parchment, so it stands 2.5-cm/1-in above the sides.

● Sift the flour into a bowl and blend in the butter until it resembles breadcrumbs, then stir in the sugar. Press the crumb mixture into the tin, making sure it is smooth and level.

● Bake for 10 to 15 minutes or until the centre is pale golden. Remove from the oven and cool while you make the filling.

● For the topping, beat the butter and sugar until light and fluffy. Gradually beat in the egg. Sift the spices and flour and fold into the mixture, together with the bran left in the sifter, the orange rind and the milk.

● Thoroughly drain the pear halves and chop. Scatter over the shortbread. Dice the dried pears and mix into a bowl of basic topping together with the chocolate chips. Pour over the chopped pears and level.

● Bake for 40 to 45 minutes or until the centres are firm. Cool in the tin for 15 minutes. Turn onto a cooling rack and when cool, cut into portions. Store in an airtight container, or freeze for up to 3 months.

# Simnel Bars

*Preparation time: 1 hour ● Cooking time: 40 to 45 minutes ● Makes: 15 pieces*

**You can make Simnel Bars less seasonal by leaving out the marzipan topping and instead, when cooked and cold, the top can be coated with a thin layer of icing.**

## INGREDIENTS

### BASIC SHORTBREAD

*75 g/3 oz plain flour*

*50 g/2 oz lightly salted butter*

*25 g/1 oz caster sugar*

### BASIC TOPPING

*50 g/2 oz lightly salted butter or margarine*

*50 g/2 oz soft brown sugar*

*1 egg, beaten*

*50 g/2 oz wholewheat flour*

*1½ tsp baking powder*

*¼ tsp mixed spice*

*¼ tsp nutmeg*

*Grated rind of ½ orange*

*1 Tbsp milk*

### FILLING

*120 g/4 oz mixed dried fruit*

*6 glacé cherries*

*2 tsp brandy*

*175 g/6 oz marzipan*

*1 Tbsp apricot jam*

Prepare the basic shortbread and basic toppping in the same way as for Double Pear Treats on the previous page.

● Chop the cherries and lightly mix into a bowl of basic topping together with the brandy and mixed dried fruit. Pour over the shortbread and level the surface.

● Bake for 40 to 45 minutes or until the centres are firm and the sides coming away from the edge of the tin. Cool in the pan for 15 minutes.

● Meanwhile, roll out the marzipan to fit half the sheet, using icing sugar to prevent it sticking to the work surface. Pre-heat the grill for 5 minutes.

● Warm the apricot jam and brush over the bake. Carefully lift the marzipan over and press lightly to fit. Using a sharp knife, mark diagonal lines across the top, making diamonds.

● Place under the grill and turn the heat down to medium. Leave until the marzipan has started to brown, checking constantly. Then gently turn onto a cooling rack covered with a folded teatowel.

● Slip onto a board and cut into portions with a sharp knife. Cool completely before storing or freezing for up to 3 months.

# Coconut and Sesame Crunch

*Preparation time: 15 minutes* ●
*Cooking time: 20 minutes* ● *Makes: 12 pieces*

**A delicious crunch bar with a distinctive nutty flavour. It is a great favourite, with a quick and easy method.**

### INGREDIENTS

120 g/4 oz margarine or butter

50 g/2 oz caster sugar

½ Tbsp golden syrup

75 g/3 oz self-raising flour

50 g/2 oz rolled oats

75 g/3 oz sweetened flaked coconut

2 Tbsp sesame seeds

Pre-heat oven to 350°F/175°C/Gas mark 4. Grease and base-line a 20 x 20-cm/8 x 8-in shallow tin.
● Melt the fat, sugar and syrup over a low heat in a large saucepan. Remove from the heat and stir in the remaining ingredients. Press into the tin. Do not worry if it looks very greasy at this stage, it is dry when cooked. Bake for 15 to 20 minutes until golden. Leave to cool for 10 minutes then cut into 12 pieces but leave to cool completely in the tin. Store in an airtight container for up to 1 week.

# Boston Brownies

*Preparation time: 20 minutes* ●
*Cooking time: 30 to 35 minutes* ●
*Makes: 9 large squares*

**Brownies are quite irresistible gooey squares of chocolate heaven and crunchy nuts. This recipe uses only cocoa which gives it a rich, full flavour – and is useful when the chocolate has disappeared from the cupboard.**

### INGREDIENTS

50 g/2 oz unsweetened cocoa powder

5 Tbsp water

¾ stick lightly salted butter

2 eggs

225 g/8 oz granulated sugar

75 g/3 oz plain flour

75 g/3 oz coarsely chopped pecan nuts

Pre-heat oven to 350°F/175°C/Gas mark 4. Grease and base-line a 20 x 20-cm/8 x 8-in tin.
● Place the cocoa in a small saucepan and gradually blend in the water. Briefly stir over a low heat to make a smooth paste. Add the butter or margarine and heat until it has melted.
● Beat the eggs and sugar until light and fluffy, then beat in the cocoa mixture.
● Sift the flour and fold in, then stir in the nuts. Spread into the tin.
● Bake for 25 to 30 minutes until risen and firm in the center. It is normal for the mixture to sink a little in the centre on cooling. Cool for 15 minutes, then cut into squares. Store in an airtight container.

# Sweet Pizza

*Preparation time: 40 minutes ● Cooking time: 20 minutes + 10 minutes ● Makes: 8 wedges*

**The rocky road cookie appears in many guises. In this version, a traditional, lemon-flavoured mixture is used to make the base.**

### INGREDIENTS

### LEMON BASE

*225 g/8 oz plain flour*

*120 g/4 oz lightly salted butter or margarine*

*120 g/4 oz caster sugar*

*Grated rind of 1 lemon*

*1 egg*

*Milk, if required*

### TOPPING

*50 g/2 oz mixed chopped nuts*

*75 g/3 oz mini marshmallows*

*50 g/2 oz milk or plain chocolate chips*

*2 Tbsp caramel topping*

Pre-heat oven to 350°F/175°C/Gas mark 4. Grease or line a baking sheet with non-stick baking parchment.

● Prepare the base. Sift the flour into a bowl and blend in the butter or margarine to make fine breadcrumbs. Stir in the sugar and lemon rind. Beat the egg and use it, together with milk if needed, to make a firm but soft dough. It must not be sticky.

● To make a 20-cm/8-in base, take three-quarters of the dough and roll out in a circle. Lift onto the baking sheet and use a flan ring or plate as a guide to the correct shape.

● Bake for about 20 minutes until pale golden and cooked in the centre. Five minutes before the end of the cooking time, place the mixed chopped nuts on a baking sheet and slip into the oven to toast. Leave there for about 10 minutes, until just starting to colour.

● Leave the "pizza" base to cool slightly, then scatter the marshmallows over the surface, followed by the nuts and the chocolate chips. Drizzle the caramel topping over and return to the oven for about 10 minutes until the pizza edges are a deeper colour and the marshmallows are just starting to melt. Serve hot or cold.

# Brazil Nut Blondies

*Preparation time: 15 minutes ● Cooking time: 20 minutes ● Makes: 12 pieces*

**Blondies are brownies without chocolate. To make up for the disappointment, there are plenty of nuts in this sweet, chewy mixture and the colour is quite dark due to the dark sugar.**

### INGREDIENTS

*1 egg*

*375 g/12 oz dark brown sugar*

*1 tsp vanilla essence*

*75 g/3 oz plain flour*

*¼ tsp bicarbonate of soda*

*1 cup chopped Brazil nuts*

*2 tsp milk*

Pre-heat oven to 350°F/175°C/Gas mark 4. Grease and base-line a 20 x 20-cm/8 x 8-in tin.

● Beat the egg and stir in the sugar and vanilla essence. Sift the flour and bicarbonate into the mixture and stir in, together with the nuts and milk. The mixture will be very stiff.

● Spread into the tin and bake for 15 to 20 minutes. Mark into squares before completely cold and leave to cool in the tin. Store in an airtight container.

# Chocolate and Raspberry Macaroon Bars

*Preparation time: 25 minutes* ● *Cooking time: 20 to 25 minutes* ● *Makes: 25*

**These are small, rich bars with an intense chocolate flavour. Use homemade raspberry jam if possible as the flavour mingles deliciously with the chocolate.**

### INGREDIENTS

#### CHOCOLATE SHORTBREAD

*75 g/3 oz plain flour*

*5 Tbsp unsweetened cocoa powder*

*75 g/3 oz lightly salted butter*

*2 egg yolks*

*3 Tbsp caster sugar*

*4-5 Tbsp good quality raspberry jam or preserve*

#### MACAROON MIXTURE

*75 g/3 oz ground almonds*

*1½ Tbsp ground rice*

*2 egg whites*

*3 drops almond essence*

*1½ tsp unsweetened cocoa powder*

Pre-heat oven to 350°F/175°C/Gas mark 4. Grease and base-line an 18 x 18-cm/7 x 11-in tin.

● Sift the flour and cocoa, blend in the butter, stir in the egg yolks and sugar. Work together to form a dough and press into the tin. Lightly spread the raspberry jam over the shortbread.

● Place the sugar, ground almonds and ground rice in a bowl and gently mix. Whisk the egg whites and almond essence until stiff peaks form. Gradually fold in the dry ingredients to a stiff mixture. Spoon over the jam and spread roughly with a fork dipped in water.

● Bake for 25 to 35 minutes until dry but not coloured. Mark into pieces while still warm and leave in the tin until cold. Lightly dust with sifted cocoa powder. Store in an airtight container.

# Cherry and Cinnamon Bars

*Preparation time: 45 minutes* ● *Cooking time: 25 minutes* ● *Makes: 10 bars*

**These ever-popular caramel fingers are combined with powdered cinnamon and dried cherries to give a new slant to a favourite recipe.**

## INGREDIENTS

### SHORTBREAD BASE

*75 g/3 oz butter or margarine*

*2 Tbsp granulated sugar*

*1 tsp ground cinnamon*

*120 g/4 oz plain flour*

### FILLING

*120 g/4 oz lightly salted butter*

*50 g/2 oz caster sugar*

*2 Tbsp golden syrup*

*225 ml/8 fl oz condensed milk*

*½ tsp almond essence*

*1 tsp ground cinnamon*

*50 g/2 oz dried cherries, halved*

### TOPPING

*75 g/3 oz plain chocolate*

*15 g/½ oz unsalted butter*

Pre-heat oven to 350°F/175°C/Gas mark 4. Grease and base-line a 20 x 20-cm/8 x 8-in tin.

● Prepare the base first by beating together the butter and sugar. Sift the flour and cinnamon and work into the mixture. Press evenly into the tin. Prick well and bake for about 20 to 25 minutes until golden. Allow to cool.

● To make the filling, place the butter, sugar, syrup and condensed milk in a heavy-bottomed saucepan and stir over a gentle heat to dissolve. Slowly bring to the boil and cook, stirring constantly, for about 7 minutes until thick and a pale toffee colour. Remove from the heat and beat in the almond essence and cinnamon. Pour half the mixture over the shortbread, sprinkle over the cherries, then the remaining filling. Leave to cool to room temperature and then place in the refrigerator.

● When this layer is cold, melt the chocolate and butter together, either over a bowl of hot water or in the microwave for 1 to 2 minutes. Stir gently and pour over the cherry caramel. Spread evenly over and leave to set. Cut into bars when cold and then store in an airtight container.

# Chocolate Chip and Pecan Shortbread

*Preparation time: 25 minutes • Cooking time: 50 to 60 minutes • Makes: 8 pieces*

**This pale, traditional shortbread is made even more tempting by the addition of nuts and chocolate.
It would make a welcome gift at any time of year but especially for Christmas.**

### INGREDIENTS

5 Tbsp chocolate chips

225 g/8 oz plain flour

50 g/2 oz ground rice

120 g/4 oz caster sugar

Pinch of salt

225 g/8 oz lightly salted butter

75 g/3 oz chopped pecan nuts

Grease a 20-cm/8-in tart tin with a removable base. Place the chocolate chips in the freezer for at least 30 minutes.

● Sift the flour and ground rice into a large bowl, mix in the sugar and salt, then blend in the butter. Stir in the nuts and the chilled chocolate and bring together to form a crumbly dough. Transfer this to the prepared tin and press down firmly using a knife. Prick the surface evenly with a skewer and mark a pattern round the edge using the flat point of a vegetable peeler. Chill for one hour. Mark into 8 portions.

● Pre-heat oven to 300°F/150°C/Gas mark 2. Bake for 50 to 60 minutes. The shortbread must look pale but be cooked in the centre. Return to the oven if necessary for up to 10 minutes longer. Score into portions again and leave to cool in the tin.

# Chocolate and Orange Slices

*Preparation time: 30 minutes* ●
*Cooking time: 20 minutes* ● *Makes: 12 slices*

**These easy slices are another example of the versatility of rolled oats. The orange flavour is only in the icing, so make sure it tastes strong enough before you pour it on.**

## INGREDIENTS

*120 g/4 oz margarine*

*120 g/4 oz self-raising flour*

*1 Tbsp unsweetened cocoa powder*

*150 g/2 oz rolled oats*

*50 g/2 oz superfine sugar*

### TOPPING

*3 Tbsp icing sugar*

*1 tsp unsweetened cocoa powder*

*Grated rind and juice of ½ orange*

*Candied orange pieces, to decorate*

Pre-heat oven to 350°F/175°C/Gas mark 4. Grease and base-line a 20 x 20-cm/8 x 8-in tin.

● Melt the margarine gently in a large saucepan. Sift the flour and cocoa and stir into the margarine with the oats and sugar.

● Press into the tin and level the surface. Bake for 15 to 20 minutes until shrinking from the sides of the tin. Leave to cool while preparing the topping.

● Sift the icing sugar and cocoa together and mix with sufficient orange juice to make a thin icing. Stir in the orange rind and pour over the cookies while still warm.

● It will look more like a glaze than a thick icing. Cut each one into slices and decorate with a small piece of candied orange.

# Date and Oat Crumb Squares

*Preparation time: 30 minutes* ●
*Cooking time: 25 to 30 minutes* ● *Makes: 18*

**This recipe can be utilized to use up dates left over after Christmas and provide snacks in the dark weeks of the New Year. The sharpness of lemon contrasts well with the dates but orange could be used instead.**

## INGREDIENTS

*375 g/12 oz rolled oats*

*120 g/4 oz wholemeal flour*

*175 g/6 oz margarine*

*50 g/2 oz soft brown sugar*

*500 g/1 lb stoned dates*

*8 Tbsp water*

*2 Tbsp lemon juice*

*2 tsp grated lemon rind*

Pre-heat oven to 375°F/190°C/Gas mark 5. Grease and base-line an 18 x 28-cm/7 x 11-in shallow tin.

● Mix the oats and flour in a large bowl and blend in the margarine. Stir in the sugar.

● Chop the dates and place in a saucepan with the remaining ingredients. Heat gently until they form a pulp.

● Press half the crumble mixture firmly into the base of the tin. Gently spread the date mixture over, then the remaining crumb mixture. Press and level the mixture. Bake for about 25 minutes until golden and the mixture is starting to shrink from the sides of the tin.

● Cool in the tin but cut into squares while still warm. Store in an airtight container.

# Cranberry and Sultana Bars

*Preparation time: 20 minutes* ●
*Cooking time: 25 to 30 minutes* ● *Makes: 16 pieces*

**Cranberries give a vivid colour and sharp flavour in contrast to the sweet base mixture. They are most widely available in the autumn, in the run-up to Christmas and freeze well. In this recipe they can be used from frozen if they are free-flowing.**

## INGREDIENTS

*120 g/4 oz margarine or butter*

*125 g/4 oz soft brown sugar*

*2 eggs, beaten*

*120 g/4 oz self-raising flour*

*50 g/2 oz ground almonds*

*120 g/4 oz cranberries*

*75 g/3 oz sultanas*

Pre-heat oven to 350°F/175°C/Gas mark 4. Grease and base-line a 20 x 20-cm/8 x 8-in tin.

● Beat the margarine and sugar until light and fluffy. Beat the eggs in gradually. Sift the flour and gently fold in, together with the ground almonds, whole cranberries and sultanas.

● Pour into the tin and bake for 25 to 35 minutes until well risen, firm in the centre and shrinking slightly from the sides of the tin. Turn out onto a wire sheet to cool, then cut into slices. These bars are best stored in the refrigerator.

# Easy Apricot Squares

*Preparation time: 15 minutes* ●
*Cooking time: 20 to 30 minutes* ● *Makes: 9 pieces*

**These are easy as only five ingredients are quickly combined into a soft, succulent bar. Do leave the apricots in large pieces to make the squares more unusual.**

## INGREDIENTS

*50 g/2 oz lightly salted butter*

*3 Tbsp set honey*

*3 Tbsp golden syrup*

*¼ cup ready to eat dried apricots, halved*

*2⅔ cups muesli*

Pre-heat oven to 325°F/160°C/Gas mark 3. Grease and base-line a 20 x 20-cm/8 x 8-in tin.

● Soften the butter, beat until light, then beat in the honey and syrup. Stir in the remaining ingredients thoroughly and press into the tin. Bake for 20 to 30 minutes. Cool for 5 minutes, then cut into 9 squares. Leave to cool completely before removing from the tin. Store in an airtight container.

# Double Chocolate and Mango Brownies

*Preparation time: 30 minutes* •
*Cooking time: 30 minutes* • *Makes: 12 pieces*

**A luscious brownie with white chocolate pieces inside. The mango contrasts well with the traditional rich chocolate and pecan mixture. This version is firmer than the other brownie recipes, to hold up all these exciting textures.**

### INGREDIENTS

*120 g/4 oz plain chocolate*

*50 g/2 oz lightly salted butter*

*2 eggs*

*120 g/4 oz soft brown sugar*

*120 g/4 oz self-raising flour*

*50 g/2 oz chopped crystallized mango*

*50 g/2 oz chopped pecan nuts*

*5 Tbsp white chocolate chips*

*5 Tbsp plain chocolate chips*

Pre-heat oven to 375°F/190°C/Gas mark 5. Grease and base-line a 20 x 20-cm/8 x 8-in tin.

• Melt the chocolate over a bowl of hot water or in the microwave for 1½ to 2 minutes. Slice the butter into the chocolate and stir to melt, reheating briefly if necessary.

• Beat the eggs and sugar until thick and stir into the chocolate mixture. Beat again, then gently fold in the flour, nuts, mango and the chocolate chips. Pour the mixture into the tin. Bake for 25 to 30 minutes or until the centre appears stable. Cool in the tin and cut into 12 pieces.

# Fig and Oat Slices

*Preparation time: 20 minutes* •
*Cooking time: 30 to 35 minutes* • *Makes: 12 pieces*

**This is a useful and economical recipe. It freezes well for up to three months, it is a welcome addition to lunch boxes and may be served warm with yoghurt for a winter dessert.**

### INGREDIENTS

*120 g/4 oz figs*

*5 Tbsp water*

*Grated rind of ½ orange*

*175 g/6 oz wholemeal flour*

*300 g/10 oz rolled oats*

*5 Tbsp packed soft brown sugar*

*175 g/6 oz margarine*

Pre-heat oven to 350°F/175°C/Gas mark 4. Meanwhile, grease and base-line a 20 x 20-cm/8 x 8-in tin.

• Chop the figs, discarding the stalks, and place in a pan with the water and orange rind. Bring to the boil and simmer for 5 minutes until very soft.

• Mix the flour and oats in a large bowl. Melt the sugar and margarine gently and stir into the oat mixture. Thoroughly combine and press half into the tin. Level the top and press well in.

• Spread the fig mixture on top and cover with the remaining oat mixture, levelling and pressing it as much as possible. Bake for 30 to 35 minutes until golden and is shrinking from the sides of the tin. Cool, cut into pieces and store in an airtight container.

### TIP

• Try to find unwaxed lemons, oranges and limes for grating, as even a good wash does not remove all the waxes from the skins.

# Exotic Fruit and Almond Slices

*Preparation time: 45 minutes ● Cooking time: 35 minutes ● Makes: 16 slices*

**This is another opportunity to use up small quantities of fruit and nuts including some of the more recent additions to the dried fruit range.**

## INGREDIENTS

### BASE

*75 g/3 oz lightly salted butter or margarine*

*5 Tbsp caster sugar*

*75 g/3 oz wholemeal flour*

*1 tsp baking powder*

*75 g/3 oz ground rice or semolina*

*3 Tbsp caster sugar*

### TOPPING

*5 Tbsp raisins*

*5 Tbsp glacé cherries*

*5 Tbsp dried mango pieces*

*5 Tbsp crystallized pineapple*

*75 g/3 oz ready-to-eat dried apricots*

*5 Tbsp chopped walnuts*

*120 g/4 oz lightly salted butter or margarine*

*225 g/8 oz caster sugar*

*1 egg, beaten*

*50 g/2 oz ground almonds*

*50 g/2 oz ground rice or semolina*

*2 Tbsp flaked almonds*

Pre-heat oven to 350°F/175°C/Gas mark 4. Grease and base-line an 18 x 28-cm/7 x 11-in shallow tin.

● Make the base by beating the sugar and butter together until light and stirring in the flour, ground rice or semolina and sugar. Press firmly into the tin.

● Coarsely chop the fruit and nuts.

● Beat the remaining butter and sugar, then beat in the egg. Fold in the ground almonds and ground rice. Stir in the chopped fruit and nuts and pour over the base. Sprinkle with the flaked almonds. Bake for about 35 minutes until the mixture and the almonds are golden-brown. Leave in the tin to cool and cut in slices. Store in an airtight container.

# Dried Cranberry Flapjacks

*Preparation time: 15 minutes* ● *Cooking time: 25 to 35 minutes* ● *Makes: 24*

**This recipe has a high percentage of fat, but it is worth using butter for the flavour and reserving the flapjacks for special occasions.**

## INGREDIENTS

*175 g/6 oz butter*

*200 g/7 oz soft brown sugar*

*2 Tbsp golden syrup*

*400 g/14 oz rolled oats*

*75 g/3 oz dried cranberries*

Pre-heat oven to 325°F/160°C/Gas mark 3. Grease and base-line an 18 x 28-cm/7 x 11-in shallow tin.

● Melt the butter, sugar and syrup until the sugar is dissolved. Stir in the oats and cranberries and press into the tin.

● Bake for 25 to 35 minutes until set. Cool in the tin and cut into pieces while still warm. Store in an airtight container.

# Fruit and Brandy Sticks

*Preparation time: 30 minutes ● Cooking time: none ● Makes: 25 small sticks*

**This recipe is an excellent way of preserving left-over fruit cake. If much of it is still left in the tin after New Year, use some of it in this recipe, freeze and use to accompany vanilla ice cream.**

### INGREDIENTS

*120 g/4 oz left-over fruit cake*

*50 g/2 oz lightly salted butter*

*2 Tbsp golden syrup*

*50 g/2 oz plain chocolate*

*1 Tbsp brandy*

### ICING

*6 Tbsp icing sugar*

*Rose flower-water or water*

*Pink food colouring*

Grease a 20 x 20-cm/8 x 8-in tin and then line the base of the pan as well.

● Crumble the cake into a bowl and chop any large pieces of fruit or nuts. Melt the butter, syrup and chocolate very gently and combine with the cake crumbs and brandy.

● Press into the tin. Level and firm the mixture and chill for at least a day before completing. The cookies may be frozen at this stage.

● Remove the mixture from the tin and place on a board. To make the icing, sift the icing sugar and mix to a thick consistency with sufficient water and/or rose flower-water to make a thin icing. However, add the rose flower-water cautiously and taste for strength before use, mixing it with water if it is too strong. Add a drop or two of pink food colouring, beat well and add a few drops more of water if the icing is too stiff. Pour evenly over the cake.

● Before the icing sets completely, cut into pieces with a sharp knife dipped into hot water. Leave to dry before storing the pieces in an airtight container.

# Flapjacks

*Preparation time: 15 minutes* ●
*Cooking time: 30 minutes* ● *Makes: 18*

**This is a delicious, basic recipe for flapjacks, suitable for everyday packed lunches and snacks. They are so easy to make, young members of the family will soon be making them for you.**

### INGREDIENTS

*120 g/4 oz margarine or lightly salted butter*

*3 Tbsp golden syrup*

*5 Tbsp soft brown sugar*

*400 g/14 oz rolled oats*

Pre-heat oven to 325°F/160°C/Gas mark 3. Grease and base line an 18 x 28-cm/7 x 11-in shallow tin. ● Place margarine, syrup, and sugar in a large pan and heat gently, stirring from time to time until the sugar has melted. Stir in the oats and press into the tin. Bake for about 30 minutes until golden. Cool slightly before cutting into 18 pieces. Leave to cool completely before removing from the tin. Store in an airtight container for up to 1 week.

# Hazelnut Flapjacks

*Preparation time: 15 minutes* ●
*Cooking time: 25 to 30 minutes* ● *Makes: 18*

**Cooks sometimes avoid hazelnuts because they need roasting and rubbing to remove their skins. In this recipe that is not necessary, all you do is chop them.**

### INGREDIENTS

*120 g/4 oz margarine or lightly salted butter*

*8 Tbsp honey*

*5 Tbsp light brown sugar*

*375 g/12 oz rolled oats*

*120 g/4 oz chopped hazelnuts*

Pre-heat oven to 350°F/175°C/Gas mark 4. Grease and base-line an 18 x 28-cm/7 x 11-in shallow tin. ● Melt the margarine or butter, honey and sugar in a large heavy-bottomed saucepan. Stir in the oats and nuts. Press into the tin and level the top. Bake for 25 to 30 minutes. Cool in the tin and cut into bars when still slightly warm. Store in an airtight container.

# Lemon Cheesecake Fingers

*Preparation time: 50 minutes ● Cooking time: 40 minutes ● Makes: 12 fingers*

**These fingers would be excellent taken on a summer picnic to round off a sumptuous meal with friends.
The cream cheese makes them a little more substantial to withstand any knocks en route.**

### INGREDIENTS

### PASTRY BASE

*175 g/6 oz plain flour*

*75 g/3 oz margarine or lightly salted butter*

*1 egg, separated*

*1 Tbsp water*

### CHEESECAKE MIXTURE

*250 g/9 oz full-fat soft cheese*

*1 egg, separated*

*120 g/4 oz caster sugar*

*Grated rind and juice of 1 lemon*

*1 Tbsp plain flour*

*5 Tbsp sultanas*

*1 Tbsp rum, optional*

Pre-heat oven to 375°F/190°C/Gas mark 4. Grease, base- and side-line an 18 x 28-cm/7 x 11-in shallow tin.

● Make the pastry by lightly blending the margarine or butter into the flour. Beat together the egg yolk (reserve the white for later) and water, add to the mixture to make a soft dough. Use a little more water if necessary as the dough must be pliable. Reserve one-quarter of the pastry.

● Roll out the remaining pastry and line the base of the tin. Press a piece of foil on top of the pastry. Bake for about 20 minutes. Remove the foil and cool. Increase oven temperature to 400°F/200°C/Gas mark 6.

● Beat the cream cheese, egg yolk, sugar, lemon rind and juice to thoroughly combine and stir in flour, sultanas and rum, if using.

● Beat the 2 egg whites to a firm peak and beat 2 tablespoons into the cheese mixture, then fold in the rest. Pour over the cooled pastry base and level gently.

● Roll out the remaining pastry and either cut strips to make a lattice or cut leaves to decorate the top. Bake for 15 minutes, then reduce temperature to 350°F/190°C/Gas mark 5 and bake for 15 minutes longer. Cool in the tin and cut into fingers. Store in an airtight container in the refrigerator for 2 to 3 days.

# Fruit and Nut Bars

*Preparation time: 45 minutes ● Cooking time: 30 minutes ● Makes: 24 bars*

**The name of this recipe could be "spring-cleaning bars" because the topping is excellent for using up ends of packets of nuts and dried fruit you come across when sorting out cupboards.**

## INGREDIENTS

### SHORTBREAD BASE

225 g/8 oz plain flour

2 Tbsp cornflour

50 g/2 oz icing sugar

300 g/10 oz butter

### TOPPING

175 g/6 oz nuts to include at least half the volume in almonds

120 g/4 oz chopped dried fruit, at least half to be glacé cherries

25 g/1 oz lightly salted butter

3 Tbsp caster sugar

1 Tbsp milk

2 tsp vanilla essence

Pre-heat oven to 400°F/200°C/Gas mark 6. Grease and base-line an 18 x 28-cm/7 x 11-in shallow tin.

● Prepare the base by sifting the flour, cornflour and icing sugar into a bowl and blending in the butter to look like breadcrumbs. Press the crumbs into the tin. Level and firm down, then bake for 15 to 20 minutes. Leave in the tin to cool.

● Prepare and chop the nuts, leaving them in large pieces. Whole almonds should first be blanched, then halved. Cut the cherries into quarters and other fruit to a similar size.

● Place the topping in a heavy-bottomed saucepan and heat gently to dissolve. Try to avoid stirring too much. Add the nuts and leave to cool.

● Stir in the fruit and pour over the base. Return to the oven and bake at the same temperature for about 15 minutes or until the nuts are browning. Cool in the tin and cut into bars when cold. Store in an airtight container.

### TIP

Suitable fruits to use in this recipe include crystallized pineapple, ginger, angelica, ready-to-eat prunes and apricots, raisins and sultanas.

# Lemon and Hazelnut Fingers

*Preparation time: 20 minutes* ●
*Cooking time: 25 minutes* ● *Makes: 16 fingers*

**These are truly heavenly. They are also incredibly easy to make and are perfect for a celebration picnic.**

### INGREDIENTS

#### PASTRY

*120 g/4 oz plain flour*

*75 g/3 oz lightly salted butter*

*3 tsp icing sugar*

#### LEMON CURD FILLING

*2 eggs, beaten*

*120 g/4 oz icing sugar*

*2 small lemons*

*50 g/2 oz unsalted butter*

*75 g/3 oz ground hazelnuts*

Pre-heat oven to 375°F/190°C/Gas mark 5. Grease, base- and side-line an 18 x 28-cm/7 x 11-in shallow tin.

● Place all the ingredients for the pastry in a food processor and process until they resemble fine breadcrumbs. Tip the pastry mixture into the tin and press into the base. Bake for 5 minutes.

● Meanwhile, make the filling. Soften the butter to the consistency of tub margarine and place in a large bowl with the remaining ingredients. Whisk well to combine. Pour the filling over the pastry and return to the oven for 15 to 20 minutes until golden and set. Leave to get cold in the tin before cutting into pieces. Best eaten when freshly made.

# Melting Almond Shortbread

*Preparation time: 10 minutes* ● *Cooking time: 45 to 50 minutes* ● *Makes: 16 bars*

**This is called "melting" for two reasons. Firstly, because it melts in the mouth. Secondly, because the butter (and it must be butter) is melted and the other ingredients are simply stirred in.**

### INGREDIENTS

*225 g/8 oz butter*

*175 g/6 oz self-raising flour*

*50 g/2 oz plain flour*

*2 Tbsp cornflour*

*50 g/2 oz caster sugar*

*4 drops almond essence*

*50 g/2 oz flaked almonds*

Pre-heat oven to 350°F/175°C/Gas mark 4. Grease and base-line a 18 x 28-cm/7 x 11-in shallow tin.
● Gently melt the butter. Meanwhile, sift the flour and cornflour together into a bowl and stir in the caster sugar. Add all but 2 tablespoons of the flaked almonds.
● Make a well in the centre and stir in the melted butter.
● Turn into the tin, press in place, and sprinkle over the remaining flaked almonds. Do not worry if the mixture seems rather sparse in the tin as it will increase in volume while cooking. Bake for 45 to 50 minutes until very pale golden but the centre looks cooked and the shortbread is beginning to shrink away from the sides of the tin. Leave in the tin to cool, then cut up into pieces.

# Linzer Bake

*Preparation time: 40 minutes* ● *Cooking time: 30 to 35 minutes* ● *Makes: 9 dessert portions*

**A cross between a cake and a pastry, Linzer Torte is a traditional Austrian dessert of raspberries and a light, spiced pastry.**

## INGREDIENTS

*175 g/6 oz self-raising flour*

*½ tsp ground cloves*

*½ tsp mixed spice*

*75 g/3 oz lightly salted butter*

*120 g/4 oz caster sugar*

*5 Tbsp ground almonds or hazelnuts*

*Grated rind of ½ lemon*

*½ tsp vanilla essence*

*1 egg*

*1–2 Tbsp milk*

*300 g/10 oz raspberry jam*

Pre-heat oven to 350°F/175°C/Gas mark 4. Grease and base-line a 20 x 20-cm/8 x 8-in tin.

● Sift the flour and spices and blend in the butter. Stir in the sugar, ground almonds and lemon rind. Beat together the egg and vanilla essence and stir in, followed by sufficient milk to make up to a firm but slightly soft dough. Gently knead to remove any cracks, wrap in clingfilm and chill for 30 minutes.

● Roll out the pastry and use to line the tin. Trim the pastry level with the top of the tin. Fill the centre with raspberry jam.

● Roll out the trimmings and cut into lattice strips. Place two or three in each direction over the jam to make an even lattice. Do not try weaving the strips as this pastry is too fragile.

● Bake in the oven for 25 to 30 minutes until the pastry is barely coloured.

# Mango and Pistachio Slices

*Preparation time: 20 minutes ● Cooking time: 30 minutes ● Makes: 16 slices*

**Lightly spiced and slightly chewy, these slices look and taste glorious, with the golden mango
contrasting beautifully with the green colour of the nuts.**

## INGREDIENTS

*120 g/4 oz lightly salted butter*

*120 g/4 oz caster sugar*

*1 egg*

*½ tsp vanilla essence*

*125 g/4 oz self-raising flour*

*½ tsp grated nutmeg*

*50 g/2 oz dried mango pieces*

*75 g/3 oz pistachio nuts*

*1 Tbsp sherry*

*4 Tbsp icing sugar*

Pre-heat oven to 350°F/175°C/Gas mark 4. Grease and base-line an 18 x 28-cm/7 x 11-in shallow tin.

● Check the dried mango packet for directions and, if necessary, soak in boiling water for 10 minutes. Drain and dry on kitchen paper and rough chop.

● Grind half the pistachio nuts to a powder and roughly chop the rest.

● Beat the butter and sugar until light and beat in the egg, vanilla essence and mango pieces.

● Stir in the nuts, flour and sherry. The mixture should be quite stiff. Spread in the tin and bake 30 minutes. Leave to cool in the tin.

● Sift the icing sugar and mix with a little water until sufficiently runny to drizzle over the bars. When set cut into pieces with a sharp knife. Store in an airtight container.

# Microwave Brownies

*Preparation time: 10 minutes* ● *Cooking time: 7 minutes* ● *Makes: 8 wedges*

**These microwaved Brownies are amazingly good and well worth trying. Eat them fresh from the microwave or at least the same day they are baked.**

## INGREDIENTS

50 g/2 oz plain chocolate, chopped

75 g/3 oz butter or margarine

75 g/3 oz dark brown sugar

2 eggs

120 g/4 oz plain flour

3 Tbsp unsweetened cocoa powder

¼ tsp baking powder

1 tsp vanilla essence

5 Tbsp chopped walnuts

2 Tbsp milk

Cook in a 25 x 15 x 5-cm/10 x 6 x 2-in heatproof glass or pottery dish lined with lightly greased greaseproof paper.

● Melt the chocolate and butter or margarine in the microwave on high for 2 minutes. Beat in the sugar and egg until smooth. Stir in the remaining ingredients to form a smooth batter. Spread in the prepared dish.

● Microwave on high for about 7 minutes until the mixture is slightly risen and a few broken bubbles break the surface. The centre will probably look damp but will set during standing time. Cool the brownies in the dish for 10 minutes then cut into 16 wedges.

### TIP

Check the brownies after 5½ minutes then check every 30 seconds until cooked, to prevent over-cooking.

# Prune and Two-Chocolate Pieces

*Preparation time: 40 minutes*
*Cooking time: 15 minutes ◦ Makes: 25*

**These delectable pieces can be served with after-dinner coffee or arranged in an attractive box as a gift. Choose the ready-to-eat type of prune to avoid having to soak them.**

### INGREDIENTS

*120 g/4 oz ready-to-eat prunes*

*1 Tbsp sweet sherry or orange juice*

*2 Tbsp water*

*50 g/2 oz self-raising flour*

*1 tsp ground cinnamon*

*150 g/5 oz rolled oats*

*75 g/3 oz lightly salted butter*

*50 g/2 oz soft brown sugar*

*5 Tbsp white chocolate chips*

*50 g/2 oz milk or plain chocolate*

Pre-heat oven to 375°F/190°C/Gas mark 5. Grease and base-line a 20 x 20-cm/8 x 8-in tin.

◦ Chop the prunes and place in a saucepan with the sherry or orange juice and water. Bring to the boil and cook for 2 minutes, stirring all the time. Leave to cool.

◦ Mix the flour, cinnamon and oats, blend in the butter and stir in the sugar.

◦ Stir in the white chocolate chips and the prune mixture. Press into the tin and bake for 12 to 15 minutes or until just starting to turn golden. Leave in the tin to cool.

◦ Melt the remaining chocolate and pour over the bake. Using a sharp knife, cut into squares while still warm. Drizzle with more melted chocolate, if liked. Store in an airtight container.

# Orange and Raisin Shortbread

*Preparation time: 30 minutes + chilling*
*Cooking time: 30 to 40 minutes ◦ Makes: 8 pieces*

**This is a delicious alternative to traditional shortbread.**

### INGREDIENTS

*75 g/3 oz plain flour*

*50 g/2 oz cornflour*

*120 g/4 oz lightly salted butter*

*50 g/2 oz caster sugar*

*25 g/1 oz ground almonds*

*Grated rind of 1 small orange*

*25 g/1 oz raisins*

*1 tsp caster sugar*

Start by lightly greasing the base and sides of a 20 x 20-cm/8-in tart tin with a removable base.

◦ Sift the flour and cornflour and blend in the butter. Stir in the sugar, ground almonds and orange rind. Press the mixture together and incorporate the raisins before the dough is fully formed. Knead lightly to evenly distribute the ingredients and ensure the dough is free from cracks.

◦ Lift onto the base of the tin. Leave the ring in place and smooth the surface to fill the base. Half-cut through to mark 8 portions and prick evenly with a fork. Chill for 1 hour.

◦ Pre-heat oven to 325°F/160°C/Gas mark 3 and bake for 30 to 40 minutes or until very pale apricot-coloured. Dust with the remaining caster sugar. Remove the ring from the tin and cut into portions. Leave on the sheet to cool and harden. Store in an airtight container.

# Spanish Date Meringue Slices

*Preparation time: 45 minutes ●*
*Cooking time: 40 minutes ● Makes: 16 slices*

**This traditional recipe uses a delicious combination of dates and oranges.**

### INGREDIENTS

#### PASTRY BASE

*50 g/2 oz lightly salted butter or margarine*

*2 Tbsp caster sugar*

*1 Tbsp beaten egg*

*Grated rind of ½ orange*

*120 g/4 oz plain flour*

#### FILLING

*225 g/8 oz stoned dates*

*1 Tbsp rum or orange juice*

*3 egg whites*

*50 g/2 oz ground almonds*

*2 Tbsp cornflour*

*5 Tbsp caster sugar*

Pre-heat oven to 350°F/175°C/Gas mark 4. Grease and base-line an 18 x 28-cm/7 x 11-in shallow tin.

● Make the pastry base. Beat the butter or margarine and sugar together until light and fluffy. Beat in the egg and orange rind, then work in the flour. Press into the base of the tin.

● Chop the dates and pour over the rum or orange juice. Mix the ground almonds, cornflour and sugar.

● Beat the egg whites to a stiff peak, fold in the soaked dates and the dry ingredients. Spread over the pastry. Bake for about 40 minutes or until the centre is firm. Leave to cool in the tin, then cut into slices. Store in an airtight container.

# Munch

*Preparation time: 15 minutes ●*
*Cooking time: 20 to 30 minutes ● Makes: 12 pieces*

**A simple, traditional American recipe. Munch used to be prepared during the morning, ready to slip into the hot oven when lunch came out.**

### INGREDIENTS

*225 g/8 oz margarine*

*225 g/8 oz soft brown sugar*

*375 g/12 oz rolled oats*

Pre-heat oven to 350°F/175°C/Gas mark 4. Grease and base-line a 20 x 20-cm/ 8 x 8-in tin.

● Beat the butter until soft and gradually beat in the sugar until light and fluffy. Stir in the oats. Press into the tin and bake for 25 to 30 minutes or until golden. Cut into pieces. Store in an airtight container.

# Stollen Bars

*Preparation time: 1 hour + rising time* ● *Cooking time: 25 to 30 minutes* ● *Makes: 30 bars*

**Here, Stollen, the traditional flat, oval German Christmas cake, is converted into bars.
Try them warmed for a special Christmas breakfast.**

### INGREDIENTS

*225 g/8 oz strong white flour*

*2 tsp easy-blend dried yeast*

*1 Tbsp lukewarm water*

*2 Tbsp sugar*

*50 g/2 oz lightly salted butter*

*1 egg*

*5 Tbsp lukewarm milk*

*Grated rind of ½ lemon*

*1 Tbsp chopped almonds*

*75 g/3 oz chopped candied citrus peel*

*50 g/2 oz glacé cherries*

*50 g/2 oz sultanas*

*175 g/6 oz marzipan*

*1 Tbsp melted butter*

*2 Tbsp icing sugar*

Grease the base of an 18 x 28-cm/7 x 11-in shallow tin and then line it.

● Take 1 teaspoon of flour from the measured amount and place in a small bowl with the yeast, warm water and a pinch of the measured sugar. Blend and leave about 10 minutes in a warm place until the mixture froths.

● Meanwhile, blend the butter into the remaining flour and stir in the sugar.

● Beat the egg. Slightly warm the milk.

● Make a well in the centre of the flour and work in the yeast mixture, egg and milk to make a pliable dough which is slightly stiffer than bread dough. Add a little more milk or flour as necessary. Turn out and knead for about 10 minutes until silky. Place in a lightly greased bowl, cover the bowl with a teatowel or clingfilm and leave in a warm, draught-free place until doubled in size.

● Punch back the dough, then knead lightly. Knead in the lemon rind, candied citrus peel, chopped glacé cherries and sultanas.

● Divide the dough in half and roll a piece to fit the base of the tin. Slice the marzipan thinly in an even layer over the top. Roll the second piece of dough to fit over.

● Cover with lightly greased clingfilm and leave in a warm draught-free place for about 20 minutes until risen and slightly puffy.

● Pre-heat oven to 450°F/230°C/Gas mark 8 and bake for about 20 minutes until golden-brown and firm in the centre. Immediately brush with melted butter. When cold dredge heavily with icing sugar and cut into 30 pieces. Store in an airtight container.

# Toffee Bars

*Preparation time: 45 minutes* ●
*Cooking time: 20 minutes* ● *Makes: 16*

**These bars hide under a multitude of recipe names but the three layers of shortbread, caramel and chocolate are universally popular with people of all ages.**

### INGREDIENTS

#### SHORTBREAD BASE

*175 g/6 oz plain flour*

*50 g/2 oz caster sugar*

*120 g/4 oz lightly salted butter*

#### FILLING

*120 g/4 oz lightly salted butter*

*225 g/8 oz caster sugar*

*225 ml/8 fl oz evaporated milk*

*Few drops vanilla essence*

#### TOPPING

*75 g/3 oz plain chocolate*

*25 g/1 oz unsalted butter*

Pre-heat oven to 350°F/175°C/Gas mark 4. Grease and base-line an 18 x 28-cm/7 x 11-in shallow tin.

● Make the base by beating the butter and sugar together until light, then working in the flour. Press the dough into the tin and bake for 20 minutes or until firm in the centre and lightly golden. Cool in the tin.

● Put the butter, sugar and evaporated milk into a heavy-bottomed saucepan and stir over a gentle heat until the sugar has dissolved. Bring to the boil and, stirring constantly, cook for about 15 minutes until thick. Remove from the heat and beat in the vanilla essence and pour over the shortbread. Allow to cool.

● Gently melt the butter and chocolate together. Pour over the caramel and cut into pieces when set. Store in an airtight container.

# Double Ginger Flapjacks

*Preparation time: 20 minutes* ●
*Cooking time: 20 to 25 minutes* ● *Makes: 8 to 16 slices*

**This flapjack has a strong gingery taste with succulent pieces of crystallized ginger hidden in the sweet, chewy cookie base.**

### INGREDIENTS

*50 g/2 oz butter*

*1½ Tbsp treacle*

*50 g/2 oz dark brown sugar*

*1 tsp ground ginger*

*300 g/10 oz rolled oats*

*75 g/3 oz chopped crystallized ginger*

*50 g/2 oz chopped pecan nuts*

*¼ tsp salt*

Pre-heat oven to 350°F/175°C/Gas mark 4. Line a 20 x 20-cm/8 x 8-in baking tin with non-stick parchment.

● In a medium saucepan, cook the butter, syrup, sugar and ground ginger over a medium heat until well-blended. Remove from the heat and stir in the oats, crystallized ginger, pecans and salt. Pour into the prepared tin and level.

● Bake until crisp and golden-brown, 20 to 25 minutes. Transfer the tin to a wire rack to cool slightly, 5 to 10 minutes. Invert onto a board and peel off the paper. While still warm, cut into 8 or 16 slices. Return to the wire rack to cool completely. Store in an airtight container.

# Chocolate Orange Dream Bars

*Preparation time: 30 minutes* ● *Cooking time: 35 to 40 minutes* ● *Makes: 18*

**These bars are made with the magical combination of chocolate and orange. They are really rich – a little goes a long way.**

## INGREDIENTS

### BASE

*120 g/4 oz plain flour*

*3 Tbsp unsweetened cocoa powder*

*¼ tsp salt*

*175 g/6 oz unsalted butter, softened*

*5 Tbsp caster sugar*

*50 g/2 oz icing sugar*

### ORANGE TOPPING

*Grated rind of 1 orange*

*125 ml/4 fl oz fresh orange juice*

*3 Tbsp water*

*4 tsp cornflour*

*1 tsp lemon juice*

*25 g/1 oz butter*

*3 Tbsp orange marmalade*

### CHOCOLATE GLAZE

*3 Tbsp double cream*

*½ tsp golden syrup*

*75 g/3 oz plain chocolate, chopped*

Pre-heat oven to 325°F/160°C/Gas mark 3. Grease and line a 20 x 20-cm/8 x 8-in baking tin.

● Sift together the flour, cocoa and salt. In a separate bowl beat the butter until creamy, add the sugars and continue beating until light and fluffy. Beat in the flour mixture in 2 or 3 batches until a dough forms. If necessary, turn the dough out onto a lightly floured surface and knead until blended.

● Pat down the dough into the base of the baking tin in an even layer. Prick the dough bottom all over with a fork. Bake until set and golden, 30 to 35 minutes. Transfer to a wire rack while preparing topping.

● In a medium saucepan, whisk together the orange rind, juice, water, cornflour and lemon juice. Over a medium heat, bring to the boil whisking constantly until mixture thickens, about 1 minute. Remove from the heat and whisk in butter and marmalade until melted and smooth. Pour over the warm pastry base and return to the oven. Bake for 5 minutes more. Transfer to a wire cooling rack to cool completely, then refrigerate until the topping is set, about 1 hour.

● In a small saucepan, bring the cream and golden syrup to the boil. Remove from the heat and all at once, stir in the chocolate until melted and smooth. Cool the chocolate slightly until thickened, stirring occasionally.

● Using the paper to help, remove the cookies from the tin. Peel off the paper and cut into bars. Spoon the cooled, thickened chocolate into a piping bag and drizzle the chocolate over the bars. Refrigerate until set, about 30 minutes. Store in the refrigerator in an airtight container.

# Savoury Cookies

Some of these cookies are served fresh from the oven, others are eaten cold. Either way this fabulous selection of savoury cookies will liven up any occasion. Unless otherwise stated, most of the cookies can be prepared in advance and frozen for up to three months.

## Cheese Cookies

*Cheese cookies make a wonderful addition to any lunch box, picnic, buffet or even formal meal. Once you start producing home-baked cheese cookies, you will never want to buy them again.*

## Meat and Fish

*A selection of tangy cookies that would be perfect for brunch or cocktail parties. Most would be good served with soft cheeses or pâtés.*

# Nuts and Seeds

# Vegetable Cookies

*A bright and tasty selection of vegetable-based cookies that are great to serve with drinks as an informal appetizer and wonderful to take to ball games and other outdoor events. They are so delicious that the kids won't object to eating vegetables.*

# Quattro Formaggi

*Preparation time: 20 minutes • Cooking time: 25 minutes • Makes: 15*

**Just like the familiar pizza topping, these cookies are flavoured with 4 different cheeses.**

### INGREDIENTS

*1 Tbsp freshly grated Parmesan cheese*

*1 Tbsp crumbled blue cheese such as Roquefort, Danish or Stilton*

*1 Tbsp grated Gruyère cheese*

*1 Tbsp grated mature Cheddar cheese*

*120 g/4 oz plain flour*

*Pinch of salt*

*120 g/4 oz lightly salted butter or margarine, softened*

*1 tsp dried oregano*

Pre-heat oven to 350°F/175°C/Gas mark 4. Grease or line two baking sheets with non-stick baking parchment.

• Mix all the cheeses together and sift in the flour and salt. Make a well in the centre and add the butter or margarine and oregano. Using a round-bladed knife, or fingertips blend the mixture together, and shape it into a soft dough.

• Divide into 15 walnut-sized balls and place on baking sheets, spaced about 5 cm/2 in apart. Flatten slightly with a fork, and bake for 20 to 25 minutes until lightly golden and firm to the touch. Cool on the sheets. Best served slightly warmed. Store in an airtight container for 3 to 4 days, or freeze for up to 3 months.

# Parmesan Paprika Crisps

*Preparation time: 15 minutes • Cooking time: 10 minutes • Makes: 18*

**These thin, nutty cheese morsels are delicious served as a snack on their own or to accompany a fine wine.**

### INGREDIENTS

*75 g/3 oz lightly salted butter or margarine*

*75 g/3 oz flaked almonds*

*50 g/2 oz ground almonds*

*225 g/8 oz freshly grated Parmesan cheese*

*¼ tsp cayenne pepper*

*1 tsp paprika*

Pre-heat oven to 350°F/175°C/Gas mark 4. Line three baking sheets with non-stick baking parchment.

• Melt the butter or margarine in a small saucepan. Remove from the heat and stir in the slivered and ground almonds. Stir in the Parmesan cheese, cayenne and paprika.

• Drop the mixture, spaced well apart, in 18 small, well-rounded heaps onto the baking sheets. Bake in the oven for 10 minutes until golden-brown. Remove from the oven and push around the edges of the cookies with the blade of a knife to neaten the shape. Leave on the sheets to cool completely. Carefully lift off using a thin, metal spatula. Store between sheets of greaseproof paper in an airtight container for 3 to 4 days, or freeze in the same way for up to 3 months.

# Feta, Olive and Sun-dried Tomato Bites

*Preparation time: 20 minutes • Cooking time: 25 minutes • Makes: 15*

**Using feta cheese gives these cookies a creamy, sharp flavour. Try a different goat's or sheep's milk cheese if preferred.**

### INGREDIENTS

*120 g/4 oz feta cheese*

*120 g/4 oz plain flour*

*2 Tbsp finely chopped sun-dried tomatoes in oil, drained*

*6 large black olives, stoned and chopped*

*120 g/4 oz lightly salted butter or margarine, softened*

Pre-heat oven to 350°F/175°C/Gas mark 4. Grease or line two baking sheets with non-stick baking parchment. Cut the cheese into very small cubes and set aside.

● Sift the flour into a bowl and mix in the chopped tomatoes and olives, then blend in the butter using a round-bladed knife. Carefully stir in the cubed cheese. Bring together the mixture with your hands to form a firm dough.

● Divide the dough into 15 walnut-sized balls and place on baking sheets, spaced about 5 cm/2 in apart. Flatten them slightly with a fork, and then bake for 20 to 25 minutes until lightly golden and firm to the touch. Leave to cool on the sheets. These cookies are best served slightly warmed. Store in an airtight container for 3 to 4 days.

# Blue Cheese Shortbread

*Preparation time: 15 minutes ● Cooking time: 40 minutes ● Serves: 8*

**This shortbread version combines with the rich flavour of blue cheese and the mild onion tang of fresh chives. Excellent served with port.**

## INGREDIENTS

| |
| --- |
| *150 g/5 oz plain flour* |
| *3 Tbsp rice flour* |
| *120 g/4 oz lightly salted butter* |
| *50 g/2 oz crumbled blue cheese* |
| *3 Tbsp freshly snipped chives* |

Pre-heat oven to 325°F/160°C/Gas mark 3. Lightly grease an 18-cm/7-in round baking tin.

● Sift the flours into a bowl. Work in the butter using your fingertips, keep it in one piece and gradually work in the dry ingredients. Stir in the blue cheese and chives and knead well.

● Pack the dough into the prepared tin, prick well with a fork and pinch the edges decoratively using your finger and thumb.

● Bake for about 35 to 40 minutes, until firm and pale golden in colour. Score into 8 triangles while still hot. Cool for 10 minutes and then transfer to a wire rack to cool completely.

● Serve split into triangles. Store in an airtight container for up to 5 days.

# Cheese and Relish Puffs

*Preparation time: 20 minutes + chilling ● Cooking time: 25 minutes ● Makes: 25*

**Serve these cheesy fingers for cocktail nibbles during the Christmas season, or at a party with a hot punch.**

## INGREDIENTS

| |
| --- |
| *150 g/5 oz grated Gruyère cheese* |
| *4 Tbsp tomato relish* |
| *Freshly ground black pepper* |
| *1 egg, beaten* |
| *350 g/12 oz puff pastry, thawed if frozen* |

Pre-heat oven to 400°F/200°C/Gas mark 6. Meanwhile, in a bowl, mix together the cheese, relish, pepper and all but 2 teaspoons of the egg. Set aside.

● Roll out the pastry on a lightly floured surface to a 30 x 40-cm/12 x 16-in rectangle. Divide the pastry evenly down the centre of the rectangle, and then divide each half into 5 equal width portions.

● Lay 5 pieces on a large ungreased baking sheet and divide the filling equally between them, spreading it out evenly, almost to the edge. Brush the edges with water and cover with remaining pastry, lightly pressing the edges to seal. Cover and chill for 30 minutes.

● Mark each pastry strip into 5 fingers and brush with the reserved egg. Bake for about 20 to 25 minutes until risen and golden-brown. Cut the pastry through into fingers, allow to cool for 10 minutes and then serve while still hot.

# Smoked Cheese Twists

*Preparation time: 25 minutes + chilling* ●
*Cooking time: 20 minutes* ● *Makes: 30*

**Long, thin twisting pastries are just the thing for parties.
Serve on their own or with a dip.**

## INGREDIENTS

75 g/3 oz lightly salted butter or margarine, softened

3 Tbsp full-fat soft cheese

1 egg yolk

175 g/6 oz plain flour

Pinch of salt

2 cloves garlic, crushed

120 g/4 oz finely grated smoked cheese

2 Tbsp cold water

In a bowl, beat the butter or margarine with the soft cheese and egg yolk. Sift in the flour and salt. Add the garlic, half the grated cheese and 2 tablespoons cold water. Stir the mixture to bring the mixture together. Turn on to a lightly floured surface and knead lightly to form a smooth dough. Wrap and chill for 30 minutes.

● Pre-heat oven to 350°F/175°C/Gas mark 4. Line two baking sheets with non-stick baking parchment.

● Roll out the dough to 5 mm/¼-in thick, and cut into ½-inch wide strips, about 15 cm/6 in long. Twist the strips and place on baking sheets, pressing down the edges well to prevent them untwisting. Sprinkle lightly with the remaining cheese. Bake for about 20 minutes until lightly golden. Transfer to wire racks and cool for about 15 minutes before serving. Cool completely and place in an airtight container for up to 10 days.

# Hot Cheese Melts

*Preparation time: 20 minutes + chilling* ●
*Cooking time: 15 minutes* ● *Makes: 16*

**For easy eating, spear each hot cookie on a cocktail stick
or small skewer before arranging them on a serving platter.**

## INGREDIENTS

120 g/4 oz finely grated mature Cheddar cheese

50 g/2 oz plain flour

1 tsp mustard powder

Pinch of salt

50 g/2 oz lightly salted butter or margarine, softened

1 Tbsp wholegrain mustard

1 tsp black mustard seeds

Place all the ingredients together in a large bowl and work the mixture until a firm dough is formed.

● Divide the mixture into 16 equal portions, and shape it into balls. Arrange the balls on a large ungreased baking sheet. Cover and chill for 1 hour until they become firm.

● Pre-heat oven to 375°F/190°C/Gas mark 5. Just prior to serving, uncover and bake in the oven for about 10 to 15 minutes until golden. Cool for 10 minutes and then serve hot.

# Cream Cheese and Chive Cornbread Cakes

*Preparation time: 20 minutes ● Cooking time: 20 minutes ● Makes: 20*

**A cross between biscuit and a cookie, these cakes can be served with soups and stews, or as part of a lunch box.**

### INGREDIENTS

*120 g/4 oz cornmeal*

*50 g/2 oz plain flour*

*2 tsp baking powder*

*50 g/2 oz lightly salted butter or margarine*

*1 egg, beaten*

*3 Tbsp freshly snipped chives*

*6 to 7 Tbsp milk*

*Full-fat soft cheese*

Pre-heat oven to 375°F/190°C/Gas mark 5. Grease or line two baking sheets.

● Sift the cornmeal, flour, baking powder, and salt into a mixing bowl and blend in the butter or margarine until well mixed. Make a well in the centre and gradually mix in the egg, 2 tablespoons of the chives and milk, to form a thick batter.

● Using a teaspoon, spoon 20 small mounds of the mixture, about 5 cm/2 in apart, on baking sheets, and bake for 15 to 20 minutes until lightly golden and firm to the touch. Transfer to wire racks to cool completely.

● Beat the soft cheese to soften and spread gently on the cookies then top with the remaining chives to serve. Best eaten on same day as topped. Store, before topping with soft cheese and chives, in an airtight container for up to 1 week.

# Red Leicester and Fruit Relish Palmiers

*Preparation time: 20 minutes ● Cooking time: 12 minutes ● Makes: 16*

**Small, heart-shaped pastry puffs filled with red cheese and tangy relish make attractive canapés.**

### INGREDIENTS

*175 g/6 oz puff pastry, thawed if frozen*

*3 Tbsp savoury fruit relish, finely chopped*

*50 g/2 oz fine grated Red Leicester cheese*

*Freshly ground black pepper*

Pre-heat oven to 425°F/220°C/Gas mark 7. Grease or line a large baking sheet with non-stick baking parchment.

● Roll out the pastry to a 40 x 20-cm/16 x 8-in rectangle. Spread thinly with 2 tablespoons of the relish and then sprinkle with two thirds of the cheese. Season with plenty of black pepper.

● Fold the pastry two ends up and over the filling, equally from each side, to meet in the middle. Spread the pastry top with the remaining relish and sprinkle with the cheese. Season with pepper. Fold the pastry ends as before, turn over and press together firmly.

● Using a sharp knife, cut the folded pastry into 16 slices and transfer to the baking sheet, leaving a small space between each. Bake for 10 to 12 minutes until lightly golden. Cool for 10 minutes then transfer to a wire rack to cool. Best served warm.

### TIP

These can be made 24 hours in advance. Store in an airtight container and re-crisp them in a hot oven for a few minutes just before serving.

# Hot Pizza Snacks

*Preparation time: 25 minutes • Cooking time: 20 minutes • Makes: 12*

**Best served warm, these tomato snacks contain the familiar ingredients you would find on a pizza, and have a soft Mozzarella cheese centre.**

## INGREDIENTS

*1 Tbsp plain flour*

*Pinch of salt*

*1 tsp dried oregano*

*125 g/4 oz lightly salted butter or margarine, softened*

*2 Tbsp freshly grated Parmesan cheese*

*2 Tbsp tomato purée*

*25-g/1-oz piece block Mozzarella cheese, cut into 12 small cubes*

*6 black olives, stoned and halved*

Pre-heat oven to 375°F/190°C/Gas mark 5. Grease or line a baking sheet with non-stick baking parchment.

● Sift the flour and salt into a bowl and stir in the oregano, butter or margarine, Parmesan and tomato purée using a round-bladed knife, and bring together with your hands to form a firm dough. Divide the mixture into 12 portions, and form into balls. Press a piece of cheese into the centre of each and reform the dough over it to enclose the cheese.

● Place on the baking sheet and lightly press an olive half on top of each. Sprinkle with a little Parmesan cheese and bake for 20 minutes until lightly golden and firm. Cool for 10 minutes before serving.

# Oaty Clusters with Cheese Crumble Top

*Preparation time: 20 minutes • Cooking time: 20 minutes • Makes: 18*

**Easy to make and delicious, these crackers have a crisp and chewy texture, with a lightly spiced, topping.**

## INGREDIENTS

*175 g/6 oz lightly salted butter or margarine*

*200 g/7 oz rolled oats*

*50 g/2 oz wholemeal flour*

*1 tsp salt*

## TOPPING

*1 Tbsp freshly grated Parmesan cheese*

*6 Tbsp wholemeal flour*

*25 g/1 oz lightly salted butter or margarine*

*1 tsp cumin seeds, crushed*

*1 tsp dried thyme*

Pre-heat oven to 375°F/190°C/Gas mark 5. Grease or line two baking sheets.

● Melt the butter or margarine for the cookies in a saucepan. Remove from the heat and stir in the oats, flour and salt. Set aside.

● Now make the crumble. Mix the cheese and flour together and blend in the butter or margarine until well mixed, and it resembles large fresh breadcrumbs.

● Drop the oat mixture onto baking sheets to form 18 walnut-sized mounds. Space them about 2.5 cm/1 in apart. Press them down lightly with a fork and then sprinkle each with a little of the crumble topping, a few cumin seeds and some thyme. Bake in the oven for 20 minutes until a rich golden-brown. Leave to cool on the baking sheets. Store in airtight containers between sheets of greaseproof paper for up to 1 week.

# Smoked Ham Rings

*Preparation time: 20 minutes • Cooking time: 20 minutes • Makes: 24*

**These cookies are good to serve with dips, or try sandwiching them together with cream cheese.**

### INGREDIENTS

*175 g/6 oz butter or margarine, softened*

*50 g/2 oz lean smoked ham, very finely chopped*

*50 g/2 oz finely grated smoked cheese*

*120 g/4 oz plain flour*

*50 g/2 oz cornflour*

*Pinch of salt*

*½ tsp mustard powder*

Pre-heat oven to 350°F/175°C/Gas mark 4. Line two baking sheets with non-stick baking parchment.

● In a bowl, beat the butter or margarine, ham and cheese together until well mixed.

● Sift the remaining ingredients into the bowl, mix well.

● Place the dough in a piping bag fitted with a 1-cm/½-in all-purpose nozzle. Pipe 24 6-cm/2½-in rings, spaced well apart, on the baking sheets. Bake in the oven for 20 minutes until lightly golden. Cool for 5 minutes then transfer to a wire rack to cool completely. Store in an airtight container for up to 4 days or freeze for up to 3 months.

# Halloumi Cookies

*Preparation time: 15 minutes • Cooking time: 25 minutes • Makes: 14*

**Halloumi cheese is mild tasting, slightly salty, and perfect for baking as it holds its shape well.**

### INGREDIENTS

*120 g/4 oz plain flour*

*75 g/3 oz Halloumi cheese, cut into small pieces*

*2 Tbsp black olives, drained, stoned and chopped*

*2 Tbsp freshly chopped coriander*

*5 Tbsp good-quality olive oil*

Pre-heat oven to 350°F/175°C/Gas mark 4. Grease or line a large baking sheet with non-stick baking parchment.

● Sift the flour into a bowl and mix in the cheese, olives and coriander. Bind together with the olive oil to form a dough. Turn on to a lightly floured surface and knead gently until smooth.

● Using a teaspoon, pile 14 small mounds onto the baking sheet, and press down lightly using a fork. Bake in the oven for 20 to 25 minutes until lightly golden and firm. Cool for 10 minutes, then transfer to a wire rack. Best served slightly warmed.

# Ham Pineapple Corn Cakes

*Preparation time: 15 minutes ● Cooking time: 20 minutes ● Makes: 15*

**Serve these soft cookies to accompany soups, stews and casseroles.**

### INGREDIENTS

120 g/4 oz cornmeal

50 g/2 oz plain flour

2 tsp baking powder

50 g/2 oz lightly salted butter or margarine

50 g/2 oz lean ham, finely chopped

50 g/2 oz finely chopped fresh or tinned pineapple

2 Tbsp freshly chopped parsley

1 egg, beaten

6 Tbsp milk

Pre-heat oven to 375°F/190°C/Gas mark 5. Line two baking sheets with non-stick baking parchment.

● Sift the cornmeal, flour, baking powder and salt into a bowl. Blend in the butter or margarine. Stir in the ham and pineapple. Make a well in the centre and add the egg, then gradually pour in the milk, stirring to form a thick batter.

● Using a teaspoon, drop 15 mounds, spaced well apart on the baking sheets. Bake for 15 to 20 minutes until lightly golden and firm. Cool for 10 minutes, then transfer to a wire rack. Store in an airtight container for up to 5 days or freeze for up to 3 months.

# Thai Prawn Crackers

*Preparation time: 30 minutes + chilling ● Cooking time: 25 minutes ● Makes: 16*

**These light and flaky cookies are flavoured with Oriental ingredients. Serve with satay sauce.**

### INGREDIENTS

225 g/8 oz self-raising flour

1 tsp salt

½ tsp ground white pepper

½ tsp hot chilli powder

50 g/2 oz lightly salted butter or margarine

2 Tbsp crunchy peanut butter

7 to 8 Tbsp cold water

4 spring onions, trimmed and finely chopped

50 g/2 oz peeled prawns, thawed if frozen, ground or finely chopped

Sift the flour, salt, pepper and chilli powder into a bowl. Blend in the butter or margarine until well mixed, and stir in the peanut butter. Mix in sufficient cold water to form a firm dough. Turn on to a lightly floured surface and knead until smooth.

● Roll out to a 38 x 15-cm/15 x 6-in rectangle. Score into three. Mix the spring onions and prawns and place one-third in the middle section. Fold up the bottom third, bring the top third over it, seal the edges and give the pastry a half-turn. Repeat twice more, sprinkling the spring onion and prawn mixture each time. Re-roll and fold again. Wrap and chill for 30 minutes.

● Pre-heat oven to 350°F/175°C/Gas mark 4. Grease and flour a baking sheet. Roll the dough out on a floured surface to form a 30-cm/12-in square and divide into 16 squares. Transfer to baking sheet, prick all over and bake for 20 to 25 minutes until golden. Cool on wire racks.

# Smoked Salmon Snacks

*Preparation time: 25 minutes + chilling* ● *Cooking time: 15 minutes* ● *Makes: 15*

**Try these luxurious cookies for a buffet lunch.**

## INGREDIENTS

75 g/3 oz lightly salted butter or margarine, softened

3 Tbsp full-fat soft cheese

1 egg yolk

175 g/6 oz plain flour

Pinch salt

4 Tbsp freshly chopped dill

2 Tbsp cold water

### FILLING

225 g/8 oz full-fat soft cheese

125 g/4 oz smoked salmon pieces, shredded fine

In a bowl, beat the butter or margarine with the soft cheese and egg yolk. Sift in the flour and salt and add the dill, then stir until evenly mixed. Stir in sufficient cold water to form a dough.

● Turn onto a floured surface and knead until smooth; place in clingfilm and chill for 30 minutes.

● Pre-heat oven to 350°F/175°C/Gas mark 4. Line two baking sheets with non-stick baking parchment.

● Roll out the pastry thinly and stamp out 30 circles using a 6-cm/2½-in cutter, re-rolling as necessary. Place on the prepared baking sheets, score lightly with a knife in diagonal lines, and then bake in the oven for about 15 minutes until lightly golden. Leave to cool on the sheets.

● To serve, beat the soft cheese until smooth and spread over half the cookies. Sprinkle with a few strips of smoked salmon and then top with the remaining cookies. Serve immediately.

● Store, unfilled, in an airtight container for up to 1 week, or freeze unfilled for up to 3 months.

# Crispy Bacon and Blue Cheese Melts

*Preparation time: 25 minutes ● Cooking time: 30 minutes ● Makes: 15*

**Basic cookie dough is transformed into a melting mixture by adding cheese. Serve these tasty snacks as an accompaniment to other cheeses or with fruit, soups and salads.**

### INGREDIENTS

*6 rashers rindless bacon*

*50 g/2 oz crumbled blue cheese*

*120 g/4 oz plain flour*

*120 g/4 oz lightly salted butter or margarine, softened*

*Pinch of cayenne pepper*

Pre-heat oven to 350°F/175°C/Gas mark 4. Grease or line two baking sheets with non-stick baking parchment.

● Pre-heat the grill to a hot setting and cook the bacon for 2 to 3 minutes on each side until golden and crispy. Drain on kitchen paper and cool. Then finely chop.

● Mix all the ingredients and the chopped bacon together using a round-bladed knife, and bring together with your hands to form a dough.

● Divide the dough into 15 portions and shape each one into a small disc. Prick the surfaces with a fork and bake in the oven for 20 to 25 minutes until lightly golden and firm to the touch. Leave to cool for 15 minutes and then serve warm. Store in an airtight container for up to 4 days.

# Pepperoni and Peppercorn Shortbreads

*Preparation time: 15 minutes + chilling* ● *Cooking time: 25 minutes* ● *Makes: 14*

**You can make and freeze these tasty pre-dinner nibbles ahead of time, and you may want to double the recipe as they will be very popular.**

## INGREDIENTS

*120 g/4 oz plain flour*

*Pinch of salt*

*75 g/3 oz unsalted butter*

*50 g/2 oz sliced pepperoni sausage, finely chopped*

*1 Tbsp pickled green peppercorns, drained*

*1 egg, beaten*

*Freshly ground black pepper*

Sift the flour and salt into a bowl, then blend in the butter until you have fine crumbs. Stir in the pepperoni and peppercorns and add enough egg to bring together to form a dough; reserve the rest for glazing.

● Turn onto a lightly floured surface and knead until smooth. Wrap and chill for 20 minutes.

● Pre-heat oven to 325°F/160°C/Gas mark 3. Line two baking sheets with non-stick baking parchment.

● Roll out to 1 cm/½ in thick. Using a 4-cm/1½-in round cutter, stamp out 14 rounds, re-rolling as necessary. Transfer to the baking sheet, brush with reserved egg and then dust with ground black pepper. Bake in the oven for 20 to 25 minutes until firm to the touch and golden. Cool for 5 minutes and then transfer to a wire rack to cool completely. To make ahead, pack into an airtight container and freeze for up to 3 months.

# Anchovy, Olive and Basil Spirals

*Preparation time: 20 minutes • Cooking time: 12 minutes • Makes: 24*

**A sophisticated puff pastry snack with a deliciously fishy flavour. They are best eaten on the day they are made, and served slightly warm.**

### INGREDIENTS

175 g/6 oz puff pastry, thawed if frozen

1 egg, beaten

50 g/2 oz anchovy fillets, drained

2 Tbsp black olives, drained, stoned and finely chopped

2 Tbsp pimiento-stuffed green olives, finely chopped

Handful fresh basil leaves

Pre-heat oven to 425°F/220°C/Gas mark 7. Line two baking sheets with non-stick baking parchment.

● Roll out the pastry on a lightly floured surface to a 30 x 20-cm/12 x 8-in rectangle. Brush the pastry with beaten egg and lay the anchovy fillets, lengthways, over the pastry. Sprinkle with the olives and lay the basil leaves on top. Starting from the long side, roll up the pastry tightly, like a Swiss roll. Press lightly to seal the end, and then slice into 24 pieces.

● Lay the pastry pieces, spaced a little apart, on the baking sheets, and brush with more egg. Bake for 10 to 12 minutes until golden and crisp. Cool for 10 minutes before serving. These are best eaten on the day they are made, and served slightly warm.

# Curried Prawn Diamond Oatcakes

*Preparation time: 20 minutes • Cooking time: 15 minutes • Makes: 18*

**These crisp oatcakes are flavoured with Chinese curry spices and chopped prawns. Good with fish pâté.**

### INGREDIENTS

25 g/1 oz plain flour

175 g/6 oz medium oatmeal

½ tsp baking powder

½ tsp salt

1½ tsp Chinese curry powder

75 g/3 oz white vegetable fat

50 g/2 oz peeled prawns, thawed if frozen, very finely chopped

1–2 tsp cold water

1 egg, beaten

2 Tbsp sesame seeds

Pre-heat oven to 400°F/200°C/Gas mark 6. Grease or line a baking sheet with non-stick baking parchment.

● Sift the flour, oatmeal, baking powder, salt and curry powder into a bowl. Blend in the white vegetable fat with your fingertips until the mixture is crumbly, then stir in the prawns and mix with sufficient water to form a firm dough.

● Roll out the dough to 5 mm/¼ in thick on a lightly floured surface. Slice the dough into 4-cm/1½-in strips, then cut each strip on the diagonal into diamond shapes (you should make about 18).

● Transfer to the baking sheet. Brush with egg and sprinkle with sesame seeds. Bake for about 15 minutes until firm and lightly golden. Leave to cool.

# Smoked Salmon and Lemon Kisses

*Preparation time: 20 minutes ● Cooking time: 25 minutes ● Makes: 12*

**These delicately flavoured melt-in-the-mouth soft-bake cookies are good served with cream cheese.
Substitute ham for the salmon if preferred.**

### INGREDIENTS

*120 g/4 oz plain flour*

*Pinch of salt*

*2 Tbsp freshly chopped parsley*

*120 g/4 oz smoked salmon, finely chopped*

*½ tsp finely grated lemon rind*

*120 g/4 oz lightly salted butter or margarine, softened*

Pre-heat oven to 350°F/175°C/Gas mark 4. Grease or line two baking sheets with non-stick baking parchment.

● Sift the flour and salt into a bowl. Stir in the parsley, smoked salmon, lemon rind and butter or margarine using a round-bladed knife. Bring together with your hands to form a dough.

● Divide the dough into 12 pieces and form them into walnut-sized balls. Place on baking sheets, spaced about 5 cm/2 in apart. Flatten slightly and bake for 20 to 25 minutes until lightly golden and firm to the touch. Leave to cool for 15 minutes. These cookies are best served slightly warm, and on the same day as baking. They can be frozen, once baked, for up to 3 months.

# Honeyed Ham and Onion Cookies

*Preparation time: 25 minutes + chilling* ● *Cooking time: 30 minutes* ● *Makes: 16*

**With a little advance preparation, these cookies make truly delicious snacks. They also make an interesting accompaniment to salads or soups.**

## INGREDIENTS

*75 g/3 oz lightly salted butter or margarine*

*1 medium onion, finely sliced*

*2 tsp honey*

*120 g/4 oz plain flour*

*Pinch of salt*

*1 Tbsp freshly chopped sage or 1 tsp dried sage*

*75 g/3 oz lean honey roast ham, finely chopped*

*2–3 tsp cold water*

*1 small egg, beaten*

*Bunch small sage leaves, optional*

Melt 25 g/1 oz of butter in a small frying pan and gently fry the onion for 5 minutes, stirring, until just softened. Add the honey, raise the heat and cook for a further 2 to 3 minutes until lightly golden. Set the mixture aside to cool.

● Sift the flour, salt and sage together into a bowl. Blend in the remaining butter and stir in the ham and prepared onion. Bind together with sufficient cold water to form a soft dough. Turn onto a lightly floured surface and knead until smooth. Wrap and chill the dough for 30 minutes.

● Pre-heat oven to 350°F/175°C/Gas mark 4. Line a large baking sheet with non-stick baking parchment.

● Divide the dough into 16 and form into small round discs. Place on the baking sheet, brush with beaten egg and press a sage leaf onto each, if using. Bake for 20 to 25 minutes until lightly golden and firm. Cool for 10 minutes and then serve warm.

# Peanut, Sesame, Carrot and Raisin Pinwheels

*Preparation time: 25 minutes + chilling* ● *Cooking time: 20 minutes* ● *Makes: 24*

**A healthy combination of ingredients makes these cookies an excellent addition to the lunch box – the peanut flavour will make them popular with children.**

## INGREDIENTS

*75 g/3 oz lightly salted butter or margarine, softened*

*3 Tbsp full-fat soft cheese*

*1 egg yolk*

*200 g/7 oz wholemeal flour*

*Pinch of salt*

*2 Tbsp cold water*

*4 Tbsp crunchy peanut butter*

*50 g/2 oz finely grated carrot*

*3 Tbsp raisins, finely chopped*

*1 Tbsp toasted sesame seeds*

In a bowl, beat together the butter, soft cheese and egg yolk. Sift the flour and salt into the bowl, adding any husks which remain in the strainer, then stir in the water until evenly mixed. Stir in to form a dough. Turn on to a lightly floured surface and knead lightly until smooth. Wrap and chill for 30 minutes.

● Pre-heat oven to 350°F/175°C/Gas mark 4. Line two baking sheets with non-stick baking parchment.

● Roll out the dough to a 30 x 23-cm/12 x 9-in rectangle. Soften the peanut butter by heating it gently and then thinly spread over the dough. Sprinkle with the carrot, raisins and sesame seeds.

● Starting at the longest side, roll up the dough tightly, like a Swiss roll, and press gently to seal the edge. Slice the roll into 24 pieces and place the pinwheels on the lined baking sheets. Bake in the oven for about 20 minutes until firm and lightly golden. Cool for 10 minutes then transfer to a wire rack to cool completely. Store in an airtight container for up to 3 days. Not suitable for freezing.

# Mixed Nut Clusters with Cajun Spices

*Preparation time: 20 minutes* ●
*Cooking time: 25 minutes* ● *Makes: 15*

**These cookies are for the real nut lover. You can use any combination of nuts for this recipe, but choose a good spread of flavours, and use unsalted varieties.**

### INGREDIENTS

3 Tbsp walnut pieces

3 Tbsp flaked whole almonds

3 Tbsp macadamia nuts, lightly crushed

3 Tbsp shelled unsalted pistachios, lightly crushed

120 g/4 oz plain flour

Pinch of celery salt

Pinch of onion salt

1 tsp paprika

¼ tsp cayenne pepper

1 tsp dried thyme

120 g/4 oz lightly salted butter or margarine, softened

Pre-heat oven to 350°F/175°C/Gas mark 4. Grease or line two baking sheets with non-stick baking parchment.

● Mix all the nuts together and place in a bowl. Sift in the flour, salts, paprika and cayenne. Add the thyme and butter or margarine and mix together with a round-bladed knife. Bring together with your hands to form a dough.

● Divide into 15 and form into walnut-sized balls. Place on baking sheets, spaced about 5 cm/2 in apart. Flatten slightly, and bake in the oven for 20 to 25 minutes until lightly golden and firm to the touch. Leave to cool on the baking sheets. Excellent served slightly warm. Store in an airtight container for up to 1 week, or freeze for up to 3 months.

# Pine Tree Shillings

*Preparation time: 15 minutes* ●
*Cooking time: 25 minutes* ● *Makes: 14*

**Pine nuts have a fragrant, resinous flavour which goes very well with the woodiness of rosemary and olives. A very Mediterranean cocktail nibble.**

### INGREDIENTS

120 g/4 oz plain flour

1 tsp salt

1 Tbsp freshly chopped rosemary or 1 tsp dried

120 g/4 oz pine nuts

3 Tbsp black olives, drained, stoned and chopped

5 Tbsp good-quality olive oil

Pre-heat oven to 350°F/175°C/Gas mark 4. Line two baking sheets with non-stick baking parchment.

● Sift the flour and salt into a bowl and stir in the rosemary, pine nuts and olives. Add the olive oil and stir to mix into a dough.

● Drop 14 teaspoonfuls of the mixture on to baking sheets and bake for 20 to 25 minutes. Cool for 10 minutes and then transfer to a rack to cool completely.

● Store in an airtight container for up to 1 week, or freeze for up to 3 months.

# Poppy Seed Spirals

*Preparation time: 25 minutes* ● *Cooking time: 27 minutes* ● *Makes: 16*

**The small black seeds in these crisp pastry rolls have a nutty flavour and crunchy texture. Substitute with sesame seeds or crushed pumpkin seeds if preferred.**

## INGREDIENTS

*150 g/5 oz lightly salted butter or margarine*

*1 medium red onion, finely sliced*

*1 Tbsp lemon juice*

*1 tsp coriander seeds, crushed*

*2 tsp honey*

*9 large sheets of filo pastry (45 x 30 cm/18 x 12 in)*

*6 Tbsp poppy seeds*

*4 Tbsp freshly chopped coriander*

Pre-heat oven to 400°F/200°C/Gas mark 6. Line a baking sheet with non-stick baking parchment.

● Melt 25 g/1 oz lightly salted butter or margarine in a small frying pan and gently fry the onion with the lemon juice and coriander seeds for 5 minutes until softened. Add the honey and cook, stirring, over a high heat for a further 2 minutes. Set aside to cool.

● In a small saucepan, gently melt the remaining butter or margarine.

● To assemble the spirals, lay a sheet of filo pastry on the work surface and brush with melted fat. Lay two more sheets on top, brushing with fat as you go. Sprinkle over 2 tablespoons poppy seeds and 1 tablespoon chopped coriander.

● Prepare three more sheets of filo as before and place on top of the seeds. Sprinkle with 2 tablespoons poppy seeds and another 1 tablespoon coriander. Spread over the cooked onion mixture. Finally, prepare the remaining three sheets of filo as before and lay over the onion layer. Sprinkle with remaining seeds and coriander. From the shortest side, carefully roll up the pastry like a Swiss roll, pressing the roll gently to seal the edge.

● Slice into 16 pieces and arrange on the baking sheet. Brush with the remaining melted fat and bake in the oven for 15 to 20 minutes until richly golden. Cool for 10 minutes and then serve. These pastries can be made up to 24 hours in advance of baking, and stored in the fridge until ready for use.

# Toasted Pecan Snacks

*Preparation time: 30 minutes + chilling* ● *Cooking time: 25 minutes* ● *Makes: 24*

**Use ready-roasted pecan halves in this recipe for a more intense flavour. Alternatively try honey-roasted pecans, available from good whole food stores.**

## INGREDIENTS

*225 g/8 oz self-raising flour*

*1 tsp salt*

*50 g/2 oz lightly salted butter or margarine*

*7–8 Tbsp cold water*

*75 g/3 oz toasted pecan nuts, finely chopped*

Sift the flour and salt into a bowl and blend in the fat. Add sufficient water to form a pliable dough. Turn on to a lightly floured surface and knead until smooth.

● Roll into a 38 x 15-cm/15 x 6-in rectangle. Mark lightly into three equal portions, and sprinkle the middle portion with one third of the nuts. Fold up the bottom third, bring the top third over it, seal the edges and give the pastry a half turn. Repeat this rolling and folding twice more, sprinkling with the nuts each time. Re-roll and fold once more. Wrap and chill.

● Pre-heat oven to 350°F175°C/Gas mark 4. Grease and flour a baking sheet.

● Roll out the pastry thinly and evenly to form a square slightly bigger than 30 cm/12 in. Trim away the edges to neaten, and then cut into 2.5 x 15-cm/1 x 6-in thin fingers. Transfer to the baking sheet, prick all over with a fork and baken for 20 to 25 minutes until lightly golden and puffed up. Transfer to a wire rack to cool. Store in an airtight container for up to 1 week.

# Mixed Seed Crunchies

*Preparation time: 10 minutes + standing* ●
*Cooking time: 15 minutes* ● *Makes: 18*

**Use small seeds in this recipe to give a very crisp texture. The oats in this recipe add a healthy touch, making them an ideal wholesome snack.**

### INGREDIENTS

175 g/6 oz rolled oats

75 g/3 oz medium oatmeal

2 Tbsp poppy seeds

2 Tbsp sesame seeds

1 tsp celery seeds

1 tsp fennel seeds, lightly crushed

125 ml/4 fl oz sunflower oil

1 tsp salt

1 egg, beaten

Place the oats, oatmeal and seeds in a bowl, and mix in the oil. Leave to stand for 1 hour.
● Pre-heat oven to 325°F/160°C/Gas mark 3. Line a baking sheet with non-stick baking parchment.
● Add the salt and egg to the oat mixture and beat together thoroughly. Place 18 teaspoonfuls of the mixture, spaced a little apart on the baking sheet and press flat with a wetted fork. Bake in the oven for about 15 minutes until golden-brown. Leave to cool on the sheets. Store in an airtight container for up to 1 week.

# Wholemeal Pumpkin Shorties

*Preparation time: 15 minutes + chilling* ●
*Cooking time: 20 to 25 minutes* ● *Makes: 14*

**Green pumpkin seeds have a nutty flavour, and they add texture to a rich, crumbly wholemeal shortbread mixture. Use white plain flour if preferred.**

### INGREDIENTS

120 g/4 oz wholemeal flour

Pinch of salt

50 g/2 oz unsalted butter

7 Tbsp pumpkin seeds, lightly crushed

1 egg yolk

2 Tbsp milk

Pre-heat oven to 325°F/160°C/Gas mark 3. Line two baking sheets with non-stick baking parchment.
● Sift the flour and salt into a bowl and blend in the butter until you have fine crumbs. Stir in the pumpkin seeds and egg yolk. Bring together with your hands to form a dough. Turn onto a lightly floured surface and knead lightly until smooth. Wrap and chill for 20 minutes.
● Roll out to 5 cm/½ in thick and cut into 14 5-cm/½-in squares, re-rolling as necessary. Place on the baking sheets and score the tops lightly with a knife. Brush lightly with the milk and bake for 20 to 25 minutes until firm and golden. Cool on the baking sheets for 5 minutes and then transfer to a wire rack to cool completely. Store in an airtight container for up to 1 week.

# Apricot and Pecan Rye Cookies

*Preparation time: 20 minutes* ● *Cooking time: 20 minutes* ● *Makes: 18*

**Rye flour has a distinctive nutty flavour and makes an interesting cookie. The addition of dried apricots gives a delicate sweetness; chopped dates or raisins could also be used.**

## INGREDIENTS

*120 g/4 oz dark rye flour*

*Pinch of salt*

*50 g/2 oz pecan nuts, lightly crushed*

*3 Tbsp finely chopped dried apricots*

*120 g/4 oz lightly salted butter or margarine, softened*

*2 Tbsp freshly chopped parsley*

Pre-heat oven to 350°F/175°C/Gas mark 4. Grease or line two baking sheets.

● Mix all the ingredients together with a round-bladed knife to form into a dough.

● Divide into 18 portions and form into small balls. Place about 2 cm/1 in apart on the baking sheets and flatten slightly with a fork. Bake for 20 minutes until golden and firm to the touch. Cool on the baking sheets. Store in an airtight container for 3 to 4 days.

# Buttery Hazelnut Hoops

*Preparation time: 20 minutes • Cooking time: 15 minutes • Makes: 24*

**Toasted hazelnuts have a rich flavour and are perfect for baking. These piped cookies look good on a platter of canapés, and taste excellent with blue cheese and grapes.**

## INGREDIENTS

*175 g/6 oz lightly salted butter or margarine, softened*

*50 g/2 oz ground toasted hazelnuts*

*120 g/4 oz plain flour*

*50 g/2 oz cornflour*

*Pinch of salt*

*3 Tbsp lightly crushed hazelnuts*

Pre-heat oven to 350°F/175°C/Gas mark 4. Line two baking sheets with non-stick baking parchment.

● Beat the butter or margarine and ground hazelnuts together. Sift in the flour, cornflour and salt, and beat well. Place in a piping bag fitted with an all-purpose 1-cm/½-in round nozzle, and pipe 24 6-cm/2½-in rings, spaced well apart, onto the baking sheets. Sprinkle the rings with the crushed hazelnuts.

● Bake in the oven for 15 minutes until golden. Cool for 5 minutes and then transfer to wire rack to cool completely. Store between layers of greaseproof paper in an airtight container for up to 5 days.

# Middle Eastern Almond Rolls

*Preparation time: 30 minutes + chilling ● Cooking time: 25 minutes ● Makes: 18*

**Mild tasting buttery almonds combine well with sweet Middle Eastern spices and sweet red onion in this filling.**

### INGREDIENTS

*75 g/3 oz lightly salted butter or margarine, softened*

*3 Tbsp full-fat soft cheese*

*1 egg yolk*

*120 g/4 oz plain flour*

*50 g/2 oz ground almonds*

*Pinch of salt*

*2 Tbsp cold water*

### FILLING

*50 g/2 oz lightly salted butter or margarine*

*1 small red onion, finely chopped*

*1 Tbsp lemon juice*

*50 g/2 oz finely chopped blanched almonds*

*1 tsp ground coriander*

*1 tsp ground cumin*

*3 Tbsp sultanas*

*2 Tbsp freshly chopped coriander*

*1 egg, beaten*

In a bowl, beat the butter or margarine, soft cheese, and egg yolk. Sift the flour and add the ground almonds and salt. Stir until evenly mixed. Add sufficient water to form a dough. Turn on to a lightly floured surface and knead lightly until smooth. Wrap and chill for 30 minutes.

● Meanwhile, make the filling. Melt the butter or margarine and gently fry the onion with the lemon juice, chopped almonds and spices, stirring, for 5 minutes until the onion is softened. Remove from the heat and add the sultanas and coriander. Set the filling aside to cool.

● Pre-heat oven to 350°F/175°C/Gas mark 4. Line a baking sheet with non-stick baking parchment.

● Roll out the dough thinly to an approximate 26-cm/ 10½-in square. Trim away the edges to neaten and divide into 9 smaller squares. Divide the mixture between each square, and form a mound down the centre of each. Brush the edges with beaten egg and carefully roll each square up. Press the edge gently to seal. Cut each roll in half.

● Transfer the rolls to the baking sheet. Score the tops lightly with a sharp knife, then brush with beaten egg to glaze and bake in the oven for 20 minutes until golden. Leave to cool on the baking sheet. Store in an airtight container for up to 1 week.

# Hot Cashew Crumbles

*Preparation time: 10 minutes + chilling ● Cooking time: 15 minutes ● Makes: 16*

**Cashews have a nutty sweetness, and are delicious flavoured with Indian spices. Serve these crumbly cookies while still warm. Replace the chickpea flour with plain flour if preferred.**

### INGREDIENTS

*50 g/2 oz ground unsalted cashew nuts*

*25 g/1 oz lightly chopped, roasted cashew nuts*

*50 g/2 oz chickpea flour*

*1 tsp mild curry powder*

*120 g/4 oz lightly salted butter or margarine, softened*

*2 Tbsp freshly chopped coriander*

*16 unsalted cashew halves*

Place the ground and chopped cashews together in a large mixing bowl and sift in the chickpea flour and curry powder. Add the butter or margarine and chopped coriander and mix all the ingredients together to form a firm dough.

● Use your hands to roll the dough out into 16 balls and arrange on a large ungreased baking sheet. Press a cashew half on to the top of each. Cover and chill for 1 hour until firm.

● Pre-heat oven to 375°F/190°C/Gas mark 5. To serve, uncover the cookies and bake in the oven for about 15 minutes until golden. Leave to stand for 10 minutes and then carefully lift the cookies off the sheets and serve them while they are still warm.

● The uncooked dough will keep covered in the refrigerator for 24 hours.

# Brazil Nut Bakes

*Preparation time: 15 minutes* ●
*Cooking time: 10 minutes* ● *Makes: 18*

**Here chips of smooth-tasting Brazil nuts combine with cheese to make crisp and slightly chewy cookies. Serve as cocktail nibbles.**

### INGREDIENTS

*120 g/4 oz lightly salted butter or margarine*

*50 g/2 oz Brazil nuts, chipped or flaked*

*50 g/2 oz ground Brazil nuts*

*225 g/8 oz freshly grated Parmesan cheese*

*Salt and pepper*

*2 Tbsp freshly chopped parsley*

Pre-heat oven to 350°F/175°C/Gas mark 4. Line a baking sheet with non-stick baking parchment.

● Melt the butter or margarine in a saucepan. Remove from the heat and stir in the remaining ingredients.

● Drop spoonfuls of the cookie mixture, spaced well apart, in 18 small mounds on the baking sheets. Flatten with a fork and bake in the oven for 10 minutes until golden-brown. Remove from the oven and push in the edges using a knife, to neaten. Cool for 5 minutes on the sheets, and then transfer to a wire rack to cool completely. Store in an airtight container between layers of greaseproof paper for 3 to 4 days.

# Roast Pepper Cookies

*Preparation time: 25 minutes* ●
*Cooking time: 25 minutes* ● *Makes: 12*

**These colourful cookies use three different coloured peppers, but you can use just one or two varieties if you prefer.**

### INGREDIENTS

*½ small red pepper, seeded*

*½ small orange pepper, seeded*

*½ small green pepper, seeded*

*120 g/4 oz plain flour*

*Pinch of salt*

*½ tsp hot chilli powder*

*120 g/4 oz lightly salted butter or margarine, softened*

*2 tsp dried chilli flakes, optional*

Pre-heat the grill to a high setting and place the peppers on the rack. Cook the peppers for 5 minutes on each side until softened and lightly charred. Cool for 10 minutes. Skin if preferred, and then finely chop the flesh. Leave to cool completely.

● Pre-heat oven to 350°F/175°C/Gas mark 4. Grease or line two baking sheets with non-stick baking parchment.

● Sift the flour, salt and chilli powder into a bowl. Stir in the peppers and butter or margarine. Using a round-bladed knife, mix to form a dough. Divide into 12, and form into walnut-sized balls. Place on the baking sheets, spaced about 5 cm/2 in apart. Flatten slightly and sprinkle each with a few chilli flakes, if using. Bake in the oven for 20 minutes until lightly golden and firm. Cool on the sheets. Best served slightly warm. Store in an airtight container for 3 to 4 days.

# Herb Crackers

*Preparation time: 25 minutes + chilling* ●
*Cooking time: 25 minutes* ● *Makes: 16*

**These crisp cookies can be made in any shape. They are ideal for serving with cheese, or could be crumbled into small pieces and used as croûtons for soups and salads.**

### INGREDIENTS

*225 g/8 oz self-raising cake flour*

*1 tsp salt*

*½ tsp ground white pepper*

*25 g/1 oz white vegetable fat*

*50 g/2 oz grated hard cheese such as Cheddar or Gruyère*

*3 Tbsp freshly chopped parsley*

*3 Tbsp freshly snipped chives*

Sift the flour, salt and pepper into a bowl and blend in the white vegetable fat. Mix to form a pliable dough by adding 7 to 8 tablespoons cold water.

● On a lightly floured surface, roll the dough into a 38 x 15-cm/15 x 6-in rectangle. Mark lightly into three equal segments. Mix the cheese and herbs together and sprinkle the middle section of pastry with one third of the herbed cheese. Fold up the bottom third, bring the top third down over it, seal the edges and give the pastry a half-turn. Repeat the rolling and folding twice more, to use up the herbed cheese. Re-roll and fold once more, then wrap and chill for 30 minutes.

● Pre-heat oven to 350°F/175°C/Gas mark 4. Lightly grease and flour a baking sheet.

● Roll out the pastry to a square slightly larger than 30 cm/12 in. Trim the edge to neaten and then divide into 16 equal square portions. Transfer to the prepared baking sheet and prick all over with a fork. Bake for 20 to 25 minutes until lightly golden and puffed up. Transfer to a wire rack to cool. Store in an airtight container for up to 1 week.

# Fried Onion and Thyme Crackers

*Preparation time: 30 minutes + chilling* ● *Cooking time: 33 minutes* ● *Makes: 16*

**These puffed wheat crackers are interlaced with a rich mixture of buttery fried onion and fresh thyme.**

### INGREDIENTS

*120 g/4 oz lightly salted butter or margarine*

*1 large onion, finely chopped*

*1 Tbsp freshly chopped thyme or 1 tsp dried thyme*

*225 g/8 oz self-raising flour*

*1 tsp salt*

*7–8 Tbsp cold water*

Melt half of the fat in a small frying pan and gently cook the onion and thyme, stirring occasionally, for 7 to 8 minutes until lightly golden. Set aside to cool.

● Sift the flour and salt into a bowl. Blend in the remaining butter or margarine, and mix in sufficient water to form a firm dough. Turn onto a lightly floured surface and knead until smooth.

● Roll out to a 38 x 15-cm/15 x 6-in rectangle. Mark lightly into three equal portions. Place one-third of the cooked onion mixture in the middle section and fold up the bottom third. Bring the top third down over it, seal the edges and give the pastry a half-turn. Repeat this rolling and folding twice, adding the onion mixture each time. Re-roll and fold once more. Wrap and chill for 30 minutes.

● Pre-heat oven to 350°F/175°C/Gas mark 4. Grease and flour a baking sheet.

● Roll the dough out thinly on a lightly floured surface to form a square slightly bigger than 30 cm/12 in. Using a 6-cm/2½-in round cutter, stamp out 16 circles; do not re-roll trimmings. Transfer to the baking sheet. Prick all over with a fork and bake for 20 to 25 minutes until lightly golden and puffed up. Transfer to wire racks to cool. Best eaten on day of baking.

# Hot Herbed Mushroom Bites

*Preparation time: 20 minutes + chilling*
*Cooking time: 21 minutes • Makes: 16*

**Serve these cookies straight from the oven for their melt-in-the-mouth texture.**

### INGREDIENTS

*120 g/4 oz lightly salted butter or margarine, softened*

*50 g/2 oz finely chopped button mushrooms*

*2 cloves garlic, crushed*

*1 tsp dried mixed herbs*

*120 g/4 oz plain flour*

*½ tsp salt*

*2 Tbsp freshly snipped chives*

Melt half the fat in a frying pan and stir-fry the mushrooms, garlic and mixed herbs over a high heat for 1 minute until softened. Leave to cool.

• Sift the flour and salt into a bowl. Blend the remaining fat into the flour and stir in the chives and mushroom mixture. Mix together to form a dough. Wrap and chill for 1 hour.

• Pre-heat oven to 375°F/190°C/Gas mark 5. Line a large baking sheet with non-stick baking parchment.

• Form into 16 balls and place on the baking sheet. Bake in the oven for about 15 to 20 minutes until lightly golden. Cool for 10 minutes and then serve. The uncooked dough will keep covered in the refrigerator for 24 hours and so this recipe can be prepared in advance.

# Courgette Flapjacks

*Preparation time: 15 minutes •*
*Cooking time: 32 minutes • Makes: 18*

**An unusual version of this popular cookie. Here grated courgettes are added to an oat-based mixture and baked.**

### INGREDIENTS

*120 g/4 oz lightly salted butter or margarine*

*175 g/6 oz grated courgettes*

*200 g/7 oz rolled oats*

*2 heaped Tbsp sesame seeds*

*150 g/5 oz wholemeal flour*

*1 tsp salt*

Pre-heat oven to 375°F/190°C/Gas mark 5. Grease and base-line an 18-cm/7-in square baking tin.

• Place the butter or margarine in a saucepan to melt. Add the courgettes and gently cook in the fat, stirring, for 4 to 5 minutes until softened. Remove from the heat and carefully stir in the rolled oats, 2 tablespoons sesame seeds, flour and salt. Mix well.

• Transfer the mixture to the tin, and press down evenly. Sprinkle the surface with the remaining sesame seeds. Bake for 30 minutes until golden and firm to the touch. Cut into 9 squares and then cut these in half diagonally to make 18 small triangles. Leave to cool in the tin. Best eaten on day of baking.

# Soft-Bake Artichoke and Olive Fingers

*Preparation time: 15 minutes* ●
*Cooking time: 45 minutes* ● *Makes: 12*

**These luxuriously moist fingers will impress guests at a party or as pre-dinner drinks are served. If preferred, replace the blue cheese with grated hard cheese such as Cheddar.**

### INGREDIENTS

120 g/4 oz plain flour

Pinch of salt

75 g/3 oz unsalted butter

75 g/3 oz crumbled blue cheese

75 g/3 oz tinned artichoke hearts, drained and finely chopped

2 Tbsp black olives, drained, stoned and finely chopped

1 egg, beaten

½ tsp paprika

Pre-heat oven to 325°F/160°C/Gas mark 3. Grease and base-line an 18-cm/7-in square baking tin.

● Sift the flour and salt into a bowl, then blend in the butter until you have fine crumbs. Stir in the cheese, artichokes and olives. Add sufficient egg to bring together to form a dough; reserve the rest of the egg for glazing. Turn on to a lightly floured surface and knead until smooth.

● Press the mixture into the prepared tin. Prick all over with a fork, brush lightly with the remaining egg and dust with paprika. Bake in the oven on the middle shelf for 40 to 45 minutes. Slice in half and then into 12 fingers. Leave to cool in the tin. Store in an airtight container for 3 to 4 days.

# Carrot, Cumin and Orange Filo Crisps

*Preparation time: 25 minutes* ●
*Cooking time: 25 minutes* ● *Makes: 16*

**Crisp, buttery filo pastry is best eaten warm.**

### INGREDIENTS

175 g/6 oz butter or margarine

50 g/2 oz grated carrots

1 Tbsp freshly squeezed orange juice

1 tsp cumin seeds, crushed

½ tsp finely grated orange rind

½ tsp salt

Fresh ground black pepper

9 large sheets filo pastry, (45 x 30 cm/18 x 12 in)

Pre-heat oven to 400°F/200°C/Gas mark 6. Line two baking sheets with non-stick baking parchment

● Melt ¼ stick of butter or margarine in a frying pan and gently cook the carrot with the orange juice and cumin seeds for 5 minutes until softened. Season and leave to cool.

● In a saucepan, melt the remaining butter or margarine.

● To assemble the filo crisps, brush a sheet of pastry with melted butter. Lay 2 more sheets on top, brushing with fat as you go. Spread over one-third of the carrot mixture. Prepare 3 more sheets of filo as before and place on top of the carrot. Spread with another third of carrot mixture. Prepare the remaining sheets of pastry, place on top and spread with carrot.

● From the shortest side, carefully roll up the pastry like a Swiss roll, pressing gently to seal the edge. Slice into 16 pieces and arrange on the baking sheets. Brush with the remaining fat and bake in the oven for 20 minutes until golden-brown. Cool for 10 minutes and serve.

# Soft-Bake Buckwheat Beetroot Snacks

*Preparation time: 20 minutes* ● *Cooking time: 20 minutes* ● *Makes: 15*

**For this recipe, use cooked beetroot that has not been soaked in vinegar. Buckwheat is a gluten-free grain with a deliciously nutty flavour.**

## INGREDIENTS

*200 g/7 oz buckwheat flour*

*Pinch of salt*

*50 g/2 oz grated cooked, peeled beetroot*

*120 g/4 oz freshly grated Parmesan cheese*

*1 tsp caraway seeds*

*120 g/4 oz lightly salted butter or margarine, softened*

Pre-heat oven to 350°F/175°C/Gas mark 4. Grease or line two baking sheets with non-stick baking parchment.

● Sift the flour and salt together into a bowl, adding any husks which remain in the sieve. Stir in the beetroot, cheese and caraway seeds. Using a round-bladed knife, stir in the butter or margarine, to form the mixture into a dough.

● Divide into 15 and form into walnut-sized balls. Place on baking sheets, spaced about 5 cm/2 in apart. Flatten slightly with a fork and bake for 15 to 20 minutes until golden and firm to the touch. Cool for 10 minutes and then transfer to a wire rack to cool. Best served slightly warm. Store in an airtight container for up to 4 days.

# Mexican Potato and Chilli Bean Corn Cakes

*Preparation time: 10 minutes ● Cooking time: 15 minutes ● Makes: 14*

**Little mounds of golden yellow corn with diced potato and kidney beans make these cookies a substantial snack and ideal lunch-box filler or tea-time treat.**

### INGREDIENTS

*120 g/4 oz cornmeal*

*50 g/2 oz plain flour*

*2 tsp baking powder*

*50 g/2 oz lightly salted butter or margarine*

*1 large cooked potato, cubed*

*5 Tbsp tinned kidney beans, drained*

*1 clove garlic, crushed*

*½ tsp chilli powder*

*2 Tbsp freshly chopped coriander*

*1 egg, beaten*

*6 Tbsp milk*

Pre-heat oven to 375°F/190°C/Gas mark 4. Grease or line two baking sheets with non-stick baking parchment.

● Sift the cornmeal, flour, baking powder and salt into a bowl. Blend the butter or margarine into the dry ingredients until well mixed. Stir in the potato, beans, garlic and coriander. Make a well in the centre and add the egg. Gradually pour in the milk, stirring until the mixture forms a thick batter.

● Using a teaspoon, drop 14 mounds, spaced about 5 cm/2 in apart on baking sheets. Bake in the oven for about 15 minutes until lightly golden and firm to the touch. Cool for 10 minutes, then transfer to a wire rack to cool completely. Store in an airtight container for up to 5 days. Not suitable for freezing.

# Index